Congressional Quarterly's
Green Guide

Congressional Quarterly's

Green Guide

100th Congress Pocket Edition

CONGRESSIONAL QUARTERLY INC.
1414 22ND ST. N.W.
WASHINGTON, D.C. 20037
(202) 887-8500

Table of Contents

Congressional Quarterly Inc. is the leading source of information on Congress. It was founded in 1945 to provide a unique news service — one devoted exclusively to comprehensive, factual, nonpartisan reporting on Congress.

The founders correctly anticipated that many people would find this service "an aid to better understanding of their government." Many services have been added over the years to fill the growing and changing needs for information on government and politics by professionals working in the news media, private business, trade and professional associations, government, libraries, campaigns and international organizations.

The *Weekly Report* has been known as the journal of record of all significant activity in Congress and the authority on national politics since 1945.

Washington Alert Service provides continuously updated, online databases encompassing a wide range of congressional information for today's government affairs specialist.

CQ publishes a variety of public affairs and reference books, including *Politics in America*, the *Washington Information Directory* and the *Federal Regulatory Directory*.

Other publications include *The Congressional Monitor*, a daily report on present and future activities of congressional committees, and *Campaign Practices Reports*, a newsletter and reference service on campaign laws, campaigning and elections.

CQ's *Professional Education Service* has added another way of presenting information on Congress and public policy and of giving public affairs managers the opportunity to question "insiders." In the past seven years, over 15,000 government affairs professionals, federal government officials and public policy analysts have attended CQ's public affairs conferences in Washington, D.C., and other cities.

The *CQ Research Department* uses CQ's databases of congressional votes, CQ's library, and other resources to provide for-pay research tailored to subscribers' special information needs.

Through an affiliated service, *Editorial Research Reports*, CQ publishes daily and weekly news and editorial research services on current events, economic, cultural, scientific, civic, foreign and social topics.

Copyright © 1987 Congressional Quarterly Inc.

Printed in the United States of America

Library of Congress Cataloging in Publication Data

Main entry under title:
Congressional Quarterly's green guide
   1. United States. Congress — Biography — Directories.
I. Congressional Quarterly, inc.   II. Title: Congressional Quarterly's green guide.
JK1012.Z5   1987   328.73'092'2   [B]   87-5321
ISBN 0-87187-435-0

Editor: Bena A. Fein

Contributors: Nancy Kervin, Michael L. Koempel, Genevieve F. Matthews, Sharon M. Page, Charles Potter, Neal Santelmann, Douglas Sery, Amy Truesdell, Lenore Webb

Cover Design: Richard A. Pottern

Page Design: William Bonn

Photographs: Stan Barouh, C-SPAN, Leonard L. Grief Jr., Rob Gurwitt, Ken Heinen, Sue Klemens, Marty LaVor, Brad Markel, Joseph McCary, Joseph Neumayer, Karen Ruckman, Art Stein, Teresa Zabala

---

Congressional Quarterly Inc.

Eugene Patterson *Editor and President*

Wayne P. Kelley *Publisher*

Neil Skene *Executive Editor*

Robert E. Cuthriell *Director of Development, Electronic Information Services*

Robert C. Hur *General Counsel*

Jonathan C. Angier *Business Manager*

John J. Coyle *General Manager, Electronic Information Services*

Research Department

Michael L. Koempel *Director*
Sharon M. Page *Assistant Director, Research*
Bena A. Fein *Research*
Nancy Kervin *Research*
Charles Potter *Research*
Neal Santelmann *Research*
Stephen F. Stine *Research*
Lenore Webb *Research*
Barbara L. Miracle *Assistant Director, Seminars*
Nancy A. Blanpied *Seminars*
Irene Cuffy *Seminars*
Karis Obrenski *Seminars*
Martha A. Alito *Library Director*
Ralph Dumain *Library*
Kathleen Kelley *Library*
Hugh Swarts *Library*
Marc Wolin *Library*

Production

I. D. Fuller *Production Manager*
Maceo Mayo *Assistant Production Manager*
Michael Emanuel *Print Services Manager*

Introduction

Congressional Quarterly's Green Guide presents the facts and faces of the 100th Congress. It is designed to help you identify members of Congress in committee, in official or informal meetings, and while watching them on C-SPAN.

Biographical information on each member (occupation before election, political career, etc.) is given. Capitol Hill offices and phone numbers are provided, but, before visiting Capitol Hill, it is a good idea to check a member's address through the CQ *Weekly Report* quarterly index, a current *Congressional Record* or directories located next to Capitol Hill elevators.

Each representative's district is described briefly and the 1980 and 1984 vote for President Ronald Reagan given. Only the 1984 vote is included in the *Green Guide* for most districts in California, Hawaii, Louisiana, Mississippi, New Jersey, Texas and Washington; no district presidential vote is given for Ohio. Redistricting made existing figures inaccurate, and recalculations will appear in the next edition of *Politics in America*.

Statewide votes for Reagan for 1980 and 1984 are given in senators' profiles.

Committee assignments are listed for each member; chairmen, ranking minority members and chamber leaders are indicated. Assignments to the Joint Committee on Printing and Joint Library Committee were not made in time for inclusion in the *Green Guide*. Additional assignments and changes will be included in the next *Politics in America*.

General and primary election results for the last two elections are given for incumbent members and the 1986 election results for freshmen. If a member was *unopposed* in an election, this is shown by *u/o*. Runoffs and special elections are indicated.

Voting studies prepared by Congressional Quarterly for 1985 and 1986 are used. The presidential support score gives the percentage of House or Senate chamber votes on which a member supported the president's position.

Party unity scores represent the percentage of a member's "yea" or "nay" votes in agreement with a majority of his party. A party unity vote is defined as a recorded vote in the House or Senate that split the parties, with a majority of Democrats opposing a majority of Republicans.

The third CQ vote study is voting participation, which is the percentage of all recorded votes on which a member voted "yea" or "nay."

Ratings of the members by four interest groups are given for 1985 and 1986. The groups chosen represent liberal, conservative, business and labor viewpoints. Ratings for 1986 by the American Conservative Union were not available, as indicated by *n/a*.

Freshmen do not have scores for CQ vote studies or interest group ratings. However, House scores are given for Senate freshmen who were members of the House in 1985-86.

Following the Senate and House profiles is a roster of members of Congress by state. Included in this list is the name of each member's chief aide.

Other parts of the *Green Guide* include sections on how to watch the House and Senate on C-SPAN, an abbreviated glossary of congressional terms, a pronunciation guide to often mispronounced members' names, and a map of Capitol Hill.

For an in-depth understanding of each member's congressional and political career, state or district, and voting record, obtain a copy of *Politics in America*. The new edition will be available in July 1987.

Bena A. Fein
February 2, 1987
Washington, D.C.

Pronunciation Guide

The following is a list of often-mispronounced names of members of Congress, followed by the correct pronunciations:

SENATE

John B. Breaux, D-La. — BRO
Alfonse M. D'Amato, R-N.Y. —
dah MAH toe
Thomas A. Daschle, D-S.D. — DASH el
Dennis DeConcini, D-Ariz. —
dee con SEE nee
Pete V. Domenici, R-N.M. —
da MEN ah chee
Wyche Fowler Jr., D-Ga. — Y-CH
Daniel K. Inouye, D-Hawaii — in NO ay

HOUSE

Les AuCoin, D-Ore. — oh COIN
Anthony C. Beilenson, D-Calif. —
BEE lin son
Douglas K. Bereuter, R-Neb. —
BEE right er
Michael Bilirakis, R-Fla. —
bill a RACK us
Sherwood Boehlert, R-N.Y. — BO lert
David E. Bonior, D-Mich. — BON yer
Frederick C. Boucher, D-Va. —
BOUGH cher
Jack Buechner, R-Mo. — BEEK ner
Tony Coelho, D-Calif. — KWELL oh
Lawrence Coughlin, R-Pa. — COFF lin
Joseph H. DioGuardi, R-N.Y. —
dee oh GWAR dee
Mervyn M. Dymally, D-Calif. —
DIE mal ee
Ben Erdreich, D-Ala. — ER dritch
Dante B. Fascell, D-Fla. — fuh SELL
Edward F. Feighan, D-Ohio — FEE an
Thomas M. Foglietta, D-Pa. —
fo lee ET ah

Jaime B. Fuster, Pop. Dem.-P.R. —
HI may FOO ster
Elton Gallegly, R-Calif. — GAL uh glee
Sam Gejdenson, D-Conn. —
GAY den son
Frank J. Guarini, D-N.J. — gwar EE nee
George Hochbrueckner, D-N.Y. —
HOCK brewk ner
Amory Houghton Jr., R-N.Y. — HO tun
John R. Kasich, R-Ohio — KAY sick
Gerald Kleczka, D-Wis. — KLETCH ka
Jim Kolbe, R-Ariz. — COLE bee
Ernest L. Konnyu, R-Calif. —
CON you
Mel Levine, D-Calif. — la VINE
Manuel Lujan Jr., R-N.M. — LOO han
Ron Marlenee, R-Mont. — MAR la nay
Bob McEwen, R-Ohio — mac YOU in
Kweisi Mfume, D-Md. — kwy E say
mm FU may
Robert J. Mrazek, D-N.Y. — ma RAH zik
Charles Pashayan Jr., R-Calif. —
Pah SHAY an
Thomas E. Petri, R-Wis. — PEE try
Arthur Ravenel Jr., R-S.C. — RAV nel
Ralph Regula, R-Ohio — REG you la
Buddy Roemer, D-La. — RO mer
Marge Roukema, R-N.J. — ROCK ah ma
Patricia Saiki, R-Hawaii — CY kee
Bill Schuette, R-Mich. — SHOO tee
Richard T. Schulze, R-Pa. — SHOOLS
Arlan Stangeland, R-Minn. —
STANG land
Fofō I.F. Sunia, D-Amer. Samoa — soo
NEE ah
Tom Tauke, R-Iowa — TAW kee
W. J. "Billy" Tauzin, D-La. — TOE zan
Robert G. Torricelli, D-N.J. —
tor ah SELL ee
Guy Vander Jagt, R-Mich. —
VAN der jack
Barbara F. Vucanovich, R-Nev. —
voo CAN oh vitch
Gus Yatron, D-Pa. — YAT ron

Brock Adams (D-Wash.)

Of Seattle — Elected 1986

Born: Jan. 13, 1927, Atlanta, Ga.
Education: U. of Washington, B.A. 1949; Harvard U., J.D. 1952.
Military Career: Navy, 1944-46.
Occupation: Lawyer.
Family: Wife, Mary Elizabeth Scott; four children.
Religion: Episcopalian.
Political Career: U.S. district attorney for the Western District of Wash., 1961-64; U.S. House, 1965-77; U.S. secretary of transportation, 1977-79.
Capitol Office: 513 Hart Bldg. 20510; 224-2621

Washington — The statewide vote for Ronald Reagan was 56% in 1984; 50% in 1980.

Committees

Commerce, Science and Transportation
Foreign Relations
Rules and Administration
Labor and Human Resources

Elections

1986	General	51%	Primary	46%

William L. Armstrong (R-Colo.)

Of Englewood — Elected 1978

Born: March 16, 1937, Fremont, Neb.
Education: Attended Tulane U., 1954-55; U. of Minnesota, 1955-56.
Military Career: Army National Guard, 1957-63.
Occupation: Broadcasting executive.
Family: Wife, Ellen Eaton; two children.
Religion: Lutheran.
Political Career: Colo. House, 1963-65; Colo. Senate, 1965-73; U.S. House, 1973-79.
Capitol Office: 528 Hart Bldg. 20510; 224-5941.

Colorado — The statewide vote for Ronald Reagan was 63% in 1984; 55% in 1980.

Committees

Banking, Housing and Urban Affairs
Budget
Finance

Elections

1984	General	64%	Primary	u/o
1978	General	59%	Primary	73%

CQ Voting Studies

	Presidential Support	Party Unity	Voting Participation
1986	94%	89%	95%
1985	72%	87%	88%

Interest Groups

	ADA	ACU	AFL-CIO	CCUS
1986	0%	n/a	0%	100%
1985	0%	90%	0%	92%

Max Baucus (D-Mont.)

Of Missoula — Elected 1978

Born: Dec. 11, 1941, Helena, Mont.
Education: Stanford U., B.A. 1964, LL.B. 1967.
Occupation: Lawyer.
Family: Wife, Wanda Minge; one child.
Religion: United Church of Christ.
Political Career: Mont. House, 1973-75; U.S. House, 1975-79.
Capitol Office: 706 Hart Bldg. 20510; 224-2651.

Montana — The statewide vote for Ronald Reagan was 60% in 1984; 57% in 1980.

Committees

Environment and Public Works
Finance
Small Business

CQ Voting Studies

	Presidential Support	Party Unity	Voting Participation
1986	30%	74%	97%
1985	30%	83%	98%

Interest Groups

	ADA	ACU	AFL-CIO	CCUS
1986	80%	n/a	60%	37%
1985	65%	9%	75%	37%

Elections

1984	General	57%	Primary	79%
1978	General	56%	Primary	65%

Lloyd Bentsen (D-Texas)

Of Houston — Elected 1970

Born: Feb. 11, 1921, Mission, Texas.
Education: U. of Texas, LL.B. 1942.
Military Career: Army Air Corps, 1942-45; Air Force Reserve, 1950-59.
Occupation: Lawyer; financial executive.
Family: Wife, Beryl Ann "B. A." Longino; three children.
Religion: Presbyterian.
Political Career: Hidalgo County judge, 1946-48; U.S. House, 1948-55.
Capitol Office: 703 Hart Bldg. 20510; 224-5922.

Texas — The statewide vote for Ronald Reagan was 64% in 1984; 55% in 1980.

Committees

Commerce, Science and Transportation
Finance   (Chairman)
Joint Taxation
Joint Economic
Select Intelligence

CQ Voting Studies

	Presidential Support	Party Unity	Voting Participation
1986	60%	46%	96%
1985	50%	54%	94%

Interest Groups

	ADA	ACU	AFL-CIO	CCUS
1986	45%	n/a	33%	68%
1985	35%	62%	53%	46%

Elections

1982	General	59%	Primary	78%
1976	General	57%	Primary	63%

Joseph R. Biden Jr.   (D-Del.)

Of Wilmington — Elected 1972

Born: Nov. 20, 1942, Scranton, Pa.
Education: U. of Delaware, B.A. 1965; Syracuse U., J.D. 1968.
Occupation: Lawyer.
Family: Wife, Jill Jacobs; three children.
Religion: Roman Catholic.
Political Career: New Castle County Council, 1970-72.
Capitol Office: 489 Russell Bldg. 20510; 224-5042.

Delaware — The statewide vote for Ronald Reagan was 60% in 1984; 47% in 1980.

Committees

Foreign Relations
Judiciary   (Chairman)

Elections

1984	General	60%	Primary	u/o	
1978	General	58%	Primary	u/o	

CQ Voting Studies

	Presidential Support	Party Unity	Voting Participation
1986	27%	83%	94%
1985	31%	77%	92%

Interest Groups

	ADA	ACU	AFL-CIO	CCUS
1986	80%	n/a	87%	38%
1985	75%	10%	81%	37%

Jeff Bingaman   (D-N.M.)

Of Santa Fe — Elected 1982

Born: Oct. 3, 1943, El Paso, Texas.
Education: Harvard U., B.A. 1965; Stanford U., J.D. 1968.
Occupation: Lawyer.
Family: Wife, Anne Kovacovich; one child.
Religion: Methodist.
Political Career: N.M. Attorney General, 1979-82.
Capitol Office: 502 Hart Bldg. 20510; 224-5521.

New Mexico — The statewide vote for Ronald Reagan was 60% in 1984; 55% in 1980.

Committees

Armed Services
Energy and Natural Resources
Governmental Affairs
Joint Economic

Elections

1982	General	54%	Primary	54%

CQ Voting Studies

	Presidential Support	Party Unity	Voting Participation
1986	41%	70%	99%
1985	33%	75%	98%

Interest Groups

	ADA	ACU	AFL-CIO	CCUS
1986	65%	n/a	73%	26%
1985	70%	13%	81%	34%

Christopher S. "Kit" Bond (R-Mo.)

Of Kansas City — Elected 1986

Born: March 6, 1939, St. Louis, Mo.
Education: Princeton U., A.B. 1960; U. of Virginia Law School, LL.B. 1963.
Occupation: Lawyer.
Family: Wife, Carolyn Reid; one child.
Religion: Presbyterian.
Political Career: Republican nominee for U.S. House, 1968; assistant attorney general, 1969-70; Missouri state auditor, 1971-73; Republican nominee for governor, 1976; governor, 1973-77, 1981-85; chairman, Republican Governors Assn., 1975.
Capitol Office: 321 Hart Bldg. 20510; 224-5721.

Missouri — The statewide vote for Ronald Reagan was 60% in 1984; 51% in 1980.

Committees

Agriculture, Nutrition and Forestry
Banking, Housing and Urban Affairs
Small Business

Elections

1986	General	53%	Primary	89%

David L. Boren (D-Okla.)

Of Seminole — Elected 1978

Born: April 21, 1941, Washington, D.C.
Education: Yale U., B.A. 1963; Oxford U., England, M.A. 1965; U. of Oklahoma, J.D. 1968.
Military Career: National Guard, 1968-75.
Occupation: Lawyer.
Family: Wife, Molly Wanda Shi; two children.
Religion: Methodist.
Political Career: Okla. House, 1967-75; Okla. governor, 1975-79.
Capitol Office: 453 Russell Bldg. 20510; 224-4721.

Oklahoma — The statewide vote for Ronald Reagan was 69% in 1984; 61% in 1980.

Committees

Agriculture, Nutrition and Forestry
Finance
Small Business
Select Intelligence   (Chairman)
Select Iran-contra

Elections

1984	General	76%	Primary	90%
1978	General	66%	Primary	60% *

** Primary runoff.*

CQ Voting Studies

	Presidential Support	Party Unity	Voting Participation
1986	67%	42%	94%
1985	47%	52%	92%

Interest Groups

	ADA	ACU	AFL-CIO	CCUS
1986	40%	n/a	27%	65%
1985	45%	55%	47%	54%

CQ Voting Studies

	Presidential Support	Party Unity	Voting Participation
1986	84%	84%	100%
1985	87%	87%	99%

Interest Groups

	ADA	ACU	AFL-CIO	CCUS
1986	15%	n/a	13%	74%
1985	5%	78%	5%	79%

Rudy Boschwitz   (R-Minn.)

Of Plymouth — Elected 1978

Born: Nov. 7, 1930, Berlin, Germany.
Education: Johns Hopkins U., B.S. 1950; New York U., LL.B. 1953.
Military Career: Army, 1954-55.
Occupation: Lawyer; plywood company owner.
Family: Wife, Ellen Lowenstein; four children.
Religion: Jewish.
Political Career: Republican national committeeman from Minnesota, 1971-79.
Capitol Office: 506 Hart Bldg. 20510; 224-5641.

Minnesota — The statewide vote for Ronald Reagan was 50% in 1984; 43% in 1980.

Committees

Agriculture, Nutrition and Forestry
Foreign Relations
Budget
Small Business

Elections

1984	General	58%	Primary	97%
1978	General	57%	Primary	87%

CQ Voting Studies

	Presidential Support	Party Unity	Voting Participation
1986	51%	66%	92%
1985	33%	69%	91%

Interest Groups

	ADA	ACU	AFL-CIO	CCUS
1986	85%	n/a	87%	31%
1985	85%	9%	81%	28%

Bill Bradley   (D-N.J.)

Of Denville — Elected 1978

Born: July 28, 1943, Crystal City, Mo.
Education: Princeton U., B.A. 1965; Oxford U., England, M.A. 1968.
Military Career: Air Force Reserve, 1967-78.
Occupation: Basketball player.
Family: Wife, Ernestine Schlant; one child.
Religion: Protestant.
Political Career: No previous office.
Capitol Office: 731 Hart Bldg. 20510; 224-3224.

New Jersey — The statewide vote for Ronald Reagan was 60% in 1984; 52% in 1980.

Committees

Energy and Natural Resources
Finance
Special Aging
Select Intelligence

Elections

1984	General	64%	Primary	93%
1978	General	55%	Primary	59%

John B. Breaux (D-La.)

Of Crowley — Elected 1986

Born: March 1, 1944, Crowley, La.
Education: U. of Southwestern Louisiana, B.A. 1964; Louisiana State U., J.D. 1967.
Occupation: Lawyer.
Family: Wife, Lois Daigle; four children.
Religion: Roman Catholic.
Political Career: U.S. House, 1972-87.
Capitol Office: 194 Dirksen Bldg. 20510; 224-4623.

Louisiana — The statewide vote for Ronald Reagan was 61% in 1984; 51% in 1980.

CQ Voting Studies — House

	Presidential Support	Party Unity	Voting Participation
1986	21%	24%	31%
1985	49%	53%	89%

Interest Groups — House

	ADA	ACU	AFL-CIO	CCUS
1986	30%	n/a	100%	25%
1985	35%	62%	53%	62%

Committees

Commerce, Science and Transportation
Environment and Public Works
Special Aging

Elections

1986	General	53%	Primary	37%

Dale Bumpers (D-Ark.)

Of Charleston — Elected 1974

Born: Aug. 12, 1925, Charleston, Ark.
Education: Attended U. of Arkansas; Northwestern U., LL.B. 1951, J.D. 1965.
Military Career: Marine Corps, 1943-46.
Occupation: Lawyer; farmer; hardware company executive.
Family: Wife, Betty Flanagan; three children.
Religion: Methodist.
Political Career: Ark. governor, 1971-75.
Capitol Office: 229 Dirksen Bldg. 20510; 224-4843.

Arkansas — The statewide vote for Ronald Reagan was 60% in 1984; 48% in 1980.

CQ Voting Studies

	Presidential Support	Party Unity	Voting Participation
1986	39%	77%	96%
1985	32%	79%	97%

Interest Groups

	ADA	ACU	AFL-CIO	CCUS
1986	70%	n/a	64%	47%
1985	70%	13%	71%	45%

Committees

Appropriations
Energy and Natural Resources
Small Business (Chairman)

Elections

1986	General	63%	Primary	u/o
1980	General	59%	Primary	u/o

Quentin N. Burdick (D-N.D.)

Of Fargo — Elected 1960

Born: June 19, 1908, Munich, N.D.
Education: U. of Minnesota, B.A. 1931, LL.B. 1932.
Occupation: Lawyer.
Family: Wife, Jocelyn Birch Peterson; three children, three stepchildren.
Religion: United Church of Christ.
Political Career: U.S. House, 1959-60; Republican candidate for N.D. Senate, 1938; Republican nominee for lieutenant governor, 1942; Democratic nominee for governor, 1946 and U.S. Senate, 1956.
Capitol Office: 511 Hart Bldg. 20510; 224-2551.

North Dakota — The statewide vote for Ronald Reagan was 65% in 1984; 64% in 1980.

Committees

Appropriations
Environment and Public Works   (Chairman)
Special Aging
Select Indian Affairs

Elections

1982	General	63%	Primary	u/o
1976	General	62%	Primary	u/o

CQ Voting Studies

	Presidential Support	Party Unity	Voting Participation
1986	18%	87%	99%
1985	25%	87%	98%

Interest Groups

	ADA	ACU	AFL-CIO	CCUS
1986	100%	n/a	93%	21%
1985	85%	9%	86%	21%

Robert C. Byrd (D-W. Va.)

Of Sophia — Elected 1958

Born: Nov. 20, 1917, North Wilkesboro, N.C.
Education: Attended Beckley College, Concord College, Morris Harvey College, 1950-51; Marshall College, 1951-52; American U., J.D. 1963.
Occupation: Lawyer.
Family: Wife, Erma Ora James; two children.
Religion: Baptist.
Political Career: W.Va. House, 1947-51; W.Va. Senate, 1951-53; U.S. House, 1953-59.
Capitol Office: 311 Hart Bldg. 20510; 224-3954.

West Virginia — The statewide vote for Ronald Reagan was 55% in 1984; 45% in 1980.

Committees

Majority Leader
Appropriations
Judiciary
Rules and Administration

Elections

1982	General	69%	Primary	u/o
1976	General	u/o	Primary	u/o

CQ Voting Studies

	Presidential Support	Party Unity	Voting Participation
1986	36%	84%	99%
1985	37%	81%	100%

Interest Groups

	ADA	ACU	AFL-CIO	CCUS
1986	75%	n/a	93%	16%
1985	65%	43%	90%	21%

John H. Chafee (R-R.I.)

Of Warwick — Elected 1976

Born: Oct. 22, 1922, Providence, R.I.
Education: Yale U., B.A. 1947; Harvard U., LL.B. 1950.
Military Career: Marine Corps, 1942-45, 1951-52.
Occupation: Lawyer.
Family: Wife, Virginia Coates; five children.
Religion: Episcopalian.
Political Career: R.I. House, 1957-63, minority leader, 1959-63; R.I. governor, 1963-69; defeated for re-election as governor, 1968; Republican nominee for U.S. Senate, 1972.
Capitol Office: 567 Dirksen Bldg. 20510; 224-2921.

Rhode Island — The statewide vote for Ronald Reagan was 52% in 1984; 37% in 1980.

Committees

Environment and Public Works
Finance
Banking, Housing and Urban Affairs
Special Aging

Elections

1982	General	51%	Primary	u/o
1976	General	58%	Primary	u/o

CQ Voting Studies

	Presidential Support	Party Unity	Voting Participation
1986	67%	64%	98%
1985	72%	68%	97%

Interest Groups

	ADA	ACU	AFL-CIO	CCUS
1986	60%	n/a	33%	63%
1985	35%	39%	24%	76%

Lawton Chiles (D-Fla.)

Of Holmes Beach — Elected 1970

Born: April 3, 1930, Lakeland, Fla.
Education: U. of Florida, B.S. 1952, LL.B. 1955.
Military Career: Army, 1952-54.
Occupation: Lawyer.
Family: Wife, Rhea May Grafton; four children.
Religion: Presbyterian.
Political Career: Fla. House, 1959-67; Fla. Senate, 1967-71.
Capitol Office: 250 Russell Bldg. 20510; 224-5274.

Florida — The statewide vote for Ronald Reagan was 65% in 1984; 56% in 1980.

Committees

Appropriations
Budget (Chairman)
Governmental Affairs
Special Aging

Elections

1982	General	62%	Primary	u/o
1976	General	63%	Primary	u/o

CQ Voting Studies

	Presidential Support	Party Unity	Voting Participation
1986	57%	56%	95%
1985	40%	59%	83%

Interest Groups

	ADA	ACU	AFL-CIO	CCUS
1986	40%	n/a	47%	58%
1985	55%	37%	89%	31%

Thad Cochran (R-Miss.)

Of Jackson — Elected 1978

Born: Dec. 7, 1937, Pontotoc County, Miss.
Education: U. of Mississippi, B.A. 1959, J.D. 1965.
Military Career: Navy, 1959-61.
Occupation: Lawyer.
Family: Wife, Rose Clayton; two children.
Religion: Baptist.
Political Career: U.S. House, 1973-79.
Capitol Office: 326 Russell Bldg. 20510; 224-5054.

Mississippi — The statewide vote for Ronald Reagan was 62% in 1984; 49% in 1980.

Committees

Agriculture, Nutrition and Forestry
Appropriations
Labor and Human Resources

Elections

1984	General	61%	Primary	u/o
1978	General	45%	Primary	69%

CQ Voting Studies

	Presidential Support	Party Unity	Voting Participation
1986	88%	88%	98%
1985	80%	81%	95%

Interest Groups

	ADA	ACU	AFL-CIO	CCUS
1986	5%	n/a	0%	89%
1985	5%	74%	15%	81%

William S. Cohen (R-Maine)

Of Bangor — Elected 1978

Born: Aug. 28, 1940, Bangor, Maine.
Education: Bowdoin College, B.A. 1962; Boston U., LL.B. 1965.
Occupation: Lawyer.
Family: Wife, Diane Dunn; two children.
Religion: Unitarian.
Political Career: Bangor City Council, 1969-72; mayor of Bangor, 1971-72; U.S. House, 1973-79.
Capitol Office: 322 Hart Bldg. 20510; 224-2523.

Maine — The statewide vote for Ronald Reagan was 61% in 1984; 46% in 1980.

Committees

Armed Services
Governmental Affairs
Special Aging
Select Intelligence   (Ranking)
Select Iran-contra

Elections

1984	General	73%	Primary	u/o
1978	General	56%	Primary	u/o

CQ Voting Studies

	Presidential Support	Party Unity	Voting Participation
1986	78%	63%	96%
1985	63%	55%	93%

Interest Groups

	ADA	ACU	AFL-CIO	CCUS
1986	50%	n/a	20%	63%
1985	35%	55%	45%	68%

Kent Conrad (D-N.D.)

Of Bismarck — Elected 1986

Born: March 12, 1948, Bismarck, N.D.
Education: Stanford U., B.A. 1971; George Washington U., M.B.A. 1975.
Occupation: Management and personnel director.
Family: Wife, Lucy Calautti; one child.
Religion: Unitarian.
Political Career: Candidate for state auditor, 1976; state tax commissioner, 1981-87.
Capitol Office: 825A Hart Bldg. 20510; 224-2043.

North Dakota — The statewide vote for Ronald Reagan was 65% in 1984; 64% in 1980.

Committees

Agriculture, Nutrition and Forestry
Budget
Energy and Natural Resources

Elections

1986	General	50%	Primary	u/o

Alan Cranston (D-Calif.)

Of Los Angeles — Elected 1968

Born: June 19, 1914, Palo Alto, Calif.
Education: Attended Pomona College, 1932-33; U. of Mexico, 1933; Stanford U., A.B. 1936.
Military Career: Army, 1944-45.
Occupation: Journalist; real estate executive; author.
Family: Wife, Norma Weintraub; one child.
Religion: Protestant.
Political Career: Calif. Controller, 1959-67; sought Democratic nomination for U.S. Senate, 1964; sought Democratic nomination for President, 1984.
Capitol Office: 112 Hart Bldg. 20510; 224-3553.

California — The statewide vote for Ronald Reagan was 58% in 1984; 53% in 1980.

Committees

Majority Whip
Banking, Housing and Urban Affairs
Foreign Relations
Veterans' Affairs (Chairman)
Select Intelligence

Elections

1986	General	51%	Primary	81%
1980	General	57%	Primary	80%

CQ Voting Studies

	Presidential Support	Party Unity	Voting Participation
1986	20%	85%	94%
1985	25%	80%	96%

Interest Groups

	ADA	ACU	AFL-CIO	CCUS
1986	95%	n/a	87%	32%
1985	100%	4%	80%	21%

Alfonse M. D'Amato (R-N.Y.)

Of Island Park — Elected 1980

Born: Aug. 1, 1937, Brooklyn, N.Y.
Education: Syracuse U., B.S. 1959; J.D. 1961.
Occupation: Lawyer.
Family: Wife, Penny Collenburg; four children.
Religion: Roman Catholic.
Political Career: Nassau County public administrator, 1965-68; receiver of taxes, town of Hempstead, 1969-71; Hempstead town supervisor, 1971-77; presiding supervisor, 1977-81; vice chairman, Nassau County Board of Supervisors, 1977-80.
Capitol Office: 520 Hart Bldg. 20510; 224-6542.

New York — The statewide vote for Ronald Reagan was 54% in 1984; 47% in 1980.

Committees

Appropriations
Banking, Housing and Urban Affairs
Small Business
Joint Economic

Elections

1986	General	57%	Primary	u/o
1980	General	45%	Primary	56%

CQ Voting Studies

	Presidential Support	Party Unity	Voting Participation
1986	77%	66%	98%
1985	71%	69%	97%

Interest Groups

	ADA	ACU	AFL-CIO	CCUS
1986	35%	n/a	53%	56%
1985	20%	70%	62%	62%

John C. Danforth (R-Mo.)

Of Newburg — Elected 1976

Born: Sept. 5, 1936, St. Louis, Mo.
Education: Princeton U., A.B. 1958; Yale U., B.D., LL.B. 1963.
Occupation: Lawyer; clergyman.
Family: Wife, Sally Dobson; five children.
Religion: Episcopalian.
Political Career: Mo. Attorney General, 1969-77; Republican nominee for U.S. Senate, 1970.
Capitol Office: 497 Russell Bldg. 20510; 224-6154.

Missouri — The statewide vote for Ronald Reagan was 60% in 1984; 51% in 1980.

Committees

Budget
Commerce, Science and Transportation (Ranking)
Finance

Elections

1982	General	51%	Primary	74%
1976	General	57%	Primary	93%

CQ Voting Studies

	Presidential Support	Party Unity	Voting Participation
1986	80%	77%	98%
1985	81%	77%	96%

Interest Groups

	ADA	ACU	AFL-CIO	CCUS
1986	30%	n/a	33%	61%
1985	15%	65%	19%	75%

Thomas A. Daschle   (D-S.D.)

Of Aberdeen — Elected 1986

Born: Dec. 9, 1947, Aberdeen, S.D.
Education: South Dakota State U., B.A. 1969.
Military Career: Air Force, 1969-72.
Occupation: Congressional aide.
Family: Wife, Linda Hall; three children.
Religion: Roman Catholic.
Political Career: U.S. House, 1979-87.
Capitol Office: 724 Hart Bldg. 20510; 224-2321.

South Dakota — The statewide vote for Ronald Reagan was 63% in 1984; 61% in 1980.

Committees

Agriculture, Nutrition and Forestry
Finance
Select Indian Affairs

Elections

1986	General	52%	Primary	u/o

CQ Voting Studies — House

	Presidential Support	Party Unity	Voting Participation
1986	20%	84%	99%
1985	16%	83%	92%

Interest Groups — House

	ADA	ACU	AFL-CIO	CCUS
1986	80%	n/a	64%	22%
1985	70%	16%	60%	38%

Dennis DeConcini   (D-Ariz.)

Of Tucson — Elected 1976

Born: May 8, 1937, Tucson, Ariz.
Education: U. of Arizona, B.A. 1959, LL.B. 1963.
Military Career: Army, 1959-60; Army Reserve, 1960-67.
Occupation: Lawyer.
Family: Wife, Susan Hurley; three children.
Religion: Roman Catholic.
Political Career: Pima County attorney, 1973-76.
Capitol Office: 328 Hart Bldg. 20510; 224-4521.

Arizona — The statewide vote for Ronald Reagan was 66% in 1984; 61% in 1980.

Committees

Appropriations
Judiciary
Rules and Administration
Veterans' Affairs
Select Indian Affairs
Select Intelligence

Elections

1982	General	57%	Primary	84%
1976	General	54%	Primary	53%

CQ Voting Studies

	Presidential Support	Party Unity	Voting Participation
1986	43%	62%	97%
1985	45%	62%	94%

Interest Groups

	ADA	ACU	AFL-CIO	CCUS
1986	45%	n/a	60%	35%
1985	45%	38%	62%	45%

Alan J. Dixon (D-Ill.)

Of Belleville — Elected 1980

Born: July 7, 1927, Belleville, Ill.
Education: U. of Illinois, B.S. 1949; Washington U., St. Louis, LL.B. 1949.
Military Career: Naval Air Cadet, 1945-46.
Occupation: Lawyer.
Family: Wife, Joan Louise Fox; three children.
Religion: Presbyterian.
Political Career: Ill. House 1951-63; Ill. Senate, 1963-71; state treasurer, 1971-77; secretary of state, 1977-81.
Capitol Office: 316 Hart Bldg. 20510; 224-2854.

Illinois — The statewide vote for Ronald Reagan was 56% in 1984; 50% in 1980.

Committees

Armed Services
Banking, Housing and Urban Affairs
Small Business

CQ Voting Studies

	Presidential Support	Party Unity	Voting Participation
1986	51%	62%	97%
1985	46%	69%	96%

Interest Groups

	ADA	ACU	AFL-CIO	CCUS
1986	65%	n/a	80%	58%
1985	60%	41%	81%	43%

Elections

1986	General	65%	Primary	85%
1980	General	56%	Primary	67%

Christopher J. Dodd (D-Conn.)

Of East Haddam — Elected 1980

Born: May 27, 1944, Willimantic, Conn.
Education: Providence College, B.A. 1966; U. of Louisville, J.D. 1972.
Military Career: Army Reserve, 1969-75.
Occupation: Lawyer.
Family: Divorced.
Religion: Roman Catholic.
Political Career: U.S. House, 1975-81.
Capitol Office: 324 Hart Bldg. 20510; 224-2823.

Connecticut — The statewide vote for Ronald Reagan was 61% in 1984; 48% in 1980.

Committees

Banking, Housing and Urban Affairs
Budget
Foreign Relations
Labor and Human Resources
Rules and Administration

CQ Voting Studies

	Presidential Support	Party Unity	Voting Participation
1986	25%	71%	99%
1985	34%	83%	96%

Interest Groups

	ADA	ACU	AFL-CIO	CCUS
1986	85%	n/a	73%	44%
1985	85%	4%	95%	41%

Elections

1986	General	65%	Primary	u/o
1980	General	56%	Primary	u/o

Robert Dole   (R-Kan.)

Of Russell — Elected 1968

Born: July 22, 1923, Russell, Kan.
Education: Attended U. of Kansas, 1941-43;
   Washburn U., A.B. 1952, LL.B. 1952.
Military Career: Army, 1943-48.
Occupation: Lawyer.
Family: Wife, Mary Elizabeth Hanford; one child.
Religion: Methodist.
Political Career: Kan. House, 1951-53; Russell County
   attorney, 1953-61; U.S. House, 1961-69; Republican nomi-
   nee for vice president, 1976; candidate for Republican
   presidential nomination, 1980.
Capitol Office: 141 Hart Bldg. 20510; 224-6521.
Kansas — The statewide vote for Ronald Reagan was 66%
in 1984; 58% in 1980.

Committees

Minority Leader
Agriculture, Nutrition and Forestry
Finance
Rules and Administration
Joint Taxation

Elections

1986	General	70%	Primary	84%
1980	General	64%	Primary	82%

CQ Voting Studies

	Presidential Support	Party Unity	Voting Participation
1986	92%	92%	99%
1985	92%	92%	99%

Interest Groups

	ADA	ACU	AFL-CIO	CCUS
1986	0%	n/a	0%	89%
1985	0%	91%	10%	90%

Pete V. Domenici   (R-N.M.)

Of Albuquerque — Elected 1972

Born: May 7, 1932, Albuquerque, N.M.
Education: U. of Albuquerque, 1950-52; U. of New Mexico,
   B.S. 1954; U. of Denver, LL.B. 1958.
Occupation: Lawyer.
Family: Wife, Nancy Burk; eight children.
Religion: Roman Catholic.
Political Career: Albuquerque City Commission, 1966-70,
   chairman and ex-officio mayor, 1967-70; Republican nomi-
   nee for governor, 1970.
Capitol Office: 434 Dirksen Bldg. 20510; 224-6621.

New Mexico — The statewide vote for Ronald Reagan was
60% in 1984; 55% in 1980.

Committees

Appropriations
Budget   (Ranking)
Energy and Natural Resources
Special Aging

Elections

1984	General	72%	Primary	u/o
1978	General	53%	Primary	u/o

CQ Voting Studies

	Presidential Support	Party Unity	Voting Participation
1986	88%	89%	99%
1985	82%	90%	96%

Interest Groups

	ADA	ACU	AFL-CIO	CCUS
1986	5%	n/a	13%	79%
1985	5%	82%	10%	83%

Dave Durenberger (R-Minn.)

Of Minneapolis — Elected 1978

Born: Aug. 19, 1934, St. Cloud, Minn.
Education: St. John's U., B.A. 1955; U. of Minnesota, J.D. 1959.
Military Career: Army Reserve, 1956-63.
Occupation: Lawyer; adhesive manufacturing executive.
Family: Wife, Gilda Beth "Penny" Baran; four children.
Religion: Roman Catholic.
Political Career: No previous office.
Capitol Office: 154 Russell Bldg. 20510; 224-3244.

Minnesota — The statewide vote for Ronald Reagan was 50% in 1984; 43% in 1980.

Committees

Environment and Public Works
Finance
Special Aging

Elections

1982	General	53%	Primary	93%
1978	General	61% *	Primary	67% *

Special election.

CQ Voting Studies

	Presidential Support	Party Unity	Voting Participation
1986	64%	65%	97%
1985	70%	59%	82%

Interest Groups

	ADA	ACU	AFL-CIO	CCUS
1986	40%	n/a	40%	58%
1985	30%	48%	47%	54%

Daniel J. Evans (R-Wash.)

Of Olympia — Elected 1983

Born: Oct. 16, 1925, Seattle, Wash.
Education: U. of Washington, B.S. 1948, M.S. 1949.
Military Career: Navy Reserve 1943-46, active duty 1951-53.
Occupation: College president; engineer.
Family: Wife, Nancy Ann Bell; three children.
Religion: Congregationalist.
Political Career: Wash. House 1957-65, minority floor leader 1961-65; governor 1965-77.
Capitol Office: 702 Hart Bldg. 20510; 224-3441.

Washington — The statewide vote for Ronald Reagan was 56% in 1984; 50% in 1980.

Committees

Energy and Natural Resources
Foreign Relations
Select Indian Affairs (Ranking)

Elections

1983	General	55% *	Primary	64% *

Special election.

CQ Voting Studies

	Presidential Support	Party Unity	Voting Participation
1986	76%	72%	96%
1985	84%	79%	98%

Interest Groups

	ADA	ACU	AFL-CIO	CCUS
1986	35%	n/a	29%	67%
1985	25%	57%	10%	79%

J. James Exon (D-Neb.)

Of Lincoln — Elected 1978

Born: Aug., 9, 1921, Geddes, S.D.
Education: Attended U. of Omaha, 1939-41.
Military Career: Army, 1941-45; Reserve, 1945-49.
Occupation: Office equipment dealer.
Family: Wife, Patricia Ann Pros; three children.
Religion: Episcopalian.
Political Career: Democratic National Committeeman from Neb., 1968-71, 1981-present; Neb. governor, 1971-79.
Capitol Office: 330 Hart Bldg. 20510; 224-4224.

Nebraska — The statewide vote for Ronald Reagan was 71% in 1984; 66% in 1980.

Committees

Armed Services
Budget
Commerce, Science and Transportation

Elections

1984	General	52%	Primary	u/o
1978	General	68%	Primary	u/o

CQ Voting Studies

	Presidential Support	Party Unity	Voting Participation
1986	34%	66%	96%
1985	43%	54%	90%

Interest Groups

	ADA	ACU	AFL-CIO	CCUS
1986	35%	n/a	53%	32%
1985	25%	59%	43%	46%

Wendell H. Ford (D-Ky.)

Of Owensboro — Elected 1974

Born: Sept. 8, 1924, Daviess County, Ky.
Education: Attended U. of Kentucky, 1942-43.
Military Career: Army, 1944-46; National Guard, 1949-62.
Occupation: Insurance executive.
Family: Wife, Jean Neel; two children.
Religion: Baptist.
Political Career: Ky. Senate, 1965-67; Ky. lieutenant governor, 1967-71; Ky. governor, 1971-74.
Capitol Office: 173A Russell Bldg. 20510; 224-4343.

Kentucky — The statewide vote for Ronald Reagan was 60% in 1984; 49% in 1980.

Committees

Commerce, Science and Transportation
Energy and Natural Resources
Rules and Administration   (Chairman)

Elections

1986	General	74%	Primary	u/o
1980	General	65%	Primary	87%

CQ Voting Studies

	Presidential Support	Party Unity	Voting Participation
1986	34%	74%	99%
1985	39%	76%	99%

Interest Groups

	ADA	ACU	AFL-CIO	CCUS
1986	55%	n/a	67%	53%
1985	50%	43%	81%	48%

Wyche Fowler Jr. (D-Ga.)

Of Atlanta — Elected 1986

Born: Oct. 6, 1940, Atlanta, Ga.
Education: Davidson College, A.B. 1962; Emory U., J.D. 1969.
Military Career: Army, 1963-65.
Occupation: Lawyer.
Family: Divorced; one child.
Religion: Presbyterian.
Political Career: Atlanta Board of Aldermen, 1970-74; president, Atlanta City Council, 1974-77; sought Democratic nomination for U.S. House, 1972; U.S. House, 1977-87.
Capitol Office: 320 Hart Bldg. 20510; 224-3643.

Georgia — The statewide vote for Ronald Reagan was 60% in 1984; 41% in 1980.

Committees

Agriculture, Nutrition and Forestry
Budget
Energy and Natural Resources

Elections

1986	General	51%	Primary	50%

CQ Voting Studies — House

	Presidential Support	Party Unity	Voting Participation
1986	17%	30%	36%
1985	24%	73%	86%

Interest Groups — House

	ADA	ACU	AFL-CIO	CCUS
1986	15%	n/a	43%	50%
1985	50%	26%	50%	50%

Jake Garn (R-Utah)

Of Salt Lake City — Elected 1974

Born: Oct. 12, 1932, Richfield, Utah.
Education: U. of Utah, B.S. 1955.
Military Career: Navy, 1956-60; Air National Guard 1960-69.
Occupation: Insurance executive.
Family: Wife, Kathleen Brewerton; seven children.
Religion: Mormon.
Political Career: Salt Lake City commissioner, 1968-72; mayor of Salt Lake City, 1972-74.
Capitol Office: 505 Dirksen Bldg. 20510; 224-5444.

Utah — The statewide vote for Ronald Reagan was 75% in 1984; 73% in 1980.

Committees

Appropriations
Banking, Housing and Urban Affairs (Ranking)
Rules and Administration

Elections

1986	General	73%	Primary	u/o
1980	General	74%	Primary	u/o

CQ Voting Studies

	Presidential Support	Party Unity	Voting Participation
1986	80%	73%	72%
1985	73%	83%	90%

Interest Groups

	ADA	ACU	AFL-CIO	CCUS
1986	0%	n/a	7%	100%
1985	0%	100%	21%	96%

John Glenn (D-Ohio)

Of Columbus — Elected 1974

Born: July 18, 1921, Cambridge, Ohio.
Education: Muskingum College, B.S. 1962.
Military Career: Marine Corps, 1942-65.
Occupation: Astronaut; soft drink company executive.
Family: Wife, Anna Margaret Castor; two children.
Religion: Presbyterian.
Political Career: Sought Democratic nomination for U.S. Senate, 1970; sought Democratic nomination for president, 1984.
Capitol Office: 503 Hart Bldg. 20510; 224-3353.

Ohio — The statewide vote for Ronald Reagan was 59% in 1984; 52% in 1980.

CQ Voting Studies

	Presidential Support	Party Unity	Voting Participation
1986	42%	74%	95%
1985	42%	79%	97%

Interest Groups

	ADA	ACU	AFL-CIO	CCUS
1986	65%	n/a	87%	44%
1985	75%	27%	86%	34%

Committees

Armed Services
Governmental Affairs   (Chairman)
Special Aging

Elections

1986	General	62%	Primary	88%
1980	General	69%	Primary	86%

Albert Gore Jr. (D-Tenn.)

Of Carthage — Elected 1984

Born: March 31, 1948, Washington, D.C.
Education: Harvard U., B.A. 1969; attended Vanderbilt School of Religion, 1972; attended Vanderbilt Law School, 1974-76.
Military Career: Army, 1969-71.
Occupation: Journalist; home builder.
Family: Wife, Mary Elizabeth "Tipper" Aitcheson; four children.
Religion: Baptist.
Political Career: U.S. House 1976-84.
Capitol Office: 393 Russell Bldg. 20510; 224-4944.

Tennessee — The statewide vote for Ronald Reagan was 58% in 1984; 49% in 1980.

CQ Voting Studies

	Presidential Support	Party Unity	Voting Participation
1986	29%	83%	99%
1985	34%	86%	99%

Interest Groups

	ADA	ACU	AFL-CIO	CCUS
1986	70%	n/a	87%	32%
1985	65%	i7%	86%	41%

Committees

Armed Services
Commerce, Science and Transportation
Rules and Administration

Elections

1984	General	61%	Primary u/o

Bob Graham   (D-Fla.)

Of Miami Lakes — Elected 1986

Born: Nov. 9, 1936, Coral Gables, Fla.
Education: U. of Florida, B.A. 1959; Harvard Law School, LL.B. 1962.
Occupation: Developer; cattleman.
Family: Wife, Adele Khoury; four children.
Religion: United Church of Christ.
Political Career: Fla. House, 1967-71; Fla. Senate, 1971-79; governor, 1979-87.
Capitol Office: 313 Hart Bldg. 20510; 224-3041.

Florida — The statewide vote for Ronald Reagan was 65% in 1984; 56% in 1980.

Committees

Banking, Housing and Urban Affairs
Environment and Public Works
Veterans' Affairs

Elections

1986	General	55%	Primary	85%

Phil Gramm   (R-Texas)

Of College Station — Elected 1984

Born: July 8, 1942, Fort Benning, Ga.
Education: U. of Georgia, B.B.A., 1964, Ph.D. 1967.
Occupation: Economics professor.
Family: Wife, Wendy Lee; two children.
Religion: Episcopalian.
Political Career: U.S. House, 1979-85; sought Democratic nomination for U.S. Senate, 1976.
Capitol Office: 370 Russell Bldg. 20510; 224-2934.

Texas — The statewide vote for Ronald Reagan was 64% in 1984; 55% in 1980.

Committees

Armed Services
Banking, Housing and Urban Affairs

Elections

1984	General	59%	Primary	73%

CQ Voting Studies

	Presidential Support	Party Unity	Voting Participation
1986	99%	95%	98%
1985	87%	95%	98%

Interest Groups

	ADA	ACU	AFL-CIO	CCUS
1986	0%	n/a	0%	89%
1985	0%	95%	0%	86%

Charles E. Grassley (R-Iowa)

Of New Hartford — Elected 1980

Born: Sept. 17, 1933, New Hartford, Iowa.
Education: U. of Northern Iowa, B.A. 1955, M.A. 1956; graduate work, U. of Iowa, 1957-58.
Occupation: Farmer.
Family: Wife, Barbara Ann Speicher; five children.
Religion: Baptist.
Political Career: Iowa House, 1959-75; U.S. House, 1975-81.
Capitol Office: 135 Hart Bldg. 20510; 224-3744.

Iowa — The statewide vote for Ronald Reagan was 53% in 1984; 51% in 1980.

CQ Voting Studies

	Presidential Support	Party Unity	Voting Participation
1986	67%	72%	99%
1985	66%	64%	99%

Interest Groups

	ADA	ACU	AFL-CIO	CCUS
1986	30%	n/a	27%	74%
1985	10%	57%	33%	69%

Committees

Appropriations
Budget
Judiciary
Special Aging

Elections

1986	General	66%	Primary	u/o
1980	General	54%	Primary	66%

Tom Harkin (D-Iowa)

Of Cumming — Elected 1984

Born: Nov. 19, 1939, Cumming, Iowa.
Education: Iowa State U., B.S. 1962; Catholic U. Law School, J.D. 1972.
Military Career: Navy, 1962-67; Naval Reserve, 1968-74.
Occupation: Lawyer.
Family: Wife, Ruth Raduenz; two children.
Religion: Roman Catholic.
Political Career: Democratic nominee for U.S. House, 1972; U.S. House 1975-85.
Capitol Office: 317 Hart Bldg. 20510; 224-3254.

Iowa — The statewide vote for Ronald Reagan was 53% in 1984; 51% in 1980.

CQ Voting Studies

	Presidential Support	Party Unity	Voting Participation
1986	19%	91%	97%
1985	22%	90%	98%

Interest Groups

	ADA	ACU	AFL-CIO	CCUS
1986	90%	n/a	93%	28%
1985	100%	5%	90%	24%

Committees

Agriculture, Nutrition and Forestry
Appropriations
Labor and Human Resources
Small Business

Elections

1984	General	56%	Primary	u/o

Orrin G. Hatch   (R-Utah)

Of Midvale — Elected 1976

Born: March 22, 1934, Pittsburgh, Pa.
Education: Brigham Young U., B.S. 1959; U. of Pittsburgh, LL.B. 1962.
Occupation: Lawyer.
Family: Wife, Elaine Hansen; six children.
Religion: Mormon.
Political Career: No previous office.
Capitol Office: 135 Russell Bldg. 20510; 224-5251.

Utah — The statewide vote for Ronald Reagan was 75% in 1984; 73% in 1980.

CQ Voting Studies

	Presidential Support	Party Unity	Voting Participation
1986	92%	92%	100%
1985	82%	85%	97%

Interest Groups

	ADA	ACU	AFL-CIO	CCUS
1986	5%	n/a	13%	95%
1985	10%	91%	19%	86%

Committees

Judiciary
Labor and Human Resources   (Ranking)
Select Intelligence
Select Iran-contra

Elections

1982	General	58%	Primary	u/o
1976	General	54%	Primary	65%

Mark O. Hatfield   (R-Ore.)

Of Tigard — Elected 1966

Born: July 12, 1922, Dallas, Ore.
Education: Willamette U., B.A. 1943; Stanford U., A.M. 1948.
Military Career: Navy, 1943-46.
Occupation: Political science professor.
Family: Wife, Antoinette Kuzmanich; four children.
Religion: Baptist.
Political Career: Ore. House, 1951-55; Ore. Senate, 1955-57; Ore. secretary of state, 1957-59; Ore. governor, 1959-67.
Capitol Office: 711 Hart Bldg. 20510; 224-3753.

Oregon — The statewide vote for Ronald Reagan was 56% in 1984; 48% in 1980.

CQ Voting Studies

	Presidential Support	Party Unity	Voting Participation
1986	42%	54%	96%
1985	45%	49%	85%

Interest Groups

	ADA	ACU	AFL-CIO	CCUS
1986	75%	n/a	47%	39%
1985	45%	18%	39%	70%

Committees

Appropriations   (Ranking)
Energy and Natural Resources
Rules and Administration

Elections

1984	General	67%	Primary	79%
1978	General	62%	Primary	66%

Chic Hecht   (R-Nev.)

Of Las Vegas — Elected 1982

Born: Nov. 30, 1928, Cape Girardeau, Mo.
Education: Washington U. (St. Louis), B.S. 1949.
Military Career: Army, 1951-53.
Occupation: Clothing store owner.
Family: Wife, Gail Kahn; two children.
Religion: Jewish.
Political Career: Nev. Senate, 1967-75.
Capitol Office: 302 Hart Bldg. 20510; 224-6244.

Nevada — The statewide vote for Ronald Reagan was 66% in 1984; 63% in 1980.

CQ Voting Studies

	Presidential Support	Party Unity	Voting Participation
1986	89%	95%	99%
1985	89%	98%	100%

Interest Groups

	ADA	ACU	AFL-CIO	CCUS
1986	0%	n/a	0%	100%
1985	0%	100%	5%	93%

Committees

Banking, Housing and Urban Affairs
Energy and Natural Resources
Select Intelligence

Elections

1982	General	50%	Primary	39%

Howell Heflin   (D-Ala.)

Of Tuscumbia — Elected 1978

Born: June 19, 1921, Poulan, Ga.
Education: Birmingham Southern College, B.A. 1942; U. of Alabama, J.D. 1948.
Military Career: Marine Corps, 1942-46.
Occupation: Lawyer; judge.
Family: Wife, Elizabeth Ann Carmichael; one child.
Religion: Methodist.
Political Career: Chief justice, Ala. Supreme Court, 1971-77.
Capitol Office: 728 Hart Bldg. 20510; 224-4124.

Alabama — The statewide vote for Ronald Reagan was 61% in 1984; 49% in 1980.

Committees

Agriculture, Nutrition and Forestry
Judiciary
Select Ethics   (Chairman)
Select Iran-contra

CQ Voting Studies

	Presidential Support	Party Unity	Voting Participation
1986	76%	42%	99%
1985	54%	56%	99%

Interest Groups

	ADA	ACU	AFL-CIO	CCUS
1986	25%	n/a	53%	58%
1985	25%	74%	67%	45%

Elections

1984	General	63%	Primary	83%
1978	General	94%	Primary	65% *

** Primary runoff.*

John Heinz (R-Pa.)

Of Pittsburgh — Elected 1976

Born: Oct. 23, 1938, Pittsburgh, Pa.
Education: Yale U., B.A. 1960; Harvard U., M.B.A. 1963.
Military Career: Air Force, 1963-69.
Occupation: Food industry executive.
Family: Wife, Teresa Simoes-Ferreira; three children.
Religion: Episcopalian.
Political Career: U.S. House, 1971-77.
Capitol Office: 277 Russell Bldg. 20510; 224-6324.

Pennsylvania — The statewide vote for Ronald Reagan was 53% in 1984; 50% in 1980.

Committees

Banking, Housing and Urban Affairs
Finance
Govermental Affairs
Special Aging   (Ranking)

Elections

1982	General	59%	Primary	u/o
1976	General	52%	Primary	38%

CQ Voting Studies

	Presidential Support	Party Unity	Voting Participation
1986	69%	56%	98%
1985	64%	54%	94%

Interest Groups

	ADA	ACU	AFL-CIO	CCUS
1986	55%	n/a	60%	59%
1985	35%	55%	67%	59%

Jesse Helms (R-N.C.)

Of Raleigh — Elected 1972

Born: Oct. 18, 1921, Monroe, N.C.
Education: Attended Wingate Jr. College and Wake Forest College, 1941.
Military Career: Navy, 1942-45.
Occupation: Journalist; broadcasting executive.
Family: Wife, Dorothy Jane Coble; three children.
Religion: Baptist.
Political Career: Raleigh City Council, 1957-61.
Capitol Office: 403 Dirksen Bldg. 20510; 224-6342.

North Carolina — The statewide vote for Ronald Reagan was 62% in 1984; 49% in 1980.

Committees

Agriculture, Nutrition and Forestry
Foreign Relations   (Ranking)
Rules and Administration
Select Ethics

Elections

1984	General	52%	Primary	91%
1978	General	55%	Primary	u/o

CQ Voting Studies

	Presidential Support	Party Unity	Voting Participation
1986	90%	95%	100%
1985	79%	94%	99%

Interest Groups

	ADA	ACU	AFL-CIO	CCUS
1986	0%	n/a	0%	95%
1985	0%	100%	5%	93%

Ernest F. Hollings (D-S.C.)

Of Charleston — Elected 1966

Born: Jan. 1, 1922, Charleston, S.C.
Education: The Citadel, B.A. 1942; U. of South Carolina, LL.B. 1947.
Military Career: Army, 1942-45.
Occupation: Lawyer.
Family: Wife, Rita Louise Liddy; four children.
Religion: Lutheran.
Political Career: S.C. House, 1949-55; S.C. lieutenant governor, 1955-59; S.C. governor, 1959-63; sought Democratic nomination for U.S. Senate, 1962; sought Democratic presidential nomination, 1984.
Capitol Office: 125 Russell Bldg. 20510; 224-6121.

South Carolina — The statewide vote for Ronald Reagan was 64% in 1984; 49% in 1980.

Committees

Appropriations
Budget
Commerce, Science and Transportation   (Chairman)
Select Intelligence

Elections

1986	General	64%	Primary	u/o
1980	General	70%	Primary	81%

CQ Voting Studies

	Presidential Support	Party Unity	Voting Participation
1986	70%	54%	100%
1985	52%	59%	100%

Interest Groups

	ADA	ACU	AFL-CIO	CCUS
1986	35%	n/a	73%	32%
1985	45%	52%	62%	55%

Gordon J. Humphrey (R-N.H.)

Of Chichester — Elected 1978

Born: Oct. 9, 1940, Bristol, Conn.
Education: Attended U. of Maryland, 1960-61; George Washington U., 1962-63; Burnside-Ott Aviation Inst., 1965.
Military Career: Air Force, 1958-62.
Occupation: Airline pilot.
Family: Wife, Patricia Greene; one child.
Religion: Baptist.
Political Career: No previous office.
Capitol Office: 531 Hart Bldg. 20510; 224-2841.

New Hampshire — The statewide vote for Ronald Reagan was 69% in 1984; 58% in 1980.

Committees

Armed Services
Judiciary
Labor and Human Resources

Elections

1984	General	59%	Primary	u/o
1978	General	51%	Primary	50%

CQ Voting Studies

	Presidential Support	Party Unity	Voting Participation
1986	92%	83%	95%
1985	80%	87%	94%

Interest Groups

	ADA	ACU	AFL-CIO	CCUS
1986	0%	n/a	0%	89%
1985	5%	90%	17%	83%

Daniel K. Inouye   (D-Hawaii)

Of Honolulu — Elected 1962

Born: Sept. 7, 1924, Honolulu, Hawaii.
Education: U. of Hawaii, A.B. 1950; George Washington U., J.D. 1952.
Military Career: Army, 1943-47.
Occupation: Lawyer.
Family: Wife, Margaret Shinobu Awamura; one child.
Religion: Methodist.
Political Career: Hawaii Territorial House, majority leader, 1954-58; Hawaii Territorial Senate, 1958-59; U.S. House, 1959-63.
Capitol Office: 722 Hart Bldg. 20510; 224-3934.

Hawaii — The statewide vote for Ronald Reagan was 55% in 1984; 45% in 1980.

Committees

Appropriations
Commerce, Science and Transportation
Rules and Administration
Select Indian Affairs   (Chairman)
Select Iran-contra   (Chairman)

Elections

1986	General	74%	Primary	u/o
1980	General	78%	Primary	88%

CQ Voting Studies

	Presidential Support	Party Unity	Voting Participation
1986	17%	72%	86%
1985	20%	80%	87%

Interest Groups

	ADA	ACU	AFL-CIO	CCUS
1986	90%	n/a	100%	38%
1985	95%	5%	95%	24%

J. Bennett Johnston   (D-La.)

Of Shreveport — Elected 1972

Born: June 10, 1932, Shreveport, La.
Education: Attended Washington and Lee U., 1950-51, 1952-53; attended U.S. Military Academy 1951-52; Louisiana State U., LL.B. 1956.
Military Career: Army, 1956-59.
Occupation: Lawyer.
Family: Wife, Mary Gunn; four children.
Religion: Baptist.
Political Career: La. House, 1964-68; La. Senate, 1968-72; sought Democratic nomination for governor, 1971.
Capitol Office: 136 Hart Bldg. 20510; 224-5824.

Louisiana — The statewide vote for Ronald Reagan was 61% in 1984; 51% in 1980.

Committees

Appropriations
Budget
Energy and Natural Resources   (Chairman)
Special Aging

Elections

1984	General	†	Primary	86%
1978	General	†	Primary	59%

†In Louisiana the primary is open to candidates of all parties. If a candidate wins 50% or more of the vote no general election is held.

CQ Voting Studies

	Presidential Support	Party Unity	Voting Participation
1986	58%	61%	98%
1985	45%	63%	95%

Interest Groups

	ADA	ACU	AFL-CIO	CCUS
1986	50%	n/a	67%	44%
1985	60%	45%	80%	28%

Nancy Landon Kassebaum   (R-Kan.)

Of Wichita — Elected 1978

Born: July 29, 1932, Topeka, Kan.
Education: U. of Kansas, B.A. 1954; U. of Michigan, M.A. 1956.
Occupation: Broadcasting executive.
Family: Divorced; four children.
Religion: Episcopalian.
Political Career: Maize School Board, 1973-75.
Capitol Office: 302 Russell Bldg. 20510; 224-4774.

Kansas — The statewide vote for Ronald Reagan was 66% in 1984; 58% in 1980.

CQ Voting Studies

	Presidential Support	Party Unity	Voting Participation
1986	70%	77%	96%
1985	76%	79%	95%

Interest Groups

	ADA	ACU	AFL-CIO	CCUS
1986	45%	n/a	21%	58%
1985	35%	48%	10%	69%

Committees

Budget
Commerce, Science and Transportation
Foreign Relations
Select Ethics

Elections

1984	General	76%	Primary	u/o
1978	General	54%	Primary	31%

Bob Kasten   (R-Wis.)

Of Milwaukee — Elected 1980

Born: June 19, 1942, Milwaukee, Wis.
Education: U. of Arizona, B.A. 1964; Columbia U., M.B.A. 1966.
Military Career: Air Force, 1967; Wis. Air National Guard, 1967-72.
Occupation: Shoe company executive.
Family: Single.
Religion: Episcopalian.
Political Career: Republican nominee for Wis. Assembly, 1970; Wis. Senate, 1973-75; U.S. House, 1975-79; sought Republican nomination for governor, 1978.
Capitol Office: 110 Hart Bldg. 20510; 224-5323.

Wisconsin — The statewide vote for Ronald Reagan was 54% in 1984; 48% in 1980.

Committees

Appropriations
Budget
Commerce, Science and Transportation
Small Business

CQ Voting Studies

	Presidential Support	Party Unity	Voting Participation
1986	81%	74%	100%
1985	74%	68%	99%

Interest Groups

	ADA	ACU	AFL-CIO	CCUS
1986	15%	n/a	27%	74%
1985	10%	70%	38%	72%

Elections

1986	General	52%	Primary	u/o
1980	General	50%	Primary	37%

Edward M. Kennedy (D-Mass.)

Of Boston — Elected 1962

Born: Feb. 22, 1932, Boston, Mass.
Education: Harvard U., A.B. 1956; U. of Virginia, LL.B. 1959.
Military Career: Army, 1951-53.
Occupation: Lawyer.
Family: Divorced; three children.
Religion: Roman Catholic.
Political Career: Suffolk County assistant district attorney, 1961-62; sought Democratic nomination for president, 1980.
Capitol Office: 113 Russell Bldg. 20510; 224-4543.

Massachusetts — The statewide vote for Ronald Reagan was 51% in 1984; 42% in 1980.

Committees

Armed Services
Judiciary
Labor and Human Resources (Chairman)
Joint Economic

Elections

1982	General	61%	Primary	u/o
1976	General	69%	Primary	u/o

CQ Voting Studies

	Presidential Support	Party Unity	Voting Participation
1986	28%	79%	95%
1985	27%	81%	89%

Interest Groups

	ADA	ACU	AFL-CIO	CCUS
1986	80%	n/a	77%	47%
1985	85%	9%	90%	39%

John Kerry (D-Mass.)

Of Boston — Elected 1984

Born: Dec. 22, 1943, Denver, Colo.
Education: Yale U., B.A. 1966; Boston College Law School, J.D. 1976.
Military Career: Navy, 1968-69.
Occupation: Lawyer.
Family: Separated, two children.
Religion: Roman Catholic.
Political Career: Mass. Lt. Gov., 1982-84; candidate for U.S. House, 1970; Democratic nominee for U.S. House, 1972.
Capitol Office: 362 Russell Bldg. 20510; 224-2742.

Massachusetts — The statewide vote for Ronald Reagan was 51% in 1984; 42% in 1980.

Committees

Commerce, Science and Transportation
Foreign Relations
Small Business

Elections

1984	General	55%	Primary	41%

CQ Voting Studies

	Presidential Support	Party Unity	Voting Participation
1986	22%	85%	95%
1985	26%	91%	98%

Interest Groups

	ADA	ACU	AFL-CIO	CCUS
1986	90%	n/a	93%	32%
1985	85%	5%	95%	38%

Frank R. Lautenberg (D-N.J.)

Of Montclair — Elected 1982

Born: Jan. 23, 1924, Paterson, N.J.
Education: Columbia U., B.S. 1949.
Military Career: Army, 1942-46.
Occupation: Computer firm executive.
Family: Wife, Lois Levinson; four children.
Religion: Jewish.
Political Career: No previous office.
Capitol Office: 717 Hart Bldg. 20510; 224-4744.

New Jersey — The statewide vote for Ronald Reagan was 60% in 1984; 52% in 1980.

CQ Voting Studies

	Presidential Support	Party Unity	Voting Participation
1986	30%	79%	95%
1985	28%	85%	98%

Interest Groups

	ADA	ACU	AFL-CIO	CCUS
1986	85%	n/a	100%	22%
1985	90%	4%	95%	32%

Committees

Appropriations
Budget
Environment and Public Works

Elections

1982	General	51%	Primary	26%

Patrick J. Leahy (D-Vt.)

Of Burlington — Elected 1974

Born: March 31, 1940, Montpelier, Vt.
Education: St. Michael's College, B.A. 1961; Georgetown U., J.D. 1964.
Occupation: Lawyer.
Family: Wife, Marcelle Pomerleau; three children.
Religion: Roman Catholic.
Political Career: Chittenden County state's attorney, 1967-75.
Capitol Office: 433 Russell Bldg. 20510; 224-4242.

Vermont — The statewide vote for Ronald Reagan was 58% in 1984; 44% in 1980.

CQ Voting Studies

	Presidential Support	Party Unity	Voting Participation
1986	24%	83%	93%
1985	29%	83%	98%

Interest Groups

	ADA	ACU	AFL-CIO	CCUS
1986	85%	n/a	87%	29%
1985	70%	13%	86%	41%

Committees

Agriculture, Nutrition and Forestry   (Chairman)
Appropriations
Judiciary

Elections

1986	General	64%	Primary	u/o
1980	General	50%	Primary	u/o

Carl Levin (D-Mich.)

Of Detroit — Elected 1978

Born: June 28, 1934, Detroit, Mich.
Education: Swarthmore College, B.A. 1956; Harvard U., LL.B. 1959.
Occupation: Lawyer.
Family: Wife, Barbara Halpern; three children.
Religion: Jewish.
Political Career: Detroit City Council, 1970-73, president, 1974-77.
Capitol Office: 459 Russell Bldg. 20510; 224-6221.

Michigan — The statewide vote for Ronald Reagan was 59% in 1984; 49% in 1980.

Committees

Armed Services
Governmental Affairs
Small Business

CQ Voting Studies

	Presidential Support	Party Unity	Voting Participation
1986	23%	91%	99%
1985	25%	89%	96%

Interest Groups

	ADA	ACU	AFL-CIO	CCUS
1986	90%	n/a	87%	26%
1985	85%	4%	90%	31%

Elections

1984	General	52%	Primary	u/o
1978	General	52%	Primary	39%

Richard G. Lugar (R-Ind.)

Of Indianapolis — Elected 1976

Born: April, 4, 1932, Indianapolis, Ind.
Education: Denison U., B.A. 1954; Oxford U., B.A., M.A. 1956.
Military Career: Navy, 1957-60.
Occupation: Agricultural industries executive.
Family: Wife, Charlene Smeltzer; four children.
Religion: Methodist.
Political Career: Indianapolis School Board, 1964-67; mayor of Indianapolis, 1968-75; Republican nominee for U.S. Senate, 1974.
Capitol Office: 306 Hart Bldg. 20510; 224-4814.

Indiana — The statewide vote for Ronald Reagan was 62% in 1984; 56% in 1980.

Committees

Agriculture, Nutrition and Forestry (Ranking)
Foreign Relations

CQ Voting Studies

	Presidential Support	Party Unity	Voting Participation
1986	88%	89%	99%
1985	89%	92%	99%

Interest Groups

	ADA	ACU	AFL-CIO	CCUS
1986	10%	n/a	0%	89%
1985	5%	74%	10%	90%

Elections

1982	General	54%	Primary	u/o
1976	General	59%	Primary	65%

Spark M. Matsunaga   (D-Hawaii)

Of Honolulu — Elected 1976

Born: Oct. 8, 1916, Kukuiula, Kauai, Hawaii.
Education: U. of Hawaii, Ed.B. 1941; Harvard U., J.D. 1951.
Military Career: Army, 1941-45.
Occupation: Lawyer.
Family: Wife, Helene Hatsumi Tokunaga; five children.
Religion: Episcopalian.
Political Career: Hawaii Territorial House, 1954-59, majority leader, 1959; U.S. House, 1963-77.
Capitol Office: 109 Hart Bldg. 20510; 224-6361.

Hawaii — The statewide vote for Ronald Reagan was 55% in 1984; 43% in 1980.

CQ Voting Studies

	Presidential Support	Party Unity	Voting Participation
1986	25%	77%	95%
1985	22%	84%	97%

Interest Groups

	ADA	ACU	AFL-CIO	CCUS
1986	85%	n/a	73%	39%
1985	95%	4%	85%	29%

Committees

Finance
Labor and Human Resources
Veterans' Affairs
Joint Taxation

Elections

1982	General	80%	Primary	u/o
1976	General	54%	Primary	51%

John McCain   (R-Ariz.)

Of Tempe — Elected 1986

Born: Aug. 29, 1936, Panama Canal Zone.
Education: U.S. Naval Academy, B.S. 1958; National War College, 1973-74.
Military Career: Navy, 1958-81.
Occupation: Naval officer; beer distributor.
Family: Wife, Cindy Lou Hensley; five children.
Religion: Episcopalian.
Political Career: U.S. House, 1983-87.
Capitol Office: 210 Hart Bldg. 20510; 224-2235.

Arizona — The statewide vote for Ronald Reagan was 66% in 1984; 61% in 1980.

CQ Voting Studies — House

	Presidential Support	Party Unity	Voting Participation
1986	68%	67%	93%
1985	68%	81%	95%

Interest Groups — House

	ADA	ACU	AFL-CIO	CCUS
1986	10%	n/a	14%	60%
1985	5%	81%	18%	91%

Committees

Armed Services
Commerce, Science and Transportation
Select Indian Affairs

Elections

1986	General	61%	Primary	u/o

James A. McClure (R-Idaho)

Of McCall — Elected 1972

Born: Dec. 27, 1924, Payette, Idaho.
Education: U. of Idaho, J.D. 1950.
Military Career: Navy, 1942-45.
Occupation: Lawyer.
Family: Wife, Louise Miller; three children.
Religion: Methodist.
Political Career: Payette County prosecuting attorney, 1951-57; Payette city attorney, 1953-59, 1962-66; Idaho Senate, 1961-67; U.S. House, 1967-73.
Capitol Office: 361 Dirksen Bldg. 20510; 224-2752.

Idaho — The statewide vote for Ronald Reagan was 72% in 1984; 66% in 1980.

Committees

Appropriations
Energy and Natural Resources   (Ranking)
Rules and Administration
Select Iran-contra

Elections

1984	General	72%	Primary	u/o
1978	General	68%	Primary	u/o

CQ Voting Studies

	Presidential Support	Party Unity	Voting Participation
1986	92%	87%	97%
1985	78%	91%	97%

Interest Groups

	ADA	ACU	AFL-CIO	CCUS
1986	0%	n/a	0%	95%
1985	0%	100%	5%	93%

Mitch McConnell (R-Ky.)

Of Louisville — Elected 1984

Born: Feb. 20, 1942, Sheffield, Ala.
Education: U. of Louisville, B.A. 1964; U. of Kentucky, J.D. 1967.
Occupation: Lawyer.
Family: Divorced; three children.
Religion: Baptist.
Political Career: Jefferson County judge/executive, 1978-85.
Capitol Office: 120 Russell Bldg. 20510; 224-2541.

Kentucky — The statewide vote for Ronald Reagan was 60% in 1984; 49% in 1980.

Committees

Agriculture, Nutrition and Forestry
Foreign Relations

Elections

1984	General	50%	Primary	79%

CQ Voting Studies

	Presidential Support	Party Unity	Voting Participation
1986	87%	90%	99%
1985	85%	82%	99%

Interest Groups

	ADA	ACU	AFL-CIO	CCUS
1986	0%	n/a	7%	89%
1985	5%	78%	10%	79%

John Melcher (D-Mont.)

Of Forsyth — Elected 1976

Born: Sept. 6, 1924, Sioux City, Iowa.
Education: Attended U. of Minnesota, 1942-43; Iowa State U., D.V.M. 1950.
Military Career: Army, 1943-45.
Profession: Veterinarian; cattle feedlot operator.
Family: Wife, Ruth Klein; five children.
Religion: Roman Catholic.
Political Career: Forsyth Board of Aldermen, 1953-55; mayor of Forsyth, 1955-61; Mont. House, 1961-63, 1969; Mont. Senate, 1963-67; U.S. House, 1969-77; Democratic nominee for U.S. House, 1966.
Capitol Office: 730 Hart Bldg. 20510; 224-2644.
Montana — The statewide vote for Ronald Reagan was 60% in 1984; 57% in 1980.

Committees

Agriculture, Nutrition and Forestry
Energy and Natural Resources
Joint Economic
Special Aging (Chairman)
Select Indian Affairs

Elections

1982	General	55%	Primary	68%
1976	General	64%	Primary	89%

CQ Voting Studies

	Presidential Support	Party Unity	Voting Participation
1986	20%	86%	99%
1985	20%	88%	95%

Interest Groups

	ADA	ACU	AFL-CIO	CCUS
1986	90%	n/a	86%	26%
1985	85%	9%	95%	29%

Howard M. Metzenbaum (D-Ohio)

Of Lyndhurst — Elected 1976

Born: June 4, 1917, Cleveland, Ohio.
Education: Ohio State U., B.A. 1939, LL.B. 1941.
Occupation: Lawyer; newspaper publisher; parking lot executive.
Family: Wife, Shirley Turoff; four children.
Religion: Jewish.
Political Career: Ohio House, 1943-47; Ohio Senate, 1947-51; Democratic nominee for U.S. Senate, 1970; sought Democratic nomination for U.S. Senate, 1974.
Capitol Office: 140 Russell Bldg. 20510; 224-2315.

Ohio — The statewide vote for Ronald Reagan was 59% in 1984; 52% in 1980.

Committees

Energy and Natural Resources
Judiciary
Labor and Human Resources
Select Intelligence

Elections

1982	General	57%	Primary	83%
1976	General	50%	Primary	54%

CQ Voting Studies

	Presidential Support	Party Unity	Voting Participation
1986	24%	86%	99%
1985	26%	87%	99%

Interest Groups

	ADA	ACU	AFL-CIO	CCUS
1986	100%	n/a	93%	21%
1985	100%	0%	100%	29%

Barbara A. Mikulski (D-Md.)

Of Baltimore — Elected 1986

Born: July 20, 1936, Baltimore, Md.
Education: Mount Saint Agnes College, B.A. 1958; U. of Maryland School of Social Work, M.S.W. 1965.
Occupation: Social worker.
Family: Single.
Religion: Roman Catholic.
Political Career: Baltimore City Council, 1971-77; Democratic nominee for U.S. Senate, 1974; U.S. House, 1977-87.
Capitol Office: 387 Russell Bldg. 20510; 224-4654.

Maryland — The statewide vote for Ronald Reagan was 53% in 1984; 44% in 1980.

Committees

Appropriations
Environment and Public Works
Labor and Human Resources
Small Business

Elections

1986	General	61%	Primary	50%

CQ Voting Studies — House

	Presidential Support	Party Unity	Voting Participation
1986	11%	75%	82%
1985	18%	89%	95%

Interest Groups — House

	ADA	ACU	AFL-CIO	CCUS
1986	90%	n/a	93%	20%
1985	80%	10%	100%	32%

George J. Mitchell (D-Maine)

Of South Portland — Elected 1982

Born: Aug. 20, 1933, Waterville, Maine.
Education: Bowdoin College, B.A. 1954; Georgetown U., LL.B. 1960.
Military Career: Army, 1954-56.
Occupation: Lawyer; judge.
Family: Wife, Sally L. Heath; one child.
Religion: Roman Catholic.
Political Career: Maine Democratic chairman, 1966-68; Democratic nominee for governor, 1974; appointed to the U.S. Senate, May 19, 1980.
Capitol Office: 176 Russell Bldg. 20510; 224-5344.

Maine — The statewide vote for Ronald Reagan was 61% in 1984; 46% in 1980.

Committees

Environment and Public Works
Finance
Governmental Affairs
Veterans' Affairs
Select Iran-contra

Elections

1982	General	61%	Primary	u/o

CQ Voting Studies

	Presidential Support	Party Unity	Voting Participation
1986	31%	84%	98%
1985	33%	87%	99%

Interest Groups

	ADA	ACU	AFL-CIO	CCUS
1986	85%	n/a	87%	32%
1985	65%	17%	86%	31%

Daniel Patrick Moynihan   (D-N.Y.)

Of Pindars Corners — Elected 1976

Born: March 16, 1927, Tulsa, Okla.
Education: Attended City U. of N.Y., 1943; Tufts U., B.N.S. 1946, B.A. 1948; Fletcher School of Law and Diplomacy, M.A. 1949, Ph.D. 1961.
Military Career: Navy, 1944-47.
Occupation: Government professor; writer.
Family: Wife, Elizabeth Brennan; three children.
Religion: Roman Catholic.
Political Career: Sought Democratic nomination, N.Y. City Council president, 1965.
Capitol Office: 464 Russell Bldg. 20510; 224-4451.

New York — The statewide vote for Ronald Reagan was 54% in 1984; 47% in 1980.

Committees

Environment and Public Works
Finance
Foreign Relations
Rules and Administration
Joint Taxation

Elections

1982	General	65%	Primary	85%
1976	General	54%	Primary	36%

CQ Voting Studies

	Presidential Support	Party Unity	Voting Participation
1986	40%	72%	96%
1985	33%	81%	96%

Interest Groups

	ADA	ACU	AFL-CIO	CCUS
1986	85%	n/a	67%	39%
1985	90%	4%	100%	33%

Frank H. Murkowski   (R-Alaska)

Of Fairbanks — Elected 1980

Born: March 28, 1933, Seattle, Wash.
Education: Attended U. of Santa Clara 1951-53; Seattle U., B.A. 1955.
Military Career: Coast Guard, 1955-56.
Occupation: Banker.
Family: Wife, Nancy Gore; six children.
Religion: Roman Catholic.
Political Career: Alaska commissioner of economic development, 1966-70; Republican nominee for U.S. House, 1970.
Capitol Office: 709 Hart Bldg. 20510; 224-6665.

Alaska — The statewide vote for Ronald Reagan was 67% in 1984; 54% in 1980.

Committees

Energy and Natural Resources
Foreign Relations
Veterans' Affairs   (Ranking)
Select Indian Affairs
Select Intelligence

Elections

1986	General	55%	Primary	u/o
1980	General	54%	Primary	59%

CQ Voting Studies

	Presidential Support	Party Unity	Voting Participation
1986	80%	81%	94%
1985	82%	78%	90%

Interest Groups

	ADA	ACU	AFL-CIO	CCUS
1986	20%	n/a	36%	65%
1985	0%	82%	26%	84%

Don Nickles (R-Okla.)

Of Ponca City — Elected 1980

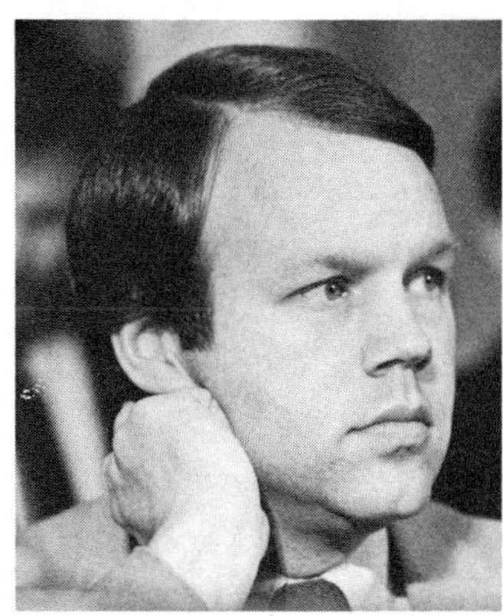

Born: Dec. 6, 1948, Ponca City, Okla.
Education: Oklahoma State U., B.B.A. 1971.
Military Career: Army National Guard, 1970-76.
Occupation: Machine company executive.
Family: Wife, Linda Lou Morrison; four children.
Religion: Roman Catholic.
Political Career: Okla. Senate, 1979-81.
Capitol Office: 713 Hart Bldg. 20510; 224-5754.

Oklahoma — The statewide vote for Ronald Reagan was 69% in 1984; 61% in 1980.

Committees

Appropriations
Budget
Energy and Natural Resources

Elections

1986	General	54%	Primary	u/o
1980	General	54%	Primary	66% *

** Primary runoff.*

CQ Voting Studies

	Presidential Support	Party Unity	Voting Participation
1986	86%	82%	100%
1985	82%	79%	99%

Interest Groups

	ADA	ACU	AFL-CIO	CCUS
1986	0%	n/a	0%	79%
1985	0%	87%	0%	90%

Sam Nunn (D-Ga.)

Of Perry — Elected 1972

Born: Sept. 8, 1938, Perry, Ga.
Education: Attended Georgia Institute of Technology, 1956-59; Emory U., A.B. 1961, LL.B. 1962.
Military Career: Coast Guard, 1959-60; Coast Guard Reserve, 1960-68.
Occupation: Farmer; lawyer.
Family: Wife, Colleen Ann O'Brien; two children.
Religion: Methodist.
Political Career: Ga. House, 1969-72.
Capitol Office: 303 Dirksen Bldg. 20510; 224-3521.

Georgia — The statewide vote for Ronald Reagan was 60% in 1984; 41% in 1980.

Committees

Armed Services (Chairman)
Governmental Affairs
Small Business
Select Intelligence
Select Iran-contra

Elections

1984	General	80%	Primary	90%
1978	General	83%	Primary	80%

CQ Voting Studies

	Presidential Support	Party Unity	Voting Participation
1986	58%	50%	95%
1985	58%	57%	98%

Interest Groups

	ADA	ACU	AFL-CIO	CCUS
1986	30%	n/a	47%	50%
1985	30%	57%	43%	59%

Bob Packwood   (R-Ore.)

Of Portland — Elected 1968

Born: Sept. 11, 1932, Portland, Ore.
Education: Willamette U., B.A. 1954; New York U. School of Law, LL.B. 1957.
Occupation: Lawyer.
Family: Wife, Georgie Oberteuffer; two children.
Religion: Unitarian.
Political Career: Ore. House, 1963-69.
Capitol Office: 259 Russell Bldg. 20510; 224-5244.

Oregon — The statewide vote for Ronald Reagan was 56% in 1984; 48% in 1980.

CQ Voting Studies

	Presidential Support	Party Unity	Voting Participation
1986	49%	58%	90%
1985	72%	67%	93%

Interest Groups

	ADA	ACU	AFL-CIO	CCUS
1986	60%	n/a	40%	58%
1985	35%	40%	43%	66%

Committees

Commerce, Science and Transportation
Finance   (Ranking)
Joint Taxation

Elections

1986	General	64%	Primary	58%
1980	General	52%	Primary	62%

Claiborne Pell   (D-R.I.)

Of Newport — Elected 1960

Born: Nov. 22, 1918, New York, N.Y.
Education: Princeton U., A.B. 1940; Columbia U., A.M. 1946.
Military Career: Coast Guard, 1941-45.
Occupation: Investment executive.
Family: Wife, Nuala O'Donnell; four children.
Religion: Episcopalian.
Political Career: No previous office.
Capitol Office: 335 Russell Bldg. 20510; 224-4642.

Rhode Island — The statewide vote for Ronald Reagan was 52% in 1984; 37% in 1980.

CQ Voting Studies

	Presidential Support	Party Unity	Voting Participation
1986	30%	75%	96%
1985	29%	82%	97%

Interest Groups

	ADA	ACU	AFL-CIO	CCUS
1986	80%	n/a	67%	42%
1985	95%	9%	95%	29%

Committees

Foreign Relations   (Chairman)
Labor and Human Resources
Rules and Administration

Elections

1984	General	73%	Primary	u/o
1978	General	75%	Primary	87%

Larry Pressler   (R-S.D.)

Of Humboldt — Elected 1978

Born: March 29, 1942, Humboldt, S.D.
Education: U. of South Dakota, B.A. 1964; Oxford U., England, 1966; Harvard U., M.A. 1971, J.D. 1971.
Military Career: Army, 1966-68.
Occupation: Lawyer.
Family: Wife, Harriet Dent, one stepchild.
Religion: Roman Catholic.
Political Career: U.S. House, 1975-79.
Capitol Office: 407A Russell Bldg. 20510; 224-5842.

South Dakota — The statewide vote for Ronald Reagan was 63% in 1984; 61% in 1980.

CQ Voting Studies

	Presidential Support	Party Unity	Voting Participation
1986	77%	72%	95%
1985	74%	72%	95%

Interest Groups

	ADA	ACU	AFL-CIO	CCUS
1986	10%	n/a	33%	68%
1985	10%	74%	20%	71%

Committees

Commerce, Science and Transportation
Environment and Public Works
Foreign Relations
Small Business
Special Aging

Elections

1984	General	74%	Primary	u/o
1978	General	67%	Primary	74%

William Proxmire   (D-Wis.)

Of Madison — Elected 1957

Born: Nov. 11, 1915, Lake Forest, Ill.
Education: Yale U., B.A. 1938; Harvard U., M.B.A. 1940, M.P.A. 1948.
Military Career: Army, 1941-46.
Occupation: Journalist; author; printing company executive.
Family: Wife, Ellen Hodges; three children.
Religion: United Church of Christ.
Political Career: Wis. Assembly, 1951-53; Democratic nominee for Wis. governor, 1952, 1954, 1956.
Capitol Office: 530 Dirksen Bldg. 20510; 224-5653.

Wisconsin — The statewide vote for Ronald Reagan was 54% in 1984; 48% in 1980.

CQ Voting Studies

	Presidential Support	Party Unity	Voting Participation
1986	28%	76%	100%
1985	48%	56%	100%

Interest Groups

	ADA	ACU	AFL-CIO	CCUS
1986	60%	n/a	60%	37%
1985	60%	26%	43%	48%

Committees

Appropriations
Banking, Housing and Urban Affairs   (Chairman)
Joint Economic

Elections

1982	General	64%	Primary	86%
1976	General	72%	Primary	u/o

David Pryor (D-Ark.)

Of Camden — Elected 1978

Born: Aug. 29, 1934, Camden, Ark.
Education: U. of Arkansas, B.A. 1957, LL.B. 1964.
Occupation: Lawyer; newspaper publisher.
Family: Wife, Barbara Lunsford; three children.
Religion: Presbyterian.
Political Career: Ark. House, 1961-67; U.S. House, 1967-73; governor, 1975-79; sought Democratic nomination for U.S. Senate, 1972.
Capitol Office: 264 Russell Bldg. 20510; 224-2353.

Arkansas — The statewide vote for Ronald Reagan was 60% in 1984; 48% in 1980.

Committees

Agriculture, Nutrition and Forestry
Finance
Governmental Affairs
Select Ethics
Special Aging

CQ Voting Studies

	Presidential Support	Party Unity	Voting Participation
1986	35%	70%	93%
1985	32%	79%	95%

Interest Groups

	ADA	ACU	AFL-CIO	CCUS
1986	60%	n/a	40%	53%
1985	80%	4%	76%	41%

Elections

1984	General	57%	Primary	u/o
1978	General	77%	Primary	55% *

* *Primary Runoff.*

Dan Quayle (R-Ind.)

Of Huntington — Elected 1980

Born: Feb. 4, 1947, Indianapolis, Ind.
Education: DePauw U., B.A. 1969; Indiana U., J.D. 1974.
Military Career: Ind. National Guard, 1969-75.
Occupation: Lawyer; newspaper publisher.
Family: Wife, Marilyn Tucker; three children.
Religion: Presbyterian.
Political Career: U.S. House, 1977-81.
Capitol Office: 524 Hart Bldg. 20510; 224-5623.

Indiana — The statewide vote for Ronald Reagan was 62% in 1984; 56% in 1980.

Committees

Armed Services
Budget
Labor and Human Resources

CQ Voting Studies

	Presidential Support	Party Unity	Voting Participation
1986	90%	94%	98%
1985	88%	93%	98%

Interest Groups

	ADA	ACU	AFL-CIO	CCUS
1986	5%	n/a	0%	89%
1985	0%	87%	10%	90%

Elections

1986	General	61%	Primary	u/o
1980	General	54%	Primary	u/o

Harry Reid (D-Nev.)

Of Searchlight — Elected 1986

Born: Dec. 2, 1939, Searchlight, Nev.
Education: Southern Utah State College, A.S.
  1959; Utah State U., B.A. 1961; George Washington U.,
  J.D. 1964.
Occupation: Lawyer.
Family: Wife, Landra Gould; five children.
Religion: Mormon.
Political Career: Nev. Assembly, 1969-71; lt. gov., 1971-75;
  Democratic nominee for U.S. Senate, 1974; candidate for
  mayor of Las Vegas, 1975; U.S. House, 1983-87.
Capitol Office: 708 Hart Bldg. 20510; 224-3542.

Nevada — The statewide vote for Ronald Reagan was 66%
in 1984; 63% in 1980.

Committees

Appropriations
Environment and Public Works
Special Aging

Elections

1986   General 51%   Primary 83%

CQ Voting Studies — House

	Presidential Support	Party Unity	Voting Participation
1986	26%	84%	99%
1985	44%	87%	99%

Interest Groups — House

	ADA	ACU	AFL-CIO	CCUS
1986	60%	n/a	93%	44%
1985	55%	29%	82%	32%

Donald W. Riegle Jr.   (D-Mich.)

Of Flint — Elected 1976

Born: Feb. 4, 1938, Flint, Mich.
Education: Attended Flint Junior College, 1956-57; Western
  Michigan U., 1957-58; U. of Michigan, B.A. 1960; Michigan
  State U., M.B.A. 1961; graduate work, Harvard Business
  School, 1964-66.
Occupation: Business executive; professor.
Family: Wife, Lori Hansen; four children.
Religion: Methodist.
Political Career: U.S. House, 1967-77.
Capitol Office: 105 Dirksen Bldg. 20510; 224-4822.

Michigan — The statewide vote for Ronald Reagan was
59% in 1984; 49% in 1980.

Committees

Banking, Housing and Urban Affairs
Budget
Commerce, Science and Transportation
Finance

Elections

1982	General	58%	Primary	u/o
1976	General	53%	Primary	44%

CQ Voting Studies

	Presidential Support	Party Unity	Voting Participation
1986	18%	96%	99%
1985	24%	87%	98%

Interest Groups

	ADA	ACU	AFL-CIO	CCUS
1986	95%	n/a	93%	26%
1985	95%	4%	90%	24%

John D. Rockefeller IV (D-W. Va.)

Of Charleston — Elected 1984

Born: June 18, 1937, New York N.Y.
Education: Attended International Christian U., Toyko, Japan, 1957-60; Harvard U., A.B., 1961.
Occupation: Public official.
Family: Wife, Sharon Percy; four children.
Religion: Presbyterian.
Political Career: W.Va. House, 1967-69; W.Va. secretary of state, 1969-73; Democratic nominee for governor, 1972; W.Va. governor, 1977-85.
Capitol Office: 241 Dirksen Bldg. 20510; 224-6472.

West Virginia — The statewide vote for Ronald Reagan was 55% in 1984; 45% in 1980.

Committees

Commerce, Science and Transportation
Finance
Veterans' Affairs

Elections

1984	General	52%	Primary	66%

CQ Voting Studies

	Presidential Support	Party Unity	Voting Participation
1986	31%	79%	98%
1985	31%	83%	93%

Interest Groups

	ADA	ACU	AFL-CIO	CCUS
1986	75%	n/a	93%	32%
1985	60%	14%	90%	36%

William V. Roth Jr. (R-Del.)

Of Wilmington — Elected 1970

Born: July 22, 1921, Great Falls, Mont.
Education: U. of Oregon, B.A. 1944; Harvard U., M.B.A. 1947, LL.B. 1949.
Military Career: Army, 1943-46.
Occupation: Lawyer.
Family: Wife, Jane Richards; two children.
Religion: Episcopalian.
Political Career: U.S. House, 1967-71; Republican nominee for lieutenant governor, 1960.
Capitol Office: 104 Hart Bldg. 20510; 224-2441.

Delaware — The statewide vote for Ronald Reagan was 60% in 1984; 47% in 1980.

Committees

Finance
Governmental Affairs (Ranking)
Joint Economic (Ranking)
Select Intelligence

Elections

1982	General	55%	Primary	u/o
1976	General	56%	Primary	u/o

CQ Voting Studies

	Presidential Support	Party Unity	Voting Participation
1986	83%	83%	97%
1985	84%	81%	98%

Interest Groups

	ADA	ACU	AFL-CIO	CCUS
1986	15%	n/a	13%	82%
1985	20%	70%	14%	83%

Warren B. Rudman   (R-N.H.)

Of Nashua — Elected 1980

Born: May 18, 1930, Boston, Mass.
Education: Syracuse U., B.S. 1952; Boston College, LL.B. 1960.
Military Career: Army, 1952-54.
Occupation: Lawyer.
Family: Wife, Shirley Wahl; three children.
Religion: Jewish.
Political Career: N.H. attorney general, 1970-76 (appointed).
Capitol Office: 530 Hart Bldg. 20510; 224-3324.

New Hampshire — The statewide vote for Ronald Reagan was 69% in 1984; 58% in 1980.

Committees

Appropriations
Budget
Governmental Affairs
Small Business
Select Ethics   (Ranking)
Select Iran-contra   (Ranking)

Elections

| 1986 | General | 66% | Primary | u/o |
| 1980 | General | 52% | Primary | 20% |

CQ Voting Studies

	Presidential Support	Party Unity	Voting Participation
1986	90%	89%	99%
1985	84%	80%	97%

Interest Groups

	ADA	ACU	AFL-CIO	CCUS
1986	10%	n/a	0%	84%
1985	10%	68%	14%	86%

Terry Sanford   (D-N.C.)

Of Durham — Elected 1986

Born: Aug. 20, 1917, Laurinburg, N.C.
Education: Presbyterian Junior College; U. of North Carolina, A.B. 1939, J.D. 1946.
Military Career: Army parachute infantry, 1942-46; North Carolina National Guard, 1948-60.
Occupation: Lawyer; president of Duke U.; FBI agent.
Family: Wife, Margaret Rose Knight; two children.
Religion: Methodist.
Political Career: State senator, 1953-55; governor, 1961-65; sought Democratic nomination for president, 1972, 1976.
Capitol Office: 716 Hart Bldg. 20510; 224-3154.

North Carolina — The statewide vote for Ronald Reagan was 62% in 1984; 49% in 1980.

Committees

Banking, Housing and Urban Affairs
Budget
Foreign Relations
Select Ethics

Elections

| 1986 | General | 52% | Primary | 60% |

"#

Paul S. Sarbanes   (D-Md.)

Of Baltimore — Elected 1976

Born: Feb. 3, 1933, Salisbury, Md.
Education: Princeton U., A.B. 1954; Oxford U., England, B.A. 1957; Harvard U., LL.B. 1960.
Occupation: Lawyer.
Family: Wife, Christine Dunbar; three children.
Religion: Greek Orthodox.
Political Career: Md. House, 1967-71; U.S. House, 1971-77.
Capitol Office: 332 Dirksen Bldg. 20510; 224-4524.

Maryland — The statewide vote for Ronald Reagan was 53% in 1984; 44% in 1980.

Committees

Banking, Housing and Urban Affairs
Foreign Relations
Joint Economic   (Chairman)
Select Iran-contra

CQ Voting Studies

	Presidential Support	Party Unity	Voting Participation
1986	18%	96%	98%
1985	22%	90%	97%

Interest Groups

	ADA	ACU	AFL-CIO	CCUS
1986	100%	n/a	100%	16%
1985	100%	0%	100%	25%

Elections

1982	General	64%	Primary	81%
1976	General	57%	Primary	55%

Jim Sasser   (D-Tenn.)

Of Nashville — Elected 1976

Born: Sept. 30, 1936, Memphis, Tenn.
Education: Attended U. of Tennessee, 1954-55; Vanderbilt U., B.A. 1958, J.D. 1961.
Military Career: Marine Corps Reserve, 1957-63.
Occupation: Lawyer.
Family: Wife, Mary Gorman; two children.
Religion: Methodist.
Political Career: No previous office.
Capitol Office: 298 Russell Bldg. 20510; 224-3344.

Tennessee — The statewide vote for Ronald Reagan was 58% in 1984; 49% in 1980.

Committees

Appropriations
Banking, Housing and Urban Affairs
Budget
Governmental Affairs
Small Business

CQ Voting Studies

	Presidential Support	Party Unity	Voting Participation
1986	24%	87%	100%
1985	33%	87%	100%

Interest Groups

	ADA	ACU	AFL-CIO	CCUS
1986	70%	n/a	87%	32%
1985	60%	26%	86%	38%

Elections

1982	General	62%	Primary	89%
1976	General	53%	Primary	44%

Richard C. Shelby (D-Ala.)

Of Tuscaloosa — Elected 1986

Born: May 6, 1934, Birmingham, Ala.
Education: U. of Alabama, A.B. 1957; LL.B. 1963.
Occupation: Lawyer.
Family: Wife, Annette Nevin; two children.
Religion: Presbyterian.
Political Career: Ala. Senate, 1971-79; U.S. House, 1979-87.
Capitol Office: 516 Hart Bldg. 20510; 224-5744.

Alabama — The statewide vote for Ronald Reagan was 61% in 1984; 49% in 1980.

Committees

Armed Services
Banking, Housing and Urban Affairs
Special Aging

Elections

1986　General　51%　　Primary　51%

CQ Voting Studies — House

	Presidential Support	Party Unity	Voting Participation
1986	44%	58%	92%
1985	52%	60%	92%

Interest Groups — House

	ADA	ACU	AFL-CIO	CCUS
1986	40%	n/a	93%	39%
1985	25%	67%	50%	57%

Paul Simon (D-Ill.)

Of Makanda — Elected 1984

Born: Nov. 29, 1928, Eugene, Ore.
Education: Attended U. of Oregon, 1945-46; Dana College, 1946-48.
Military Career: Army, 1951-53.
Occupation: Author; newspaper publisher.
Family: Wife, Jeanne Hurley; two children.
Religion: Lutheran.
Political Career: Ill. House, 1955-63; Ill. Senate, 1963-69; Ill. lt. gov., 1969-73; sought Democratic gubernatorial nomination, 1972; U.S. House 1975-85.
Capitol Office: 462 Dirksen Bldg. 20510; 224-2152.

Illinois — The statewide vote for Ronald Reagan was 56% in 1984; 50% in 1980.

Committees

Budget
Foreign Relations
Judiciary
Labor and Human Resources

Elections

1984　General　50%　　Primary　36%

CQ Voting Studies

	Presidential Support	Party Unity	Voting Participation
1986	19%	89%	99%
1985	25%	89%	93%

Interest Groups

	ADA	ACU	AFL-CIO	CCUS
1986	80%	n/a	80%	32%
1985	85%	5%	95%	34%

Alan K. Simpson   (R-Wyo.)

Of Cody — Elected 1978

Born: Sept. 2, 1931, Denver, Colo.
Education: U. of Wyoming, B.S.L. 1954, LL.B. 1958.
Military Career: Army, 1954-56.
Occupation: Lawyer.
Family: Wife, Ann Schroll; three children.
Religion: Episcopalian.
Political Career: Cody City attorney, 1959-69; Wyo. House, 1965-77.
Capitol Office: 261 Dirksen Bldg. 20510; 224-3424.

Wyoming — The statewide vote for Ronald Reagan was 71% in 1984; 63% in 1980.

CQ Voting Studies

	Presidential Support	Party Unity	Voting Participation
1986	92%	90%	97%
1985	90%	91%	100%

Interest Groups

	ADA	ACU	AFL-CIO	CCUS
1986	10%	n/a	0%	76%
1985	10%	78%	10%	90%

Committees

Assistant Minority Leader
Environment and Public Works
Judiciary
Veterans' Affairs
Special Aging

Elections

1984	General	78%	Primary	88%
1978	General	62%	Primary	55%

Arlen Specter   (R-Pa.)

Of Philadelphia — Elected 1980

Born: Feb. 12, 1930, Wichita, Kan.
Education: U. of Pennsylvania, B.A. 1951; Yale U., LL.B. 1956.
Military Career: Air Force, 1951-53.
Occupation: Lawyer; law professor.
Family: Wife, Joan Lois Levy; two children.
Religion: Jewish.
Political Career: Philadelphia district attorney, 1966-74; Republican nominee for mayor of Philadelphia, 1967; defeated for re-election as district attorney, 1973; sought Republican nomination for U.S. Senate, 1976; sought Republican nomination for governor, 1978.
Capitol Office: 331 Hart Bldg. 20510; 224-4254.

Pennsylvania — The statewide vote for Ronald Reagan was 53% in 1984; 50% in 1980.

Committees

Appropriations
Judiciary
Veterans' Affairs
Select Intelligence

CQ Voting Studies

	Presidential Support	Party Unity	Voting Participation
1986	31%	27%	95%
1985	61%	51%	94%

Interest Groups

	ADA	ACU	AFL-CIO	CCUS
1986	75%	n/a	87%	44%
1985	55%	36%	71%	55%

Elections

1986	General	57%	Primary	76%
1980	General	51%	Primary	36%

Robert T. Stafford (R-Vt.)

Of Rutland — Elected 1972

Born: Aug. 8, 1913, Rutland, Vt.
Education: Middlebury College, B.S. 1935; attended U. of Michigan, 1935-36; Boston U., LL.B. 1938.
Military Career: Navy, 1942-46, 1951-53.
Occupation: Lawyer.
Family: Wife, Helen Kelley; four children.
Religion: Congregationalist.
Political Career: Rutland County state's attorney, 1947-51; Vt. deputy attorney general, 1953-55; Vt. attorney general, 1955-57; lt. gov., 1957-59; governor, 1959-61; U.S. House, 1961-71.
Capitol Office: 133 Hart Bldg. 20510; 224-5141.

Vermont — The statewide vote for Ronald Reagan was 58% in 1984; 44% in 1980.

Committees

Environment and Public Works   (Ranking)
Labor and Human Resources
Veterans' Affairs

CQ Voting Studies

	Presidential Support	Party Unity	Voting Participation
1986	55%	53%	85%
1985	69%	62%	93%

Interest Groups

	ADA	ACU	AFL-CIO	CCUS
1986	60%	n/a	50%	25%
1985	45%	25%	43%	59%

Elections

1982	General	50%	Primary	46%
1976	General	50%	Primary	69%

John C. Stennis (D-Miss.)

Of De Kalb — Elected 1947

Born: Aug. 3, 1901, Kemper County, Miss.
Education: Mississippi State U., B.S. 1923; U. of Virginia, LL.B. 1928.
Occupation: Lawyer; judge.
Family: Widowed; two children.
Religion: Presbyterian.
Political Career: Miss. House, 1928-32; prosecuting attorney, 16th Judicial District, 1931-37; circuit judge, 1937-47.
Capitol Office: 205 Russell Bldg. 20510; 224-6253.

Mississippi — The statewide vote for Ronald Reagan was 62% in 1984; 49% in 1980.

Committees

Appropriations   (Chairman)
Armed Services

CQ Voting Studies

	Presidential Support	Party Unity	Voting Participation
1986	63%	29%	83%
1985	41%	46%	73%

Interest Groups

	ADA	ACU	AFL-CIO	CCUS
1986	35%	n/a	50%	56%
1985	25%	67%	58%	50%

Elections

1982	General	64%	Primary	u/o
1976	General	u/o	Primary	u/o

Ted Stevens (R-Alaska)

Of Girdwood — Elected 1970

Born: Nov. 18, 1923, Indianapolis, Ind.
Education: U.C.L.A., B.A. 1947; Harvard U. Law School, LL.B. 1950.
Military Career: Army Air Corps, 1943-46.
Occupation: Lawyer.
Family: Wife, Catherine Chandler; six children.
Religion: Episcopalian.
Political Career: Alaska House, 1965-68; Republican nominee for U.S. Senate, 1962; sought Republican U.S. Senate nomination, 1968; appointed to U.S. Senate, 1968.
Capitol Office: 522 Hart Bldg. 20510; 224-3004.

Alaska — The statewide vote for Ronald Reagan was 67% in 1984; 54% in 1980.

CQ Voting Studies

	Presidential Support	Party Unity	Voting Participation
1986	83%	83%	95%
1985	75%	71%	90%

Interest Groups

	ADA	ACU	AFL-CIO	CCUS
1986	15%	n/a	33%	74%
1985	10%	64%	25%	78%

Committees

Appropriations
Commerce, Science and Transportation
Governmental Affairs
Rules and Administration   (Ranking)

Elections

1984	General	71%	Primary	u/o
1978	General	76%	Primary	u/o

Steve Symms (R-Idaho)

Of Caldwell — Elected 1980

Born: April 23, 1938, Nampa, Idaho.
Education: U. of Idaho, B.S. 1960.
Military Career: Marines, 1960-63.
Occupation: Fruit grower, fitness club owner.
Family: Wife, Frances E. Stockdale; four children.
Religion: Methodist.
Political Career: U.S. House, 1973-81.
Capitol Office: 509 Hart Bldg. 20510; 224-6142.

Idaho — The statewide vote for Ronald Reagan was 72% in 1984; 66% in 1980.

CQ Voting Studies

	Presidential Support	Party Unity	Voting Participation
1986	86%	84%	85%
1985	81%	91%	97%

Interest Groups

	ADA	ACU	AFL-CIO	CCUS
1986	0%	n/a	0%	100%
1985	0%	100%	0%	90%

Committees

Armed Services
Budget
Environment and Public Works
Joint Economic

Elections

1986	General	52%	Primary	u/o
1980	General	50%	Primary	u/o

Strom Thurmond (R-S.C.)

Of Aiken — Elected 1954

Born: Dec. 5, 1902, Edgefield, S.C.
Education: Clemson College, B.S. 1923.
Military Career: Army, 1942-46.
Occupation: Lawyer.
Family: Wife, Nancy Moore; four children.
Religion: Baptist.
Political Career: S.C. Senate, 1933-38; S.C. governor, 1947-51; States Rights nominee for president, 1948; sought Democratic nomination for U.S. Senate, 1950.
Capitol Office: 218 Russell Bldg. 20510; 224-5972.

South Carolina — The statewide vote for Ronald Reagan was 64% in 1984; 49% in 1980.

Committees

Armed Services
Judiciary (Ranking)
Labor and Human Resources
Veterans' Affairs

Elections

1984	General	67%	Primary	94%
1978	General	56%	Primary	u/o

CQ Voting Studies

	Presidential Support	Party Unity	Voting Participation
1986	89%	91%	99%
1985	87%	92%	99%

Interest Groups

	ADA	ACU	AFL-CIO	CCUS
1986	5%	n/a	0%	78%
1985	0%	91%	14%	97%

Paul S. Trible Jr. (R-Va.)

Of Newport News — Elected 1982

Born: Dec. 29, 1946, Baltimore, Md.
Education: Hampden-Sydney College, B.A. 1968; Washington and Lee U., J.D. 1971.
Occupation: Lawyer.
Family: Wife, Rosemary Dunaway; two children.
Religion: Episcopalian.
Political Career: Commonwealth's Attorney, Essex County, Va., 1974-76; U.S. House, 1977-83.
Capitol Office: 517 Hart Bldg. 20510; 224-4024.

Virginia — The statewide vote for Ronald Reagan was 62% in 1984; 53% in 1980.

Committees

Commerce, Science and Transportation
Foreign Relations
Governmental Affairs
Select Iran-contra

Elections

1982	General	51%	Primary	u/o

CQ Voting Studies

	Presidential Support	Party Unity	Voting Participation
1986	83%	85%	98%
1985	86%	85%	97%

Interest Groups

	ADA	ACU	AFL-CIO	CCUS
1986	5%	n/a	7%	79%
1985	0%	78%	20%	90%

Malcolm Wallop (R-Wyo.)

Of Big Horn — Elected 1976

Born: Feb. 27, 1933, New York, N.Y.
Education: Yale U., B.A. 1954.
Military Career: Army, 1955-57.
Occupation: Rancher; meatpacking executive.
Family: Wife, French Carter Gamble; four children.
Religion: Episcopalian.
Political Career: Wyo. House, 1969-73; Wyo. Senate, 1973-77; sought Republican nomination for Wyo. governor, 1974.
Capitol Office: 206 Russell Bldg. 20510; 224-6441.

Wyoming — The statewide vote for Ronald Reagan was 71% in 1984; 63% in 1980.

Committees

Energy and Natural Resources
Finance
Small Business

Elections

1982	General	57%	Primary	81%
1976	General	55%	Primary	76%

CQ Voting Studies

	Presidential Support	Party Unity	Voting Participation
1986	93%	94%	95%
1985	73%	88%	91%

Interest Groups

	ADA	ACU	AFL-CIO	CCUS
1986	0%	n/a	0%	95%
1985	0%	95%	5%	97%

John W. Warner (R-Va.)

Of Middleburg — Elected 1978

Born: Feb. 18, 1927, Washington, D.C.
Education: Washington and Lee U., B.S. 1949; U. of Virginia, LL.B. 1953.
Military Career: Navy, 1944-46; Marine Corps, 1950-52.
Occupation: Lawyer, farmer.
Family: Divorced; three children.
Religion: Episcopalian.
Political Career: No previous office.
Capitol Office: 421 Russell Bldg. 20510; 224-2023.

Virginia — The statewide vote for Ronald Reagan was 62% in 1984; 53% in 1980.

Committees

Armed Services
Environment and Public Works
Rules and Administration
Select Intelligence

Elections

1984	General	70%	Primary	u/o
1978	General	50%	Primary	u/o

CQ Voting Studies

	Presidential Support	Party Unity	Voting Participation
1986	87%	86%	99%
1985	82%	82%	100%

Interest Groups

	ADA	ACU	AFL-CIO	CCUS
1986	5%	n/a	7%	79%
1985	5%	74%	19%	79%

Lowell P. Weicker Jr. (R-Conn.)

Of Greenwich — Elected 1970

Born: May 16, 1931, Paris, France.
Education: Yale U., B.A. 1953; U. of Virginia, LL.B 1958.
Military Career: Army, 1953-55; Army Reserve, 1959-64.
Occupation: Lawyer.
Family: Wife, Claudia Testa Ingram; seven children.
Religion: Episcopalian.
Political Career: Conn. House, 1963-69; first selectman of Greenwich, 1963-67; U.S. House, 1969-71.
Capitol Office: 225 Russell Bldg. 20510; 224-4041.

Connecticut — The statewide vote for Ronald Reagan was 61% in 1984; 48% in 1980.

Committees

Appropriations
Energy and Natural Resources
Labor and Human Resources
Small Business   (Ranking)

Elections

1982	General	50%	Primary	u/o
1976	General	58%	Primary	u/o

CQ Voting Studies

	Presidential Support	Party Unity	Voting Participation
1986	45%	47%	91%
1985	42%	41%	91%

Interest Groups

	ADA	ACU	AFL-CIO	CCUS
1986	80%	n/a	62%	50%
1985	70%	13%	52%	50%

Pete Wilson (R-Calif.)

Of San Diego — Elected 1982

Born: Aug. 23, 1933, Lake Forest, Ill.
Education: Yale U., B.A. 1955; U. of California, Berkeley, LL.B. 1962.
Military Career: Marine Corps, 1955-58.
Occupation: Lawyer.
Family: Wife, Gayle Graham.
Religion: Protestant.
Political Career: Calif. Assembly, 1967-71; San Diego mayor, 1971-83.
Capitol Office: 720 Hart Bldg. 20510; 224-3841.

California — The statewide vote for Ronald Reagan was 58% in 1984; 53% in 1980.

Committees

Agriculture, Nutrition and Forestry
Armed Services
Commerce, Science and Transportation
Joint Economic
Special Aging

Elections

1982	General	52%	Primary	38%

CQ Voting Studies

	Presidential Support	Party Unity	Voting Participation
1986	82%	88%	100%
1985	75%	74%	91%

Interest Groups

	ADA	ACU	AFL-CIO	CCUS
1986	5%	n/a	7%	89%
1985	10%	77%	18%	93%

Timothy E. Wirth (D-Colo.)

Of Boulder — Elected 1986

Born: Sept. 22, 1939, Santa Fe, N.M.
Education: Harvard U., A.B. 1961, M.Ed. 1964; Stanford U., Ph.D. 1973.
Military Career: Army Reserve, 1961-67.
Occupation: Education official.
Family: Wife, Wren Winslow; two children.
Religion: Episcopalian.
Political Career: U.S. House, 1975-87.
Capitol Office: 237 Russell Bldg. 20510; 224-5852.

Colorado — The statewide vote for Ronald Reagan was 63% in 1984; 55% in 1980.

Committees

Armed Services
Budget
Energy and Natural Resources

Elections

1986	General	51%	Primary	u/o

CQ Voting Studies — House

	Presidential Support	Party Unity	Voting Participation
1986	27%	76%	91%
1985	21%	81%	92%

Interest Groups — House

	ADA	ACU	AFL-CIO	CCUS
1986	75%	n/a	92%	54%
1985	70%	10%	71%	38%

Edward Zorinsky (D-Neb.)

Of Omaha — Elected 1976
Died March 6, 1987.

Born: Nov. 11, 1928, Omaha, Neb.
Education: Attended U. of Minnesota, 1945-46; Creighton U., 1946-47; U. of Nebraska, B.S. 1949; graduate work, Harvard U., 1966.
Military Career: Army Reserve, 1950-66.
Occupation: Candy and tobacco wholesaler.
Family: Wife, Cece Rottman; three children.
Religion: Jewish.
Political Career: Omaha Public Power District Board, 1968-73; mayor of Omaha, 1973-77.
Capitol Office: 443 Russell Bldg. 20510; 224-6551.

Nebraska — The statewide vote for Ronald Reagan was 71% in 1984; 66% in 1980.

Committees

Agriculture, Nutrition and Forestry
Foreign Relations

Elections

1982	General	67%	Primary	u/o
1976	General	52%	Primary	49%

CQ Voting Studies

	Presidential Support	Party Unity	Voting Participation
1986	64%	44%	99%
1985	53%	46%	95%

Interest Groups

	ADA	ACU	AFL-CIO	CCUS
1986	15%	n/a	33%	78%
1985	25%	55%	38%	70%

Gary L. Ackerman (D-N.Y.)

Of Queens — Elected 1983

Born: Nov. 19, 1942, Brooklyn, N.Y.
Education: Queens College, B.A. 1965.
Occupation: Teacher; newspaper publisher and editor; advertising executive.
Family: Wife, Rita Gail Tewel; three children.
Religion: Jewish.
Political Career: N.Y. Senate, 1979-83; sought Democratic nomination for N.Y. City councilman at large, 1977.
Capitol Office: 1725 Longworth Bldg. 20515; 225-2601.

New York 7th: Central Queens — Hollis and Kew Gardens. The district vote for Ronald Reagan was 47% in 1984; 44% in 1980.

Committees

Foreign Affairs
Post Office and Civil Service
Select Hunger

Elections

1986	General	76%	Primary	u/o
1984	General	69%	Primary	u/o

CQ Voting Studies

	Presidential Support	Party Unity	Voting Participation
1986	12%	91%	88%
1985	20%	87%	90%

Interest Groups

	ADA	ACU	AFL-CIO	CCUS
1986	85%	n/a	100%	13%
1985	100%	10%	100%	20%

Daniel K. Akaka (D-Hawaii)

Of Honolulu — Elected 1976

Born: Sept. 11, 1924, Honolulu, Hawaii.
Education: U. of Hawaii, B.Ed. 1952, M.Ed. 1966.
Military Career: Army, 1945-47.
Occupation: Elementary school teacher; public official.
Family: Wife, Mary Mildred Chong; five children.
Religion: Congregationalist.
Political Career: Sought Democratic nomination for lieutenant governor, 1974.
Capitol Office: 2301 Rayburn Bldg. 20515; 225-4906.

Hawaii 2nd: Honolulu Suburbs and Outer Islands. The district vote for Ronald Reagan was 55% in 1984.

Committees

Appropriations
Select Narcotics Abuse and Control

Elections

1986	General	78%	Primary	u/o
1984	General	82%	Primary	u/o

CQ Voting Studies

	Presidential Support	Party Unity	Voting Participation
1986	18%	89%	94%
1985	26%	86%	91%

Interest Groups

	ADA	ACU	AFL-CIO	CCUS
1986	90%	n/a	86%	18%
1985	65%	14%	88%	22%

Bill Alexander (D-Ark.)

Of Osceola — Elected 1968

Born: Jan. 16, 1934, Memphis, Tenn.
Education: Southwestern at Memphis, B.A. 1957; Vanderbilt U., LL.B. 1960.
Military Career: Army, 1951-53.
Occupation: Lawyer.
Family: Divorced; one child.
Religion: Episcopalian.
Political Career: No previous office.
Capitol Office: 233 Cannon Bldg. 20515; 225-4076.

Arkansas 1st: East — Jonesboro. The district vote for Ronald Reagan was 57% in 1984; 45% in 1980.

Committee

Appropriations

CQ Voting Studies

	Presidential Support	Party Unity	Voting Participation
1986	22%	80%	90%
1985	25%	84%	90%

Interest Groups

	ADA	ACU	AFL-CIO	CCUS
1986	75%	n/a	100%	29%
1985	70%	5%	82%	23%

Elections

1986	General	64%	Primary	52%
1984	General	97%	Primary	77%

Glenn M. Anderson (D-Calif.)

Of San Pedro — Elected 1968

Born: Feb. 21, 1913, Hawthorne, Calif.
Education: U.C.L.A., B.A. 1936.
Military Career: Army, 1943-45.
Occupation: Banker; home builder.
Family: Wife, Lee Dutton; three children.
Religion: Episcopalian.
Political Career: Mayor of Hawthorne, 1941-43; Calif. Assembly, 1943-51; Democratic nominee for Calif. Senate, 1950; Calif. lt. gov., 1959-67; defeated for re-election, 1966.
Capitol Office: 2329 Rayburn Bldg. 20515; 225-6676.

California 32nd: San Pedro and Long Beach. The district vote for Ronald Reagan was 58% in 1984.

Committees

Merchant Marine and Fisheries
Public Works and Transportation

CQ Voting Studies

	Presidential Support	Party Unity	Voting Participation
1986	22%	84%	99%
1985	39%	84%	96%

Interest Groups

	ADA	ACU	AFL-CIO	CCUS
1986	75%	n/a	79%	28%
1985	70%	38%	88%	19%

Elections

1986	General	70%	Primary	91%
1984	General	61%	Primary	87%

Michael A. Andrews   (D-Texas)

Of Houston — Elected 1982

Born: Feb. 7, 1944, Houston, Texas.
Education: U. of Texas, B.A. 1967; Southern Methodist U., J.D. 1970.
Occupation: Lawyer.
Family: Wife, Ann Bowman; two children.
Religion: Methodist.
Political Career: Democratic nominee for U.S. House, 1980.
Capitol Office: 322 Cannon Bldg. 20515; 225-7508.

Texas 25th: South Houston and Southeast Suburbs. The district vote for Ronald Reagan was 52% in 1984; 49% in 1980.

Committee

Ways and Means

Elections

1986	General	u/o	Primary	94%
1984	General	64%	Primary	94%

CQ Voting Studies

	Presidential Support	Party Unity	Voting Participation
1986	37%	72%	97%
1985	39%	77%	99%

Interest Groups

	ADA	ACU	AFL-CIO	CCUS
1986	50%	n/a	64%	61%
1985	30%	57%	50%	71%

Frank Annunzio   (D-Ill.)

Of Chicago — Elected 1964

Born: Jan. 12, 1915, Chicago, Ill.
Education: De Paul U., B.S. 1940, M.A. 1942.
Occupation: Teacher; labor official.
Family: Wife, Angeline Alesia; three children.
Religion: Roman Catholic.
Political Career: Illinois labor director, 1949-52.
Capitol Office: 2303 Rayburn Bldg. 20515; 225-6661.

Illinois 11th: Northwest Chicago and Suburbs. The district vote for Ronald Reagan was 61% in 1984; 46% in 1980.

Committees

Banking, Finance and Urban Affairs
House Administration   (Chairman)

Elections

1986	General	71%	Primary	85%
1984	General	63%	Primary	88%

CQ Voting Studies

	Presidential Support	Party Unity	Voting Participation
1986	23%	90%	96%
1985	29%	89%	97%

Interest Groups

	ADA	ACU	AFL-CIO	CCUS
1986	70%	n/a	93%	39%
1985	75%	5%	100%	23%

Beryl Anthony Jr. (D-Ark.)

Of El Dorado — Elected 1978

Born: Feb. 21, 1938, El Dorado, Ark.
Education: U. of Arkansas, B.S., B.A. 1961, J.D. 1963.
Occupation: Lawyer.
Family: Wife, Sheila Foster; two children.
Religion: Episcopalian.
Political Career: Prosecuting attorney, Ark. 13th Judicial District, 1971-77.
Capitol Office: 1117 Longworth Bldg. 20515; 225-3772.

Arkansas 4th: South — Pine Bluff. The district vote for Ronald Reagan was 56% in 1984; 43% in 1980.

Committees

Ways and Means
Select Children, Youth and Families

CQ Voting Studies

	Presidential Support	Party Unity	Voting Participation
1986	27%	78%	90%
1985	28%	81%	94%

Interest Groups

	ADA	ACU	AFL-CIO	CCUS
1986	50%	n/a	54%	40%
1985	55%	33%	59%	32%

Elections

1986	General	82%	Primary	u/o
1984	General	98%	Primary	u/o

Douglas Applegate (D-Ohio)

Of Steubenville — Elected 1976

Born: March 27, 1928, Steubenville, Ohio.
Education: Graduated from Steubenville H.S.; 1947.
Occupation: Real estate salesman.
Family: Wife, Betty Engstrom; two children.
Religion: Presbyterian.
Political Career: Ohio House, 1961-69; Ohio Senate, 1969-77.
Capitol Office: 2183 Rayburn Bldg. 20515; 225-6265.

Ohio 18th: East — Steubenville.

Committees

Public Works and Transportation
Veterans' Affairs

CQ Voting Studies

	Presidential Support	Party Unity	Voting Participation
1986	24%	75%	96%
1985	29%	63%	91%

Interest Groups

	ADA	ACU	AFL-CIO	CCUS
1986	65%	n/a	93%	35%
1985	55%	19%	59%	50%

Elections

1986	General	u/o	Primary	91%
1984	General	76%	Primary	91%

Bill Archer (R-Texas)

Of Houston — Elected 1970

Born: March 22, 1928, Houston, Texas.
Education: Attended Rice U., 1945-46; U. of Texas, B.B.A. 1949, LL.B. 1951.
Military Career: Air Force, 1951-53.
Occupation: Lawyer; feed company executive.
Family: Wife, Sharon Sawyer; five children; two stepchildren.
Religion: Roman Catholic.
Political Career: Hunters Creek Village Council, 1955-62; Texas House, 1967-71.
Capitol Office: 1135 Longworth Bldg. 20515; 225-2571.

Texas 7th: Western Houston and Suburbs. The district vote for Ronald Reagan was 82% in 1984; 78% in 1980.

Committees

Ways and Means
Joint Taxation

CQ Voting Studies

	Presidential Support	Party Unity	Voting Participation
1986	82%	81%	96%
1985	88%	80%	95%

Interest Groups

	ADA	ACU	AFL-CIO	CCUS
1986	0%	n/a	0%	94%
1985	5%	100%	0%	100%

Elections

1986	General	88%	Primary	u/o
1984	General	87%	Primary	u/o

Dick Armey (R-Texas)

Of Lewisville — Elected 1984

Born: July 7, 1940, Cando, N.D.
Education: Jamestown College, B.A. 1963; U. of North Dakota, M.A. 1964; U. of Oklahoma, Ph.D. 1969.
Occupation: Economist.
Family: Wife, Susan K. Byrd; five children.
Religion: Presbyterian.
Political Career: No previous office.
Capitol Office: 514 Cannon Bldg. 20515; 225-7772.

Texas 26th: Fort Worth Suburbs — Arlington and Denton. The district vote for Ronald Reagan was 77% in 1984.

Committees

Budget
Education and Labor

CQ Voting Studies

	Presidential Support	Party Unity	Voting Participation
1986	82%	97%	99%
1985	88%	94%	98%

Interest Groups

	ADA	ACU	AFL-CIO	CCUS
1986	0%	n/a	7%	100%
1985	15%	95%	0%	95%

Elections

1986	General	68%	Primary	85%
1984	General	51%	Primary	u/o

Les Aspin (D-Wis.)

Of East Troy — Elected 1970

Born: July 21, 1938, Milwaukee, Wis.
Education: Yale U., B.A. 1960; Oxford U., England, M.A. 1962; Massachusetts Institute of Technology, Ph.D. 1965.
Military Career: Army, 1966-68.
Occupation: Professor of economics.
Family: Divorced.
Religion: Episcopalian.
Political Career: Sought Democratic nomination for Wis. treasurer, 1968.
Capitol Office: 2336 Rayburn Bldg. 20515; 225-3031.

Wisconsin 1st: Southeast — Racine and Kenosha. The district vote for Ronald Reagan was 54% in 1984; 50% in 1980.

Committees

Armed Services (Chairman)
Select Iran-contra

CQ Voting Studies

	Presidential Support	Party Unity	Voting Participation
1986	28%	83%	91%
1985	33%	82%	89%

Interest Groups

	ADA	ACU	AFL-CIO	CCUS
1986	50%	n/a	80%	42%
1985	65%	19%	100%	10%

Elections

1986	General	75%	Primary	u/o
1984	General	56%	Primary	u/o

Chester G. Atkins (D-Mass.)

Of Concord — Elected 1984

Born: April 14, 1948, Geneva, Switzerland.
Education: Antioch College, B.A. 1970.
Occupation: Public official.
Family: Wife, Corinne Hobbs; two children.
Religion: Unitarian.
Political Career: Mass. House, 1971-73; Mass. Senate, 1973-85.
Capitol Office: 504 Cannon Bldg. 20515; 225-3411.

Massachusetts 5th: North — Lowell and Lawrence. The district vote for Ronald Reagan was 57% in 1984; 44% in 1980.

Committees

Budget
Education and Labor
Foreign Affairs
Standards of Official Conduct

CQ Voting Studies

	Presidential Support	Party Unity	Voting Participation
1986	18%	86%	92%
1985	20%	86%	93%

Interest Groups

	ADA	ACU	AFL-CIO	CCUS
1986	90%	n/a	92%	25%
1985	90%	5%	81%	33%

Elections

1986	General	u/o	Primary	u/o
1984	General	53%	Primary	53%

Les AuCoin (D-Ore.)

Of Forest Grove — Elected 1974

Born: Oct. 21, 1942, Redmond, Ore.
Education: Pacific U., B.A. 1969.
Military Career: Army, 1961-64.
Occupation: Journalist; public relations executive.
Family: Wife, Susan Swearinger; two children.
Religion: Protestant.
Political Career: Ore. House, 1971-75, majority leader, 1973-75.
Capitol Office: 2159 Rayburn Bldg. 20515; 225-0855.

Oregon 1st: Western Portland and Suburbs. The district vote for Ronald Reagan was 55% in 1984; 47% in 1980.

Committee

Appropriations

Elections

1986	General	62%	Primary	88%
1984	General	53%	Primary	u/o

CQ Voting Studies

	Presidential Support	Party Unity	Voting Participation
1986	29%	82%	94%
1985	24%	71%	89%

Interest Groups

	ADA	ACU	AFL-CIO	CCUS
1986	90%	n/a	86%	33%
1985	65%	29%	71%	64%

Robert E. Badham (R-Calif.)

Of Newport Beach — Elected 1976

Born: June 9, 1929, Los Angeles, Calif.
Education: Attended Occidental College, 1947-48; Stanford U., B.A. 1951.
Military Career: Navy, 1951-54.
Occupation: Hardware company executive.
Family: Wife, Anne Carroll; five children.
Religion: Lutheran.
Political Career: Calif. Assembly, 1963-77.
Capitol Office: 2427 Rayburn Bldg. 20515; 225-5611.

California 40th: Coastal and Central Orange County. The district vote for Ronald Reagan was 75% in 1984.

Committees

Armed Services
House Administration

Elections

1986	General	61%	Primary	66%
1984	General	64%	Primary	u/o

CQ Voting Studies

	Presidential Support	Party Unity	Voting Participation
1986	64%	73%	83%
1985	61%	82%	85%

Interest Groups

	ADA	ACU	AFL-CIO	CCUS
1986	0%	n/a	8%	100%
1985	0%	95%	6%	89%

Richard Baker (R-La.)

Of Baton Rouge — Elected 1986

Born: May 22, 1948, New Orleans, La.
Education: Louisiana State U., B.A. 1971.
Occupation: Real estate broker.
Family: Wife, Kay Carpenter; two children.
Religion: Methodist.
Political Career: La. House, 1973-87; candidate for La. Senate, 1980.
Capitol Office: 506 Cannon Bldg. 20515; 225-3901.

Louisiana 6th: East Central — Baton Rouge. The district vote for Ronald Reagan was 64% in 1984; 53% in 1980.

Committees

Interior and Insular Affairs
Small Business

Elections

1986   General   †   Primary   51%

†In Louisiana the primary is open to candidates of all parties. If a candidate wins 50% or more of the vote no general election is held.

Cass Ballenger (R-N.C.)

Of Hickory — Elected 1986

Born: Dec. 6, 1926, Hickory, N.C.
Education: Attended U. of North Carolina, 1944-45; Amherst College, B.A. 1948.
Military Career: Naval Air Corps, 1944-45.
Occupation: President of plastics packaging company.
Family: Wife, Donna Davis; three children.
Religion: Episcopalian.
Political Career: Catawba County Board of Commissioners, 1966-74, chairman, 1970-74; N.C. House, 1975-77; N.C. Senate, 1977-87.
Capitol Office: 116 Cannon Bldg. 20515; 225-2576.

North Carolina 10th: West — Gastonia and Hickory. The district vote for Ronald Reagan was 69% in 1984; 55% in 1980.

Committees

Education and Labor
Public Works and Transportation

Elections

1986   General   57%   Primary   53%

Doug Barnard Jr. (D-Ga.)

Of Augusta — Elected 1976

Born: March 20, 1922, Augusta, Ga.
Education: Mercer U., B.A. 1943, LL.B. 1948.
Military Career: Army, 1943-45.
Occupation: Banker.
Family: Wife, Naomi Elizabeth Holt; three children.
Religion: Baptist.
Political Career: No previous office.
Capitol Office: 2227 Rayburn Bldg. 20515; 225-4101.

Georgia 10th: North Central — Athens and Augusta. The district vote for Ronald Reagan was 65% in 1984; 44% in 1980.

Committees

Banking, Finance and Urban Affairs
Government Operations

Elections

1986	General	67%	Primary	u/o
1984	General	100%	Primary	u/o

CQ Voting Studies

	Presidential Support	Party Unity	Voting Participation
1986	54%	52%	81%
1985	54%	53%	92%

Interest Groups

	ADA	ACU	AFL-CIO	CCUS
1986	25%	n/a	23%	79%
1985	15%	71%	44%	50%

Steve Bartlett (R-Texas)

Of Dallas — Elected 1982

Born: Sept. 19, 1947, Los Angeles, Calif.
Education: U. of Texas, B.A. 1971.
Occupation: Owner of tool and plastics company.
Family: Wife, Gail Coke; three children.
Religion: Presbyterian.
Political Career: Dallas City Council, 1977-81.
Capitol Office: 1709 Longworth Bldg. 20515; 225-4201.

Texas 3rd: North Dallas and Northern Suburbs. The district vote for Ronald Reagan was 82% in 1984.

Committees

Banking, Finance and Urban Affairs
Education and Labor

Elections

1986	General	u/o	Primary	u/o
1984	General	83%	Primary	u/o

CQ Voting Studies

	Presidential Support	Party Unity	Voting Participation
1986	77%	91%	99%
1985	89%	93%	98%

Interest Groups

	ADA	ACU	AFL-CIO	CCUS
1986	5%	n/a	7%	94%
1985	5%	95%	0%	100%

Joe L. Barton (R-Texas)

Of Ennis — Elected 1984

Born: Sept. 15, 1949, Waco, Texas.
Education: Texas A&M U., B.S. 1972; Purdue U., M.S. 1973.
Occupation: Engineering consultant.
Family: Wife, Janet Sue Winslow; three children.
Religion: Methodist.
Political Career: No previous office.
Capitol Office: 1225 Longworth Bldg. 20515; 225-2002.

Texas 6th: Suburban Dallas-Fort Worth, Suburban Houston and Bryan. The district vote for Ronald Reagan was 69% in 1984.

CQ Voting Studies

	Presidential Support	Party Unity	Voting Participation
1986	76%	93%	97%
1985	85%	94%	94%

Interest Groups

	ADA	ACU	AFL-CIO	CCUS
1986	0%	n/a	7%	94%
1985	5%	100%	0%	95%

Committee

Energy and Commerce

Elections

1986	General	56%	Primary	u/o
1984	General	57%	Primary	50% *

** Primary runoff.*

Herbert H. Bateman (R-Va.)

Of Newport News — Elected 1982

Born: Aug. 7, 1928, Elizabeth City, N.C.
Education: College of William and Mary, B.A. 1949; Georgetown U., J.D. 1956.
Military Career: Air Force, 1951-53.
Occupation: Lawyer.
Family: Wife, Laura Yacobi; two children.
Religion: Presbyterian.
Political Career: Va. Senate, 1968-82.
Capitol Office: 1527 Longworth Bldg. 20515; 225-4261.

Virginia 1st: East — Newport News and Hampton. The district vote for Ronald Reagan was 62% in 1984; 50% in 1980.

CQ Voting Studies

	Presidential Support	Party Unity	Voting Participation
1986	69%	64%	97%
1985	69%	67%	97%

Interest Groups

	ADA	ACU	AFL-CIO	CCUS
1986	0%	n/a	7%	78%
1985	10%	71%	6%	77%

Committees

Armed Services
Merchant Marine and Fisheries

Elections

1986	General	56%	Primary	u/o
1984	General	59%	Primary	u/o

Jim Bates (D-Calif.)

Of San Diego — Elected 1982

Born: July 21, 1941, Denver, Colo.
Education: San Diego State U., B.A. 1975.
Military Career: Marine Corps, 1959-63.
Occupation: Marketing analyst.
Family: Wife, Marilyn Brewer; one child.
Religion: Protestant.
Political Career: San Diego City Council, 1971-74; San Diego County Board of Supervisors, 1975-82; sought Democratic nomination for U.S. House, 1980.
Capitol Office: 1404 Longworth Bldg. 20515; 225-5452.

California 44th: Central San Diego. The district vote for Ronald Reagan was 52% in 1984.

Committees

Energy and Commerce
House Administration

Elections

1986	General	65%	Primary	u/o
1984	General	70%	Primary	87%

CQ Voting Studies

	Presidential Support	Party Unity	Voting Participation
1986	19%	83%	98%
1985	30%	79%	96%

Interest Groups

	ADA	ACU	AFL-CIO	CCUS
1986	90%	n/a	86%	44%
1985	80%	29%	75%	41%

Anthony C. Beilenson (D-Calif.)

Of Los Angeles — Elected 1976

Born: Oct. 26, 1932, New Rochelle, N.Y.
Education: Harvard U., A.B. 1954; Harvard Law School, LL.B. 1957.
Occupation: Lawyer.
Family: Wife, Dolores Martin; three children.
Religion: Jewish.
Political Career: Calif. Assembly, 1963-67; Calif. Senate, 1967-77; sought Democratic nomination for U.S. Senate, 1968.
Capitol Office: 1025 Longworth Bldg. 20515; 225-5911.

California 23rd: Beverly Hills and Part of San Fernando Valley. The district vote for Ronald Reagan was 53% in 1984.

Committees

Rules
Select Intelligence

Elections

1986	General	68%	Primary	88%
1984	General	62%	Primary	88%

CQ Voting Studies

	Presidential Support	Party Unity	Voting Participation
1986	18%	89%	97%
1985	23%	88%	92%

Interest Groups

	ADA	ACU	AFL-CIO	CCUS
1986	80%	n/a	50%	18%
1985	95%	5%	88%	24%

Charles E. Bennett   (D-Fla.)

Of Jacksonville — Elected 1948

Born: Dec. 2, 1910, Canton, N.Y.
Education: U. of Florida, B.A., J.D. 1934.
Military Career: Army, 1942-47.
Occupation: Lawyer.
Family: Wife, Jean Fay; two children.
Religion: Disciples of Christ.
Political Career: Fla. House, 1941.
Capitol Office: 2107 Rayburn Bldg. 20515; 225-2501.

Florida 3rd: Northeast — Jacksonville. The district vote for Ronald Reagan was 59% in 1984; 45% in 1980.

Committees

Armed Services
Merchant Marine and Fisheries

CQ Voting Studies

	Presidential Support	Party Unity	Voting Participation
1986	33%	82%	100%
1985	35%	82%	100%

Interest Groups

	ADA	ACU	AFL-CIO	CCUS
1986	55%	n/a	64%	50%
1985	70%	19%	88%	32%

Elections

1986	General	u/o	Primary	u/o
1984	General	u/o	Primary	u/o

Helen Delich Bentley   (R-Md.)

Of Lutherville — Elected 1984

Born: Nov. 28, 1923, Ruth, Nev.
Education: U. of Missouri, B.A. 1944.
Occupation: Journalist; international trade consultant.
Family: Husband, William Roy Bentley.
Religion: Greek Orthodox.
Political Career: Republican nominee for U.S. House, 1980, 1982.
Capitol Office: 1610 Longworth Bldg. 20515; 225-3061.

Maryland 2nd: Baltimore Suburbs. The district vote for Ronald Reagan was 66% in 1984; 47% in 1980.

Committees

Merchant Marine and Fisheries
Public Works and Transportation
Select Aging

CQ Voting Studies

	Presidential Support	Party Unity	Voting Participation
1986	57%	60%	91%
1985	64%	74%	92%

Interest Groups

	ADA	ACU	AFL-CIO	CCUS
1986	15%	n/a	67%	63%
1985	20%	76%	24%	73%

Elections

1986	General	59%	Primary	u/o
1984	General	51%	Primary	51%

Doug Bereuter   (R-Neb.)

Of Utica — Elected 1978.

Born: Oct. 6, 1939, York, Neb.
Education: U. of Nebraska, B.A. 1961; Harvard U., M.C.P. 1963, M.P.A. 1973.
Military Career: Army, 1963-65.
Occupation: City planner.
Family: Wife, Louise Anna Meyer; two children.
Religion: Lutheran.
Political Career: Neb. Legislature, 1975-79.
Capitol Office: 2446 Rayburn Bldg. 20515; 225-4806.

Nebraska 1st: East Central — Lincoln. The district vote for Ronald Reagan was 67% in 1984; 62% in 1980.

CQ Voting Studies

	Presidential Support	Party Unity	Voting Participation
1986	58%	73%	98%
1985	58%	74%	98%

Interest Groups

	ADA	ACU	AFL-CIO	CCUS
1986	15%	n/a	21%	72%
1985	15%	67%	12%	82%

Committees

Banking, Finance and Urban Affairs
Foreign Affairs
Select Hunger

Elections

1986	General	64%	Primary	91%
1984	General	74%	Primary	u/o

Howard L. Berman   (D-Calif.)

Of Studio City — Elected 1982

Born: April 15, 1941, Los Angeles, Calif.
Education: U. of California, Los Angeles, B.A. 1962, LL.B. 1965.
Occupation: Lawyer.
Family: Wife, Janis Schwartz; two children.
Religion: Jewish.
Political Career: Calif. Assembly, 1973-83
Capitol Office: 137 Cannon Bldg. 20515; 225-4695.

California 26th: Santa Monica Mountains and Central San Fernando Valley. The district vote for Ronald Reagan was 54% in 1984.

CQ Voting Studies

	Presidential Support	Party Unity	Voting Participation
1986	18%	89%	95%
1985	24%	91%	93%

Interest Groups

	ADA	ACU	AFL-CIO	CCUS
1986	95%	n/a	92%	19%
1985	100%	10%	94%	24%

Committees

Foreign Affairs
Judiciary

Elections

1986	General	65%	Primary	u/o
1984	General	63%	Primary	85%

Tom Bevill (D-Ala.)

Of Jasper — Elected 1966

Born: March 27, 1921, Townley, Ala.
Education: U. of Alabama, B.S. 1943, LL.B. 1948.
Military Career: Army, 1943-46.
Occupation: Lawyer.
Family: Wife, Lou Betts; three children.
Religion: Baptist.
Political Career: Ala. House, 1959-67; sought Democratic nomination for U.S. House, 1964.
Capitol Office: 2302 Rayburn Bldg. 20515; 225-4876.

Alabama 4th: North Central — Gadsden. The district vote for Ronald Reagan was 59% in 1984; 46% in 1980.

Committee

Appropriations

CQ Voting Studies

	Presidential Support	Party Unity	Voting Participation
1986	40%	67%	94%
1985	54%	66%	91%

Interest Groups

	ADA	ACU	AFL-CIO	CCUS
1986	40%	n/a	79%	29%
1985	25%	57%	53%	35%

Elections

1986	General	77%	Primary	u/o
1984	General	100%	Primary	88%

Mario Biaggi (D-N.Y.)

Of The Bronx — Elected 1968

Born: Oct. 26, 1917, New York, N.Y.
Education: New York Law School, LL.B. 1963.
Occupation: Lawyer; police detective.
Family: Wife, Marie Wassil; four children.
Religion: Roman Catholic.
Political Career: Sought Democratic nomination for N.Y. City mayor, 1973.
Capitol Office: 2428 Rayburn Bldg. 20515; 225-2464.

New York 19th: South Yonkers and East and Central Bronx. The district vote for Ronald Reagan was 52% in 1984; 43% in 1980.

Committees

Education and Labor
Merchant Marine and Fisheries
Select Aging

CQ Voting Studies

	Presidential Support	Party Unity	Voting Participation
1986	27%	82%	90%
1985	38%	75%	87%

Interest Groups

	ADA	ACU	AFL-CIO	CCUS
1986	65%	n/a	100%	21%
1985	55%	25%	100%	28%

Elections

1986	General	90%	Primary	u/o
1984	General	95%	Primary	u/o

James H. Bilbray (D-Nev.)

Of Las Vegas — Elected 1986

Born: May 19, 1938, Las Vegas, Nev.
Education: American U., B.A. 1962; Washington College of
Law, J.D. 1964.
Military Career: National Guard, 1955-63; Reserves, 1963-
present.
Occupation: Lawyer.
Family: Wife, Michaelene Mercer; four children.
Religion: Roman Catholic.
Political Career: Nev. Senate 1981-87; Democratic nominee
for U.S. House, 1972.
Capitol Office: 1431 Longworth Bldg. 20515; 225-5965.

Nevada 1st: South — Las Vegas. The district vote for
Ronald Reagan was 63% in 1984; 59% in 1980.

Committees

Foreign Affairs
Small Business
Select Hunger

Elections

1986	General	55%	Primary	36%

Michael Bilirakis (R-Fla.)

Of Palm Harbor — Elected 1982

Born: July 16, 1930, Tarpon Springs, Fla.
Education: U. of Pittsburgh, B.S. 1959; attended George
Washington U., 1959-60; U. of Florida, J.D. 1963.
Military Career: Air Force, 1951-55.
Occupation: Lawyer; restaurant owner.
Family: Wife, Evelyn Miaoulis; two children.
Religion: Greek Orthodox.
Political Career: No previous office.
Capitol Office: 1530 Longworth Bldg. 20515; 225-5755.

Florida 9th: West — Clearwater, Parts of Pasco and
Hillsborough Counties. The district vote for Ronald Reagan
was 67% in 1984; 56% in 1980.

Committees

Energy and Commerce
Veterans' Affairs

Elections

1986	General	71%	Primary	u/o
1984	Generai	79%	Primary	u/o

CQ Voting Studies

	Presidential Support	Party Unity	Voting Participation
1986	77%	88%	97%
1985	75%	84%	94%

Interest Groups

	ADA	ACU	AFL-CIO	CCUS
1986	15%	n/a	29%	67%
1985	10%	71%	29%	77%

Thomas J. Bliley Jr. (R-Va.)

Of Richmond — Elected 1980

Born: Jan. 28, 1932, Chesterfield County, Va.
Education: Georgetown U., B.A. 1952.
Military Career: Navy, 1952-55.
Occupation: Funeral director.
Family: Wife, Mary Virginia Kelley; two children.
Religion: Roman Catholic.
Political Career: Richmond City Council, 1968-77; mayor, 1970-77.
Capitol Office: 213 Cannon Bldg. 20515; 225-2815.

Virginia 3rd: Richmond and Suburbs. The district vote for Ronald Reagan was 65% in 1984; 57% in 1980.

Committees

District of Columbia
Energy and Commerce
Select Children, Youth and Families

Elections

1986	General	69%	Primary	u/o
1984	General	86%	Primary	u/o

CQ Voting Studies

	Presidential Support	Party Unity	Voting Participation
1986	69%	82%	97%
1985	74%	83%	99%

Interest Groups

	ADA	ACU	AFL-CIO	CCUS
1986	5%	n/a	14%	88%
1985	5%	81%	24%	82%

Sherwood Boehlert (R-N.Y.)

Of New Hartford — Elected 1982

Born: Sept. 28, 1936, Utica, N.Y.
Education: Utica College, A.B. 1961.
Military Career: Army, 1956-58.
Occupation: Congressional aide.
Family: Wife, Marianne Willey; four children.
Religion: Roman Catholic.
Political Career: Oneida County Executive, 1979-82; sought Republican nomination for U.S. House, 1972.
Capitol Office: 1641 Longworth Bldg. 20515; 225-3665.

New York 25th: Central — Rome and Utica. The district vote for Ronald Reagan was 63% in 1984; 51% in 1980.

Committees

Public Works and Transportation
Science, Space and Technology
Select Aging

Elections

1986	General	69%	Primary	67%
1984	General	73%	Primary	u/o

CQ Voting Studies

	Presidential Support	Party Unity	Voting Participation
1986	46%	53%	98%
1985	41%	54%	97%

Interest Groups

	ADA	ACU	AFL-CIO	CCUS
1986	50%	n/a	93%	56%
1985	45%	52%	65%	57%

Lindy (Mrs. Hale) Boggs (D-La.)

Of New Orleans — Elected 1973

Born: March 13, 1916, Brunswick Plantation, La.
Education: Tulane U., B.A. 1935.
Occupation: High school teacher.
Family: Widow of Rep. Hale Boggs; three children.
Religion: Roman Catholic.
Political Career: No previous office.
Capitol Office: 2353 Rayburn Bldg. 20515; 225-6636.

Louisiana 2nd: New Orleans. The district vote for Ronald Reagan was 38% in 1984.

Committees

Appropriations
Select Children, Youth and Families

Elections

1986	General	†	Primary	91%
1984	General	†	Primary	60%

† In Louisiana the primary is open to candidates of all parties. If a candidate wins 50% or more of the vote no general election is held.

CQ Voting Studies

	Presidential Support	Party Unity	Voting Participation
1986	22%	85%	95%
1985	28%	82%	92%

Interest Groups

	ADA	ACU	AFL-CIO	CCUS
1986	80%	n/a	100%	25%
1985	65%	19%	88%	29%

Edward P. Boland (D-Mass.)

Of Springfield — Elected 1952

Born: Oct. 1, 1911, Springfield, Mass.
Education: Attended Boston College Law School.
Military Career: Army, 1942-46.
Occupation: Public official.
Family: Wife, Mary Egan; four children.
Religion: Roman Catholic.
Political Career: Mass. House, 1935-41; Hampden County register of deeds, 1941-42 and 1946-52.
Capitol Office: 2426 Rayburn Bldg. 20515; 225-5601.

Massachusetts 2nd: West-Central — Springfield. The district vote for Ronald Reagan was 54% in 1984; 40% in 1980.

Committees

Appropriations
Select Iran-contra

Elections

1986	General	66%	Primary	u/o
1984	General	69%	Primary	65%

CQ Voting Studies

	Presidential Support	Party Unity	Voting Participation
1986	20%	82%	83%
1985	28%	82%	88%

Interest Groups

	ADA	ACU	AFL-CIO	CCUS
1986	70%	n/a	100%	17%
1985	75%	10%	88%	27%

Bill Boner (D-Tenn.)

Of Nashville — Elected 1978

Born: Feb. 14, 1945, Nashville, Tenn.

Education: Middle Tennessee State U., B.S. 1967; George Peabody College, M.A. 1969; YMCA Night Law School, J.D. 1978.

Occupation: High school and college teacher and coach; banker; lawyer.

Family: Wife, Betty Fowlkes; two children.

Religion: Methodist.

Political Career: Tenn. House, 1971-73, 1975-77; Tenn. Senate, 1977-79.

Capitol Office: 107 Cannon Bldg. 20515; 225-4311.

Tennessee 5th: Nashville. The district vote for Ronald Reagan was 52% in 1984; 37% in 1980.

CQ Voting Studies

	Presidential Support	Party Unity	Voting Participation
1986	30%	70%	84%
1985	44%	81%	95%

Interest Groups

	ADA	ACU	AFL-CIO	CCUS
1986	50%	n/a	100%	18%
1985	40%	33%	81%	41%

Committees

Appropriations
Select Aging

Elections

1986	General	59%	Primary	58%
1984	General	100%	Primary	u/o

David E. Bonior (D-Mich.)

Of Mount Clemens — Elected 1976

Born: June 6, 1945, Detroit, Mich.

Education: U. of Iowa, B.A., 1967; Chapman College, M.A. 1972.

Military Career: Air Force, 1968-72.

Occupation: Probation officer.

Family: Divorced; two children.

Religion: Roman Catholic.

Political Career: Mich. House, 1973-77.

Capitol Office: 2242 Rayburn Bldg. 20515; 225-2106.

Michigan 12th: Southeast — Macomb County and Port Huron. The district vote for Ronald Reagan was 67% in 1984; 54%. in 1980.

CQ Voting Studies

	Presidential Support	Party Unity	Voting Participation
1986	16%	90%	92%
1985	19%	90%	91%

Interest Groups

	ADA	ACU	AFL-CIO	CCUS
1986	95%	n/a	100%	6%
1985	90%	5%	94%	25%

Committee

Rules

Elections

1986	General	66%	Primary	90%
1984	General	58%	Primary	u/o

Don Bonker (D-Wash.)

Of Vancouver — Elected 1974

Born: March 7, 1937, Denver, Colo.
Education: Clark College, A.A., 1962; Lewis and Clark College, B.A. 1964.
Military Career: Coast Guard, 1955-59; Coast Guard Reserve, 1959-64.
Occupation: Auditor.
Family: Wife, Carolyn Jo Ekern; two children.
Religion: Presbyterian.
Political Career: Clark County auditor, 1966-74; Democratic nominee for Wash. secretary of state, 1972.
Capitol Office: 434 Cannon Bldg. 20515; 225-3536.

Washington 3rd: Southwest — Olympia and Vancouver. The district vote for Ronald Reagan was 53% in 1984.

Committees

Foreign Affairs
Merchant Marine and Fisheries
Select Aging

Elections

1986	General	74%	Primary	75%
1984	General	71%	Primary	u/o

CQ Voting Studies

	Presidential Support	Party Unity	Voting Participation
1986	23%	80%	87%
1985	23%	81%	87%

Interest Groups

	ADA	ACU	AFL-CIO	CCUS
1986	70%	n/a	79%	40%
1985	85%	14%	88%	20%

Robert A. Borski (D-Pa.)

Of Philadelphia — Elected 1982

Born: Oct. 20, 1948, Philadelphia, Pa.
Education: U. of Baltimore, B.A. 1971.
Occupation: Stockbroker.
Family: Wife, Barbara Joniek; three children.
Religion: Roman Catholic.
Political Career: Pa. House, 1977-83.
Capitol Office: 314 Cannon Bldg. 20515; 225-8251.

Pennsylvania 3rd: Northeast Philadelphia. The district vote for Ronald Reagan was 54% in 1984; 50% in 1980.

Committees

Merchant Marine and Fisheries
Public Works and Transportation
Select Aging

Elections

1986	General	61%	Primary	96%
1984	General	64%	Primary	u/o

CQ Voting Studies

	Presidential Support	Party Unity	Voting Participation
1986	20%	93%	98%
1985	24%	94%	97%

Interest Groups

	ADA	ACU	AFL-CIO	CCUS
1986	75%	n/a	100%	33%
1985	80%	5%	88%	23%

Douglas H. Bosco (D-Calif.)

Of Occidental — Elected 1982

Born: July 28, 1946, Brooklyn, N.Y.
Education: Willamette U., B.A. 1968, J.D. 1971.
Occupation: Lawyer.
Family: Single.
Religion: Roman Catholic.
Political Career: Calif. Assembly, 1979-83; Sought Democratic nomination for U.S. House, 1976.
Capitol Office: 408 Cannon Bldg. 20515; 225-3311.

California 1st: Northern Coast — Santa Rosa and Eureka. The district vote for Ronald Reagan was 52% in 1984.

CQ Voting Studies

	Presidential Support	Party Unity	Voting Participation
1986	21%	78%	86%
1985	26%	74%	84%

Interest Groups

	ADA	ACU	AFL-CIO	CCUS
1986	70%	n/a	100%	23%
1985	65%	19%	63%	33%

Committees

Merchant Marine and Fisheries
Public Works and Transportation

Elections

1986	General	72%	Primary	75%
1984	General	62%	Primary	u/o

Frederick C. Boucher (D-Va.)

Of Abingdon — Elected 1982

Born: Aug. 1, 1946, Abingdon, Va.
Education: Roanoke College, B.A. 1968; U. of Virginia, J.D. 1971.
Occupation: Lawyer.
Family: Single.
Religion: Methodist.
Political Career: Va. Senate, 1975-83.
Capitol Office: 428 Cannon Bldg. 20515; 225-3861.

Virginia 9th: Southwest — Blacksburg and Bristol. The district vote for Ronald Reagan was 58% in 1984; 48% in 1980.

Committees

Energy and Commerce
Judiciary
Science, Space and Technology
Select Aging

CQ Voting Studies

	Presidential Support	Party Unity	Voting Participation
1986	23%	83%	90%
1985	29%	87%	94%

Interest Groups

	ADA	ACU	AFL-CIO	CCUS
1986	70%	n/a	86%	20%
1985	60%	19%	65%	48%

Elections

1986	General	u/o	Primary	u/o
1984	General	52%	Primary	u/o

Beau Boulter (R-Texas)

Of Amarillo — Elected 1984

Born: Feb. 23, 1942, El Paso, Texas.
Education: U. of Texas, B.A. 1965; Baylor U., J.D. 1968.
Occupation: Lawyer.
Family: Wife, Rosemary Rutherford; three children.
Religion: Independent Bible Church.
Political Career: Amarillo city commissioner, 1981-83; sought Republican nomination for U.S. House, 1982.
Capitol Office: 124 Cannon Bldg. 20515; 225-3706.

Texas 13th: The Panhandle — Amarillo and Wichita Falls. The district vote for Ronald Reagan was 75% in 1984; 62% in 1980.

Committees

Budget
Government Operations
Select Children, Youth and Families

CQ Voting Studies

	Presidential Support	Party Unity	Voting Participation
1986	66%	85%	97%
1985	78%	87%	95%

Interest Groups

	ADA	ACU	AFL-CIO	CCUS
1986	5%	n/a	14%	89%
1985	0%	100%	0%	95%

Elections

1986	General	65%	Primary	u/o
1984	General	53%	Primary	u/o

Barbara Boxer (D-Calif.)

Of Greenbrae — Elected 1982

Born: Nov. 11, 1940, Brooklyn, N.Y.
Education: Brooklyn College, B.A. 1962.
Occupation: Stockbroker; journalist.
Family: Husband, Stewart Boxer; two children.
Religion: Jewish.
Political Career: Marin County Board of Supervisors, 1977-82; candidate for Marin County Board of Supervisors, 1972.
Capitol Office: 307 Cannon Bldg. 20515; 225-5161.

California 6th: Northwest San Francisco, Marin County and Parts of Sonoma and Solano Counties. The district vote for Ronald Reagan was 42% in 1984.

Committees

Armed Services
Budget
Select Children, Youth and Families

CQ Voting Studies

	Presidential Support	Party Unity	Voting Participation
1986	13%	84%	88%
1985	11%	88%	91%

Interest Groups

	ADA	ACU	AFL-CIO	CCUS
1986	90%	n/a	100%	13%
1985	95%	5%	100%	19%

Elections

1986	General	74%	Primary	90%
1984	General	68%	Primary	u/o

Joseph E. Brennan   (D-Maine)

Of Portland — Elected 1986

Born: Nov. 2, 1934, Portland, Maine.
Education: Boston College, B.S. 1956, M.A. 1958; U. of Maine Law School, LL.B. 1963.
Military Career: Army, 1953-55.
Occupation: Lawyer.
Family: Divorced; two children.
Religion: Roman Catholic.
Political Career: Maine House, 1965-71; Cumberland County district attorney, 1970-72; Maine Senate, 1973-75; Maine attorney general, 1975-79; governor 1979-87; sought Democratic gubernatorial nomination, 1974.
Capitol Office: 1428 Longworth Bldg. 20515; 225-6116.

Maine 1st: South — Portland and Augusta. The district vote for Ronald Reagan was 60% in 1984; 45% in 1980.

Committees

Armed Services
Merchant Marine and Fisheries

Elections

1986	General	54%	Primary	u/o

CQ Voting Studies

	Presidential Support	Party Unity	Voting Participation
1986	21%	76%	83%
1985	24%	87%	91%

Interest Groups

	ADA	ACU	AFL-CIO	CCUS
1986	70%	n/a	100%	33%
1985	70%	11%	94%	28%

Jack Brooks   (D-Texas)

Of Beaumont — Elected 1952

Born: Dec. 18, 1922, Crowley, La.
Education: Attended Lamar College, 1939-41; U. of Texas, B.J. 1943, J.D. 1949.
Military Career: Marine Corps, 1942-45; Marine Corps Reserve, 1945-72.
Occupation: Lawyer.
Family: Wife, Charlotte Collins; three children.
Religion: Methodist.
Political Career: Texas House, 1947-51.
Capitol Office: 2449 Rayburn Bldg. 20515; 225-6565

Texas 9th: Southeast — Beaumont and Galveston. The district vote for Ronald Reagan was 52% in 1984; 47% in 1980.

Committees

Government Operations   (Chairman)
Judiciary
Select Iran-contra

Elections

1986	General	62%	Primary	u/o
1984	General	59%	Primary	u/o

William S. Broomfield (R-Mich.)

Of Birmingham — Elected 1956

Born: April 28, 1922, Royal Oak, Mich.
Education: Attended Michigan State U., 1951.
Military Career: Army Air Corps, 1942.
Occupation: Insurance agency owner.
Family: Wife, Jane Smith Thompson; three children.
Religion: Presbyterian.
Political Career: Mich. House, 1949-55; Mich. Senate, 1955-57.
Capitol Office: 2306 Rayburn Bldg. 20515; 225-6135.

Michigan 18th: Oakland County. The district vote for Ronald Reagan was 74% in 1984; 62% in 1980.

Committees

Foreign Affairs (Ranking)
Small Business
Select Iran-contra

Elections

1986	General	74%	Primary	u/o
1984	General	79%	Primary	u/o

CQ Voting Studies

	Presidential Support	Party Unity	Voting Participation
1986	70%	69%	92%
1985	73%	67%	94%

Interest Groups

	ADA	ACU	AFL-CIO	CCUS
1986	5%	n/a	7%	100%
1985	5%	85%	13%	71%

George E. Brown Jr. (D-Calif.)

Of Riverside — Elected 1962

Born: March 6, 1920, Holtville, Calif.
Education: Graduated from El Centro Jr. College, 1938; U.C.L.A., B.A. 1946.
Military Career: Army, 1942-46.
Occupation: Physicist; management consultant.
Family: Wife, Rowena Somerindyke; four children.
Religion: Methodist.
Political Career: Monterey Park City Council, 1954-55, mayor, 1955-58; Calif. Assembly, 1959-63; sought Democratic nomination for U.S. Senate, 1970.
Capitol Office: 2256 Rayburn Bldg. 20515; 225-6161.

California 36th: San Bernardino and Riverside. The district vote for Ronald Reagan was 56% in 1984.

Committees

Agriculture
Science, Space and Technology
Select Intelligence

Elections

1986	General	57%	Primary	u/o
1984	General	57%	Primary	u/o

CQ Voting Studies

	Presidential Support	Party Unity	Voting Participation
1986	18%	82%	85%
1985	20%	84%	90%

Interest Groups

	ADA	ACU	AFL-CIO	CCUS
1986	95%	n/a	92%	21%
1985	85%	6%	93%	28%

Hank Brown   (R-Colo.)

Of Greeley — Elected 1980

Born: Feb. 12, 1940, Denver, Colo.
Education: U. of Colorado, B.S. 1961, J.D. 1969.
Military Career: Navy, 1962-66.
Occupation: Tax accountant; meatpacking company executive; lawyer.
Family: Wife, Nan Morrison; three children.
Religion: United Church of Christ.
Political Career: Colo. Senate, 1973-77; Republican nominee for Colo. lt. gov., 1978.
Capitol Office: 1424 Longworth Bldg. 20515; 225-4676.

Colorado 4th: North and East — Fort Collins and Greeley. The district vote for Ronald Reagan was 67% in 1984; 58% in 1980.

Committee

Ways and Means

Elections

1986	General	70%	Primary	u/o
1984	General	71%	Primary	u/o

CQ Voting Studies

	Presidential Support	Party Unity	Voting Participation
1986	67%	92%	99%
1985	70%	87%	98%

Interest Groups

	ADA	ACU	AFL-CIO	CCUS
1986	10%	n/a	0%	94%
1985	30%	67%	12%	82%

Terry L. Bruce   (D-Ill.)

Of Olney — Elected 1984

Born: March 25, 1944, Olney, Ill.
Education: U. of Illinois, B.S. 1966; J.D. 1969.
Occupation: Lawyer; farmer.
Family: Wife, Charlotte Roberts; two children.
Religion: Methodist.
Political Career: Ill. Senate, 1971-85; Democratic nominee for U.S. House, 1978.
Capitol Office: 419 Cannon Bldg. 20515; 225-5001.

Illinois 19th: Southeast — Danville and Champaign-Urbana. The district vote for Ronald Reagan was 62% in 1984; 57% in 1980.

Committees

Energy and Commerce
Science, Space and Technology

Elections

1986	General	66%	Primary	u/o
1984	General	52%	Primary	37%

CQ Voting Studies

	Presidential Support	Party Unity	Voting Participation
1986	20%	88%	100%
1985	29%	89%	99%

Interest Groups

	ADA	ACU	AFL-CIO	CCUS
1986	80%	n/a	100%	33%
1985	70%	19%	76%	36%

John Bryant (D-Texas)

Of Dallas — Elected 1982

Born: Feb. 22, 1947, Lake Jackson, Texas.
Education: Southern Methodist U., B.A. 1969, J.D. 1972.
Occupation: Lawyer.
Family: Wife, Janet Elizabeth Watts; three children.
Religion: Methodist.
Political Career: Texas House, 1974-83.
Capitol Office: 412 Cannon Bldg. 20515; 225-2231.

Texas 5th: Downtown Dallas and Eastern and Southern Suburbs. The district vote for Ronald Reagan was 59% in 1984; 51% in 1980.

Committees

Energy and Commerce
Judiciary
Veterans' Affairs

Elections

1986	General	59%	Primary	93%
1984	General	u/o	Primary	u/o

CQ Voting Studies

	Presidential Support	Party Unity	Voting Participation
1986	18%	84%	96%
1985	23%	89%	97%

Interest Groups

	ADA	ACU	AFL-CIO	CCUS
1986	65%	n/a	93%	44%
1985	55%	10%	88%	41%

Jack Buechner (R-Mo.)

Of Kirkwood — Elected 1986

Born: June 6, 1940, St. Louis, Mo.
Education: Benedictine College, B.A. 1962; St. Louis U., J.D. 1965.
Occupation: Lawyer; real estate developer.
Family: Wife, Marietta Coon; two children.
Religion: Roman Catholic.
Political Career: Mo. House, 1973-83.
Capitol Office: 502 Cannon Bldg. 20515; 225-2561.

Missouri 2nd: Western St. Louis County. The district vote for Ronald Reagan was 69% in 1984; 60% in 1980.

Committees

Budget
Science, Space and Technology

Elections

1986	General	52%	Primary	72%

Jim Bunning (R-Ky.)

Of Fort Thomas — Elected 1986

Born: Oct. 23, 1931, Campbell County, Ky.
Education: Xavier U., B.S. 1953.
Occupation: Professional baseball player; investment broker.
Family: Wife, Mary Catherine Theis; nine children.
Religion: Roman Catholic.
Political Career: Fort Thomas City Council, 1977-79; Ky. Senate, 1979-83; GOP gubernatorial nominee, 1983.
Capitol Office: 1123 Longworth Bldg. 20515; 225-3465.

Kentucky 4th: Louisville Suburbs, Covington and Newport. The district vote for Ronald Reagan was 69% in 1984; 56% in 1980.

Committees

Banking, Finance and Urban Affairs
Merchant Marine and Fisheries

Elections

1986	General	56%	Primary	u/o

CQ Voting Studies

	Presidential Support	Party Unity	Voting Participation
1986	81%	94%	97%
1985	80%	94%	95%

Interest Groups

	ADA	ACU	AFL-CIO	CCUS
1986	5%	n/a	21%	89%
1985	5%	100%	0%	86%

Dan Burton (R-Ind.)

Of Indianapolis — Elected 1982

Born: June 21, 1938, Indianapolis, Ind.
Education: Attended Indiana U., 1958-59; Cincinnati Bible Seminary, 1959-60.
Military Career: Army, 1956-57.
Occupation: Insurance and real estate agent.
Family: Wife, Barbara Logan; three children.
Religion: Protestant.
Political Career: Ind. Senate, 1969-71, 1981-83; Ind. House, 1967-69, 1977-81; Republican nominee for U.S. House, 1970; sought Republican nomination for U.S. House, 1972.
Capitol Office: 120 Cannon Bldg. 20515; 225-2276.

Indiana 6th: Northern Indianapolis and Anderson. The district vote for Ronald Reagan was 66% in 1984; 65% in 1980.

Committees

Foreign Affairs
Post Office and Civil Service
Veterans' Affairs

Elections

1986	General	69%	Primary	93%
1984	General	73%	Primary	u/o

Sala Burton (D-Calif.)

Of San Francisco — Elected 1983
Died Feb. 1, 1987.

Born: April 1, 1925, Bialystok, Poland.
Education: Attended San Francisco State U.
Occupation: Political activist.
Family: Widow of Rep. Phillip Burton; one child.
Religion: Jewish.
Political Career: No previous office.
Capitol Office: 1408 Longworth Bldg. 20515; 225-4965.

California 5th: Most of San Francisco. A special election will be held April 7, 1987. The district vote for Ronald Reagan was 33% in 1984.

Committees

Rules   (Burton was replaced by Bart Gordon, D-Tenn.)
Select Hunger   (Burton was replaced by Liz Patterson, D-S.C.)

CQ Voting Studies

	Presidential Support	Party Unity	Voting Participation
1986	11%	63%	61%
1985	15%	95%	95%

Elections

1986	General	77%	Primary	89%
1984	General	72%	Primary	87%

Interest Groups

	ADA	ACU	AFL-CIO	CCUS
1986	55%	n/a	100%	10%
1985	95%	0%	100%	14%

Albert G. Bustamante (D-Texas)

Of San Antonio — Elected 1984

Born: April 8, 1935, Asherton, Texas.
Education: Sul Ross State College, B.A. 1961.
Military Career: Army, 1954-56.
Occupation: Teacher.
Family: Wife, Rebecca Pounders; three children.
Religion: Roman Catholic.
Political Career: Bexar County commissioner, 1972-78; Bexar County judge, 1978-83.
Capitol Office: 1116 Longworth Bldg. 20515; 225-4511.

Texas 23rd: Southwest — San Antonio Suburbs and Laredo. The district vote for Ronald Reagan was 59% in 1984.

Committees

Armed Services
Government Operations

CQ Voting Studies

	Presidential Support	Party Unity	Voting Participation
1986	32%	82%	92%
1985	34%	85%	93%

Elections

1986	General	u/o	Primary	u/o
1984	General	u/o	Primary	59%

Interest Groups

	ADA	ACU	AFL-CIO	CCUS
1986	50%	n/a	100%	20%
1985	65%	19%	88%	24%

Beverly B. Byron   (D-Md.)

Of Frederick — Elected 1978

Born: July 27, 1932, Baltimore, Md.
Education: Attended Hood College, 1963-64.
Occupation: Civic leader.
Family: Husband, Kirk Walsh; three children.
Religion: Episcopalian.
Political Career: No previous office.
Capitol Office: 2430 Rayburn Bldg. 20515; 225-2721.

Maryland 6th: West — Hagerstown and Cumberland. The district vote for Ronald Reagan was 69% in 1984; 58% in 1980.

CQ Voting Studies

	Presidential Support	Party Unity	Voting Participation
1986	50%	55%	94%
1985	52%	63%	92%

Interest Groups

	ADA	ACU	AFL-CIO	CCUS
1986	20%	n/a	46%	63%
1985	10%	65%	47%	59%

Committees

Armed Services
Interior and Insular Affairs
Select Aging

Elections

1986	General	72%	Primary	84%
1984	General	65%	Primary	74%

Sonny Callahan   (R-Ala.)

Of Mobile — Elected 1984

Born: Sept. 11, 1932, Mobile, Ala.
Education: Graduated from McGill High School, Mobile, 1950.
Military Career: Navy, 1952-54.
Occupation: Moving and storage company executive.
Family: Wife, Karen Reed; six children.
Religion: Roman Catholic.
Political Career: Alabama House, served as Democrat, 1971-79; Alabama Senate, served as Democrat, 1979-83; sought Democratic nomination for lieutenant governor, 1982.
Capitol Office: 1232 Longworth Bldg. 20515; 225-4931.

Alabama 1st: Southwest — Mobile. The district vote for Ronald Reagan was 64% in 1984; 56% in 1980.

CQ Voting Studies

	Presidential Support	Party Unity	Voting Participation
1986	73%	75%	96%
1985	74%	82%	99%

Interest Groups

	ADA	ACU	AFL-CIO	CCUS
1986	0%	n/a	29%	89%
1985	0%	86%	12%	86%

Committee

Energy and Commerce

Elections

1986	General	u/o	Primary	u/o
1984	General	51%	Primary	61%

Ben Nighthorse Campbell   (D-Colo.)

Of Ignacio — Elected 1986

Born: April 13, 1933, Auburn, Calif.
Education: San Jose State U., B.A. 1957; attended Meiji U., Tokyo, 1960-64.
Military Career: Air Force, 1952-54.
Occupation: Jewelry designer; rancher.
Family: Wife, Linda Price; two children.
Religion: Unspecified.
Political Career: Colo. House, 1983-87.
Capitol Office: 1724 Longworth Bldg. 20515; 225-4761.

Colorado 3rd: Western Slope and Pueblo. The district vote for Ronald Reagan was 63% in 1984; 57% in 1980.

Committees

Agriculture
Interior and Insular Affairs
Small Business

Elections

1986	General	52%	Primary	u/o

Benjamin L. Cardin   (D-Md.)

Of Baltimore — Elected 1986

Born: Oct. 5, 1943, Baltimore, Md.
Education: U. of Pittsburgh, B.A. 1964; U. of Maryland School of Law, LL.B. 1967.
Occupation: Lawyer.
Family: Wife, Myrna Edelman; two children.
Religion: Jewish.
Political Career: Md. House of Delegates, 1967-87, Speaker, 1979-87.
Capitol Office: 507 Cannon Bldg. 20515; 225-4016.

Maryland 3rd: Baltimore and Northern and Southern Suburbs. The district vote for Ronald Reagan was 50% in 1984; 37% in 1980.

Committees

Judiciary
Public Works and Transportation

Elections

1986	General	79%	Primary	82%

Thomas R. Carper (D-Del.)

Of Wilmington — Elected 1982

Born: Jan. 23, 1947, Beckley, W.Va.
Education: Ohio State U., B.A., 1968; U. of Delaware, M.B.A., 1975.
Military Career: Navy, 1968-1973; Naval Reserve, 1973-present.
Occupation: Public official.
Family: Wife, Martha Ann Stacy.
Religion: Presbyterian.
Political Career: Delaware State Treasurer, 1977-83.
Capitol Office: 131 Cannon Bldg. 20515; 225-4165.

Delaware: At-large. The district vote for Ronald Reagan was 60% in 1984; 47% in 1980.

Committees

Banking, Finance and Urban Affairs
Merchant Marine and Fisheries

CQ Voting Studies

	Presidential Support	Party Unity	Voting Participation
1986	30%	78%	99%
1985	43%	75%	98%

Interest Groups

	ADA	ACU	AFL-CIO	CCUS
1986	55%	n/a	86%	50%
1985	55%	24%	71%	50%

Elections

1986	General	66%	Primary	u/o
1984	General	59%	Primary	u/o

Bob Carr (D-Mich.)

Of Okemos — Elected 1974

Born: March 27, 1943, Janesville, Wis.
Education: U. of Wisconsin, B.S. 1965, J.D. 1968.
Occupation: Lawyer.
Family: Separated.
Religion: Baptist.
Political Career: U.S. House, 1975-81; Democratic nominee for U.S. House, 1972, 1980.
Capitol Office: 2439 Rayburn Bldg. 20515; 225-4872.

Michigan 6th: Central — Lansing and Pontiac. The district vote for Ronald Reagan was 64% in 1984; 50% in 1980.

Committees

Appropriations
Select Hunger

CQ Voting Studies

	Presidential Support	Party Unity	Voting Participation
1986	21%	75%	97%
1985	29%	81%	94%

Interest Groups

	ADA	ACU	AFL-CIO	CCUS
1986	70%	n/a	86%	33%
1985	65%	15%	76%	50%

Elections

1986	General	57%	Primary	94%
1984	General	52%	Primary	u/o

Rod Chandler (R-Wash.)

Of Bellevue — Elected 1982

Born: July 13, 1942, La Grande, Ore.
Education: Attended Eastern Oregon State College, 1961-62; Oregon State U., B.S. 1968.
Occupation: Public relations consultant; newscaster.
Military Career: Oregon National Guard, 1959-64.
Family: Wife, Joyce Elaine Laremore; two children.
Religion: Protestant.
Political Career: Wash. House, 1975-1983.
Capitol Office: 223 Cannon Bldg. 20515; 225-7761.

Washington 8th: Seattle Suburbs — Bellevue. The district vote for Ronald Reagan was 63% in 1984.

Committee

Ways and Means

Elections

1986	General	65%	Primary	64%
1984	General	62%	Primary	u/o

CQ Voting Studies

	Presidential Support	Party Unity	Voting Participation
1986	56%	66%	91%
1985	61%	72%	94%

Interest Groups

	ADA	ACU	AFL-CIO	CCUS
1986	20%	n/a	21%	71%
1985	15%	67%	18%	95%

Jim Chapman (D-Texas)

Of Sulfur Springs — Elected 1985

Born: March 8, 1945, Washington, D.C.
Education: U. of Texas, B.A. 1968; Southern Methodist U., J.D. 1970.
Occupation: Lawyer.
Family: Wife, Betty Brice, two children.
Religion: Methodist.
Political Career: District attorney, 8th Judicial District of Texas, 1977-85; sought Democratic nomination for Texas Senate, 1984.
Capitol Office: 429 Cannon Bldg. 20515; 225-3035.

Texas 1st: Northeast — Texarkana. The district vote for Ronald Reagan was 58% in 1984; 49% in 1980.

Committees

Public Works and Transportation
Science, Space and Technology

Elections

1986	General	u/o	Primary	u/o
1985	General	51% *	Primary	30% *

** Special election.*

CQ Voting Studies

	Presidential Support	Party Unity	Voting Participation
1986	37%	69%	94%
1985	42%	59%	91%

Interest Groups

	ADA	ACU	AFL-CIO	CCUS
1986	40%	n/a	69%	50%
1985	n/a	71%	20%	92%

Bill Chappell Jr. (D-Fla.)

Of Ormond Beach — Elected 1968

Born: Feb. 3, 1922, Kendrick, Fla.
Education: U. of Florida, B.A. 1947, LL.B. 1949, J.D. 1967.
Military Career: Navy; active reserve 1942-47, reserve 1947-82.
Occupation: Lawyer.
Family: Wife, Jeane Brown; four children, two stepchildren.
Religion: Methodist.
Political Career: Fla. House, 1955-65 and 1967-69; Speaker, 1961-63.
Capitol Office: 2468 Rayburn Bldg. 20515; 225-4035.

Florida 4th: Northeast — Daytona Beach. The district vote for Ronald Reagan was 67% in 1984; 56% in 1980.

Committee

Appropriations

Elections

1986	General	u/o	Primary	u/o
1984	General	65%	Primary	63%

CQ Voting Studies

	Presidential Support	Party Unity	Voting Participation
1986	43%	65%	90%
1985	52%	70%	92%

Interest Groups

	ADA	ACU	AFL-CIO	CCUS
1986	30%	n/a	64%	31%
1985	40%	57%	53%	33%

Dick Cheney (R-Wyo.)

Of Casper — Elected 1978

Born: Jan. 30, 1941, Lincoln, Neb.
Education: U. of Wyoming, B.A. 1965, M.A. 1966.
Occupation: Financial consultant.
Family: Wife, Lynne Vincent; two children.
Religion: Methodist.
Political Career: No previous office.
Capitol Office: 104 Cannon Bldg. 20515; 225-2311.

Wyoming: At-large. The district vote for Ronald Reagan was 71% in 1984; 63% in 1980.

Committees

Interior and Insular Affairs
Select Intelligence
Select Iran-contra (Ranking)

Elections

1986	General	69%	Primary	87%
1984	General	74%	Primary	u/o

CQ Voting Studies

	Presidential Support	Party Unity	Voting Participation
1986	81%	81%	91%
1985	86%	90%	93%

Interest Groups

	ADA	ACU	AFL-CIO	CCUS
1986	0%	n/a	7%	100%
1985	0%	100%	0%	95%

James McClure Clarke   (D-N.C.)

Of Fairview — Elected 1986

Born: June 12, 1917, Manchester, Vt.
Education: Princeton U., A.B. 1939.
Military Career: Navy, 1942-45.
Occupation: Farmer.
Family: Wife, Elspeth McClure; eight children.
Religion: Presbyterian.
Political Career: N.C. House, 1977-81; N.C. Senate, 1981-83; U.S. House, 1983-85; Democratic nominee for U.S. House, 1984.
Capitol Office: 217 Cannon Bldg. 20515; 225-6401.

North Carolina 11th: West — Asheville. The district vote for Ronald Reagan was 63% in 1984; 51% in 1980.

Committees

Foreign Affairs
Interior and Insular Affairs
Select Aging

Elections

1986	General	51%	Primary	75%

William L. Clay   (D-Mo.)

Of St. Louis — Elected 1968

Born: April 30, 1931, St. Louis, Mo.
Education: St. Louis U., B.S. 1953.
Military Career: Army, 1953-55.
Occupation: Real estate salesman; insurance executive.
Family: Wife, Carol Ann Johnson; three children.
Religion: Roman Catholic.
Political Career: St. Louis Board of Aldermen, 1959-64; St. Louis Democratic committeeman, 1964-67.
Capitol Office: 2470 Rayburn Bldg. 20515; 225-2406.

Missouri 1st: North St. Louis and Northeast St. Louis County. The district vote for Ronald Reagan was 35% in 1984; 31% in 1980.

Committees

Education and Labor
House Administration
Post Office and Civil Service

Elections

1986	General	66%	Primary	80%
1984	General	68%	Primary	u/o

CQ Voting Studies

	Presidential Support	Party Unity	Voting Participation
1986	8%	71%	83%
1985	15%	73%	90%

Interest Groups

	ADA	ACU	AFL-CIO	CCUS
1986	75%	n/a	100%	15%
1985	100%	5%	100%	24%

William F. Clinger Jr.   (R-Pa.)

Of Warren — Elected 1978

Born: April 4, 1929, Warren, Pa.
Education: Johns Hopkins U., B.A. 1951; U. of Virginia Law School, LL.B. 1965.
Military Career: Navy, 1951-55.
Occupation: Lawyer.
Family: Wife, Julia Whitla; four children.
Religion: Presbyterian.
Political Career: No previous office.
Capitol Office: 1122 Longworth Bldg. 20515; 225-5121.

Pennsylvania 23rd: Northwest, Central — State College. The district vote for Ronald Reagan was 63% in 1984; 55% in 1980.

Committees

Government Operations
Public Works and Transportation
Select Aging

CQ Voting Studies

	Presidential Support	Party Unity	Voting Participation
1986	52%	48%	95%
1985	50%	54%	92%

Interest Groups

	ADA	ACU	AFL-CIO	CCUS
1986	50%	n/a	86%	44%
1985	35%	48%	59%	57%

Elections

1986	General	55%	Primary	u/o
1984	General	52%	Primary	u/o

Dan Coats   (R-Ind.)

Of Fort Wayne — Elected 1980

Born: May 16, 1943, Jackson, Mich.
Education: Wheaton College, B.A. 1965; Indiana U., J.D. 1971.
Military Career: Army Corps of Engineers, 1966-68.
Occupation: Lawyer.
Family: Wife, Marcia Anne Crawford; three children.
Religion: Baptist.
Political Career: No previous office.
Capitol Office: 1417 Longworth Bldg. 20515; 225-4436.

Indiana 4th: Northeast — Fort Wayne. The district vote for Ronald Reagan was 67% in 1984; 58% in 1980.

Committees

Energy and Commerce
Select Children, Youth and Families   (Ranking)

CQ Voting Studies

	Presidential Support	Party Unity	Voting Participation
1986	70%	84%	98%
1985	74%	81%	98%

Interest Groups

	ADA	ACU	AFL-CIO	CCUS
1986	10%	n/a	14%	94%
1985	20%	86%	18%	86%

Elections

1986	General	70%	Primary	u/o
1984	General	61%	Primary	u/o

Howard Coble (R-N.C.)

Of Greensboro — Elected 1984

Born: March 18, 1931, Greensboro, N.C.
Education: Attended Appalachian State U., 1949-50; Guilford College, 1950-1952, 1957-58, A.B. 1958; U. of North Carolina School of Law, J.D. 1962.
Military Career: Coast Guard, 1952-56; Coast Guard Reserve, 1960-81.
Occupation: Lawyer.
Family: Single.
Religion: Presbyterian.
Political Career: N.C. House, 1969, 1979-83; secretary, N.C. Department of Revenue, 1973-76; Republican nominee for state treasurer, 1976.
Capitol Office: 430 Cannon Bldg. 20515; 225-3065.

North Carolina 6th: Central — Greensboro and High Point. The district vote for Ronald Reagan was 65% in 1984; 54% in 1980.

Committees

Judiciary
Merchant Marine and Fisheries

Elections

1986	General	50%	Primary	u/o
1984	General	51%	Primary	51%

CQ Voting Studies

	Presidential Support	Party Unity	Voting Participation
1986	68%	84%	98%
1985	69%	87%	97%

Interest Groups

	ADA	ACU	AFL-CIO	CCUS
1986	10%	n/a	36%	89%
1985	0%	81%	12%	91%

Tony Coelho (D-Calif.)

Of Merced — Elected 1978

Born: June 15, 1942, Los Banos, Calif.
Education: Loyola U. (Los Angeles), B.A. 1964.
Occupation: Congressional aide.
Family: Wife, Phyllis Butler; two children.
Religion: Roman Catholic.
Political Career: No previous office.
Capitol Office: 403 Cannon Bldg. 20515; 225-6131.

California 15th: Mid-San Joaquin Valley — Modesto. The district vote for Ronald Reagan was 59% in 1984.

Committees

Majority Whip
Agriculture
House Administration
Interior and Insular Affairs

Elections

1986	General	72%	Primary	u/o
1984	General	66%	Primary	u/o

CQ Voting Studies

	Presidential Support	Party Unity	Voting Participation
1986	21%	87%	90%
1985	20%	88%	92%

Interest Groups

	ADA	ACU	AFL-CIO	CCUS
1986	70%	n/a	100%	14%
1985	80%	0%	88%	26%

E. Thomas Coleman   (R-Mo.)

Of Kansas City — Elected 1976

Born: May 29, 1943, Kansas City, Mo.
Education: William Jewell College, B.A. 1965; New York U., M.P.A. 1966; Washington U., J.D. 1969.
Occupation: Lawyer.
Family: Wife, Marilyn Anderson; three children.
Religion: Protestant.
Political Career: Mo. House, 1973-77; unsuccessful campaign for Clay County clerk, 1970.
Capitol Office: 2344 Rayburn Bldg. 20515; 225-7041.

Missouri 6th: Northwest — St. Joseph. The district vote for Ronald Reagan was 60% in 1984; 50% in 1980.

Committees

Agriculture
Education and Labor

CQ Voting Studies

	Presidential Support	Party Unity	Voting Participation
1986	67%	76%	94%
1985	56%	76%	95%

Interest Groups

	ADA	ACU	AFL-CIO	CCUS
1986	5%	n/a	21%	75%
1985	10%	67%	29%	75%

Elections

1986	General	57%	Primary	u/o
1984	General	65%	Primary	u/o

Ronald D. Coleman   (D-Texas)

Of El Paso — Elected 1982

Born: Nov. 29, 1941, El Paso, Texas.
Education: U. of Texas at El Paso, B.A. 1963; U. of Texas at Austin, J.D. 1967.
Military Career: Army, 1967-69.
Occupation: Lawyer.
Family: Wife, Tammy Biel; two children.
Religion: Presbyterian.
Political Career: Texas House, 1973-83.
Capitol Office: 416 Cannon Bldg. 20515; 225-4831.

Texas 16th: West — El Paso. The district vote for Ronald Reagan was 57% in 1984; 54% in 1980.

Committee

Appropriations

CQ Voting Studies

	Presidential Support	Party Unity	Voting Participation
1986	29%	81%	98%
1985	31%	89%	98%

Interest Groups

	ADA	ACU	AFL-CIO	CCUS
1986	70%	n/a	86%	56%
1985	60%	19%	71%	33%

Elections

1986	General	66%	Primary	u/o
1984	General	57%	Primary	u/o

Cardiss Collins (D-Ill.)

Of Chicago — Elected 1973

Born: Sept. 24, 1931, St. Louis, Mo.
Education: Attended Northwestern U.
Occupation: Auditor.
Family: Widow of Rep. George W. Collins; one child.
Religion: Baptist.
Political Career: No previous office.
Capitol Office: 2264 Rayburn Bldg. 20515; 225-5006.

Illinois 7th: Chicago — Downtown and West Side. The district vote for Ronald Reagan was 25% in 1984; 23% in 1980.

Committees

Energy and Commerce
Government Operations
Select Narcotics Abuse and Control

CQ Voting Studies

	Presidential Support	Party Unity	Voting Participation
1986	12%	78%	81%
1985	16%	87%	87%

Interest Groups

	ADA	ACU	AFL-CIO	CCUS
1986	95%	n/a	100%	13%
1985	95%	5%	100%	10%

Elections

1986	General	81%	Primary	60%
1984	General	78%	Primary	49%

Larry Combest (R-Texas)

Of Lubbock — Elected 1984

Born: March 20, 1945, Memphis, Texas.
Education: West Texas State U., B.A. 1969.
Occupation: Congressional aide; electronics wholesaler.
Family: Wife, Sharon McCurry; two children.
Religion: Methodist.
Political Career: No previous office.
Capitol Office: 1529 Longworth Bldg. 20515; 225-4005.

Texas 19th: Northwest — Lubbock and Odessa. The district vote for Ronald Reagan was 75% in 1984; 68% in 1980.

Committees

Agriculture
District of Columbia
Small Business

CQ Voting Studies

	Presidential Support	Party Unity	Voting Participation
1986	78%	82%	100%
1985	75%	89%	99%

Interest Groups

	ADA	ACU	AFL-CIO	CCUS
1986	5%	n/a	21%	94%
1985	5%	100%	0%	91%

Elections

1986	General	62%	Primary	u/o
1984	General	58%	Primary	58% *

** Primary runoff.*

Silvio O. Conte (R-Mass.)

Of Pittsfield — Elected 1958

Born: Nov. 9, 1921, Pittsfield, Mass.
Education: Boston College, LL.B. 1949.
Military Career: Navy, 1942-44.
Occupation: Lawyer.
Family: Wife, Corinne Duval; four children.
Religion: Roman Catholic.
Political Career: Mass. Senate, 1951-59.
Capitol Office: 2300 Rayburn Bldg. 20515; 225-5335.

Massachusetts 1st: West — Berkshire Hills and Pioneer Valley. The district vote for Ronald Reagan was 51% in 1984; 40% in 1980.

CQ Voting Studies

	Presidential Support	Party Unity	Voting Participation
1986	27%	25%	99%
1985	36%	43%	97%

Interest Groups

	ADA	ACU	AFL-CIO	CCUS
1986	75%	n/a	100%	22%
1985	75%	14%	100%	32%

Committees

Appropriations (Ranking)
Small Business

Elections

1986	General	78%	Primary	u/o
1984	General	73%	Primary	u/o

John Conyers Jr. (D-Mich.)

Of Detroit — Elected 1964

Born: May 16, 1929, Detroit, Mich.
Education: Wayne State U., B.A. 1957, LL.B. 1958.
Military Career: National Guard, 1948-52; Army, 1952-53; Army Reserve, 1953-57.
Occupation: Lawyer.
Family: Single.
Religion: Baptist.
Political Career: No previous office.
Capitol Office: 2313 Rayburn Bldg. 20515; 225-5126.

Michigan 1st: Detroit — North Central and Highland Park. The district vote for Ronald Reagan was 14% in 1984; 12% in 1980.

CQ Voting Studies

	Presidential Support	Party Unity	Voting Participation
1986	11%	71%	75%
1985	13%	69%	75%

Interest Groups

	ADA	ACU	AFL-CIO	CCUS
1986	85%	n/a	92%	9%
1985	75%	12%	92%	28%

Committees

Government Operations
Judiciary
Small Business

Elections

1986	General	90%	Primary	90%
1984	General	89%	Primary	u/o

Jim Cooper (D-Tenn.)

Of Shelbyville — Elected 1982

Born: June 19, 1954, Shelbyville, Tenn.
Education: U. of North Carolina, B.A. 1975; Oxford U., B.A., M.A. 1977; Harvard Law School, J.D. 1980.
Occupation: Lawyer.
Family: Wife, Martha Hays.
Religion: Episcopalian.
Political Career: No previous office.
Capitol Office: 125 Cannon Bldg. 20515; 225-6831.

Tennessee 4th: Northeast and South Central. The district vote for Ronald Reagan was 57% in 1984; 49% in 1980.

Committees

Energy and Commerce
Small Business

Elections

1986	General	u/o	Primary	u/o
1984	General	75%	Primary	u/o

CQ Voting Studies

	Presidential Support	Party Unity	Voting Participation
1986	31%	80%	95%
1985	43%	85%	99%

Interest Groups

	ADA	ACU	AFL-CIO	CCUS
1986	70%	n/a	64%	53%
1985	55%	24%	71%	45%

Lawrence Coughlin (R-Pa.)

Of Villanova — Elected 1968

Born: April 11, 1929, Wilkes-Barre, Pa.
Education: Yale U., A.B. 1950; Harvard U., M.B.A. 1954; Temple U., LL.B. 1958.
Military Career: Marine Corps Reserve, 1948-58, active duty, 1951-52.
Occupation: Lawyer.
Family: Wife, Susan MacGregor; four children.
Religion: Episcopalian.
Political Career: Pa. House, 1965-67; Pa. Senate, 1967-69.
Capitol Office: 2467 Rayburn Bldg. 20515; 225-6111.

Pennsylvania 13th: Northwest Philadelphia Suburbs — The Main Line. The district vote for Ronald Reagan was 60% in 1984; 55% in 1980.

Committees

Appropriations
Select Narcotics Abuse and Control

Elections

1986	General	58%	Primary	u/o
1984	General	56%	Primary	91%

CQ Voting Studies

	Presidential Support	Party Unity	Voting Participation
1986	48%	51%	97%
1985	50%	63%	96%

Interest Groups

	ADA	ACU	AFL-CIO	CCUS
1986	45%	n/a	71%	61%
1985	50%	43%	59%	57%

Jim Courter (R-N.J.)

Of Hackettstown — Elected 1978

Born: Oct. 14, 1941, Montclair, N.J.
Education: Colgate U., B.A. 1963; Duke U., J.D. 1966.
Occupation: Lawyer.
Family: Wife, Carmen McCalman; two children.
Religion: Methodist.
Political Career: Allamuchy Township attorney, 1975-78.
Capitol Office: 2422 Rayburn Bldg. 20515; 225-5801.

New Jersey 12th: North and Central — Morristown. The district vote for Ronald Reagan was 56% in 1984.

Committees

Armed Services
Select Aging
Select Iran-contra

Elections

1986	General	64%	Primary	u/o
1984	General	65%	Primary	u/o

CQ Voting Studies

	Presidential Support	Party Unity	Voting Participation
1986	69%	75%	97%
1985	70%	76%	94%

Interest Groups

	ADA	ACU	AFL-CIO	CCUS
1986	25%	n/a	57%	61%
1985	15%	86%	35%	57%

William J. Coyne (D-Pa.)

Of Pittsburgh — Elected 1980

Born: Aug. 24, 1936, Pittsburgh, Pa.
Education: Robert Morris College, B.S. 1965.
Military Career: Army, 1955-57.
Occupation: Accountant.
Family: Single.
Religion: Roman Catholic.
Political Career: Pa. House, 1971-73; Pittsburgh City Council, 1974-81; sought Democratic nomination for Pa. Senate, 1972.
Capitol Office: 424 Cannon Bldg. 20515; 225-2301.

Pennsylvania 14th: Pittsburgh. The district vote for Ronald Reagan was 30% in 1984; 33% in 1980.

Committee

Ways and Means

Elections

1986	General	95%	Primary	86%
1984	General	77%	Primary	82%

CQ Voting Studies

	Presidential Support	Party Unity	Voting Participation
1986	17%	95%	98%
1985	19%	94%	97%

Interest Groups

	ADA	ACU	AFL-CIO	CCUS
1986	100%	n/a	100%	22%
1985	95%	0%	100%	19%

Larry E. Craig (R-Idaho)

Of Midvale — Elected 1980

Born: July 20, 1945, Council, Idaho.
Education: U. of Idaho, B.A. 1969; graduate work,
  George Washington U, 1970.
Military Career: National Guard, 1970-72.
Occupation: Farmer; real estate salesman.
Family: Wife, Suzanne Scott; three stepchildren.
Religion: Methodist.
Political Career: Idaho Senate, 1975-81.
Capitol Office: 1034 Longworth Bldg. 20515; 225-6611.

Idaho 1st: North and West — Lewiston and Boise. The
district vote for Ronald Reagan was 68% in 1984; 59% in
1980.

Committees

Government Operations
Interior and Insular Affairs
Standards of Official Conduct

CQ Voting Studies

	Presidential Support	Party Unity	Voting Participation
1986	79%	85%	95%
1985	75%	91%	96%

Elections

1986	General	67%	Primary	u/o
1984	General	69%	Primary	u/o

Interest Groups

	ADA	ACU	AFL-CIO	CCUS
1986	5%	n/a	21%	100%
1985	0%	90%	0%	91%

Philip M. Crane (R-Ill.)

Of Mount Prospect — Elected 1969

Born: Nov. 3, 1930, Chicago, Ill.
Education: Attended DePauw U., 1948-50;
  Hillsdale College, B.A. 1952; attended U. of Michigan,
  1952-54; U. of Vienna, 1953-56; Indiana U., M.A. 1961,
  Ph.D. 1963.
Military Career: Army, 1954-56.
Occupation: Author; history professor.
Family: Wife, Arlene Catherine Johnson; eight children.
Religion: Methodist.
Political Career: Sought Republican nomination for presi-
  dent, 1980.
Capitol Office: 1035 Longworth Bldg. 20515; 225-3711.

Illinois 12th: Far Northwest Suburbs — Palatine. The district vote for Ronald Reagan was 76% in 1984; 64% in 1980.

Committee

Ways and Means

CQ Voting Studies

	Presidential Support	Party Unity	Voting Participation
1986	82%	87%	92%
1985	80%	79%	84%

Elections

1986	General	78%	Primary	u/o
1984	General	78%	Primary	u/o

Interest Groups

	ADA	ACU	AFL-CIO	CCUS
1986	0%	n/a	0%	93%
1985	5%	95%	6%	82%

George W. Crockett Jr.   (D-Mich.)

Of Detroit — Elected 1980

Born: Aug. 10, 1909, Jacksonville, Fla.
Education: Morehouse College, A.B. 1931; U. of Michigan, J.D. 1934.
Occupation: Lawyer; judge.
Family: Wife, Harriette Clark; three children.
Religion: Baptist.
Political Career: Judge, Detroit Recorder's Court, 1966-78.
Capitol Office: 1531 Longworth Bldg. 20515; 225-2261.

Michigan 13th: Downtown Detroit. The district vote for Ronald Reagan was 15% in 1984; 6% in 1980.

Committees

Foreign Affairs
Judiciary
Select Aging

CQ Voting Studies

	Presidential Support	Party Unity	Voting Participation
1986	12%	77%	84%
1985	19%	78%	85%

Interest Groups

	ADA	ACU	AFL-CIO	CCUS
1986	95%	n/a	92%	15%
1985	80%	10%	92%	18%

Elections

1986	General	86%	Primary	80%
1984	General	87%	Primary	87%

Dan Daniel   (D-Va.)

Of Danville — Elected 1968

Born: May 12, 1914, Chatham, Va.
Education: Graduated from Danville H.S., 1948.
Military Career: Navy, 1944.
Occupation: Textile company executive.
Family: Wife, Ruby McGregor; one child.
Religion: Baptist.
Political Career: Va. House, 1960-69.
Capitol Office: 2308 Rayburn Bldg. 20515; 225-4711.

Virginia 5th: South — Danville. The district vote for Ronald Reagan was 66% in 1984; 55% in 1980.

Committees

Armed Services
Select Intelligence

CQ Voting Studies

	Presidential Support	Party Unity	Voting Participation
1986	61%	44%	96%
1985	66%	46%	91%

Interest Groups

	ADA	ACU	AFL-CIO	CCUS
1986	5%	n/a	23%	88%
1985	10%	67%	29%	67%

Elections

1986	General	u/o	Primary	u/o
1984	General	u/o	Primary	u/o

William E. Dannemeyer   (R-Calif.)

Of Fullerton — Elected 1978

Born: Sept. 22, 1929, Los Angeles, Calif.
Education: Santa Maria Jr. College, 1946-47; Valparaiso U., B.A. 1950; U. of California, Hastings College of Law, J.D. 1952.
Military Career: Army, 1952-54.
Occupation: Lawyer.
Family: Wife, Evelyn Hoemann; three children.
Religion: Lutheran.
Political Career: Calif. Assembly, served as a Democrat, 1963-67, served as a Republican, 1977-79; Democratic nominee for Calif. Senate, 1966; Republican nominee for Calif. Assembly, 1972.
Capitol Office: 1214 Longworth Bldg. 20515; 225-4111.

California 39th: Northern Orange County — Anaheim and Fullerton. The district vote for Ronald Reagan was 77% in 1984.

Committees

Energy and Commerce
Judiciary

Elections

1986	General	76%	Primary	u/o
1984	General	76%	Primary	u/o

CQ Voting Studies

	Presidential Support	Party Unity	Voting Participation
1986	81%	90%	95%
1985	78%	89%	91%

Interest Groups

	ADA	ACU	AFL-CIO	CCUS
1986	5%	n/a	0%	87%
1985	10%	90%	6%	95%

George "Buddy" Darden   (D-Ga.)

Of Marietta — Elected 1983

Born: Nov. 22, 1943, Hancock Co., Ga.
Education: University of Georgia, B.A. 1965, J.D. 1967.
Occupation: Lawyer.
Family: Wife, Lillian Budd; two children.
Religion: Methodist.
Political Career: Cobb County district attorney, 1973-77; Georgia House, 1981-83.
Capitol Office: 1330 Longworth Bldg. 20515; 225-2931.

Georgia 7th: Northwest — Rome and Marietta. The district vote for Ronald Reagan was 73% in 1984; 49% in 1980.

Committees

Armed Services
Interior and Insular Affairs

Elections

1986	General	67%	Primary	u/o
1984	General	55%	Primary	u/o

CQ Voting Studies

	Presidential Support	Party Unity	Voting Participation
1986	49%	60%	97%
1985	51%	67%	98%

Interest Groups

	ADA	ACU	AFL-CIO	CCUS
1986	10%	n/a	31%	82%
1985	15%	71%	44%	64%

Hal Daub (R-Neb.)

Of Omaha — Elected 1980

Born: April 23, 1941, Fort Bragg, N.C.
Education: Washington U., St. Louis, B.S. 1963; U. of Nebraska, J.D. 1966.
Military Career: Army, 1966-68.
Occupation: Feed company executive; lawyer.
Family: Wife, Cindy Shin; three children.
Religion: Presbyterian.
Political Career: Douglas County Republican chairman, 1974-77; Republican nominee for U.S. House, 1978.
Capitol Office: 1019 Longworth Bldg. 20515; 225-4155.

Nebraska 2nd: East — Omaha. The district vote for Ronald Reagan was 67% in 1984; 61% in 1980.

CQ Voting Studies

	Presidential Support	Party Unity	Voting Participation
1986	78%	89%	98%
1985	74%	91%	99%

Interest Groups

	ADA	ACU	AFL-CIO	CCUS
1986	5%	n/a	7%	78%
1985	5%	81%	18%	73%

Committee

Ways and Means

Elections

1986	General	59%	Primary	u/o
1984	General	65%	Primary	u/o

Jack Davis (R-Ill.)

Of New Lenox — Elected 1986

Born: Sept. 6, 1935, Chicago, Ill.
Education: Southern Illinois U., B.S. 1956, attended Southern Illinois U., 1959-61.
Military Career: Navy, 1965-69.
Occupation: Businessman.
Family: Wife, Virginia Griffin; three children.
Religion: Protestant.
Political Career: Ill. House, 1977-87.
Capitol Office: 1234 Longworth Bldg. 20515; 225-3635.

Illinois 4th: Southern Chicago Suburbs, Joliet and Aurora. The district vote for Ronald Reagan was 61% in 1984; 56% in 1980.

Committees

Armed Services
Veterans' Affairs

Elections

1986	General	52%	Primary	u/o

Robert W. Davis   (R-Mich.)

Of Gaylord — Elected 1978

Born: July 31, 1932, Marquette, Mich.
Education: Attended Northern Michigan U., 1950-52; Hillsdale College, 1951-52; Wayne State U. College of Mortuary Science, B.S. 1954.
Occupation: Funeral director.
Family: Wife, Martha Cole; four children.
Religion: Episcopalian.
Political Career: St. Ignace City Council, 1964-66; Mich. House, 1967-71; Mich. Senate, 1971-79, Senate Republican leader, 1974-79.
Capitol Office: 2417 Rayburn Bldg. 20515; 225-4735.

Michigan 11th: Upper Peninsula and Northern Lower Peninsula. The district vote for Ronald Reagan was 65% in 1984; 50% in 1980.

Committees

Armed Services
Merchant Marine and Fisheries   (Ranking)

CQ Voting Studies

	Presidential Support	Party Unity	Voting Participation
1986	39%	36%	82%
1985	49%	55%	95%

Interest Groups

	ADA	ACU	AFL-CIO	CCUS
1986	35%	n/a	92%	57%
1985	35%	62%	65%	55%

Elections

1986	General	64%	Primary	u/o
1984	General	59%	Primary	u/o

Peter A. DeFazio   (D-Ore.)

Of Springfield — Elected 1986

Born: May 27, 1947, Needham, Mass.
Education: Tufts U., B.A. 1969; U. of Oregon, M.S. 1977.
Military Career: Air Force, 1967-71.
Occupation: Congressional aide.
Family: Wife, Myrnie L. Daut.
Religion: Roman Catholic.
Political Career: Lane County commissioner, 1983-87.
Capitol Office: 1729 Longworth Bldg. 20515; 225-6416.

Oregon 4th: Southwest — Eugene. The district vote for Ronald Reagan was 53% in 1984; 49% in 1980.

Committees

Interior and Insular Affairs
Public Works and Transportation
Small Business

Elections

1986	General	54%	Primary	34%

E. "Kika" de la Garza   (D-Texas)

Of Mission — Elected 1964

Born: Sept. 22, 1927, Mercedes, Texas.
Education: St. Mary's U., LL.B. 1952.
Military Career: Navy, 1945-46; Army, 1950-52.
Occupation: Lawyer.
Family: Wife, Lucille Alamia; three children.
Religion: Roman Catholic.
Political Career: Texas House, 1953-65.
Capitol Office: 1401 Longworth Bldg. 20515; 225-2531.

Texas 15th: South — McAllen. The district vote for Ronald Reagan was 46% in 1984; 42% in 1980.

CQ Voting Studies

	Presidential Support	Party Unity	Voting Participation
1986	27%	72%	85%
1985	34%	75%	89%

Interest Groups

	ADA	ACU	AFL-CIO	CCUS
1986	55%	n/a	85%	39%
1985	60%	24%	76%	20%

Committee

Agriculture   (Chairman)

Elections

1986	General	u/o	Primary	u/o
1984	General	u/o	Primary	u/o

Thomas D. DeLay   (R-Texas)

Of Sugar Land — Elected 1984

Born: April 8, 1947, Laredo, Texas.
Education: Attended Baylor U., 1965-67; U. of Houston, B.S. 1970.
Occupation: Pest control company owner.
Family: Wife, Christine Ann Furrh; one child.
Religion: Baptist.
Political Career: Texas House, 1979-85.
Capitol Office: 1039 Longworth Bldg. 20515; 225-5951.

Texas 22nd: Southwest Houston and Suburbs, Fort Bend and Brazoria Counties. The district vote for Ronald Reagan was 70% in 1984; 65% in 1980.

CQ Voting Studies

	Presidential Support	Party Unity	Voting Participation
1986	83%	91%	95%
1985	85%	87%	95%

Interest Groups

	ADA	ACU	AFL-CIO	CCUS
1986	0%	n/a	7%	94%
1985	5%	100%	0%	95%

Committee

Appropriations

Elections

1986	General	72%	Primary	u/o
1984	General	65%	Primary	53%

Ronald V. Dellums (D-Calif.)

Of Oakland — Elected 1970

Born: Nov. 24, 1935, Oakland, Calif.
Education: San Francisco State College, B.A. 1960; U. of California, Berkeley, M.S.W. 1962.
Military Career: Marine Corps, 1954-56.
Occupation: Psychiatric social worker.
Family: Wife, Leola Higgs; three children.
Religion: Protestant.
Political Career: Berkeley City Council, 1967-71.
Capitol Office: 2136 Rayburn Bldg. 20515; 225-2661.

California 8th: North Alameda County — Oakland and Berkeley. The district vote for Ronald Reagan was 34% in 1984.

Committees

Armed Services
District of Columbia   (Chairman)

Elections

1986	General	61%	Primary	83%
1984	General	60%	Primary	79%

CQ Voting Studies

	Presidential Support	Party Unity	Voting Participation
1986	12%	89%	93%
1985	16%	91%	94%

Interest Groups

	ADA	ACU	AFL-CIO	CCUS
1986	100%	n/a	86%	12%
1985	95%	5%	100%	19%

Butler Derrick (D-S.C.)

Of Edgefield — Elected 1974

Born: Sept. 30, 1936, Springfield, Mass.
Education: Attended U. of South Carolina, 1954-1958; U. of Georgia, LL.B. 1965.
Occupation: Lawyer.
Family: Divorced; two children.
Religion: Episcopalian.
Political Career: S.C. House, 1969-75.
Capitol Office: 201 Cannon Bldg. 20515; 225-5301.

South Carolina 3rd: West — Anderson and Aiken. The district vote for Ronald Reagan was 67% in 1984; 47% in 1980.

Committees

Budget
Rules
Select Aging

Elections

1986	General	68%	Primary	u/o
1984	General	58%	Primary	u/o

CQ Voting Studies

	Presidential Support	Party Unity	Voting Participation
1986	28%	81%	94%
1985	29%	74%	92%

Interest Groups

	ADA	ACU	AFL-CIO	CCUS
1986	55%	n/a	57%	44%
1985	60%	10%	53%	36%

Michael DeWine (R-Ohio)

Of Cedarville — Elected 1982

Born: Jan. 5, 1947, Springfield, Ohio.
Education: Miami U. (Ohio), B.S. 1969; Ohio Northern U., J.D. 1972.
Occupation: Lawyer.
Family: Wife, Frances Struewing; six children.
Religion: Roman Catholic.
Political Career: Greene County prosecuting attorney, 1977-81; Ohio Senate, 1981-83.
Capitol Office: 1705 Longworth Bldg. 20515; 225-4324.

Ohio 7th: West Central — Springfield and Marion.

Committees

Foreign Affairs
Judiciary
Select Iran-contra

Elections

1986	General	u/o	Primary	u/o
1984	General	77%	Primary	u/o

CQ Voting Studies

	Presidential Support	Party Unity	Voting Participation
1986	78%	85%	97%
1985	78%	87%	97%

Interest Groups

	ADA	ACU	AFL-CIO	CCUS
1986	0%	n/a	14%	94%
1985	10%	86%	18%	64%

William L. Dickinson (R-Ala.)

Of Montgomery — Elected 1964

Born: June 5, 1925, Opelika, Ala.
Education: U. of Alabama Law School, LL.B. 1950.
Military Career: Navy, 1943-46; Air Force Reserve.
Occupation: Lawyer; judge; railroad executive.
Family: Wife, Barbara Edwards; four children.
Religion: Methodist.
Political Career: Opelika city judge, 1951-53; Lee County Court of Common Pleas and Juvenile Court judge, 1953-59; 5th Judicial Circuit judge, 1959-63.
Capitol Office: 2406 Rayburn Bldg. 20515; 225-2901.

Alabama 2nd: Southeast — Montgomery and Dothan. The district vote for Ronald Reagan was 63% in 1984; 53% in 1980.

Committees

Armed Services (Ranking)
House Administration

Elections

1986	General	66%	Primary	u/o
1984	General	60%	Primary	u/o

CQ Voting Studies

	Presidential Support	Party Unity	Voting Participation
1986	71%	78%	92%
1985	63%	76%	93%

Interest Groups

	ADA	ACU	AFL-CIO	CCUS
1986	15%	n/a	38%	73%
1985	10%	65%	18%	82%

Norman D. Dicks   (D-Wash.)

Of Bremerton — Elected 1976

Born: Dec. 16, 1940, Bremerton, Wash.
Education: U. of Washington, B.A. 1963, J.D. 1968.
Occupation: Lawyer; congressional aide.
Family: Wife, Suzanne Callison; two children.
Religion: Lutheran.
Political Career: No previous office.
Capitol Office: 2429 Rayburn Bldg. 20515; 225-5916.

Washington 6th: Puget Sound — Bremerton and Tacoma. The district vote for Ronald Reagan was 57% in 1984.

Committee

Appropriations

Elections

1986	General	72%	Primary	72%
1984	General	66%	Primary	93%

CQ Voting Studies

	Presidential Support	Party Unity	Voting Participation
1986	27%	90%	97%
1985	35%	85%	95%

Interest Groups

	ADA	ACU	AFL-CIO	CCUS
1986	70%	n/a	79%	28%
1985	70%	24%	88%	38%

John D. Dingell   (D-Mich.)

Of Trenton — Elected 1955

Born: July 8, 1926, Colorado Springs, Colo.
Education: Georgetown U., B.S. 1949, LL.B. 1952.
Military Career: Army, 1944-46.
Occupation: Lawyer.
Family: Wife, Deborah Insley; four children.
Religion: Roman Catholic.
Political Career: Assistant Wayne County prosecutor, 1953-55.
Capitol Office: 2221 Rayburn Bldg. 20515; 225-4071.

Michigan 16th: Southeast Wayne County and Monroe County. The district vote for Ronald Reagan was 64% in 1984; 48% in 1980.

Committee

Energy and Commerce   (Chairman)

Elections

1986	General	78%	Primary	92%
1984	General	64%	Primary	u/o

CQ Voting Studies

	Presidential Support	Party Unity	Voting Participation
1986	24%	80%	88%
1985	23%	76%	85%

Interest Groups

	ADA	ACU	AFL-CIO	CCUS
1986	75%	n/a	92%	6%
1985	85%	14%	88%	25%

Joseph J. DioGuardi (R-N.Y.)

Of New Rochelle — Elected 1984

Born: Sept. 20, 1940, New York, N.Y.
Education: Fordham U., B.S. 1962.
Military Career: Army Reserve, 1963-69.
Occupation: Accountant.
Family: Wife, Carol Asselta; two children.
Religion: Roman Catholic.
Political Career: No previous office.
Capitol Office: 325 Cannon Bldg. 20515; 225-6506

New York 20th: Central and Southern Westchester County. The district vote for Ronald Reagan was 56% in 1984; 52% in 1980.

CQ Voting Studies

	Presidential Support	Party Unity	Voting Participation
1986	57%	55%	98%
1985	60%	69%	96%

Interest Groups

	ADA	ACU	AFL-CIO	CCUS
1986	35%	n/a	64%	78%
1985	10%	67%	35%	76%

Committees

Government Operations
Merchant Marine and Fisheries
Select Narcotics Abuse and Control

Elections

1986	General	54%	Primary	u/o
1984	General	50%	Primary	u/o

Julian C. Dixon (D-Calif.)

Of Culver City — Elected 1978

Born: Aug. 8, 1934, Washington, D.C.
Education: California State U., Los Angeles, B.S. 1962; Southwestern U., LL.B. 1967.
Military Career: Army, 1957-60.
Occupation: Legislative aide; lawyer.
Family: Wife, Betty Lee; one child.
Religion: Episcopalian.
Political Career: Calif. Assembly, 1973-79.
Capitol Office: 2400 Rayburn Bldg. 20515; 225-7084.

California 28th: Southern Los Angeles and Culver City. The district vote for Ronald Reagan was 32% in 1984.

CQ Voting Studies

	Presidential Support	Party Unity	Voting Participation
1986	13%	80%	85%
1985	18%	84%	85%

Interest Groups

	ADA	ACU	AFL-CIO	CCUS
1986	85%	n/a	100%	25%
1985	80%	0%	100%	15%

Committees

Appropriations
Standards of Official Conduct (Chairman)

Elections

1986	General	78%	Primary	93%
1984	General	76%	Primary	91%

Brian J. Donnelly (D-Mass.)

Of Dorchester — Elected 1978

Born: March 2, 1946, Dorchester, Mass.
Education: Boston U., B.S. 1970.
Occupation: High school teacher.
Family: Wife, Virginia Norton; two children.
Religion: Roman Catholic.
Political Career: Mass. House, 1973-79; asst. majority leader, 1977-79.
Capitol Office: 438 Cannon Bldg. 20515; 225-3215.

Massachusetts 11th: Part of Boston and South Shore Suburbs. The district vote for Ronald Reagan was 52% in 1984; 44% in 1980.

Committee

Ways and Means

Elections

1986	General	u/o	Primary	77%
1984	General	u/o	Primary	91%

CQ Voting Studies

	Presidential Support	Party Unity	Voting Participation
1986	18%	86%	92%
1985	26%	90%	96%

Interest Groups

	ADA	ACU	AFL-CIO	CCUS
1986	75%	n/a	93%	29%
1985	80%	5%	100%	23%

Byron L. Dorgan (D-N.D.)

Of Bismarck — Elected 1980

Born: May 14, 1942, Regent, N.D.
Education: U. of North Dakota, B.S. 1965; U. of Denver, M.B.A. 1966.
Occupation: Public official.
Family: Divorced; two children.
Religion: Lutheran.
Political Career: N.D. tax commissioner, 1969-80; Democratic nominee for U.S. House, 1974.
Capitol Office: 238 Cannon Bldg. 20515; 225-2611.

North Dakota: At-large. The district vote for Ronald Reagan was 65% in 1984; 64% in 1980.

Committees

Ways and Means
Select Hunger

Elections

1986	General	76%	Primary	u/o
1984	General	79%	Primary	u/o

CQ Voting Studies

	Presidential Support	Party Unity	Voting Participation
1986	26%	82%	96%
1985	23%	83%	97%

Interest Groups

	ADA	ACU	AFL-CIO	CCUS
1986	70%	n/a	71%	29%
1985	65%	10%	76%	27%

Bob Dornan (R-Calif.)

Of Garden Grove — Elected 1976

Born: April 3, 1933, New York, N.Y.
Education: Attended Loyola U. (California), 1950-53.
Military Career: Air Force, 1953-58.
Occupation: Broadcast journalist and producer.
Family: Wife, Sallie Hansen; five children.
Religion: Roman Catholic.
Political Career: Candidate for mayor of Los Angeles, 1973; served in U.S. House, 1977-83; sought Republican nomination for U.S. Senate, 1982.
Capitol Office: 301 Cannon Bldg. 20515; 225-2965.

California 38th: Northwestern Orange County, Santa Ana and Garden Grove. The district vote for Ronald Reagan was 69% in 1984.

Committees

Foreign Affairs
Veterans' Affairs
Select Narcotics Abuse and Control

CQ Voting Studies

	Presidential Support	Party Unity	Voting Participation
1986	80%	82%	94%
1985	80%	79%	92%

Interest Groups

	ADA	ACU	AFL-CIO	CCUS
1986	5%	n/a	8%	81%
1985	10%	95%	12%	81%

Elections

1986	General	57%	Primary	u/o
1984	General	53%	Primary	65%

Wayne Dowdy (D-Miss.)

Of McComb — Elected 1981

Born: July 27, 1943, Fitzgerald, Ga.
Education: Millsaps College, B.A. 1965; Jackson School of Law, LL.B. 1968.
Military Career: Miss. National Guard; Army Reserve, 1966-72.
Occupation: Lawyer; broadcasting executive.
Family: Wife, Susan Tenney; three children.
Religion: Methodist.
Political Career: City judge 1970-74; Mayor of McComb, 1978-81.
Capitol Office: 240 Cannon Bldg. 20515; 225-5865.

Mississippi 4th: Southwest — Jackson. The district vote for Ronald Reagan was 59% in 1984.

Committees

Energy and Commerce
Veterans' Affairs

CQ Voting Studies

	Presidential Support	Party Unity	Voting Participation
1986	29%	68%	84%
1985	36%	66%	86%

Interest Groups

	ADA	ACU	AFL-CIO	CCUS
1986	45%	n/a	77%	29%
1985	45%	48%	69%	45%

Elections

1986	General	71%	Primary	86%
1984	General	55%	Primary	u/o

Thomas J. Downey   (D-N.Y.)

Of Amityville — Elected 1974

Born: Jan. 28, 1949, Ozone Park, N.Y.
Education: Cornell U., B.S. 1970; attended St. John's U. Law School, 1972-74; American U., J.D. 1979.
Occupation: Personnel manager.
Family: Wife, D. Chris Milanos; two children.
Religion: Methodist.
Political Career: Suffolk County Legislature, 1972-75.
Capitol Office: 2232 Rayburn Bldg. 20515; 225-3335.

New York 2nd: Long Island — Western Suffolk County. The district vote for Ronald Reagan was 66% in 1984; 58% in 1980.

CQ Voting Studies

	Presidential Support	Party Unity	Voting Participation
1986	18%	91%	95%
1985	21%	91%	95%

Interest Groups

	ADA	ACU	AFL-CIO	CCUS
1986	95%	n/a	79%	17%
1985	85%	5%	94%	26%

Committees

Ways and Means
Select Aging

Elections

1986	General	63%	Primary	u/o
1984	General	55%	Primary	u/o

David Dreier   (R-Calif.)

Of La Verne — Elected 1980

Born: July 5, 1952, Kansas City, Mo.
Education: Claremont Men's College, B.A. 1975; Claremont Graduate School, M.A. 1976.
Occupation: Public relations executive.
Family: Single.
Religion: Christian Scientist.
Political Career: Republican nominee for U.S. House, 1978.
Capitol Office: 410 Cannon Bldg. 20515; 225-2305.

California 33rd: Eastern Los Angeles — Pomona and Whittier. The district vote for Ronald Reagan was 70% in 1984.

CQ Voting Studies

	Presidential Support	Party Unity	Voting Participation
1986	83%	95%	98%
1985	84%	92%	98%

Interest Groups

	ADA	ACU	AFL-CIO	CCUS
1986	0%	n/a	0%	100%
1985	10%	90%	0%	95%

Committees

Banking, Finance and Urban Affairs
Small Business

Elections

1986	General	73%	Primary	u/o
1984	General	71%	Primary	u/o

John J. Duncan (R-Tenn.)

Of Knoxville — Elected 1964

Born: March 24, 1919, Scott County, Tenn.
Education: U. of Tennessee, B.S. 1942; Cumberland U., J.D. 1948.
Military Career: Army, 1942-45.
Occupation: Lawyer.
Family: Wife, Lois Swisher; four children.
Religion: Presbyterian.
Political Career: Mayor of Knoxville, 1959-64.
Capitol Office: 2206 Rayburn Bldg. 20515; 225-5435.

Tennessee 2nd: East — Knoxville. The district vote for Ronald Reagan was 64% in 1984; 58% in 1980.

Committees

Ways and Means (Ranking)
Joint Taxation (Ranking)

CQ Voting Studies

	Presidential Support	Party Unity	Voting Participation
1986	69%	62%	98%
1985	65%	60%	97%

Interest Groups

	ADA	ACU	AFL-CIO	CCUS
1986	10%	n/a	21%	72%
1985	15%	71%	35%	68%

Elections

1986	General	76%	Primary	u/o
1984	General	77%	Primary	u/o

Richard J. Durbin (D-Ill.)

Of Springfield — Elected 1982

Born: Nov. 21, 1944, East St. Louis, Ill.
Education: Georgetown U., B.S. (Foreign Service) 1966, J.D. 1969.
Occupation: Lawyer.
Family: Wife, Loretta Schaefer; three children.
Religion: Roman Catholic.
Political Career: Democratic nominee for Ill. Senate, 1976; Democratic nominee for lieutenant governor, 1978.
Capitol Office: 417 Cannon Bldg. 20515; 225-5271.

Illinois 20th: Central — Springfield, Decatur and Quincy. The district vote for Ronald Reagan was 58% in 1984; 57% in 1980.

Committees

Appropriations
Budget
Select Children, Youth and Families

CQ Voting Studies

	Presidential Support	Party Unity	Voting Participation
1986	17%	90%	99%
1985	28%	79%	98%

Interest Groups

	ADA	ACU	AFL-CIO	CCUS
1986	85%	n/a	93%	22%
1985	65%	19%	82%	36%

Elections

1986	General	68%	Primary	u/o
1984	General	61%	Primary	92%

Bernard J. Dwyer (D-N.J.)

Of Edison — Elected 1980

Born: Jan. 24, 1921, Perth Amboy, N.J.
Education: Attended Rutgers U.
Military Career: Navy, 1940-45.
Occupation: Insurance salesman and executive.
Family: Wife, Lilyan Sudzina; one child.
Religion: Roman Catholic.
Political Career: Edison Township Council, 1958-69; Edison mayor, 1969-73; N.J. Senate, 1974-80, majority leader, 1980.
Capitol Office: 404 Cannon Bldg. 20515; 225-6301.

New Jersey 6th: Central — New Brunswick and Perth Amboy. The district vote for Ronald Reagan was 59% in 1984.

Committees

Appropriations
Standards of Official Conduct
Select Intelligence

Elections

1986	General	70%	Primary	88%
1984	General	56%	Primary	86%

CQ Voting Studies

	Presidential Support	Party Unity	Voting Participation
1986	19%	95%	97%
1985	25%	97%	99%

Interest Groups

	ADA	ACU	AFL-CIO	CCUS
1986	80%	n/a	100%	22%
1985	80%	0%	100%	23%

Mervyn M. Dymally (D-Calif.)

Of Compton — Elected 1980

Born: May 12, 1926, Cedros, Trinidad.
Education: California State U., Los Angeles, B.A. 1954; California State U., Sacramento, M.A. 1969; U.S. International U., Ph.D. 1978.
Occupation: Special education teacher; data processing executive.
Family: Wife, Alice M. Gueno; two children.
Religion: Episcopalian.
Political Career: Calif. Assembly, 1963-67; Calif. Senate, 1967-75; Calif. lieutenant governor, 1975-79, defeated for re-election, 1978.
Capitol Office: 1717 Longworth Bldg. 20515; 225-5425.

California 31st: Southern Los Angeles County — Compton and Carson. The district vote for Ronald Reagan was 41% in 1984.

Committees

District of Columbia
Foreign Affairs
Post Office and Civil Service

Elections

1986	General	72%	Primary	85%
1984	General	71%	Primary	84%

CQ Voting Studies

	Presidential Support	Party Unity	Voting Participation
1986	13%	92%	94%
1985	15%	63%	76%

Interest Groups

	ADA	ACU	AFL-CIO	CCUS
1986	100%	n/a	93%	19%
1985	90%	10%	87%	24%

Roy Dyson (D-Md.)

Of Great Mills — Elected 1980

Born: Nov. 15, 1948, Great Mills, Md.
Education: Attended U. of Baltimore, 1970-71; U. of Maryland, 1971-72.
Occupation: Lumber company executive.
Family: Single.
Religion: Roman Catholic.
Political Career: Md. House, 1975-81; Democratic nominee for U.S. House, 1976.
Capitol Office: 224 Cannon Bldg. 20515; 225-5311.

Maryland 1st: Eastern Shore and Southern Maryland. The district vote for Ronald Reagan was 65% in 1984; 52% in 1980.

Committees

Armed Services
Merchant Marine and Fisheries

Elections

1986	General	67%	Primary	89%
1984	General	58%	Primary	87%

CQ Voting Studies

	Presidential Support	Party Unity	Voting Participation
1986	53%	57%	97%
1985	55%	66%	97%

Interest Groups

	ADA	ACU	AFL-CIO	CCUS
1986	30%	n/a	69%	50%
1985	30%	65%	59%	50%

Joseph D. Early (D-Mass.)

Of Worcester — Elected 1974

Born: Jan. 31, 1933, Worcester, Mass.
Education: College of the Holy Cross, B.S. 1955.
Military Career: Navy, 1955-57.
Occupation: Teacher and basketball coach.
Family: Wife, Marilyn Powers; eight children.
Religion: Roman Catholic.
Political Career: Mass. House, 1963-75.
Capitol Office: 2349 Rayburn Bldg. 20515; 225-6101.

Massachusetts 3rd: Central — Worcester. The district vote for Ronald Reagan was 57% in 1984; 44% in 1980.

Committee

Appropriations

Elections

1986	General	u/o	Primary	u/o
1984	General	67%	Primary	u/o

CQ Voting Studies

	Presidential Support	Party Unity	Voting Participation
1986	13%	80%	87%
1985	28%	82%	88%

Interest Groups

	ADA	ACU	AFL-CIO	CCUS
1986	85%	n/a	93%	20%
1985	80%	10%	100%	21%

Dennis E. Eckart (D-Ohio)

Of Mentor — Elected 1980

Born: April 6, 1950, Cleveland, Ohio.
Education: Xavier U., B.S. 1971; Cleveland State U., J.D. 1974.
Occupation: Lawyer.
Family: Wife, Sandra Pestotnik; one child.
Religion: Roman Catholic.
Political Career: Assistant prosecutor, Lake County, 1974; Ohio House, 1975-81.
Capitol Office: 1210 Longworth Bldg. 20515; 225-6331.

Ohio 11th: Northeast — Cleveland Suburbs.

Committees

Energy and Commerce
Small Business

Elections

1986	General	74%	Primary	92%
1984	General	67%	Primary	u/o

CQ Voting Studies

	Presidential Support	Party Unity	Voting Participation
1986	21%	87%	99%
1985	24%	88%	99%

Interest Groups

	ADA	ACU	AFL-CIO	CCUS
1986	65%	n/a	86%	22%
1985	70%	19%	76%	36%

Don Edwards (D-Calif.)

Of San Jose — Elected 1962

Born: Jan. 6, 1915, San Jose, Calif.
Education: Stanford U., A.B. 1936; graduate work, Stanford Law School, 1936-38.
Military Career: Navy, 1942-45.
Occupation: Title company executive; lawyer; FBI agent.
Family: Wife, Edith Wilke; five children.
Religion: Unitarian.
Political Career: No previous office.
Capitol Office: 2307 Rayburn Bldg. 20515; 225-3072.

California 10th: Southeast Bay Area — Downtown San Jose and Fremont. The district vote for Ronald Reagan was 51% in 1984.

Committees

Judiciary
Veterans' Affairs

Elections

1986	General	73%	Primary	u/o
1984	General	62%	Primary	86%

CQ Voting Studies

	Presidential Support	Party Unity	Voting Participation
1986	16%	95%	99%
1985	20%	97%	99%

Interest Groups

	ADA	ACU	AFL-CIO	CCUS
1986	100%	n/a	93%	12%
1985	100%	0%	100%	18%

Mickey Edwards (R-Okla.)

Of Oklahoma City — Elected 1976

Born: July 12, 1937, Cleveland, Ohio.
Education: U. of Oklahoma, B.S. 1958; Oklahoma City U. Law School, J.D. 1969.
Occupation: Lawyer; journalist.
Family: Wife, Lisa Reagan; one child.
Religion: Episcopalian.
Political Career: Republican nominee for U.S. House, 1974.
Capitol Office: 2434 Rayburn Bldg. 20515; 225-2132.

Oklahoma 5th: North Central — Part of Oklahoma City and Bartlesville. The district vote for Ronald Reagan was 76% in 1984; 69% in 1980.

Committees

Appropriations
Budget

CQ Voting Studies

	Presidential Support	Party Unity	Voting Participation
1986	71%	72%	90%
1985	71%	79%	91%

Interest Groups

	ADA	ACU	AFL-CIO	CCUS
1986	5%	n/a	14%	81%
1985	5%	90%	0%	85%

Elections

1986	General	70%	Primary	u/o
1984	General	76%	Primary	89%

Bill Emerson (R-Mo.)

Of Cape Girardeau — Elected 1980

Born: Jan. 1, 1938, St. Louis, Mo.
Education: Westminster College, B.A. 1959; U. of Baltimore LL.B. 1964.
Military Career: Air Force Reserves, 1964-present.
Occupation: Government relations executive.
Family: Wife, Jo Ann Hermann; four children.
Religion: Presbyterian.
Political Career: No previous office.
Capitol Office: 418 Cannon Bldg. 20515; 225-4404.

Missouri 8th: Southeast — Cape Girardeau. The district vote for Ronald Reagan was 61% in 1984; 54% in 1980.

Committees

Agriculture
Interior and Insular Affairs
Select Hunger

CQ Voting Studies

	Presidential Support	Party Unity	Voting Participation
1986	69%	82%	100%
1985	60%	78%	97%

Interest Groups

	ADA	ACU	AFL-CIO	CCUS
1986	10%	n/a	29%	72%
1985	10%	80%	25%	81%

Elections

1986	General	53%	Primary	u/o
1984	General	65%	Primary	u/o

Glenn English (D-Okla.)

Of Cordell — Elected 1974

Born: Nov. 30, 1940, Cordell, Okla.
Education: Southwestern State College, B.A. 1964.
Military Career: Army Reserve, 1965-71.
Occupation: Petroleum landman.
Family: Wife, Jan Pangle; two children.
Religion: Methodist.
Political Career: No previous office.
Capitol Office: 2235 Rayburn Bldg. 20515; 225-5565.

Oklahoma 6th: West, Panhandle and Part of Oklahoma City. The district vote for Ronald Reagan was 69% in 1984; 64% in 1980.

Committees

Agriculture
Government Operations

Elections

1986	General	u/o	Primary	u/o
1984	General	59%	Primary	u/o

CQ Voting Studies

	Presidential Support	Party Unity	Voting Participation
1986	43%	63%	96%
1985	58%	53%	97%

Interest Groups

	ADA	ACU	AFL-CIO	CCUS
1986	35%	n/a	50%	61%
1985	15%	76%	24%	82%

Ben Erdreich (D-Ala.)

Of Birmingham — Elected 1982

Born: Dec. 9, 1938, Birmingham, Ala.
Education: Yale U., B.A. 1960; U. of Alabama School of Law, J.D. 1963.
Military Career: Army, 1963-65.
Occupation: Lawyer.
Family: Wife, Ellen Cooper; two children.
Religion: Jewish.
Political Career: Ala. House, 1971-75; Jefferson County Commission, 1975-83; Democratic nominee for U.S. House, 1972.
Capitol Office: 439 Cannon Bldg. 20515; 225-4921.

Alabama 6th: Birmingham and Suburbs. The district vote for Ronald Reagan was 59% in 1984; 51% in 1980.

Committees

Banking, Finance and Urban Affairs
Government Operations
Select Aging

Elections

1986	General	73%	Primary	u/o
1984	General	60%	Primary	88%

CQ Voting Studies

	Presidential Support	Party Unity	Voting Participation
1986	40%	67%	97%
1985	52%	68%	97%

Interest Groups

	ADA	ACU	AFL-CIO	CCUS
1986	55%	n/a	92%	50%
1985	35%	52%	59%	45%

Mike Espy   (D-Miss.)

Of Yazoo City — Elected 1986

Born: Nov. 30, 1953, Yazoo City, Miss.
Education: Howard U., B.A. 1975; U. of Santa Clara School of Law, J.D. 1978.
Occupation: Lawyer; businessman.
Family: Wife, Sheila Bell; two children.
Religion: Baptist.
Political Career: Miss. assistant secretary of state, 1980-84; assistant state attorney general, 1984-85.
Capitol Office: 216 Cannon Bldg. 20515; 225-5876.

Mississippi 2nd: West Central — Mississippi Delta. The district vote for Ronald Reagan was 50% in 1984.

Committees

Agriculture
Budget
Select Hunger

Elections

1986	General	52%	Primary	50%

CQ Voting Studies

	Presidential Support	Party Unity	Voting Participation
1986	13%	95%	99%
1985	14%	96%	97%

Interest Groups

	ADA	ACU	AFL-CIO	CCUS
1986	100%	n/a	93%	11%
1985	100%	5%	100%	18%

Lane Evans   (D-Ill.)

Of Rock Island — Elected 1982

Born: Aug. 4, 1951, Rock Island, Ill.
Education: Augustana College (Ill.), A.B. 1974; Georgetown U., J.D. 1978.
Military Career: Marine Corps, 1969-71.
Occupation: Lawyer.
Family: Single.
Religion: Roman Catholic.
Political Career: No previous office.
Capitol Office: 328 Cannon Bldg. 20515; 225-5905.

Illinois 17th: West — Rock Island, Moline and Galesburg. The district vote for Ronald Reagan was 54% in 1984; 56% in 1980.

Committees

Agriculture
Veterans' Affairs
Select Children, Youth and Families

Elections

1986	General	56%	Primary	u/o
1984	General	57%	Primary	u/o

Dante B. Fascell   (D-Fla.)

Of Miami — Elected 1954

Born: March 9, 1917, Bridgehampton, N.Y.
Education: U. of Miami, J.D. 1938.
Military Career: Army, 1941-46.
Profession: Lawyer.
Family: Wife, Jeanne-Marie Pelot; two children.
Religion: Protestant.
Political Career: Fla. House, 1951-54.
Capitol Office: 2354 Rayburn Bldg. 20515; 225-4506.

Florida 19th: South — Coral Gables and Key West. The district vote for Ronald Reagan was 64% in 1984; 55% in 1980.

Committees

Foreign Affairs   (Chairman)
Select Iran-contra
Select Narcotics Abuse and Control

CQ Voting Studies

	Presidential Support	Party Unity	Voting Participation
1986	28%	88%	96%
1985	34%	88%	94%

Interest Groups

	ADA	ACU	AFL-CIO	CCUS
1986	70%	n/a	93%	24%
1985	60%	24%	94%	11%

Elections

1986	General	69%	Primary	u/o
1984	General	64%	Primary	u/o

Harris W. Fawell   (R-Ill.)

Of Naperville — Elected 1984

Born: March 25, 1929, West Chicago, Ill.
Education: Attended North Central College, 1947-49; Chicago-Kent College of Law, J.D. 1952.
Occupation: Lawyer.
Family: Wife, Ruth Johnson; three children.
Religion: Methodist.
Political Career: Ill. Senate, 1963-77; candidate for Ill. Supreme Court, 1976.
Capitol Office: 318 Cannon Bldg. 20515; 225-3515.

Illinois 13th: Southwest Chicago Suburbs — Downers Grove. The district vote for Ronald Reagan was 74% in 1984; 62% in 1980.

Committees

Education and Labor
Science, Space and Technology
Select Aging

CQ Voting Studies

	Presidential Support	Party Unity	Voting Participation
1986	69%	83%	99%
1985	85%	79%	98%

Interest Groups

	ADA	ACU	AFL-CIO	CCUS
1986	20%	n/a	14%	89%
1985	15%	81%	6%	95%

Elections

1986	General	73%	Primary	u/o
1984	General	67%	Primary	30%

Vic Fazio (D-Calif.)

Of West Sacramento — Elected 1978

Born: Oct. 11, 1942, Winchester, Mass.
Education: Union College, B.A. 1965.
Occupation: Journalist.
Family: Wife, Judy Kern; two children, one stepchild.
Religion: Episcopalian.
Political Career: Calif. Assembly, 1975-79.
Capitol Office: 2433 Rayburn Bldg. 20515; 225-5716.

California 4th: Suburban Sacramento to Bay Area. The district vote for Ronald Reagan was 56% in 1984.

CQ Voting Studies

	Presidential Support	Party Unity	Voting Participation
1986	20%	93%	98%
1985	26%	90%	95%

Interest Groups

	ADA	ACU	AFL-CIO	CCUS
1986	80%	n/a	93%	24%
1985	75%	14%	82%	32%

Committees

Appropriations
Budget
Standards of Official Conduct
Select Hunger

Elections

1986	General	69%	Primary	u/o
1984	General	61%	Primary	u/o

Edward F. Feighan (D-Ohio)

Of Lakewood — Elected 1982

Born: Oct. 22, 1947, Lakewood, Ohio.
Education: Attended Borromeo College of Ohio, 1965-66; Loyola University (La.), B.A. 1969; Cleveland-Marshall College of Law, J.D. 1978.
Occupation: Lawyer.
Family: Wife, Nadine Hopwood; three children.
Religion: Roman Catholic.
Political Career: Ohio House, 1973-1979; Cuyahoga County Commission, 1979-1983; candidate for mayor of Cleveland, 1977.
Capitol Office: 1124 Longworth Bldg. 20515; 225-5731.

Ohio 19th: Cleveland Suburbs.

CQ Voting Studies

	Presidential Support	Party Unity	Voting Participation
1986	17%	90%	97%
1985	29%	88%	97%

Interest Groups

	ADA	ACU	AFL-CIO	CCUS
1986	95%	n/a	100%	33%
1985	70%	10%	82%	32%

Committees

Foreign Affairs
Judiciary

Elections

1986	General	55%	Primary	87%
1984	General	55%	Primary	80%

Jack Fields (R-Texas)

Of Humble — Elected 1980

Born: Feb. 3, 1952, Humble, Texas.
Education: Baylor U., B.A. 1974, J.D. 1977.
Occupation: Lawyer; cemetery executive.
Family: Wife, Roni Sue Haddock.
Religion: Baptist.
Political Career: No previous office.
Capitol Office: 413 Cannon Bldg. 20515; 225-4901.

Texas 8th: Houston Suburbs and Eastern Harris County. The district vote for Ronald Reagan was 60% in 1984; 57% in 1980.

Committees

Energy and Commerce
Merchant Marine and Fisheries

Elections

1986	General	68%	Primary	u/o
1984	General	65%	Primary	u/o

CQ Voting Studies

	Presidential Support	Party Unity	Voting Participation
1986	79%	95%	98%
1985	74%	89%	95%

Interest Groups

	ADA	ACU	AFL-CIO	CCUS
1986	5%	n/a	0%	94%
1985	10%	90%	6%	91%

Hamilton Fish Jr. (R-N.Y.)

Of Milbrook — Elected 1968

Born: June 3, 1926, Washington, D.C.
Education: Harvard College, A.B. 1949; New York U., LL.B. 1957.
Military Career: Naval Reserve, 1944-46.
Occupation: Lawyer.
Family: Widowed; four children.
Religion: Episcopalian.
Political Career: Republican nominee for U.S. House, 1966.
Capitol Office: 2269 Rayburn Bldg. 20515; 225-5441.

New York 21st: Hudson Valley — Poughkeepsie. The district vote for Ronald Reagan was 68% in 1984; 59% in 1980.

Committees

Judiciary (Ranking)
Joint Economic

Elections

1986	General	76%	Primary	u/o
1984	General	78%	Primary	u/o

CQ Voting Studies

	Presidential Support	Party Unity	Voting Participation
1986	40%	33%	92%
1985	45%	42%	87%

Interest Groups

	ADA	ACU	AFL-CIO	CCUS
1986	45%	n/a	57%	44%
1985	35%	40%	80%	55%

Floyd H. Flake   (D-N.Y.)

Of Queens — Elected 1986

Born: Jan. 30, 1945, Los Angeles, Calif.
Education: Wilberforce U., B.A. 1967; attended Payne Theological Seminary, 1968-70; Northeastern U., 1974-75; St. John's U., 1982-85.
Occupation: Clergyman.
Family: Wife, M. Elaine McCollins; four children.
Religion: African Methodist Episcopal.
Political Career: No previous office.
Capitol Office: 1427 Longworth Bldg. 20515; 225-3461.

New York 6th: Southern Queens — Ozone Park and Jamaica. The district vote for Ronald Reagan was 30% in 1984; 36% in 1980.

Committees

Banking, Finance and Urban Affairs
Small Business
Select Hunger

Elections

1986	General	68%	Primary	49%

Ronnie G. Flippo   (D-Ala.)

Of Florence — Elected 1976

Born: Aug. 15, 1937, Florence, Ala.
Education: U. of North Alabama, B.S. 1965; U. of Alabama, M.A. 1966.
Occupation: Accountant.
Family: Wife, Faye Cooper; six children.
Religion: Church of Christ.
Political Career: Ala. House, 1971-75; Ala. Senate, 1975-77.
Capitol Office: 2334 Rayburn Bldg. 20515; 225-4801.

Alabama 5th: North — Huntsville. The district vote for Ronald Reagan was 59% in 1984; 41% in 1980.

Committee

Ways and Means

Elections

1986	General	79%	Primary	90%
1984	General	96%	Primary	u/o

CQ Voting Studies

	Presidential Support	Party Unity	Voting Participation
1986	33%	64%	82%
1985	45%	69%	93%

Interest Groups

	ADA	ACU	AFL-CIO	CCUS
1986	40%	n/a	77%	29%
1985	35%	58%	53%	43%

James J. Florio (D-N.J.)

Of Pine Hill — Elected 1974

Born: Aug. 29, 1937, Brooklyn, N.Y.

Education: Trenton State College, B.A. 1962; graduate work, Columbia U., 1962-63; Rutgers U. Law School, J.D. 1967.

Military Career: Navy, 1955-58, Naval Reserve, 1958-74.

Occupation: Lawyer.

Family: Divorced; three children.

Religion: Roman Catholic.

Political Career: N.J. Assembly, 1970-74; Democratic nominee for U.S. House, 1972; sought Democratic gubernatorial nomination, 1977; Democratic nominee for governor, 1981.

Capitol Office: 2162 Rayburn Bldg. 20515; 225-6501.

New Jersey 1st: Southwest — Camden. The district vote for Ronald Reagan was 55% in 1984.

Committees

Energy and Commerce
Veterans' Affairs
Select Aging

Elections

1986	General	76%	Primary	96%
1984	General	72%	Primary	93%

CQ Voting Studies

	Presidential Support	Party Unity	Voting Participation
1986	19%	87%	94%
1985	25%	89%	94%

Interest Groups

	ADA	ACU	AFL-CIO	CCUS
1986	70%	n/a	100%	15%
1985	85%	10%	100%	14%

Thomas M. Foglietta (D-Pa.)

Of Philadelphia — Elected 1980

Born: Dec. 3, 1928, Philadelphia, Pa.

Education: St. Joseph's College, B.A. 1949; Temple U., J.D. 1952.

Occupation: Lawyer.

Family: Single.

Religion: Roman Catholic.

Political Career: Philadelphia City Council, 1955-75; Republican nominee for mayor of Philadelphia, 1975.

Capitol Office: 231 Cannon Bldg. 20515; 225-4731.

Pennsylvania 1st: South and Central Philadelphia. The district vote for Ronald Reagan was 35% in 1984; 31% in 1980.

Committees

Armed Services
Merchant Marine and Fisheries

Elections

1986	General	75%	Primary	61%
1984	General	75%	Primary	52%

CQ Voting Studies

	Presidential Support	Party Unity	Voting Participation
1986	16%	79%	83%
1985	20%	90%	94%

Interest Groups

	ADA	ACU	AFL-CIO	CCUS
1986	90%	n/a	100%	14%
1985	90%	5%	94%	14%

Thomas S. Foley (D-Wash.)

Of Spokane — Elected 1964

Born: March 6, 1929, Spokane, Wash.
Education: U. of Washington, B.A. 1951, LL.B. 1957.
Occupation: Lawyer.
Family: Wife, Heather Strachan.
Religion: Roman Catholic.
Political Career: No previous office.
Capitol Office: 1201 Longworth Bldg. 20515; 225-2006.

Washington 5th: East — Spokane. The district vote for Ronald Reagan was 60% in 1984.

CQ Voting Studies

	Presidential Support	Party Unity	Voting Participation
1986	23%	91%	95%
1985	29%	90%	93%

Interest Groups

	ADA	ACU	AFL-CIO	CCUS
1986	75%	n/a	86%	33%
1985	75%	10%	76%	27%

Committees

Majority Leader
Budget
Select Iran-contra

Elections

1986	General	75%	Primary	73%
1984	General	70%	Primary	u/o

Harold E. Ford (D-Tenn.)

Of Memphis — Elected 1974

Born: May 20, 1945, Memphis Tenn.
Education: Tennessee State U., B.S. 1967; John Gupton Mortuary, L.F.D., L.E.D. 1969; Howard U., M.B.A. 1982.
Occupation: Mortician.
Family: Wife, Dorothy Bowles; three children.
Religion: Baptist.
Political Career: Tenn. House, 1971-75.
Capitol Office: 2305 Rayburn Bldg. 20515; 225-3265.

Tennessee 9th: Memphis. The district vote for Ronald Reagan was 36% in 1984; 34% in 1980.

CQ Voting Studies

	Presidential Support	Party Unity	Voting Participation
1986	16%	71%	78%
1985	18%	87%	90%

Interest Groups

	ADA	ACU	AFL-CIO	CCUS
1986	100%	n/a	91%	8%
1985	90%	0%	94%	14%

Committees

Ways and Means
Select Aging

Elections

1986	General	u/o	Primary	73%
1984	General	72%	Primary	80%

William D. Ford (D-Mich.)

Of Taylor — Elected 1964

Born: Aug. 6, 1927, Detroit, Mich.
Education: Attended Nebraska State Teachers College, 1946; Wayne State U., 1947-48; U. of Denver, B.S. 1949, LL.B. 1951.
Military Career: Navy, 1944-46; Air Force Reserve, 1950-58.
Occupation: Lawyer.
Family: Divorced; three children.
Religion: United Church of Christ.
Political Career: Taylor Township justice of the peace, 1955-57; Melvindale city attorney, 1957-59; Taylor Township attorney, 1957-64; Mich. Senate, 1963-65.
Capitol Office: 239 Cannon Bldg. 20515; 225-6261.

Michigan 15th: Southwestern Wayne County. The district vote for Ronald Reagan was 61% in 1984; 49% in 1980.

Committees

Education and Labor
Post Office and Civil Service   (Chairman)

Elections

1986	General	76%	Primary	91%
1984	General	60%	Primary	u/o

CQ Voting Studies

	Presidential Support	Party Unity	Voting Participation
1986	18%	84%	91%
1985	16%	71%	79%

Interest Groups

	ADA	ACU	AFL-CIO	CCUS
1986	80%	n/a	93%	6%
1985	80%	5%	100%	20%

Barney Frank (D-Mass.)

Of Newton — Elected 1980

Born: March 31, 1940, Bayonne, N.J.
Education: Harvard U., B.A. 1962, J.D. 1977.
Occupation: Lawyer.
Family: Single.
Religion: Jewish.
Political Career: Mass. House, 1973-81.
Capitol Office: 1030 Longworth Bldg. 20515; 225-5931.

Massachusetts 4th: Boston Suburbs and Fall River. The district vote for Ronald Reagan was 48% in 1984; 40% in 1980.

Committees

Banking, Finance and Urban Affairs
Government Operations
Judiciary
Select Aging

Elections

1986	General	u/o	Primary	84%
1984	General	74%	Primary	u/o

CQ Voting Studies

	Presidential Support	Party Unity	Voting Participation
1986	18%	91%	98%
1985	25%	91%	95%

Interest Groups

	ADA	ACU	AFL-CIO	CCUS
1986	100%	n/a	86%	17%
1985	100%	10%	94%	23%

Bill Frenzel (R-Minn.)

Of Golden Valley — Elected 1970

Born: July 31, 1928, St. Paul, Minn.
Education: Dartmouth College, B.A. 1950, M.B.A. 1951.
Military Career: Naval Reserve, 1951-54.
Profession: Warehouse company executive.
Family: Wife, Ruth Purdy; three children.
Religion: Unspecified.
Political Career: Minn. House, 1963-71.
Capitol Office: 1026 Longworth Bldg. 20515; 225-2871.

Minnesota 3rd: Southern and Western Twin Cities Suburbs. The district vote for Ronald Reagan was 59% in 1984; 47% in 1980.

Committees

House Administration (Ranking)
Ways and Means

CQ Voting Studies

	Presidential Support	Party Unity	Voting Participation
1986	66%	74%	95%
1985	63%	72%	92%

Interest Groups

	ADA	ACU	AFL-CIO	CCUS
1986	25%	n/a	0%	81%
1985	20%	67%	19%	90%

Elections

1986	General	70%	Primary	u/o
1984	General	73%	Primary	90%

Martin Frost (D-Texas)

Of Dallas — Elected 1978

Born: Jan. 1, 1942, Glendale, Calif.
Education: U. of Missouri, B.A. and B.J. 1964; Georgetown U. Law Center, J.D. 1970.
Military Career: Army Reserve, 1966-72.
Occupation: Lawyer.
Family: Wife, Valerie Hall; three children.
Religion: Jewish.
Political Career: Sought Democratic nomination for U.S. House, 1974.
Capitol Office: 2459 Rayburn Bldg. 20515; 225-3605.

Texas 24th: South Dallas and Western Suburbs. The district vote for Ronald Reagan was 53% in 1984.

Committees

Budget
Rules

CQ Voting Studies

	Presidential Support	Party Unity	Voting Participation
1986	23%	74%	86%
1985	26%	83%	93%

Interest Groups

	ADA	ACU	AFL-CIO	CCUS
1986	45%	n/a	73%	43%
1985	55%	24%	82%	35%

Elections

1986	General	67%	Primary	93%
1984	General	59%	Primary	92%

Elton Gallegly   (R-Calif.)

Of Simi Valley — Elected 1986

Born: March 7, 1944, Huntington Park, Calif.
Education: Attended Los Angeles State College, 1962-63.
Occupation: Real estate broker.
Family: Wife, Janice Shrader; four children.
Religion: Protestant.
Political Career: Simi Valley City Council, 1979-80; mayor, Simi Valley, 1980-86.
Capitol Office: 1020 Longworth Bldg. 20515; 225-5811.

California 21st: Part of Ventura County and Western San Fernando Valley. The district vote for Ronald Reagan was 72% in 1984.

Committees

Interior and Insular Affairs
Small Business

Elections

1986	General	70%	Primary	50%

Dean A. Gallo   (R-N.J.)

Of Parsippany — Elected 1984

Born: Nov. 23, 1935, Hackensack, N.J.
Education: Boonton, N.J. High School
Occupation: Real estate broker.
Family: Divorced; two children.
Religion: Methodist.
Political Career: Parsippany-Troy Hills Township Council, 1968-71; Morris County Freeholder, 1971-75; N.J. Assembly, 1976-84.
Capitol Office: 1318 Longworth Bldg. 20515; 225-5034.

New Jersey 11th: North — Morris County. The district vote for Ronald Reagan was 69% in 1984.

Committees

Public Works and Transportation
Small Business

Elections

1986	General	68%	Primary	87%
1984	General	56%	Primary	u/o

CQ Voting Studies

	Presidential Support	Party Unity	Voting Participation
1986	70%	71%	98%
1985	63%	80%	99%

Interest Groups

	ADA	ACU	AFL-CIO	CCUS
1986	35%	n/a	57%	61%
1985	20%	81%	29%	68%

Robert Garcia   (D-N.Y.)

Of The Bronx — Elected 1978

Born: Jan. 9, 1933, New York, N.Y.
Education: Attended City College of New York; Community College of New York; RCA Institute, 1957.
Military Career: Army, 1950-53.
Occupation: Computer engineer.
Family: Wife, Jane Lee; two children; one stepchild.
Religion: Pentecostal.
Political Career: N.Y. Assembly, 1965-67; N.Y. Senate, 1967-78.
Capitol Office: 2338 Rayburn Bldg. 20515; 225-4361.

New York 18th: South Bronx. The district vote for Ronald Reagan was 19% in 1984; 22% in 1980.

Committees

Banking, Finance and Urban Affairs
Post Office and Civil Service

CQ Voting Studies

	Presidential Support	Party Unity	Voting Participation
1986	13%	83%	85%
1985	21%	82%	84%

Interest Groups

	ADA	ACU	AFL-CIO	CCUS
1986	95%	n/a	100%	17%
1985	95%	0%	100%	19%

Elections

1986	General	94%	Primary	u/o
1984	General	89%	Primary	u/o

Joseph M. Gaydos   (D-Pa.)

Of McKeesport — Elected 1968

Born: July 3, 1926, Braddock, Pa.
Education: Attended Duquesne U., 1945-47; U. of Notre Dame Law School, LL.B. 1951.
Military Career: Naval Reserve, 1944-46.
Occupation: Lawyer.
Family: Wife, Alice Gray; five children.
Religion: Roman Catholic.
Political Career: Pa. Senate, 1967-68.
Capitol Office: 2186 Rayburn Bldg. 20515; 225-4631.

Pennsylvania 20th: Pittsburgh Suburbs — McKeesport. The district vote for Ronald Reagan was 37% in 1984; 39% in 1980.

Committees

Education and Labor
House Administration
Standards of Official Conduct

CQ Voting Studies

	Presidential Support	Party Unity	Voting Participation
1986	33%	73%	92%
1985	28%	78%	94%

Interest Groups

	ADA	ACU	AFL-CIO	CCUS
1986	55%	n/a	100%	31%
1985	70%	15%	71%	32%

Elections

1986	General	u/o	Primary	u/o
1984	General	76%	Primary	69%

Sam Gejdenson (D-Conn.)

Of Bozrah — Elected 1980

Born: May 20, 1948, Eschwege, Germany.
Education: Mitchell Junior College, A.S. 1968;
U. of Connecticut, B.A. 1970.
Occupation: Dairy farmer.
Family: Wife, Karen Flemming; two children.
Religion: Jewish.
Political Career: Conn. House, 1975-79.
Capitol Office: 1410 Longworth Bldg. 20515; 225-2076.

Connecticut 2nd: East — New London. The district vote
for Ronald Reagan was 61% in 1984; 46% in 1980.

Committees

Foreign Affairs
House Administration
Interior and Insular Affairs
Select Hunger

Elections

1986	General	67%	Primary	u/o
1984	General	54%	Primary	u/o

CQ Voting Studies

	Presidential Support	Party Unity	Voting Participation
1986	13%	96%	99%
1985	23%	92%	96%

Interest Groups

	ADA	ACU	AFL-CIO	CCUS
1986	95%	n/a	100%	41%
1985	90%	10%	94%	23%

George W. Gekas (R-Pa.)

Of Harrisburg — Elected 1982

Born: April 14, 1930, Harrisburg, Pa.
Education: Dickinson College, B.A. 1952; Dickinson School
of Law, LL.B., J.D. 1958.
Military Career: Army, 1953-55.
Occupation: Lawyer.
Family: Wife, Evangeline Charas.
Religion: Greek Orthodox.
Political Career: Pa. House, 1967-75; Pa. Senate, 1977-83.
Capitol Office: 1519 Longworth Bldg. 20515; 225-4315.

Pennsylvania 17th: Central — Harrisburg and Williams-
port. The district vote for Ronald Reagan was 66% in 1984;
61% in 1980.

Committee

Judiciary

Elections

1986	General	74%	Primary	u/o
1984	General	73%	Primary	u/o

CQ Voting Studies

	Presidential Support	Party Unity	Voting Participation
1986	76%	83%	99%
1985	73%	85%	99%

Interest Groups

	ADA	ACU	AFL-CIO	CCUS
1986	10%	n/a	36%	83%
1985	15%	76%	29%	73%

Richard A. Gephardt   (D-Mo.)

Of St. Louis — Elected 1976

Born: Jan. 31, 1941, St. Louis, Mo.
Education: Northwestern U., B.S. 1962; U. of Michigan, J.D. 1965.
Military Career: Air National Guard, 1965-71.
Occupation: Lawyer.
Family: Wife, Jane Ann Byrnes; three children.
Religion: Baptist.
Political Career: St. Louis Board of Aldermen, 1971-76.
Capitol Office: 1436 Longworth Bldg. 20515; 225-2671.

Missouri 3rd: South St. Louis, Southeast St. Louis County and Jefferson County. The district vote for Ronald Reagan was 65% in 1984; 54% in 1980.

Committee

Ways and Means

Elections

1986	General	69%	Primary	u/o
1984	General	u/o	Primary	u/o

CQ Voting Studies

	Presidential Support	Party Unity	Voting Participation
1986	16%	69%	70%
1985	26%	84%	91%

Interest Groups

	ADA	ACU	AFL-CIO	CCUS
1986	70%	n/a	100%	18%
1985	60%	19%	88%	19%

Sam Gibbons   (D-Fla.)

Of Tampa — Elected 1962

Born: Jan. 20, 1920, Tampa, Fla.
Education: U. of Florida, 1938-41; L.L.B. 1947.
Military Career: Army, 1941-45.
Occupation: Lawyer.
Family: Wife, Martha Hanley; three children.
Religion: Presbyterian.
Political Career: Fla. House, 1953-59; Fla. Senate, 1959-63.
Capitol Office: 2204 Rayburn Bldg. 20515; 225-3376.

Florida 7th: West — Tampa. The district vote for Ronald Reagan was 63% in 1984; 51% in 1980.

Committees

Ways and Means
Joint Taxation

Elections

1986	General	u/o	Primary	u/o
1984	General	59%	Primary	u/o

CQ Voting Studies

	Presidential Support	Party Unity	Voting Participation
1986	33%	71%	92%
1985	50%	69%	91%

Interest Groups

	ADA	ACU	AFL-CIO	CCUS
1986	50%	n/a	31%	57%
1985	40%	38%	53%	50%

Benjamin A. Gilman (R-N.Y.)

Of Middletown — Elected 1972

Born: Dec. 6, 1922, Poughkeepsie, N.Y.
Education: U. of Pennsylvania Wharton School, B.S. 1946; New York Law School, LL.B. 1950.
Military Career: Army Air Corps, 1943-45.
Occupation: Lawyer.
Family: Wife, Rita Gail Kelhoffer; four children; two stepchildren.
Religion: Jewish.
Political Career: N.Y. Assembly, 1967-73.
Capitol Office: 2160 Rayburn Bldg. 20515; 225-3776.

New York 22nd: Lower Hudson Valley. The district vote for Ronald Reagan was 60% in 1984; 55% in 1980.

Committees

Foreign Affairs
Post Office and Civil Service
Select Hunger
Select Narcotics Abuse and Control   (Ranking)

Elections

1986	General	69%	Primary	u/o
1984	General	69%	Primary	u/o

CQ Voting Studies

	Presidential Support	Party Unity	Voting Participation
1986	43%	31%	98%
1985	44%	43%	96%

Interest Groups

	ADA	ACU	AFL-CIO	CCUS
1986	40%	n/a	92%	28%
1985	45%	43%	82%	27%

Newt Gingrich (R-Ga.)

Of Jonesboro — Elected 1978

Born: June 17, 1943, Harrisburg, Pa.
Education: Emory U., B.A. 1965; Tulane U., M.A. 1968, Ph.D. 1971.
Occupation: History professor.
Family: Wife, Marianne Ginther; two children.
Religion: Baptist.
Political Career: Republican nominee for U.S. House, 1974, 1976.
Capitol Office: 2438 Rayburn Bldg. 20515; 225-4501.

Georgia 6th: West Central — Atlanta Suburbs. The district vote for Ronald Reagan was 69% in 1984; 45% in 1980.

Committees

House Administration
Public Works and Transportation

Elections

1986	General	60%	Primary	u/o
1984	General	69%	Primary	u/o

CQ Voting Studies

	Presidential Support	Party Unity	Voting Participation
1986	72%	85%	92%
1985	68%	84%	92%

Interest Groups

	ADA	ACU	AFL-CIO	CCUS
1986	0%	n/a	14%	94%
1985	10%	81%	12%	95%

Dan Glickman (D-Kan.)

Of Wichita — Elected 1976

Born: Nov. 24, 1944, Wichita, Kan.
Education: U. of Michigan, B.A. 1966; George Washington U., J.D. 1969.
Occupation: Lawyer.
Family: Wife, Rhoda Yura; two children.
Religion: Jewish.
Political Career: Wichita Board of Education, 1973-76, president, 1975-76.
Capitol Office: 1212 Longworth Bldg. 20515; 225-6216.

Kansas 4th: Central — Wichita. The district vote for Ronald Reagan was 63% in 1984; 53% in 1980.

Committees

Agriculture
Judiciary
Science, Space and Technology

CQ Voting Studies

	Presidential Support	Party Unity	Voting Participation
1986	28%	76%	98%
1985	36%	76%	98%

Interest Groups

	ADA	ACU	AFL-CIO	CCUS
1986	55%	n/a	64%	50%
1985	55%	35%	59%	41%

Elections

1986	General	64%	Primary	93%
1984	General	74%	Primary	u/o

Henry B. Gonzalez (D-Texas)

Of San Antonio — Elected 1961

Born: May 3, 1916, San Antonio, Texas.
Education: Graduated from San Antonio Junior College, 1937; attended U. of Texas at Austin, 1937-39; St. Mary's U. School of Law, LL.B. 1943.
Occupation: Lawyer; business consultant; translator.
Family: Wife, Bertha Cuellar; eight children.
Religion: Roman Catholic.
Political Career: San Antonio City Council, 1953-56; San Antonio mayor pro tem, 1954; Texas Senate, 1957-61; sought Democratic nomination for governor, 1958; candidate for U.S. Senate, special election, 1961.
Capitol Office: 2413 Rayburn Bldg. 20515; 225-3236.

Texas 20th: Central San Antonio. The district vote for Ronald Reagan was 41% in 1984; 33% in 1980.

Committees

Banking, Finance and Urban Affairs
Small Business

CQ Voting Studies

	Presidential Support	Party Unity	Voting Participation
1986	17%	90%	98%
1985	21%	94%	95%

Interest Groups

	ADA	ACU	AFL-CIO	CCUS
1986	95%	n/a	93%	17%
1985	85%	0%	88%	14%

Elections

1986	General	u/o	Primary	u/o
1984	General	u/o	Primary	u/o

Bill Goodling (R-Pa.)

Of Jacobus — Elected 1974

Born: Dec. 5, 1927, Loganville, Pa.
Education: U. of Maryland, B.S. 1953; Western Maryland College, M.Ed. 1956.
Military Career: Army, 1946-48.
Occupation: Public school superintendent.
Family: Wife, Hilda Wright; two children.
Religion: Methodist.
Political Career: Dallastown School Board president, 1964-67.
Capitol Office: 2263 Rayburn Bldg. 20515; 225-5836.

Pennsylvania 19th: South Central — York. The district vote for Ronald Reagan was 69% in 1984; 61% in 1980.

Committees

Budget
Education and Labor

Elections

1986	General	73%	Primary	u/o
1984	General	76%	Primary	u/o

CQ Voting Studies

	Presidential Support	Party Unity	Voting Participation
1986	60%	69%	96%
1985	61%	74%	93%

Interest Groups

	ADA	ACU	AFL-CIO	CCUS
1986	25%	n/a	43%	88%
1985	25%	57%	18%	77%

Bart Gordon (D-Tenn.)

Of Murfreesboro — Elected 1984

Born: Jan. 24, 1949, Murfreesboro, Tenn.
Education: Middle Tennessee State U., B.S. 1971; U. of Tennessee Law School, J.D. 1973.
Occupation: Lawyer.
Family: Single.
Religion: Methodist.
Political Career: Tenn. Democratic chairman, 1981-83.
Capitol Office: 1517 Longworth Bldg. 20515; 225-4231.

Tennessee 6th: North Central — Murfreesboro. The district vote for Ronald Reagan was 59% in 1984; 43% in 1980.

Committees

Rules
Select Aging

Elections

1986	General	77%	Primary	u/o
1984	General	63%	Primary	28%

CQ Voting Studies

	Presidential Support	Party Unity	Voting Participation
1986	27%	83%	96%
1985	33%	79%	93%

Interest Groups

	ADA	ACU	AFL-CIO	CCUS
1986	75%	n/a	86%	39%
1985	55%	20%	63%	45%

Bill Gradison (R-Ohio)

Of Cincinnati — Elected 1974

Born: Dec. 28, 1928, Cincinnati, Ohio.
Education: Yale U., B.A. 1948; Harvard Business School, M.B.A. 1951; Harvard U., D.C.S. 1954.
Occupation: Investment broker.
Family: Wife, Heather Jane Stirton; eight children.
Religion: Jewish.
Political Career: Cincinnati City Council, 1961-74; mayor of Cincinnati, 1971.
Capitol Office: 2311 Rayburn Bldg. 20515; 225-3164.

Ohio 2nd: Hamilton County — Eastern Cincinnati and Suburbs.

CQ Voting Studies

	Presidential Support	Party Unity	Voting Participation
1986	61%	59%	96%
1985	65%	63%	95%

Interest Groups

	ADA	ACU	AFL-CIO	CCUS
1986	15%	n/a	7%	94%
1985	20%	60%	8%	85%

Committees

Budget
Ways and Means

Elections

1986	General	71%	Primary	u/o
1984	General	69%	Primary	u/o

Fred Grandy (R-Iowa)

Of Sioux City — Elected 1986

Born: June 29, 1948, Sioux City, Iowa.
Education: Harvard U., B.A. 1970.
Occupation: Actor.
Family: Engaged, Catherine Mann; two children.
Religion: Episcopalian.
Political Career: No previous office.
Capitol Office: 1711 Longworth Bldg. 20515; 225-5476.

Iowa 6th: Northwest — Sioux City. The district vote for Ronald Reagan was 57% in 1984; 57% in 1980.

Committees

Agriculture
Education and Labor
Select Children, Youth and Families

Elections

1986	General	51%	Primary	68%

Bill Grant (D-Fla.)

Of Madison — Elected 1986

Born: Feb. 21, 1943, Lake City, Fla.
Education: Florida State U., B.A. 1963.
Occupation: Banker.
Family: Divorced; two children.
Religion: Baptist.
Political Career: Fla. Senate, 1983-87.
Capitol Office: 1331 Longworth Bldg. 20515; 225-5235.

Florida 2nd: North — Tallahassee. The district vote for Ronald Reagan was 53% in 1984; 43% in 1980.

Committees

Government Operations
Public Works and Transportation

Elections

1986	General	u/o	Primary	51%

Kenneth J. Gray (D-Ill.)

Of West Frankfort — Elected 1984

Born: Nov. 14, 1924, West Frankfort, Ill.
Education: Attended West Frankfort High School.
Military Career: Army Air Corps, 1943-46.
Occupation: Auctioneer; car dealer.
Family: Wife, Gwendolyn June Croslin; three children.
Religion: Baptist.
Political Career: U.S. House, 1955-75.
Capitol Office: 2109 Rayburn Bldg. 20515; 225-5201.

Illinois 22nd: South — Carbondale. The district vote for Ronald Reagan was 56% in 1984; 54% in 1980.

Committees

Public Works and Transportation
Veterans' Affairs

Elections

1986	General	53%	Primary	u/o
1984	General	50%	Primary	56%

CQ Voting Studies

	Presidential Support	Party Unity	Voting Participation
1986	28%	84%	93%
1985	26%	75%	86%

Interest Groups

	ADA	ACU	AFL-CIO	CCUS
1986	65%	n/a	100%	35%
1985	55%	26%	82%	37%

William H. Gray III (D-Pa.)

Of Philadelphia — Elected 1978

Born: Aug. 20, 1941, Baton Rouge, La.

Education: Franklin and Marshall College, B.A. 1963; Drew Theological Seminary, M.Div. 1966; Princeton Theological Seminary, Th.M. 1970.

Occupation: Clergyman.

Family: Wife, Andrea Dash; three children.

Religion: Baptist.

Political Career: Sought Democratic nomination for U.S. House, 1976.

Capitol Office: 204 Cannon Bldg. 20515; 225-4001.

Pennsylvania 2nd: North and West Philadelphia. The district vote for Ronald Reagan was 10% in 1984; 9% in 1980.

Committees

Appropriations
Budget   (Chairman)
District of Columbia

CQ Voting Studies

	Presidential Support	Party Unity	Voting Participation
1986	13%	88%	90%
1985	15%	82%	86%

Interest Groups

	ADA	ACU	AFL-CIO	CCUS
1986	80%	n/a	92%	33%
1985	95%	0%	93%	15%

Elections

1986	General	u/o	Primary	97%
1984	General	91%	Primary	84%

Bill Green (R-N.Y.)

Of Manhattan — Elected 1978

Born: Oct. 16, 1929, New York, N.Y.

Education: Harvard College, B.A. 1950; Harvard Law School, J.D. 1953.

Military Career: Army, 1953-55.

Occupation: Lawyer.

Family: Wife, Patricia Freiberg; two children.

Religion: Jewish.

Political Career: N.Y. Assembly, 1965-68; sought GOP nomination to U.S. House, 1968.

Capitol Office: 1110 Longworth Bldg. 20515; 225-2436.

New York 15th: Manhattan — East Side. The district vote for Ronald Reagan was 39% in 1984; 36% in 1980.

Committee

Appropriations

CQ Voting Studies

	Presidential Support	Party Unity	Voting Participation
1986	38%	26%	99%
1985	35%	34%	96%

Interest Groups

	ADA	ACU	AFL-CIO	CCUS
1986	70%	n/a	64%	39%
1985	60%	35%	65%	57%

Elections

1986	General	58%	Primary	u/o
1984	General	56%	Primary	u/o

Judd Gregg (R-N.H.)

Of Greenfield — Elected 1980

Born: Feb. 14, 1947, Nashua, N.H.
Education: Columbia U., A.B. 1969; Boston U., J.D. 1972, LL.M. 1975.
Occupation: Lawyer.
Family: Wife, Kathleen McLellan; three children.
Religion: Protestant.
Political Career: N.H. Governor's Executive Council, 1979-81.
Capitol Office: 308 Cannon Bldg. 20515; 225-5206.

New Hampshire 2nd: West — Concord and Nashua. The district vote for Ronald Reagan was 67% in 1984; 55% in 1980.

Committee

Ways and Means

Elections

1986	General	74%	Primary	u/o
1984	General	76%	Primary	u/o

CQ Voting Studies

	Presidential Support	Party Unity	Voting Participation
1986	74%	85%	94%
1985	70%	78%	92%

Interest Groups

	ADA	ACU	AFL-CIO	CCUS
1986	20%	n/a	21%	88%
1985	10%	76%	29%	86%

Frank J. Guarini (D-N.J.)

Of Jersey City — Elected 1978

Born: Aug. 20, 1924, Jersey City, N.J.
Education: Dartmouth College, B.A. 1947; New York U. Law School, J.D. 1950, LL.M. 1955.
Military Career: Navy, 1944-46.
Occupation: Lawyer.
Family: Single.
Religion: Roman Catholic.
Political Career: N.J. Senate 1966-72; sought Democratic nomination for U.S. Senate, 1970.
Capitol Office: 2458 Rayburn Bldg. 20515; 225-2765.

New Jersey 14th: North — Jersey City. The district vote for Ronald Reagan was 53% in 1984.

Committees

Budget
Ways and Means
Select Narcotics Abuse and Control

Elections

1986	General	73%	Primary	87%
1984	General	66%	Primary	72%

CQ Voting Studies

	Presidential Support	Party Unity	Voting Participation
1986	22%	89%	97%
1985	21%	93%	95%

Interest Groups

	ADA	ACU	AFL-CIO	CCUS
1986	80%	n/a	93%	17%
1985	85%	5%	94%	20%

Steve Gunderson (R-Wis.)

Of Osseo — Elected 1980

Born: May 10, 1951, Eau Claire, Wis.
Education: U. of Wisconsin, B.A. 1973.
Occupation: Public official.
Family: Single.
Religion: Lutheran.
Political Career: Wis. House, 1975-79.
Capitol Office: 227 Cannon Bldg. 20515; 225-5506.

Wisconsin 3rd: West — Eau Claire and La Crosse. The district vote for Ronald Reagan was 55% in 1984; 48% in 1980.

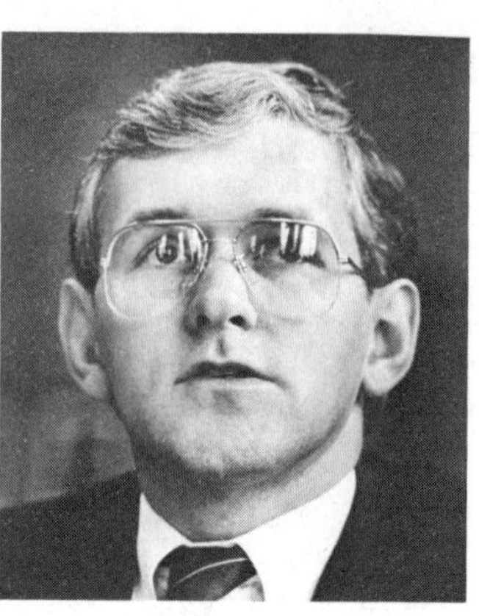

Committees

Agriculture
Education and Labor

Elections

1986	General	64%	Primary	u/o
1984	General	68%	Primary	u/o

CQ Voting Studies

	Presidential Support	Party Unity	Voting Participation
1986	52%	66%	96%
1985	50%	74%	97%

Interest Groups

	ADA	ACU	AFL-CIO	CCUS
1986	40%	n/a	67%	72%
1985	35%	43%	29%	77%

Ralph M. Hall (D-Texas)

Of Rockwall — Elected 1980

Born: May 3, 1923, Rockwall County, Texas.
Education: Attended Texas Christian U., 1943; U. of Texas, 1946-47; Southern Methodist U., LL.B. 1951.
Military Career: Navy, 1942-45.
Occupation: Lawyer; businessman.
Family: Wife, Mary Ellen Murphy; three children.
Religion: Methodist.
Political Career: Rockwall County judge, 1950-62; Texas Senate, 1963-73; sought Democratic nomination for lt. gov., 1972.
Capitol Office: 236 Cannon Bldg. 20515; 225-6673.

Texas 4th: Northeast — Tyler and Longview. The district vote for Ronald Reagan was 69% in 1984; 58% in 1980.

Committees

Energy and Commerce
Science, Space and Technology

Elections

1986	General	72%	Primary	u/o
1984	General	58%	Primary	u/o

CQ Voting Studies

	Presidential Support	Party Unity	Voting Participation
1986	56%	38%	98%
1985	58%	45%	92%

Interest Groups

	ADA	ACU	AFL-CIO	CCUS
1986	10%	n/a	33%	80%
1985	15%	70%	31%	67%

Tony P. Hall (D-Ohio)

Of Dayton — Elected 1978

Born: Jan. 16, 1942, Dayton, Ohio.
Education: Denison U., A.B. 1964.
Occupation: Real estate salesman.
Family: Wife, Janet Dick; two children.
Religion: Christian.
Political Career: Ohio House, 1969-73; Ohio Senate, 1973-79; Democratic nominee for Ohio secretary of state, 1974.
Capitol Office: 2448 Rayburn Bldg. 20515; 225-6465.

Ohio 3rd: Southwest — Dayton.

Committees

Rules
Select Hunger

Elections

1986	General	74%	Primary	92%
1984	General	u/o	Primary	u/o

CQ Voting Studies

	Presidential Support	Party Unity	Voting Participation
1986	14%	78%	92%
1985	29%	81%	94%

Interest Groups

	ADA	ACU	AFL-CIO	CCUS
1986	65%	n/a	64%	44%
1985	65%	11%	88%	41%

Lee H. Hamilton (D-Ind.)

Of Nashville — Elected 1964

Born: April 20, 1931, Daytona Beach, Fla.
Education: DePauw U., B.A. 1952; attended Goethe U., Frankfurt, West Germany, 1952-53; Indiana U., J.D. 1956.
Occupation: Lawyer.
Family: Wife, Nancy Nelson; three children.
Religion: Methodist.
Political Career: No previous office.
Capitol Office: 2187 Rayburn Bldg. 20515; 225-5315.

Indiana 9th: Southeast — Bloomington and New Albany. The district vote for Ronald Reagan was 60% in 1984; 52% in 1980.

Committees

Foreign Affairs
Science, Space and Technology
Joint Economic
Select Iran-contra   (Chairman)

Elections

1986	General	73%	Primary	92%
1984	General	65%	Primary	91%

CQ Voting Studies

	Presidential Support	Party Unity	Voting Participation
1986	33%	83%	99%
1985	38%	82%	99%

Interest Groups

	ADA	ACU	AFL-CIO	CCUS
1986	55%	n/a	57%	56%
1985	60%	33%	69%	57%

John Paul Hammerschmidt   (R-Ark.)

Of Harrison — Elected 1966

Born: May, 4, 1922, Harrison, Ark.
Education: Attended The Citadel, 1938-39; U. of Arkansas, 1940-41; Oklahoma State U., 1945-46.
Military Career: Army, 1942-45; Air Force Reserve.
Occupation: Lumber company executive.
Family: Wife, Virginia Sharp; one child.
Religion: Presbyterian.
Political Career: Ark. Republican chairman, 1964-66.
Capitol Office: 2207 Rayburn Bldg. 20515; 225-4301.

Arkansas 3rd: Northwest — Ozark Plateau and Fort Smith. The district vote for Ronald Reagan was 70% in 1984; 58% in 1980.

Committees

Public Works and Transportation   (Ranking)
Veterans' Affairs
Select Aging

CQ Voting Studies

	Presidential Support	Party Unity	Voting Participation
1986	69%	69%	98%
1985	64%	71%	98%

Interest Groups

	ADA	ACU	AFL-CIO	CCUS
1986	5%	n/a	14%	78%
1985	25%	81%	12%	77%

Elections

1986	General	81%	Primary	u/o
1984	General	u/o	Primary	u/o

James V. Hansen   (R-Utah)

Of Farmington — Elected 1980

Born: Aug. 14, 1932, Salt Lake City, Utah.
Education: U. of Utah, B.S. 1960.
Military Career: Navy, 1952-54.
Occupation: Insurance executive; land developer.
Family: Wife, Anne Burgoyne; five children.
Religion: Mormon.
Political Career: Farmington City Council, 1963-72; Utah House, 1973-81, Speaker, 1979-81.
Capitol Office: 1113 Longworth Bldg. 20515; 225-0453.

Utah 1st: Ogden and Rural Utah. The district vote for Ronald Reagan was 78% in 1984; 76% in 1980.

Committees

Armed Services
Interior and Insular Affairs
Standards of Official Conduct

CQ Voting Studies

	Presidential Support	Party Unity	Voting Participation
1986	79%	80%	88%
1985	81%	85%	94%

Interest Groups

	ADA	ACU	AFL-CIO	CCUS
1986	0%	n/a	0%	93%
1985	5%	95%	0%	86%

Elections

1986	General	52%	Primary	u/o
1984	General	71%	Primary	u/o

Claude Harris   (D-Ala.)

Of Tuscaloosa — Elected 1986

Born: June 29, 1940, Bessemer, Ala.
Education: U. of Alabama, B.S. 1962, LL.B. 1965.
Military Career: Army National Guard, 1967-present.
Occupation: Lawyer.
Family: Wife, Barbara Cork; two children.
Religion: Baptist.
Political Career: Alabama circuit judge, 6th Circuit, 1977-85.
Capitol Office: 1009 Longworth Bldg. 20515; 225-2665.

Alabama 7th: West Central — Tuscaloosa and Bessemer. The district vote for Ronald Reagan was 59% in 1984; 48% in 1980.

Committees

Agriculture
Veterans' Affairs

Elections

1986   General   59%   Primary   35%

J. Dennis Hastert   (R-Ill.)

Of Yorkville — Elected 1986

Born: Jan. 2, 1942, Aurora, Ill.
Education: Wheaton College, B.A. 1964; Northern Illinois U., M.S. 1967.
Occupation: Teacher.
Family: Wife, Jean Kahl; two children.
Religion: Protestant.
Political Career: Ill. House, 1981-87.
Capitol Office: 515 Cannon Bldg. 20515; 225-2976.

Illinois 14th: North Central — De Kalb and Elgin. The district vote for Ronald Reagan was 69% in 1984; 61% in 1980.

Committees

Government Operations
Public Works and Transportation
Select Children, Youth and Families

Elections

1986   General   52%   Primary   u/o

Charles Hatcher   (D-Ga.)

Of Newton — Elected 1980

Born: July 1, 1939, Doerun, Ga.
Education: Georgia Southern U., B.S. 1965; U. of Georgia, J.D. 1969.
Military Career: Air Force, 1958-62.
Occupation: Lawyer.
Family: Wife, Ellen Wilson; three children.
Religion: Episcopalian.
Political Career: Ga. House, 1973-81.
Capitol Office: 405 Cannon Bldg. 20515; 225-3631.

Georgia 2nd: Southwest — Albany and Valdosta. The district vote for Ronald Reagan was 58% in 1984; 42% in 1980.

Committees

Agriculture
Small Business

CQ Voting Studies

	Presidential Support	Party Unity	Voting Participation
1986	34%	67%	86%
1985	49%	73%	89%

Interest Groups

	ADA	ACU	AFL-CIO	CCUS
1986	30%	n/a	64%	69%
1985	35%	52%	44%	42%

Elections

1986	General	u/o	Primary	u/o
1984	General	u/o	Primary	u/o

Augustus F. Hawkins   (D-Calif.)

Of Los Angeles — Elected 1962

Born: Aug. 31, 1907, Shreveport, La.
Education: U.C.L.A., A.B. 1931; graduate work, U. of Southern California Institute of Government.
Occupation: Real estate salesman.
Family: Wife, Elsie Taylor.
Religion: Methodist.
Political Career: Calif. Assembly, 1935-63.
Capitol Office: 2371 Rayburn Bldg. 20515; 225-2201.

California 29th: South-Central Los Angeles, Watts and Downey. The district vote for Ronald Reagan was 22% in 1984.

Committees

Education and Labor   (Chairman)
Joint Economic

CQ Voting Studies

	Presidential Support	Party Unity	Voting Participation
1986	19%	77%	89%
1985	14%	81%	82%

Interest Groups

	ADA	ACU	AFL-CIO	CCUS
1986	85%	n/a	92%	15%
1985	85%	0%	100%	22%

Elections

1986	General	85%	Primary	93%
1984	General	87%	Primary	91%

Charles A. Hayes (D-Ill.)

Of Chicago — Elected 1983

Born: Feb. 17, 1918, Cairo, Ill.
Education: High school graduate.
Occupation: Labor official; packinghouse worker.
Family: Wife, Edna Miller; two children, two step-children.
Religion: Baptist.
Political Career: No previous office.
Capitol Office: 1028 Longworth Bldg. 20515; 225-4372.

Illinois 1st: Chicago — South Side. The district vote for Ronald Reagan was 5% in 1984; 6% in 1980.

CQ Voting Studies

	Presidential Support	Party Unity	Voting Participation
1986	13%	89%	94%
1985	15%	93%	95%

Interest Groups

	ADA	ACU	AFL-CIO	CCUS
1986	95%	n/a	100%	6%
1985	100%	0%	100%	14%

Committees

Education and Labor
Small Business

Elections

1986	General	96%	Primary	93%
1984	General	96%	Primary	83%

Jimmy Hayes (D-La.)

Of Lafayette — Elected 1986

Born: Dec. 21, 1946, Lafayette, La.
Education: U. of Southwestern Louisiana, B.S. 1967; Tulane U. School of Law, J.D. 1970.
Military Career: Louisiana Air National Guard, 1968-74.
Occupation: Lawyer; real estate developer.
Family: Wife, Leslie Owen; three children.
Religion: Methodist.
Political Career: Louisiana commissioner of financial institutions, 1984-85.
Capitol Office: 503 Cannon Bldg. 20515; 225-2031.

Louisiana 7th: Southwest — Lake Charles and Lafayette. The district vote for Ronald Reagan was 59% in 1984; 49% in 1980.

Committees

Public Works and Transportation
Science, Space and Technology

Elections

1986	General	57%	Primary	30%

Joel Hefley (R-Colo.)

Of Colorado Springs — Elected 1986

Born: April 18, 1935, Ardmore, Okla.
Education: Oklahoma Baptist U., B.A. 1957; Oklahoma State U., M.A. 1962.
Occupation: Community planner.
Family: Wife, Olivia Lynn Christian; three children.
Religion: Presbyterian.
Political Career: Colo. House, 1977-79; Colo. Senate, 1979-87.
Capitol Office: 508 Cannon Bldg. 20515; 225-4422.

Colorado 5th: South Central — Colorado Springs. The district vote for Ronald Reagan was 75% in 1984; 64% in 1980.

Committees

Science, Space and Technology
Small Business

Elections

1986	General	70%	Primary	57%

CQ Voting Studies

	Presidential Support	Party Unity	Voting Participation
1986	30%	80%	92%
1985	35%	63%	73%

Interest Groups

	ADA	ACU	AFL-CIO	CCUS
1986	50%	n/a	57%	40%
1985	25%	46%	53%	37%

W. G. "Bill" Hefner (D-N.C.)

Of Concord — Elected 1974

Born: April 11, 1930, Elora, Tenn.
Education: High school graduate.
Occupation: Broadcasting executive.
Family: Wife, Nancy Hill; two children.
Religion: Baptist.
Political Career: No previous office.
Capitol Office: 2161 Rayburn Bldg. 20515; 225-3715.

North Carolina 8th: South Central — Kannapolis and Salisbury. The district vote for Ronald Reagan was 65% in 1984; 52% in 1980.

Committee

Appropriations

Elections

1986	General	58%	Primary	u/o
1984	General	51%	Primary	84%

Paul B. Henry (R-Mich.)

Of Grand Rapids — Elected 1984

Born: July 9, 1942, Chicago, Ill.
Education: Wheaton College, B.A. 1963; Duke U., M.A. 1968, Ph. D. 1970.
Occupation: Political science professor.
Family: Wife, Karen Anne Borthistle; three children.
Religion: Christian Reformed.
Political Career: Mich. House, 1979-83; Mich. Senate, 1983-85.
Capitol Office: 215 Cannon Bldg. 20515; 225-3831.

Michigan 5th: West Central — Grand Rapids. The district vote for Ronald Reagan was 68% in 1984; 55% in 1980.

Committees

Education and Labor
Science, Space and Technology
Select Aging

Elections

1986	General	71%	Primary	u/o
1984	General	62%	Primary	63%

CQ Voting Studies

	Presidential Support	Party Unity	Voting Participation
1986	43%	67%	98%
1985	60%	69%	99%

Interest Groups

	ADA	ACU	AFL-CIO	CCUS
1986	40%	n/a	43%	89%
1985	25%	67%	24%	68%

Wally Herger (R-Calif.)

Of Rio Oso — Elected 1986

Born: May 20, 1945, Sutter County, Calif.
Education: American River Community College, A.A. 1967; attended California State U., 1968-69.
Occupation: Rancher; gas company president; state assemblyman.
Family: Wife, Pamela Sargent; eight children.
Religion: Mormon.
Political Career: Calif. Assembly, 1981-87.
Capitol Office: 1630 Longworth Bldg. 20515; 225-3076.

California 2nd: North Central — Chico and Redding. The district vote for Ronald Reagan was 63% in 1984.

Committees

Agriculture
Merchant Marine and Fisheries

Elections

1986	General	59%	Primary	72%

Dennis M. Hertel (D-Mich.)

Of Harper Woods — Elected 1980

Born: Dec. 7, 1948, Detroit, Mich.
Education: Eastern Michigan U., B.A. 1971; Wayne State U., J.D. 1974.
Occupation: Lawyer.
Family: Wife, Cynthia S. Grosscup; four children.
Religion: Roman Catholic.
Political Career: Candidate for Detroit City Council, 1973; Mich. House, 1975-81.
Capitol Office: 218 Cannon Bldg. 20515; 225-6276.

Michigan 14th: Detroit Suburbs — Warren. The district vote for Ronald Reagan was 62% in 1984; 50% in 1980.

Committees

Armed Services
Merchant Marine and Fisheries
Select Aging

Elections

1986	General	73%	Primary	96%
1984	General	59%	Primary	u/o

CQ Voting Studies

	Presidential Support	Party Unity	Voting Participation
1986	14%	90%	97%
1985	29%	88%	99%

Interest Groups

	ADA	ACU	AFL-CIO	CCUS
1986	85%	n/a	93%	19%
1985	80%	14%	88%	27%

John Hiler (R-Ind.)

Of La Porte — Elected 1980

Born: April 24, 1953, Chicago, Ill.
Education: Williams College, B.A. 1975; U. of Chicago, M.B.A. 1977.
Occupation: Foundry executive.
Family: Wife, Catherine Sands; one child.
Religion: Roman Catholic.
Political Career: Republican nominee for Ind. House, 1978.
Capitol Office: 407 Cannon Bldg. 20515; 225-3915.

Indiana 3rd: North Central — South Bend. The district vote for Ronald Reagan was 62% in 1984; 56% in 1980.

Committees

Banking, Finance and Urban Affairs
Small Business

Elections

1986	General	50%	Primary	u/o
1984	General	52%	Primary	u/o

CQ Voting Studies

	Presidential Support	Party Unity	Voting Participation
1986	78%	89%	98%
1985	80%	95%	98%

Interest Groups

	ADA	ACU	AFL-CIO	CCUS
1986	0%	n/a	0%	94%
1985	5%	90%	12%	91%

George J. Hochbrueckner (D-N.Y.)

Of Coram — Elected 1986

Born: Sept. 20, 1938, Queens, N.Y.

Education: Attended State U. of New York, 1959-60; Hofstra U., 1960-61; Pierce College, 1961-62; U. of California, Northridge, 1962-63.

Military Career: Navy, 1956-59.

Occupation: Aerospace engineer.

Family: Wife, Carol Ann Joan Seifert; four children.

Religion: Roman Catholic.

Political Career: N.Y. Assembly, 1975-85; Democratic nominee for U.S. House, 1984.

Capitol Office: 1008 Longworth Bldg. 20515; 225-3826.

New York 1st: Long Island — Eastern Suffolk County. The district vote for Ronald Reagan was 66% in 1984; 57% in 1980.

Committees

Armed Services
Merchant Marine and Fisheries

Elections

1986   General   51%   Primary   u/o

Clyde Holloway (R-La.)

Of Forest Hill — Elected 1986

Born: Nov. 28, 1943, Lecompte, La.

Education: Attended National School of Aeronautics, Kansas City, Mo., 1966.

Occupation: Nursery owner.

Family: Wife, Cathy Kohlhepp; four children.

Religion: Baptist.

Political Career: Sought Republican nomination for U.S. House, 1980, 1985.

Capitol Office: 1207 Longworth Bldg. 20515; 225-4926.

Louisiana 8th: Central — Alexandria. The district vote for Ronald Reagan was 50% in 1984; 42% in 1980.

Committees

Agriculture
Select Children, Youth and Families

Elections

1986   General   51%   Primary   23%

Larry J. Hopkins (R-Ky.)

Of Lexington — Elected 1978

Born: Oct. 25, 1933, Detroit, Mich.
Education: Attended Murray State U., 1952-54.
Military Career: Marine Corps, 1954-56.
Occupation: Stockbroker.
Family: Wife, Carolyn Pennebaker; three children.
Religion: Methodist.
Political Career: Ky. House, 1972-78; Ky. Senate, 1978-79; Republican nominee for Fayette County Commission, 1970.
Capitol Office: 2437 Rayburn Bldg. 20515; 225-4706.

Kentucky 6th: North Central — Lexington and Frankfort. The district vote for Ronald Reagan was 62% in 1984; 45% in 1980.

Committees

Agriculture
Armed Services

CQ Voting Studies

	Presidential Support	Party Unity	Voting Participation
1986	72%	82%	98%
1985	61%	71%	98%

Interest Groups

	ADA	ACU	AFL-CIO	CCUS
1986	10%	n/a	21%	94%
1985	10%	71%	24%	81%

Elections

1986	General	74%	Primary	u/o
1984	General	71%	Primary	u/o

Frank Horton (R-N.Y.)

Of Beighton — Elected 1962

Born: Dec. 12, 1919, Cuero, Texas.
Education: Louisiana State U., B.A. 1941; Cornell U., LL.B. 1947.
Military Career: Army, 1941-45.
Occupation: Lawyer.
Family: Wife, Nancy Richmond; two children.
Religion: Presbyterian.
Political Career: Rochester City Council, 1955-61.
Capitol Office: 2229 Rayburn Bldg. 20515; 225-4916.

New York 29th: West — Part of Rochester. The district vote for Ronald Reagan was 63% in 1984; 49% in 1980.

Committees

Government Operations   (Ranking)
Post Office and Civil Service

CQ Voting Studies

	Presidential Support	Party Unity	Voting Participation
1986	27%	18%	92%
1985	31%	25%	89%

Interest Groups

	ADA	ACU	AFL-CIO	CCUS
1986	75%	n/a	100%	31%
1985	50%	30%	82%	35%

Elections

1986	General	70%	Primary	u/o
1984	General	70%	Primary	62%

Amo Houghton (R-N.Y.)

Of Corning — Elected 1986

Born: Aug. 7, 1926, Corning, N.Y.
Education: Harvard U., B.A. 1950, M.B.A. 1952.
Military Career: Marine Corps, 1945-46.
Occupation: Glassworks company executive.
Family: Wife, Ruth West; four children.
Religion: Episcopalian.
Political Career: No previous office.
Capitol Office: 1217 Longworth Bldg. 20515; 225-3161.

New York 34th: Southern Tier — Jamestown and Elmira. The district vote for Ronald Reagan was 68% in 1984; 54% in 1980.

Committees

Budget
Government Operations

Elections

1986	General	59%	Primary	u/o

James J. Howard (D-N.J.)

Of Spring Lake Heights — Elected 1964

Born: July 24, 1927, Irvington, N.J.
Education: St. Bonaventure U., B.A. 1952; Rutgers U., M.Ed. 1958.
Military Career: Navy, 1944-46.
Occupation: Elementary school teacher, principal.
Family: Wife, Marlene Vetrano; three children.
Religion: Roman Catholic.
Political Career: No previous office.
Capitol Office: 2188 Rayburn Bldg. 20515; 225-4671.

New Jersey 3rd: Central Coast — Asbury Park and Long Branch. The district vote for Ronald Reagan was 67% in 1984.

Committee

Public Works and Transportation (Chairman)

Elections

1986	General	59%	Primary	95%
1984	General	53%	Primary	91%

CQ Voting Studies

	Presidential Support	Party Unity	Voting Participation
1986	21%	93%	97%
1985	21%	94%	97%

Interest Groups

	ADA	ACU	AFL-CIO	CCUS
1986	85%	n/a	100%	18%
1985	90%	0%	100%	23%

Steny H. Hoyer   (D-Md.)

Of Berkshire — Elected 1981

Born: June 14, 1939, New York, N.Y.
Education: U. of Maryland, B.S. 1963; Georgetown U., J.D. 1966.
Occupation: Lawyer.
Family: Wife, Judith Pickett; three children.
Religion: Baptist.
Political Career: Md. Senate, 1967-79, president, 1975-79; sought Democratic nomination for lt. gov., 1978.
Capitol Office: 1513 Longworth Bldg. 20515; 225-4131.

Maryland 5th: Northern Prince George's County. The district vote for Ronald Reagan was 42% in 1984; 40% in 1980.

Committee

Appropriations

CQ Voting Studies

	Presidential Support	Party Unity	Voting Participation
1986	21%	95%	98%
1985	29%	93%	98%

Interest Groups

	ADA	ACU	AFL-CIO	CCUS
1986	95%	n/a	93%	22%
1985	75%	14%	94%	32%

Elections

1986	General	82%	Primary	91%
1984	General	72%	Primary	88%

Carroll Hubbard Jr.   (D-Ky.)

Of Mayfield — Elected 1974

Born: July 7, 1937, Murray, Ky.
Education: Georgetown College, B.S. 1959; U. of Louisville, J.D. 1962.
Military Career: Ky. Air National Guard, 1962-67; Ky. Army National Guard, 1968-70.
Occupation: Lawyer.
Family: Wife, Carol Brown; two children; three stepchildren.
Religion: Baptist.
Political Career: Ky. Senate, 1968-75; sought Democratic gubernatorial nomination, 1979.
Capitol Office: 2182 Rayburn Bldg. 20515; 225-3115.

Kentucky 1st: West — Paducah. The district vote for Ronald Reagan was 54% in 1984; 44% in 1980.

Committees

Banking, Finance and Urban Affairs
Merchant Marine and Fisheries

CQ Voting Studies

	Presidential Support	Party Unity	Voting Participation
1986	52%	49%	99%
1985	59%	48%	92%

Interest Groups

	ADA	ACU	AFL-CIO	CCUS
1986	35%	n/a	86%	50%
1985	20%	63%	63%	68%

Elections

1986	General	u/o	Primary	81%
1984	General	u/o	Primary	79%

Jerry Huckaby (D-La.)

Of Ringgold — Elected 1976

Born: July 19, 1941, Hodge, La.
Education: Louisiana State U., B.S. 1963; Georgia State U.,
    M.B.A. 1968.
Occupation: Farmer; engineer.
Family: Wife, Suzanna Woodward; two children.
Religion: Methodist.
Political Career: No previous office.
Capitol Office: 2421 Rayburn Bldg. 20515; 225-2376.

Louisiana 5th: North — Monroe. The district vote for
Ronald Reagan was 66% in 1984; 56% in 1980.

Committees

Agriculture
Interior and Insular Affairs

Elections

1986	General	†	Primary	69%
1984	General	†	Primary	u/o

*† In Louisiana the primary is open to candidates of all parties. If a
candidate wins 50% or more of the vote no general election is held.*

CQ Voting Studies

	Presidential Support	Party Unity	Voting Participation
1986	41%	53%	86%
1985	49%	51%	89%

Interest Groups

	ADA	ACU	AFL-CIO	CCUS
1986	20%	n/a	31%	73%
1985	35%	57%	41%	71%

William J. Hughes (D-N.J.)

Of Ocean City — Elected 1974

Born: Oct. 17, 1932, Salem, N.J.
Education: Rutgers U., A.B. 1955, J.D. 1958.
Occupation: Lawyer.
Family: Wife, Nancy L. Gibson; four children.
Religion: Episcopalian.
Political Career: Assistant prosecutor, Cape May County,
    1960-70; Ocean City Solicitor, 1970-74; Democratic nomi-
    nee for U.S. House, 1970.
Capitol Office: 341 Cannon Bldg. 20515; 225-6572.

New Jersey 2nd: South — Atlantic City and Vineland. The
district vote for Ronald Reagan was 62% in 1984.

Committees

Judiciary
Merchant Marine and Fisheries
Select Aging
Select Narcotics Abuse and Control

Elections

1986	General	71%	Primary	95%
1984	General	63%	Primary	u/o

CQ Voting Studies

	Presidential Support	Party Unity	Voting Participation
1986	28%	78%	99%
1985	30%	76%	99%

Interest Groups

	ADA	ACU	AFL-CIO	CCUS
1986	75%	n/a	79%	22%
1985	75%	19%	82%	41%

Duncan L. Hunter (R-Calif.)

Of Coronado — Elected 1980

Born: May 31, 1948, Riverside, Calif.
Education: Attended U. of Montana, 1966-67, U. of California, Santa Barbara, 1967-68; Western State U., B.S.L. 1976, J.D. 1976.
Military Career: Army, 1969-71.
Occupation: Lawyer.
Family: Wife, Lynne Layh; two children.
Religion: Baptist.
Political Career: No previous office.
Capitol Office: 133 Cannon Bldg. 20515; 225-5672.

California 45th: Imperial Valley and Part of San Diego. The district vote for Ronald Reagan was 71% in 1984.

CQ Voting Studies

	Presidential Support	Party Unity	Voting Participation
1986	78%	85%	96%
1985	74%	75%	91%

Interest Groups

	ADA	ACU	AFL-CIO	CCUS
1986	0%	n/a	29%	100%
1985	10%	86%	19%	76%

Committees

Armed Services
Select Narcotics Abuse and Control

Elections

1986	General	78%	Primary	u/o
1984	General	75%	Primary	u/o

Earl Hutto (D-Fla.)

Of Panama City — Elected 1978

Born: May 12, 1926, Midland City, Ala.
Education: Troy State U., Ala., B.S. 1949; graduate work, Northwestern U., 1951.
Military Career: Navy, 1944-46.
Occupation: High school English teacher; sportscaster; advertising and broadcast executive.
Family: Wife, Nancy Myers; two children.
Religion: Baptist.
Political Career: Fla. House, 1973-79.
Capitol Office: 2435 Rayburn Bldg. 20515; 225-4136.

Florida 1st: Northwest — Pensacola and Panama City. The district vote for Ronald Reagan was 76% in 1984; 61% in 1980.

Committees

Armed Services
Merchant Marine and Fisheries

Elections

1986	General	65%	Primary	u/o
1984	General	u/o	Primary	u/o

CQ Voting Studies

	Presidential Support	Party Unity	Voting Participation
1986	57%	51%	96%
1985	56%	56%	97%

Interest Groups

	ADA	ACU	AFL-CIO	CCUS
1986	5%	n/a	29%	89%
1985	15%	76%	25%	86%

Henry J. Hyde (R-Ill.)

Of Bensenville — Elected 1974

Born: April 18, 1924, Chicago, Ill.
Education: Attended Duke U., 1944; Georgetown U., B.S.
1947; Loyola U., J.D. 1949.
Military Career: Navy, 1944-46.
Occupation: Lawyer.
Family: Wife, Jeanne Simpson; four children.
Religion: Roman Catholic.
Political Career: Ill. House, 1967-75, majority leader, 1971-
72; Republican nominee for U.S. House, 1962.
Capitol Office: 2104 Rayburn Bldg. 20515; 225-4561.

Illinois 6th: Far West Chicago Suburbs — Wheaton. The
district vote for Ronald Reagan was 76% in 1984; 63% in
1980.

Committees

Foreign Affairs
Judiciary
Select Intelligence   (Ranking)
Select Iran-contra

Elections

1986	General	75%	Primary	u/o
1984	General	75%	Primary	u/o

CQ Voting Studies

	Presidential Support	Party Unity	Voting Participation
1986	76%	75%	94%
1985	71%	75%	92%

Interest Groups

	ADA	ACU	AFL-CIO	CCUS
1986	5%	n/a	7%	75%
1985	15%	81%	21%	74%

James M. Inhofe (R-Okla.)

Of Tulsa — Elected 1986

Born: Nov. 11, 1934, Des Moines, Iowa.
Education: U. of Tulsa, B.A. 1959.
Military Career: Army, 1954-56.
Occupation: Real estate developer; insurance company
executive.
Family: Wife, Kay Kirkpatrick; four children.
Religion: Presbyterian.
Political Career: Okla. House, 1967-69; Okla. Senate, 1969-
77; Republican nominee for governor, 1974; Republican
nominee for U.S. House, 1976; mayor of Tulsa, 1977-85;
defeated for reelection, 1984.
Capitol Office: 1017 Longworth Bldg. 20515; 225-2211.

Oklahoma 1st: Tulsa and Parts of Osage, Creek and Washington Counties. The district vote for Ronald Reagan was
71% in 1984; 64% in 1980.

Committees

Government Operations
Public Works and Transportation

Elections

1986	General	56%	Primary	54%

Andy Ireland (R-Fla.)

Of Winter Haven — Elected 1976

Born: Aug. 23, 1930, Cincinnati, Ohio.
Education: Yale U., B.S. 1952; Louisiana State U. School of Banking, graduated 1959; attended Columbia U. School of Business, 1953-54.
Occupation: Banker.
Family: Wife, Nancy Haydock; four children.
Religion: Episcopalian.
Political Career: Winter Haven City Commission, 1966-68; Democratic nominee for Fla. Senate, 1972.
Capitol Office: 2416 Rayburn Bldg. 20515; 225-5015.

Florida 10th: Central — Lakeland, Winter Haven and Bradenton. The district vote for Ronald Reagan was 71% in 1984; 58% in 1980.

Committees

Armed Services
Small Business

Elections

1986	General	72%	Primary	u/o
1984	General	62%	Primary	u/o

CQ Voting Studies

	Presidential Support	Party Unity	Voting Participation
1986	74%	87%	92%
1985	80%	88%	94%

Interest Groups

	ADA	ACU	AFL-CIO	CCUS
1986	0%	n/a	8%	100%
1985	5%	90%	6%	82%

Andrew Jacobs Jr. (D-Ind.)

Of Indianapolis — Elected 1964

Born: Feb. 24, 1932, Indianapolis, Ind.
Education: Indiana U., B.S. 1954, LL.B. 1958.
Military Career: Marine Corps, 1950-52.
Occupation: Lawyer.
Family: Divorced.
Religion: Roman Catholic.
Political Career: Ind. House, 1959-61; Democratic nominee for U.S. House, 1962; defeated for reelection to U.S. House, 1972; re-elected, 1974.
Capitol Office: 1533 Longworth Bldg. 20515; 225-4011.

Indiana 10th: Indianapolis. The district vote for Ronald Reagan was 55% in 1984; 45% in 1980.

Committee

Ways and Means

Elections

1986	General	58%	Primary	95%
1984	General	59%	Primary	95%

CQ Voting Studies

	Presidential Support	Party Unity	Voting Participation
1986	17%	61%	98%
1985	35%	53%	95%

Interest Groups

	ADA	ACU	AFL-CIO	CCUS
1986	85%	n/a	79%	50%
1985	80%	24%	65%	59%

James M. Jefford (R-Vt.)

Of Rutland — Elected 1974

Born: May 11, 1934, Rutland, Vt.
Education: Yale U., B.S.I.A. 1956; Harvard U., LL.B. 1962.
Military Career: Navy, 1956-59; Navy Reserve, 1959-present.
Occupation: Lawyer.
Family: Wife, Elizabeth Daley; two children.
Religion: Congregationalist.
Political Career: Vt. Senate, 1967-69; Vt. attorney general, 1969-73; sought Republican gubernatorial nomination, 1972.
Capitol Office: 2431 Rayburn Bldg. 20515; 225-4115.

Vermont: At-large. The district vote for Ronald Reagan was 58% in 1984; 44% in 1980.

Committees

Agriculture
Education and Labor   (Ranking)
Select Aging

Elections

1986	General	96%	Primary	u/o
1984	General	65%	Primary	72%

CQ Voting Studies

	Presidential Support	Party Unity	Voting Participation
1986	41%	29%	98%
1985	30%	37%	91%

Interest Groups

	ADA	ACU	AFL-CIO	CCUS
1986	60%	n/a	71%	56%
1985	55%	16%	65%	59%

Ed Jenkins (D-Ga.)

Of Jasper — Elected 1976

Born: Jan. 4, 1933, Young Harris, Ga.
Education: Young Harris College, A.A. 1951; U. of Georgia, LL.B. 1959.
Military Career: Coast Guard, 1952-55.
Occupation: Lawyer.
Family: Wife, Jo Thomasson; two children.
Religion: Baptist.
Political Career: No previous office.
Capitol Office: 203 Cannon Bldg. 20515; 225-5211.

Georgia 9th: Northeast — Gainesville. The district vote for Ronald Reagan was 69% in 1984; 40% in 1980.

Committees

Budget
Ways and Means
Select Iran-contra

Elections

1986	General	u/o	Primary	88%
1984	General	67%	Primary	u/o

CQ Voting Studies

	Presidential Support	Party Unity	Voting Participation
1986	41%	65%	94%
1985	48%	69%	96%

Interest Groups

	ADA	ACU	AFL-CIO	CCUS
1986	35%	n/a	36%	53%
1985	25%	55%	47%	50%

Nancy L. Johnson   (R-Conn.)

Of New Britain — Elected 1982

Born: Jan. 5, 1935, Chicago, Ill.
Education: Attended U. of Chicago, 1951, 1953; Radcliffe College, B.A. 1957; attended U. of London, 1957-58.
Occupation: Civic leader.
Family: Husband, Theodore Johnson; three children.
Religion: Unitarian.
Political Career: Conn. Senate, 1977-83; Republican candidate for New Britain Common Council, 1975.
Capitol Office: 119 Cannon Bldg. 20515; 225-4476.

Connecticut 6th: Northwest — New Britain. The district vote for Ronald Reagan was 63% in 1984; 47% in 1980.

CQ Voting Studies

	Presidential Support	Party Unity	Voting Participation
1986	52%	38%	97%
1985	50%	45%	97%

Interest Groups

	ADA	ACU	AFL-CIO	CCUS
1986	40%	n/a	79%	72%
1985	40%	48%	47%	64%

Committees

Budget
Public Works and Transportation
Select Children, Youth and Families

Elections

1986	General	65%	Primary	u/o
1984	General	64%	Primary	u/o

Tim Johnson   (D-S.D.)

Of Vermillion — Elected 1986

Born: Dec. 28, 1946, Canton, S.D.
Education: U. of South Dakota, B.A. 1969, M.A. 1970, J.D. 1975.
Occupation: Lawyer.
Family: Wife, Barbara Brooks; three children.
Religion: Lutheran.
Political Career: S.D. House, 1979-83; S.D. Senate, 1983-87.
Capitol Office: 513 Cannon Bldg. 20515; 225-2801.

South Dakota: At-large. The district vote for Ronald Reagan was 63% in 1984; 61% in 1980.

Committees

Agriculture
Veterans' Affairs

Elections

1986	General	59%	Primary	48%

Ed Jones (D-Tenn.)

Of Yorkville — Elected 1969

Born: April 20, 1912, Yorkville, Tenn.
Education: U. of Tennessee, B.S. 1934.
Occupation: Dairy farmer; agriculture official.
Family: Wife, Llewellyn Wyatt; one child.
Religion: Presbyterian.
Political Career: No previous office.
Capitol Office: 108 Cannon Bldg. 20515; 225-4714.

Tennessee 8th: West — Jackson and Part of Shelby County. The district vote for Ronald Reagan was 57% in 1984; 47% in 1980.

Committees

Agriculture
House Administration

Elections

1986	General	81%	Primary	u/o
1984	General	u/o	Primary	u/o

CQ Voting Studies

	Presidential Support	Party Unity	Voting Participation
1986	29%	69%	88%
1985	45%	78%	95%

Interest Groups

	ADA	ACU	AFL-CIO	CCUS
1986	45%	n/a	62%	40%
1985	35%	43%	53%	35%

Walter B. Jones (D-N.C.)

Of Farmville — Elected 1966

Born: Aug. 19, 1913, Fayetteville, N.C.
Education: North Carolina State U., B.S. 1934.
Occupation: Office supply company executive.
Family: Wife, Elizabeth Fisher; two children.
Religion: Baptist.
Political Career: Mayor of Farmville, 1949-53; N.C. House, 1955-59; N.C. Senate, 1965-66; sought Democratic nomination for U.S. House, 1960.
Capitol Office: 241 Cannon Bldg. 20515; 225-3101.

North Carolina 1st: Northeast — Greenville and Kinston. The district vote for Ronald Reagan was 57% in 1984; 45% in 1980.

Committees

Agriculture
Merchant Marine and Fisheries (Chairman)

Elections

1986	General	70%	Primary	u/o
1984	General	67%	Primary	61%

CQ Voting Studies

	Presidential Support	Party Unity	Voting Participation
1986	27%	76%	87%
1985	20%	76%	85%

Interest Groups

	ADA	ACU	AFL-CIO	CCUS
1986	55%	n/a	77%	40%
1985	70%	5%	71%	25%

Jim Jontz (D-Ind.)

Of Brookston — Elected 1986

Born: Dec. 18, 1951, Indianapolis, Ind.
Education: Indiana U., B.S. 1973.
Occupation: State legislator.
Family: Single.
Religion: Methodist.
Political Career: Ind. House, 1975-85; Ind. Senate, 1985-87.
Capitol Office: 1005 Longworth Bldg. 20515; 225-5037.

Indiana 5th: North — Kokomo. The district vote for Ronald Reagan was 69% in 1984; 63% in 1980.

Committees

Agriculture
Education and Labor
Veterans' Affairs

Elections

1986	General	52%	Primary	u/o

Paul E. Kanjorski (D-Pa.)

Of Nanticoke — Elected 1984

Born: April 2, 1937, Nanticoke, Pa.
Education: Temple U., B.A. 1961; Dickinson School of Law, J.D. 1965.
Military Career: Army, 1960-61.
Occupation: Lawyer.
Family: Wife, Nancy Hickerson; one child.
Religion: Roman Catholic.
Political Career: Sought Democratic nomination for U.S. House, special election 1980, regular primary 1980.
Capitol Office: 1518 Longworth Bldg. 20515; 225-6511.

Pennsylvania 11th: Northeast — Wilkes-Barre. The district vote for Ronald Reagan was 56% in 1984; 51% in 1980.

Committees

Banking, Finance and Urban Affairs
Veterans' Affairs

Elections

1986	General	71%	Primary	94%
1984	General	59%	Primary	47%

CQ Voting Studies

	Presidential Support	Party Unity	Voting Participation
1986	22%	83%	98%
1985	33%	80%	98%

Interest Groups

	ADA	ACU	AFL-CIO	CCUS
1986	65%	n/a	93%	28%
1985	55%	19%	76%	32%

Marcy Kaptur (D-Ohio)

Of Toledo — Elected 1982

Born: June 17, 1946, Toledo, Ohio
Education: U. of Wisconsin, B.A. 1968; U. of Michigan, M.U.P. 1974; attended University of Manchester, England, 1974.
Occupation: Urban planner.
Family: Single.
Religion: Roman Catholic.
Political Career: No previous office.
Capitol Office: 1228 Longworth Bldg. 20515; 225-4146.

Ohio 9th: Northwest — Toledo.

Committees

Banking, Finance and Urban Affairs
Veterans' Affairs

CQ Voting Studies

	Presidential Support	Party Unity	Voting Participation
1986	17%	84%	88%
1985	26%	84%	94%

Interest Groups

	ADA	ACU	AFL-CIO	CCUS
1986	75%	n/a	93%	33%
1985	60%	14%	88%	41%

Elections

1986	General	77%	Primary	u/o
1984	General	55%	Primary	93%

John R. Kasich (R-Ohio)

Of Westerville — Elected 1982

Born: May 13, 1952, McKees Rocks, Pa.
Education: Ohio State U., B.A. 1974.
Occupation: Legislative aide.
Family: Divorced.
Religion: Roman Catholic.
Political Career: Ohio Senate, 1979-1983.
Capitol Office: 1133 Longworth Bldg. 20515; 225-5355.

Ohio 12th: Northeast Columbus and Suburbs.

Committee

Armed Services

CQ Voting Studies

	Presidential Support	Party Unity	Voting Participation
1986	70%	75%	98%
1985	74%	90%	97%

Interest Groups

	ADA	ACU	AFL-CIO	CCUS
1986	10%	n/a	29%	89%
1985	5%	90%	12%	86%

Elections

1986	General	73%	Primary	u/o
1984	General	70%	Primary	u/o

Robert W. Kastenmeier (D-Wis.)

Of Sun Prairie — Elected 1958

Born: Jan. 24, 1924, Beaver Dam, Wis.
Education: U. of Wisconsin, LL.B. 1952.
Military Career: Army, 1943-46.
Occupation: Lawyer.
Family: Wife, Dorothy Chambers; three children.
Religion: Unspecified.
Political Career: Democratic nominee for U.S. House, 1956.
Capitol Office: 2328 Rayburn Bldg. 20515; 225-2906.

Wisconsin 2nd: South — Madison. The district vote for Ronald Reagan was 49% in 1984; 40% in 1980.

CQ Voting Studies

	Presidential Support	Party Unity	Voting Participation
1986	16%	92%	98%
1985	16%	91%	97%

Interest Groups

	ADA	ACU	AFL-CIO	CCUS
1986	100%	n/a	86%	17%
1985	100%	5%	94%	24%

Committees

Judiciary
Select Intelligence

Elections

1986	General	56%	Primary	u/o
1984	General	64%	Primary	82%

Jack F. Kemp (R-N.Y.)

Of Hamburg — Elected 1970

Born: July 13, 1935, Los Angeles, Calif.
Education: Occidental College, B.A. 1957.
Military Career: Army Reserve, 1958-62.
Occupation: Professional football player.
Family: Wife, Joanne Main; four children.
Religion: Presbyterian.
Political Career: No previous office.
Capitol Office: 2252 Rayburn Bldg. 20515; 225-5265.

New York 31st: West — Buffalo Suburbs and Canandaigua. The district vote for Ronald Reagan was 62% in 1984; 50% in 1980.

CQ Voting Studies

	Presidential Support	Party Unity	Voting Participation
1986	69%	52%	81%
1985	79%	71%	88%

Interest Groups

	ADA	ACU	AFL-CIO	CCUS
1986	15%	n/a	31%	58%
1985	10%	81%	12%	79%

Committees

Appropriations
Select Children, Youth and Families

Elections

1986	General	57%	Primary	u/o
1984	General	75%	Primary	u/o

Joseph P. Kennedy II   (D-Mass.)

Of Boston — Elected 1986

Born: Sept. 24, 1952, Brighton, Mass.
Education: U. of Mass., B.A. 1976.
Occupation: Energy company executive.
Family: Wife, Sheila Rauch; two children.
Religion: Roman Catholic.
Political Career: No previous office.
Capitol Office: 1631 Longworth Bldg. 20515; 225-5111.

Massachusetts 8th: Boston and Suburbs — Cambridge. The district vote for Ronald Reagan was 37% in 1984; 32% in 1980.

Committees

Banking, Finance and Urban Affairs
Veterans' Affairs
Select Aging

Elections

1986	General	73%	Primary	51%

Barbara B. Kennelly   (D-Conn.)

Of Hartford — Elected 1982

Born: July 10, 1936, Hartford, Conn.
Education: Trinity College (Washington, D.C.), B.A. 1958;
  Trinity College (Hartford, Conn.), M.A. 1971;
  Harvard-Radcliffe Business Administration Program, 1959
Occupation: Public official.
Family: Husband, James J. Kennelly; four children.
Religion: Roman Catholic.
Political Career: Hartford Court of Common Council, 1975-
  79; Conn. secretary of state, 1979-82.
Capitol Office: 1230 Longworth Bldg. 20515; 225-2265.

Connecticut 1st: Central — Hartford. The district vote for Ronald Reagan was 53% in 1984; 39% in 1980.

Committees

Ways and Means
Select Intelligence

Elections

1986	General	74%	Primary	u/o
1984	General	62%	Primary	u/o

CQ Voting Studies

	Presidential Support	Party Unity	Voting Participation
1986	20%	91%	96%
1985	23%	91%	97%

Interest Groups

	ADA	ACU	AFL-CIO	CCUS
1986	85%	n/a	93%	35%
1985	90%	10%	94%	27%

Dale E. Kildee (D-Mich.)

Of Flint — Elected 1976

Born: Sept. 16, 1929, Flint, Mich.
Education: Sacred Heart Seminary, B.A. 1952; U. of Detroit, teaching certificate, 1954; U. of Michigan, M.A. 1961.
Occupation: Latin teacher.
Family: Wife, Gayle Heyn; three children.
Religion: Roman Catholic.
Political Career: Mich. House, 1965-75; Mich. Senate, 1975-77.
Capitol Office: 2262 Rayburn Bldg. 20515; 225-3611.

Michigan 7th: East Central — Flint. The district vote for Ronald Reagan was 54% in 1984; 45% in 1980.

Committees

Education and Labor
Interior and Insular Affairs

Elections

1986	General	80%	Primary	94%
1984	General	93%	Primary	u/o

CQ Voting Studies

	Presidential Support	Party Unity	Voting Participation
1986	13%	97%	99%
1985	18%	94%	97%

Interest Groups

	ADA	ACU	AFL-CIO	CCUS
1986	95%	n/a	100%	17%
1985	85%	5%	100%	25%

Gerald D. Kleczka (D-Wis.)

Of Milwaukee — Elected 1984

Born: Nov. 26, 1943, Milwaukee, Wis.
Education: Attended U. of Wisconsin, 1961-62, 1967, 1970.
Military Career: Wis. Air National Guard, 1963-69.
Occupation: Accountant.
Family: Wife, Bonnie Scott.
Religion: Roman Catholic.
Political Career: Wis. Assembly 1969-73; Wis. Senate 1975-84.
Capitol Office: 226 Cannon Bldg. 20515; 225-4572.

Wisconsin 4th: Southern Milwaukee and Suburbs — Waukesha. The district vote for Ronald Reagan was 47% in 1984; 44% in 1980.

Committees

Banking, Finance and Urban Affairs
Government Operations

Elections

1986	General	u/o	Primary	u/o
1984	General	67%	Primary	u/o

CQ Voting Studies

	Presidential Support	Party Unity	Voting Participation
1986	24%	85%	95%
1985	28%	87%	94%

Interest Groups

	ADA	ACU	AFL-CIO	CCUS
1986	75%	n/a	86%	25%
1985	75%	14%	82%	23%

Jim Kolbe (R-Ariz.)

Of Tucson — Elected 1984

Born: June 28, 1942, Evanston, Ill.
Education: Northwestern U., B.A. 1965; Stanford U., M.B.A. 1967.
Military Career: Navy, 1967-69.
Occupation: Real estate consultant.
Family: Wife, Sarah Dinham; one child.
Religion: Methodist.
Political Career: Arizona Senate, 1977-83; Republican nominee for U.S. House in 1982.
Capitol Office: 1222 Longworth Bldg. 20515; 225-2542.

Arizona 5th: Southeast. The district vote for Ronald Reagan was 62% in 1984; 55% in 1980.

Committee

Appropriations

Elections

1986	General	65%	Primary	u/o
1984	General	51%	Primary	u/o

CQ Voting Studies

	Presidential Support	Party Unity	Voting Participation
1986	69%	84%	96%
1985	78%	86%	97%

Interest Groups

	ADA	ACU	AFL-CIO	CCUS
1986	20%	n/a	7%	88%
1985	0%	76%	6%	95%

Joe Kolter (D-Pa.)

Of Beaver Falls — Elected 1982

Born: Sept. 3, 1926, McDonald, Ohio.
Education: Geneva College, B.S. and B.A. 1950.
Military Career: Air Force, 1945-46.
Occupation: Accountant.
Family: Wife, Dorothy Gray; four children.
Religion: Roman Catholic.
Political Career: New Brighton City Council, 1962-66; Pa. House, 1968-83; sought Democratic nomination for U.S. House, 1974.
Capitol Office: 212 Cannon Bldg. 20515; 225-2565.

Pennsylvania 4th: West — New Castle. The district vote for Ronald Reagan was 48% in 1984; 48% in 1980.

Committees

Government Operations
Public Works and Transportation

Elections

1986	General	61%	Primary	81%
1984	General	57%	Primary	82%

CQ Voting Studies

	Presidential Support	Party Unity	Voting Participation
1986	26%	83%	97%
1985	28%	80%	92%

Interest Groups

	ADA	ACU	AFL-CIO	CCUS
1986	70%	n/a	100%	33%
1985	65%	10%	69%	23%

Ernie Konnyu (R-Calif.)

Of Saratoga — Elected 1986

Born: May 17,1937, Tamasi, Hungary.
Education: Ohio State U., B.S. 1965.
Occupation: Auditor.
Family: Wife, Lillian Muenks; four children.
Religion: Roman Catholic.
Political Career: Calif. Assembly, 1981-87; Republican nominee for U.S. House, 1976.
Capitol Office: 511 Cannon Bldg. 20515; 225-5411.

California 12th: Parts of San Mateo and Santa Clara Counties. The district vote for Ronald Reagan was 57% in 1984.

Committees

Government Operations
Science, Space and Technology

Elections

1986   General   61%   Primary   53%

CQ Voting Studies

	Presidential Support	Party Unity	Voting Participation
1986	17%	87%	97%
1985	29%	90%	98%

Interest Groups

	ADA	ACU	AFL-CIO	CCUS
1986	90%	n/a	100%	39%
1985	90%	19%	76%	36%

Peter H. Kostmayer (D-Pa.)

Of New Hope — Elected 1976

Born: Sept. 27, 1946, New York, N.Y.
Education: Columbia U., B.A. 1971.
Occupation: Public relations consultant.
Family: Wife, Pamela Rosenberg; two stepchildren.
Religion: Episcopalian.
Political Career: U.S. House, 1977-81.
Capitol Office: 123 Cannon Bldg. 20515; 225-4276.

Pennsylvania 8th: Northern Philadelphia Suburbs and Bucks County. The district vote for Ronald Reagan was 64% in 1984; 56% in 1980.

Committees

Foreign Affairs
Interior and Insular Affairs
Select Hunger

Elections

1986   General   55%   Primary   91%
1984   General   51%   Primary   u/o

Jon Kyl (R-Ariz.)

Of Phoenix — Elected 1986

Born: April 25, 1942, Oakland, Neb.
Education: U. of Arizona, B.A. 1964, LL.B. 1966.
Occupation: Lawyer.
Family: Wife, Caryll Collins; two children.
Religion: Presbyterian.
Political Career: No previous office.
Capitol Office: 313 Cannon Bldg. 20515; 225-3361.

Arizona 4th: Northeast — Northern Phoenix and Scotts-
dale. The district vote for Ronald Reagan was 71% in 1984;
67% in 1980.

Committees

Armed Services
Government Operations

Elections

1986	General	65%	Primary	59%

John J. LaFalce (D-N.Y.)

Of Buffalo — Elected 1974

Born: Oct. 6, 1939, Buffalo, N.Y.
Education: Canisius College, B.S. 1961; Villanova U., J.D.
1964.
Military Career: Army, 1965-67.
Occupation: Lawyer, law lecturer.
Family: Wife, Patricia Fisher; one child.
Religion: Roman Catholic.
Political Career: N.Y. Senate, 1971-73; N.Y. Assembly,
1973-75.
Capitol Office: 2367 Rayburn Bldg. 20515; 225-3231.

New York 32nd: West — Niagara Falls and Part of Rochester. The district vote for Ronald Reagan was 55% in 1984;
45% in 1980.

Committees

Banking, Finance and Urban Affairs
Small Business (Chairman)

Elections

1986	General	91%	Primary	92%
1984	General	69%	Primary	95%

CQ Voting Studies

	Presidential Support	Party Unity	Voting Participation
1986	19%	80%	93%
1985	30%	77%	92%

Interest Groups

	ADA	ACU	AFL-CIO	CCUS
1986	85%	n/a	83%	25%
1985	70%	14%	94%	38%

Robert J. Lagomarsino   (R-Calif.)

Of Ventura — Elected 1974

Born: Sept. 4, 1926, Ventura, Calif.
Education: U. of California, Santa Barbara, B.A. 1950; U. of Santa Clara, LL.B. 1953.
Military Career: Navy, 1944-46.
Occupation: Lawyer.
Family: Wife, Norma Smith; three children.
Religion: Roman Catholic.
Political Career: Ojai City Council, 1958; Mayor of Ojai, 1958-61; Calif. Senate, 1961-74.
Capitol Office: 2332 Rayburn Bldg. 20515; 225-3601.

California 19th: South Central Coast — Santa Barbara. The district vote for Ronald Reagan was 62% in 1984.

CQ Voting Studies

	Presidential Support	Party Unity	Voting Participation
1986	80%	92%	99%
1985	80%	94%	99%

Interest Groups

	ADA	ACU	AFL-CIO	CCUS
1986	5%	n/a	7%	89%
1985	5%	90%	6%	82%

Committees

Foreign Affairs
Interior and Insular Affairs

Elections

1986	General	73%	Primary	u/o
1984	General	67%	Primary	u/o

Martin H. Lancaster   (D-N.C.)

Of Goldsboro — Elected 1986

Born: March 24, 1943, Wayne County, N.C.
Education: U. of North Carolina, B.A. 1965; U. of North Carolina School of Law, J.D. 1967.
Military Career: Navy, 1967-70.
Occupation: Lawyer.
Family: Wife, Alice Matheny; two children.
Religion: Presbyterian.
Political Career: N.C. House, 1979-87.
Capitol Office: 1632 Longworth Bldg. 20515; 225-3415.

North Carolina 3rd: Southeast Central — Goldsboro. The district vote for Ronald Reagan was 61% in 1984; 47% in 1980.

Committees

Public Works and Transportation
Small Business

Elections

1986	General	64%	Primary	44%

Tom Lantos (D-Calif.)

Of San Mateo — Elected 1980

Born: Feb. 1, 1928, Budapest, Hungary.
Education: U. of Washington, B.A. 1949, M.A. 1950; U. of California, Berkeley, Ph.D. 1953.
Occupation: Professor of economics.
Family: Wife, Annette Tilleman; two children.
Religion: Jewish.
Political Career: Millbrae Board of Education, 1958-66.
Capitol Office: 1707 Longworth Bldg. 20515; 225-3531.

California 11th: Most of San Mateo County. The district vote for Ronald Reagan was 50% in 1984.

CQ Voting Studies

	Presidential Support	Party Unity	Voting Participation
1986	23%	89%	94%
1985	19%	88%	93%

Interest Groups

	ADA	ACU	AFL-CIO	CCUS
1986	70%	n/a	100%	31%
1985	70%	5%	94%	22%

Committees

Foreign Affairs
Government Operations
Select Aging

Elections

1986	General	74%	Primary	u/o
1984	General	70%	Primary	89%

Delbert L. Latta (R-Ohio)

Of Bowling Green — Elected 1958

Born: March 5, 1920, Weston, Ohio.
Education: Attended Findlay College, 1938-40; Ohio Northern U., LL.B. 1943; B.A. 1950.
Military Career: Ohio National Guard (federalized), 1938-41; Marine Corps Reserve, 1942-43.
Occupation: Lawyer.
Family: Wife, Rose Mary Kiene; two children.
Religion: Church of Christ.
Political Career: Ohio Senate, 1953-59.
Capitol Office: 2309 Rayburn Bldg. 20515; 225-6405.

Ohio 5th: Northwest — Bowling Green and Sandusky.

CQ Voting Studies

	Presidential Support	Party Unity	Voting Participation
1986	63%	71%	84%
1985	85%	88%	95%

Interest Groups

	ADA	ACU	AFL-CIO	CCUS
1986	5%	n/a	27%	86%
1985	5%	90%	6%	86%

Committees

Budget (Ranking)
Rules

Elections

1986	General	64%	Primary	85%
1984	General	63%	Primary	u/o

Jim Leach (R-Iowa)

Of Davenport — Elected 1976

Born: Oct. 15, 1942, Davenport, Iowa.
Education: Princeton U., B.A. 1964; Johns Hopkins U., M.A. 1966; graduate work, London School of Economics, 1966-68.
Occupation: Foreign service officer; propane gas company executive.
Family: Wife, Elisabeth Ann "Deba" Foxley; one child.
Religion: Episcopalian.
Political Career: Republican nominee for U.S. House, 1974.
Capitol Office: 1514 Longworth Bldg. 20515; 225-6576.

Iowa 1st: Southeast — Davenport. The district vote for Ronald Reagan was 52% in 1984; 50% in 1980.

Committees

Banking, Finance and Urban Affairs
Foreign Affairs

CQ Voting Studies

	Presidential Support	Party Unity	Voting Participation
1986	47%	58%	98%
1985	34%	53%	95%

Interest Groups

	ADA	ACU	AFL-CIO	CCUS
1986	55%	n/a	21%	61%
1985	60%	33%	53%	50%

Elections

1986	General	66%	Primary	u/o
1984	General	67%	Primary	u/o

Marvin Leath (D-Texas)

Of Waco — Elected 1978

Born: May 6, 1931, Henderson, Texas.
Education: Attended Kilgore Jr. College, 1949-50; U. of Texas, B.B.A. 1954.
Military Career: Army, 1954-56.
Occupation: Banker.
Family: Wife, Alta Ruth Neill; one child.
Religion: Presbyterian.
Political Career: No previous office.
Capitol Office: 336 Cannon Bldg. 20515; 225-6105.

Texas 11th: Central — Waco. The district vote for Ronald Reagan was 66% in 1984; 53% in 1980.

Committees

Armed Services
Budget

CQ Voting Studies

	Presidential Support	Party Unity	Voting Participation
1986	53%	55%	90%
1985	52%	46%	95%

Interest Groups

	ADA	ACU	AFL-CIO	CCUS
1986	45%	n/a	50%	50%
1985	10%	76%	18%	77%

Elections

1986	General	u/o	Primary	u/o
1984	General	u/o	Primary	u/o

Richard H. Lehman   (D-Calif.)

Of Fresno — Elected 1982

Born: July 20, 1948, Sanger, Calif.
Education: Attended Fresno City College, 1967-68; California State U. (Fresno), 1969; California State U. (Santa Cruz), 1970.
Military Career: Army National Guard, 1970-76.
Occupation: Legislative aide.
Family: Wife, Patricia Ann Kandarian.
Religion: Lutheran.
Political Career: Calif. Assembly, 1977-83.
Capitol Office: 1319 Longworth Bldg. 20515; 225-4540.

California 18th: Central Valley and Fresno. The district vote for Ronald Reagan was 51% in 1984.

Committees

Banking, Finance and Urban Affairs
Interior and Insular Affairs

Elections

1986	General	71%	Primary	u/o
1984	General	67%	Primary	u/o

CQ Voting Studies

	Presidential Support	Party Unity	Voting Participation
1986	20%	87%	91%
1985	16%	83%	86%

Interest Groups

	ADA	ACU	AFL-CIO	CCUS
1986	75%	n/a	100%	25%
1985	80%	0%	88%	15%

William Lehman   (D-Fla.)

Of Miami — Elected 1972

Born: Oct. 5, 1913, Selma, Ala.
Education: U. of Alabama, B.S. 1934.
Occupation: Automobile dealer; high school English teacher.
Family: Wife, Joan Feibelman; two children.
Religion: Jewish.
Political Career: Dade County School Board, 1966-72, chairman, 1971-72.
Capitol Office: 2347 Rayburn Bldg. 20515; 225-4211.

Florida 17th: Southeast — North Miami and Part of Hialeah. The district vote for Ronald Reagan was 46% in 1984; 41% in 1980.

Committees

Appropriations
Select Children, Youth and Families

Elections

1986	General	u/o	Primary	u/o
1984	General	u/o	Primary	u/o

CQ Voting Studies

	Presidential Support	Party Unity	Voting Participation
1986	20%	92%	96%
1985	23%	95%	96%

Interest Groups

	ADA	ACU	AFL-CIO	CCUS
1986	100%	n/a	83%	20%
1985	95%	5%	100%	24%

Mickey Leland (D-Texas)

Of Houston — Elected 1978

Born: Nov. 27, 1944, Lubbock, Texas.
Education: Texas Southern U., B.S. 1970.
Occupation: Pharmacist.
Family: Alison Walton; one child.
Religion: Roman Catholic.
Political Career: Texas House, 1973-79.
Capitol Office: 2236 Rayburn Bldg. 20515; 225-3816.

Texas 18th: Central Houston. The district vote for Ronald Reagan was 26% in 1984; 28% in 1980.

Committees

Energy and Commerce
Post Office and Civil Service
Select Hunger   (Chairman)

Elections

1986	General	u/o	Primary	91%
1984	General	79%	Primary	91%

CQ Voting Studies

	Presidential Support	Party Unity	Voting Participation
1986	9%	88%	89%
1985	20%	90%	94%

Interest Groups

	ADA	ACU	AFL-CIO	CCUS
1986	100%	n/a	93%	12%
1985	100%	0%	94%	10%

Norman F. Lent (R-N.Y.)

Of East Rockaway — Elected 1970

Born: March 23, 1931, Oceanside, N.Y.
Education: Hofstra U., B.A. 1952; Cornell U., J.D. 1957.
Military Career: Naval Reserve, 1952-54.
Occupation: Lawyer.
Family: Wife, Barbara Morris; three children.
Religion: Methodist.
Political Career: N.Y. Senate, 1963-71.
Capitol Office: 2408 Rayburn Bldg. 20515; 225-7896.

New York 4th: Long Island — Southeastern Nassau County. The district vote for Ronald Reagan was 64% in 1984; 57% in 1980.

Committees

Energy and Commerce   (Ranking)
Merchant Marine and Fisheries

Elections

1986	General	65%	Primary	u/o
1984	General	69%	Primary	u/o

CQ Voting Studies

	Presidential Support	Party Unity	Voting Participation
1986	61%	65%	93%
1985	65%	72%	96%

Interest Groups

	ADA	ACU	AFL-CIO	CCUS
1986	20%	n/a	46%	64%
1985	10%	75%	31%	57%

Sander M. Levin (D-Mich.)

Of Southfield — Elected 1982

Born: Sept. 6, 1931, Detroit, Mich.
Education: U. of Chicago, B.A. 1952; Columbia U., M.A. 1954; Harvard U., LL.B. 1957.
Occupation: Lawyer.
Family: Wife, Victoria Schlafer; four children.
Religion: Jewish.
Political Career: Mich. Senate, 1965-1971; Democratic nominee for governor, 1970, 1974.
Capitol Office: 323 Cannon Bldg. 20515; 225-4961.

Michigan 17th: Northwest Detroit and Southeast Oakland County. The district vote for Ronald Reagan was 54% in 1984; 43% in 1980.

Committees

Ways and Means
Select Children, Youth and Families

Elections

1986	General	77%	Primary	94%
1984	General	u/o	Primary	u/o

CQ Voting Studies

	Presidential Support	Party Unity	Voting Participation
1986	19%	97%	99%
1985	23%	97%	99%

Interest Groups

	ADA	ACU	AFL-CIO	CCUS
1986	85%	n/a	100%	33%
1985	85%	10%	88%	32%

Mel Levine (D-Calif.)

Of Pacific Palisades — Elected 1982

Born: June 7, 1943, Los Angeles, Calif.
Education: U. of California, Berkeley, A.B. 1964; Princeton U., M.P.A. 1966; Harvard U., J.D. 1969.
Occupation: Lawyer.
Family: Wife, Jan Greenberg; three children.
Religion: Jewish.
Political Career: Calif. Assembly, 1977-83.
Capitol Office: 132 Cannon Bldg. 20515; 225-6451.

California 27th: Pacific Coast — Santa Monica. The district vote for Ronald Reagan was 52% in 1984.

Committees

Foreign Affairs
Interior and Insular Affairs
Select Narcotics Abuse and Control

Elections

1986	General	65%	Primary	u/o
1984	General	55%	Primary	89%

CQ Voting Studies

	Presidential Support	Party Unity	Voting Participation
1986	16%	92%	96%
1985	24%	94%	97%

Interest Groups

	ADA	ACU	AFL-CIO	CCUS
1986	85%	n/a	75%	15%
1985	100%	10%	94%	27%

Jerry Lewis (R-Calif.)

Of Redlands — Elected 1978

Born: Oct. 21, 1934, Seattle, Wash.
Education: U.C.L.A., B.A. 1956.
Occupation: Insurance executive.
Family: Wife, Arlene Willis; four children, three stepchildren.
Religion: Presbyterian.
Political Career: San Bernardino School Board, 1965-68; Calif. Assembly, 1969-79; GOP nominee for Calif. Senate, 1973.
Capitol Office: 326 Cannon Bldg. 20515; 225-5861.

California 35th: San Bernardino County. The district vote for Ronald Reagan was 71% in 1984.

CQ Voting Studies

	Presidential Support	Party Unity	Voting Participation
1986	63%	63%	80%
1985	65%	75%	91%

Interest Groups

	ADA	ACU	AFL-CIO	CCUS
1986	0%	n/a	15%	64%
1985	10%	76%	27%	62%

Committee

Appropriations

Elections

1986	General	77%	Primary	u/o
1984	General	85%	Primary	u/o

John Lewis (D-Ga.)

Of Atlanta — Elected 1986

Born: Feb. 21, 1940, Troy, Ala.
Education: American Baptist Theological Seminary, B.A. 1961; Fisk U., B.A. 1963.
Occupation: Civil rights activist; associate director, AC-TION.
Family: Wife, Lillian Miles; one child.
Religion: Baptist.
Political Career: Atlanta City Council, 1982-86; sought Democratic nomination for U.S. House, 1977.
Capitol Office: 501 Cannon Bldg. 20515; 225-3801.

Georgia 5th: Atlanta. The district vote for Ronald Reagan was 33% in 1984; 35% in 1980.

Committees

Interior and Insular Affairs
Public Works and Transportation

Elections

1986	General	75%	Primary	35%

Tom Lewis (R-Fla.)

Of North Palm Beach — Elected 1982

Born: Oct. 26, 1924, Philadelphia, Pa.
Education: Attended Palm Beach Junior College, 1956-57; U. of Florida, 1958-59.
Military Career: Air Force, 1943-54.
Occupation: Real estate broker; aircraft testing specialist.
Family: Wife, Marian Vastine; three children.
Religion: Methodist.
Political Career: Mayor and councilman, North Palm Beach, 1964-71; Fla. House, 1972-80; Fla. Senate, 1980-82.
Capitol Office: 1216 Longworth Bldg. 20515; 225-5792.

Florida 12th: South Central — West Palm Beach and Parts of Palm Beach. The district vote for Ronald Reagan was 67% in 1984; 61% in 1980.

Committees

Agriculture
Science, Space and Technology

Elections

1986	General	u/o	Primary	u/o
1984	General	u/o	Primary	u/o

CQ Voting Studies

	Presidential Support	Party Unity	Voting Participation
1986	71%	82%	96%
1985	66%	85%	97%

Interest Groups

	ADA	ACU	AFL-CIO	CCUS
1986	15%	n/a	21%	76%
1985	5%	81%	6%	86%

Jim Lightfoot (R-Iowa)

Of Shenandoah — Elected 1984

Born: Sept. 27, 1939, Sioux City, Iowa.
Education: Attended Univ. of Iowa, Univ. of Tulsa.
Military Career: Army, 1955-56; Army Reserve, 1956-63.
Occupation: Radio broadcaster, store owner.
Family: Wife, Nancy Harrison; four children.
Religion: Roman Catholic.
Political Career: Corsicana, Texas, City Commission, 1974-76.
Capitol Office: 1609 Longworth Bldg. 20515; 225-3806.

Iowa 5th: Southwest — Council Bluffs and Fort Dodge. The district vote for Ronald Reagan was 58% in 1984; 58% in 1980.

Committees

Government Operations
Public Works and Transportation
Select Aging

Elections

1986	General	59%	Primary	u/o
1984	General	51%	Primary	58%

CQ Voting Studies

	Presidential Support	Party Unity	Voting Participation
1986	70%	83%	99%
1985	63%	85%	99%

Interest Groups

	ADA	ACU	AFL-CIO	CCUS
1986	10%	n/a	14%	94%
1985	10%	81%	24%	82%

William O. Lipinski   (D-Ill.)

Of Chicago — Elected 1982

Born: Dec. 22, 1937, Chicago, Ill.
Education: Attended Loras College, 1957-58.
Military Career: Army Reserve, 1961-67.
Occupation: Parks supervisor.
Family: Wife, Rose Lapinski; two children.
Religion: Roman Catholic.
Political Career: Chicago city alderman, 1975-83.
Capitol Office: 1032 Longworth Bldg. 20515; 225-5701.

Illinois 5th: South Central Chicago and Suburbs. The district vote for Ronald Reagan was 58% in 1984; 42% in 1980.

CQ Voting Studies

	Presidential Support	Party Unity	Voting Participation
1986	42%	74%	93%
1985	36%	78%	90%

Interest Groups

	ADA	ACU	AFL-CIO	CCUS
1986	45%	n/a	92%	27%
1985	55%	33%	100%	14%

Committees

Merchant Marine and Fisheries
Public Works and Transportation

Elections

1986	General	70%	Primary	u/o
1984	General	64%	Primary	83%

Bob Livingston   (R-La.)

Of Metairie — Elected 1977

Born: April 30, 1943, Colorado Springs, Colo.
Education: Tulane U., B.A. 1967, J.D. 1968.
Military Career: Navy, 1961-63.
Occupation: Lawyer.
Family: Wife, Bonnie Robichaux; four children.
Religion: Episcopalian.
Political Career: Republican nominee for U.S. House, 1976.
Capitol Office: 2412 Rayburn Bldg. 20515; 225-3015.

Louisiana 1st: Southeast — Jefferson Parish. The district vote for Ronald Reagan was 77% in 1984.

Committees

Appropriations
Select Intelligence

Elections

1986	General	†	Primary	u/o
1984	General	†	Primary	88%

† In Louisiana the primary is open to candidates of all parties. If a candidate wins 50% or more of the vote no general election is held.

CQ Voting Studies

	Presidential Support	Party Unity	Voting Participation
1986	76%	71%	92%
1985	74%	81%	95%

Interest Groups

	ADA	ACU	AFL-CIO	CCUS
1986	0%	n/a	21%	78%
1985	0%	86%	12%	86%

Marilyn Lloyd   (D-Tenn.)

Of Chattanooga — Elected 1974

Born: Jan. 3, 1929, Fort Smith, Ark.
Education: Attended Shorter College, 1958-60 and 1962-63.
Occupation: Radio station owner and manager.
Family: Widowed; four children.
Religion: Church of Christ.
Political Career: No previous office.
Capitol Office: 2266 Rayburn Bldg. 20515; 225-3271.

Tennessee 3rd: Southeast — Chattanooga and Oak Ridge. The district vote for Ronald Reagan was 63% in 1984; 56% in 1980.

Committees

Armed Services
Science, Space and Technology
Select Aging

CQ Voting Studies

	Presidential Support	Party Unity	Voting Participation
1986	53%	39%	95%
1985	52%	56%	95%

Interest Groups

	ADA	ACU	AFL-CIO	CCUS
1986	20%	n/a	50%	53%
1985	35%	48%	75%	45%

Elections

1986	General	54%	Primary	u/o
1984	General	52%	Primary	87%

Trent Lott   (R-Miss.)

Of Pascagoula — Elected 1972

Born: Oct. 9, 1941, Grenada, Miss.
Education: U. of Mississippi, B.P.A., 1963, J.D. 1967.
Occupation: Lawyer.
Family: Wife, Patricia Elizabeth Thompson; two children.
Religion: Baptist.
Political Career: No previous office.
Capitol Office: 2185 Rayburn Bldg. 20515; 225-5772.

Mississippi 5th: Southeast — Gulf Coast and Hattiesburg. The district vote for Ronald Reagan was 73% in 1984.

Committees

Minority Whip
Rules

CQ Voting Studies

	Presidential Support	Party Unity	Voting Participation
1986	78%	79%	93%
1985	73%	82%	93%

Interest Groups

	ADA	ACU	AFL-CIO	CCUS
1986	5%	n/a	23%	86%
1985	0%	90%	12%	95%

Elections

1986	General	82%	Primary	u/o
1984	General	85%	Primary	u/o

Bill Lowery   (R-Calif.)

Of San Diego — Elected 1980

Born: May 2, 1947, San Diego, Calif.
Education: Attended San Diego State U., 1965-69.
Occupation: Public relations executive.
Family: Wife, Kathleen Brown; three children.
Religion: Roman Catholic.
Political Career: San Diego City Council, 1977-80; San Diego deputy mayor, 1979-80.
Capitol Office: 225 Cannon Bldg. 20515; 225-3201.

California 41st: North San Diego and Suburbs. The district vote for Ronald Reagan was 64% in 1984.

CQ Voting Studies

	Presidential Support	Party Unity	Voting Participation
1986	76%	68%	92%
1985	71%	74%	91%

Interest Groups

	ADA	ACU	AFL-CIO	CCUS
1986	5%	n/a	8%	75%
1985	5%	81%	6%	86%

Committee

Appropriations

Elections

1986	General	69%	Primary	u/o
1984	General	63%	Primary	u/o

Mike Lowry   (D-Wash.)

Of Renton — Elected 1978

Born: March 8, 1939, St. John, Wash.
Education: Washington State U., B.A. 1962.
Occupation: Public official.
Family: Wife, Mary Carlson; one child.
Religion: Baptist.
Political Career: King County Council, 1975-78; candidate for King County executive, 1973; Democratic nominee, U.S. Senate, 1983 special election.
Capitol Office: 2454 Rayburn Bldg. 20515; 225-3106.

Washington 7th: Seattle and Suburbs. The district vote for Ronald Reagan was 39% in 1984.

CQ Voting Studies

	Presidential Support	Party Unity	Voting Participation
1986	17%	88%	99%
1985	18%	91%	97%

Interest Groups

	ADA	ACU	AFL-CIO	CCUS
1986	95%	n/a	71%	6%
1985	100%	10%	88%	27%

Committees

Budget
Merchant Marine and Fisheries

Elections

1986	General	73%	Primary	72%
1984	General	70%	Primary	92%

Manuel Lujan Jr. (R-N.M.)

Of Albuquerque — Elected 1968

Born: May 12, 1928, San Ildefonso, N.M.
Education: Attended St. Mary's College, 1946-47; College of Santa Fe, B.A. 1950.
Occupation: Insurance broker.
Family: Wife, Jean Kay Couchman; four children.
Religion: Roman Catholic.
Political Career: Republican nominee for N.M. Senate, 1964.
Capitol Office: 1323 Longworth Bldg. 20515; 225-6316.

New Mexico 1st: Central — Albuquerque. The district vote for Ronald Reagan was 60% in 1984; 54% in 1980.

Committees

Interior and Insular Affairs
Science, Space and Technology   (Ranking)

Elections

1986	General	71%	Primary	u/o
1984	General	65%	Primary	u/o

CQ Voting Studies

	Presidential Support	Party Unity	Voting Participation
1986	57%	60%	82%
1985	71%	73%	97%

Interest Groups

	ADA	ACU	AFL-CIO	CCUS
1986	5%	n/a	18%	80%
1985	15%	67%	24%	77%

Thomas A. Luken (D-Ohio)

Of Cincinnati — Elected 1976

Born: July 9, 1925, Cincinnati, Ohio.
Education: Attended Bowling Green State U., 1943-44; Xavier U., A.B. 1947; Chase Law School, LL.B. 1950.
Military Career: Marine Corps, 1943-45.
Occupation: Lawyer.
Family: Wife, Shirley Ast; eight children.
Religion: Roman Catholic.
Political Career: Cincinnati City Council, 1965-67, 1969-71, 1973; mayor of Cincinnati, 1971-72; elected to U.S. House in special election, March 1974; defeated for re-election, 1974; re-elected to U.S. House, 1976.
Capitol Office: 2368 Rayburn Bldg. 20515; 225-2216.

Ohio 1st: Hamilton County — Western Cincinnati and Suburbs.

Committees

Energy and Commerce
Small Business
Select Aging

Elections

1986	General	62%	Primary	88%
1984	General	55%	Primary	88%

CQ Voting Studies

	Presidential Support	Party Unity	Voting Participation
1986	21%	84%	93%
1985	33%	74%	90%

Interest Groups

	ADA	ACU	AFL-CIO	CCUS
1986	80%	n/a	86%	25%
1985	65%	32%	71%	41%

Donald E. "Buz" Lukens   (R-Ohio)

Of Middletown — Elected 1986

Born: Feb. 11, 1931, Warren County, Ohio.
Education: Ohio State U., B.A. 1954; attended U. of Maryland, 1955-56.
Military Career: Air Force, 1954-60; Air Force Reserve, 1971-83.
Occupation: Business consultant.
Family: Divorced.
Religion: Protestant.
Political Career: U.S. House, 1967-71; Ohio Senate, 1971-87; sought GOP gubernatorial nomination, 1970; GOP nominee for state auditor, 1978.
Capitol Office: 117 Cannon Bldg. 20515; 225-6205.

Ohio 8th: Southwest — Middletown and Hamilton.

Committees

Foreign Affairs
Government Operations

Elections

1986	General	68%	Primary	u/o

Dan Lungren   (R-Calif.)

Of Long Beach — Elected 1978

Born: Sept. 22, 1946, Long Beach, Calif.
Education: U. of Notre Dame, B.A. 1968; Georgetown U., J.D. 1971.
Occupation: Lawyer.
Family: Wife, Barbara Kolls; three children.
Religion: Roman Catholic.
Political Career: Republican nominee for U.S. House, 1976.
Capitol Office: 2440 Rayburn Bldg. 20515; 225-2415.

California 42nd: Coastal Los Angeles and Orange Counties. The district vote for Ronald Reagan was 72% in 1984.

Committees

Judiciary
Select Intelligence

Elections

1986	General	75%	Primary	u/o
1984	General	73%	Primary	u/o

CQ Voting Studies

	Presidential Support	Party Unity	Voting Participation
1986	86%	87%	96%
1985	80%	87%	96%

Interest Groups

	ADA	ACU	AFL-CIO	CCUS
1986	0%	n/a	7%	100%
1985	5%	90%	6%	90%

Connie Mack (R-Fla.)

Of Cape Coral — Elected 1982

Born: Oct. 29, 1940, Philadelphia, Pa.
Education: Univ. of Florida, B.S. 1966.
Occupation: Banker.
Family: Wife, Priscilla Hobbs; two children.
Religion: Roman Catholic.
Political Career: No previous office.
Capitol Office: 228 Cannon Bldg. 20515; 225-2536.

Florida 13th: Southwest — Sarasota and Fort Myers. The district vote for Ronald Reagan was 74% in 1984; 67% in 1980.

Committees

Budget
Foreign Affairs

Elections

1986	General	75%	Primary	u/o
1984	General	u/o	Primary	u/o

CQ Voting Studies

	Presidential Support	Party Unity	Voting Participation
1986	86%	94%	98%
1985	85%	91%	99%

Interest Groups

	ADA	ACU	AFL-CIO	CCUS
1986	0%	n/a	7%	100%
1985	10%	95%	18%	86%

Buddy MacKay (D-Fla.)

Of Ocala — Elected 1982

Born: March 22, 1933, Ocala, Fla.
Education: Attended Davidson College, 1950-51; U. of Florida, B.S. 1954, LL.B. 1961.
Military Career: Air Force, 1954-58.
Occupation: Lawyer; citrus grower.
Family: Wife, Anne Selph; four children.
Religion: Presbyterian.
Political Career: Fla. House, 1969-75; Fla. Senate, 1975-81; sought Democratic nomination for U.S. Senate, 1980.
Capitol Office: 330 Cannon Bldg. 20515; 225-5744.

Florida 6th: North Central — Gainesville and Ocala. The district vote for Ronald Reagan was 65% in 1984; 53% in 1980.

Committees

Budget
Science, Space and Technology
Special Aging

Elections

1986	General	69%	Primary	86%
1984	General	99%	Primary	u/o

CQ Voting Studies

	Presidential Support	Party Unity	Voting Participation
1986	29%	72%	91%
1985	40%	76%	94%

Interest Groups

	ADA	ACU	AFL-CIO	CCUS
1986	55%	n/a	43%	61%
1985	50%	38%	53%	62%

Edward R. Madigan   (R-Ill.)

Of Lincoln — Elected 1972

Born: Jan. 13, 1936, Lincoln, Ill.
Education: Lincoln College, A.A. 1956.
Occupation: Automobile leasing executive.
Family: Wife, Evelyn M. George; three children.
Religion: Roman Catholic.
Political Career: Ill. House, 1967-73.
Capitol Office: 2312 Rayburn Bldg. 20515; 225-2371.

Illinois 15th: Central — Bloomington and Kankakee. The district vote for Ronald Reagan was 68% in 1984; 64% in 1980.

Committees

Agriculture   (Ranking)
Energy and Commerce

Elections

1986	General	u/o	Primary	u/o
1984	General	73%	Primary	u/o

CQ Voting Studies

	Presidential Support	Party Unity	Voting Participation
1986	67%	70%	90%
1985	60%	71%	92%

Interest Groups

	ADA	ACU	AFL-CIO	CCUS
1986	0%	n/a	25%	79%
1985	30%	71%	29%	71%

Thomas J. Manton   (D-N.Y.)

Of Queens — Elected 1984

Born: Nov. 3, 1932, New York, N.Y.
Education: St. John's U., B.B.A. 1958; St. John's U. Law School, LL.B. 1962.
Military Career: Marine Corps, 1951-53.
Occupation: Lawyer.
Family: Wife, Diane Mason Schley; four children.
Religion: Roman Catholic.
Political Career: New York City councilman, 1970-84; sought Democratic nomination for U.S. House, 1972, 1978.
Capitol Office: 327 Cannon Bldg. 20515; 225-3965.

New York 9th: Western Queens — Astoria and Jackson Heights. The district vote for Ronald Reagan was 57% in 1984; 53% in 1980.

Committees

Banking, Finance and Urban Affairs
Merchant Marine and Fisheries
Select Aging

Elections

1986	General	69%	Primary	u/o
1984	General	53%	Primary	30%

CQ Voting Studies

	Presidential Support	Party Unity	Voting Participation
1986	18%	88%	92%
1985	23%	88%	94%

Interest Groups

	ADA	ACU	AFL-CIO	CCUS
1986	75%	n/a	100%	29%
1985	70%	10%	81%	27%

Edward J. Markey   (D-Mass.)

Of Malden — Elected 1976

Born: July 11, 1946, Malden, Mass.
Education: Boston College, B.A. 1968, J.D. 1972.
Military Career: Army Reserve, 1968-73.
Occupation: Lawyer.
Family: Single.
Religion: Roman Catholic.
Political Career: Mass. House, 1973-77.
Capitol Office: 2133 Rayburn Bldg. 20515; 225-2836.

Massachusetts 7th: Northern Suburbs — Medford and Malden. The district vote for Ronald Reagan was 50% in 1984; 42% in 1980.

Committees

Energy and Commerce
Interior and Insular Affairs

Elections

1986	General	u/o	Primary	u/o
1984	General	71%	Primary	54%

CQ Voting Studies

	Presidential Support	Party Unity	Voting Participation
1986	11%	86%	90%
1985	23%	90%	95%

Interest Groups

	ADA	ACU	AFL-CIO	CCUS
1986	95%	n/a	85%	13%
1985	100%	10%	100%	29%

Ron Marlenee   (R-Mont.)

Of Scobey — Elected 1976

Born: Aug. 8, 1935, Scobey, Mont.
Education: Attended U. of Montana, 1953, 1960; Montana State U., 1960.
Occupation: Rancher.
Family: Wife, Cynthia Tiemann; three children.
Religion: Lutheran.
Political Career: No previous office.
Capitol Office: 2465 Rayburn Bldg. 20515; 225-1555.

Montana 2nd: East. The district vote for Ronald Reagan was 63% in 1984; 59% in 1980.

Committees

Agriculture
Interior and Insular Affairs

Elections

1986	General	53%	Primary	u/o
1984	General	66%	Primary	u/o

CQ Voting Studies

	Presidential Support	Party Unity	Voting Participation
1986	74%	80%	91%
1985	61%	71%	88%

Interest Groups

	ADA	ACU	AFL-CIO	CCUS
1986	0%	n/a	7%	82%
1985	10%	95%	18%	71%

David O' B. Martin   (R-N.Y.)

Of Canton — Elected 1980

Born: April 26, 1944, Ogdensburg, N.Y.
Education: U. of Notre Dame, B.B.A. 1966; Albany Law
  School, J.D. 1973.
Military Career: Marine Corps, 1966-70.
Occupation: Lawyer.
Family: Wife, DeeAnn Hedlund; three children.
Religion: Roman Catholic.
Political Career: St. Lawrence County Legislature, 1974-77;
  N.Y. Assembly, 1977-81.
Capitol Office: 442 Cannon Bldg. 20515; 225-4611.

New York 26th: North — Plattsburgh and Watertown. The
district vote for Ronald Reagan was 67% in 1984; 49% in
1980.

Committee

Armed Services

CQ Voting Studies

	Presidential Support	Party Unity	Voting Participation
1986	53%	56%	89%
1985	59%	66%	91%

Interest Groups

	ADA	ACU	AFL-CIO	CCUS
1986	15%	n/a	42%	79%
1985	15%	71%	47%	71%

Elections

1986	General	u/o	Primary	u/o
1984	General	71%	Primary	u/o

Lynn Martin   (R-Ill.)

Of Loves Park — Elected 1980

Born: Dec. 26, 1939, Chicago, Ill.
Education: U. of Illinois, B.A. 1960.
Occupation: English teacher.
Family: Husband, Harry D. Leinenweber; two children, five
  step children.
Religion: Roman Catholic.
Political Career: Winnebago County Board, 1972-76; Ill.
  House, 1977-79; Ill. Senate, 1979-81.
Capitol Office: 1208 Longworth Bldg. 20515; 225-5676.

Illinois 16th: Northwest — Rockford. The district vote for
Ronald Reagan was 63% in 1984; 55% in 1980.

Committee

Armed Services

CQ Voting Studies

	Presidential Support	Party Unity	Voting Participation
1986	74%	81%	98%
1985	61%	84%	95%

Interest Groups

	ADA	ACU	AFL-CIO	CCUS
1986	15%	n/a	38%	94%
1985	20%	67%	18%	81%

Elections

1986	General	67%	Primary	u/o
1984	General	58%	Primary	82%

Matthew G. Martinez (D-Calif.)

Of Monterey Park — Elected 1982

Born: Feb. 14, 1929, Walsenburg, Colo.
Education: Graduated from Los Angeles Trade-Technical College, 1959.
Military Career: Marine Corps, 1947-1950.
Occupation: Upholstery company owner.
Family: Divorced; five children.
Religion: Roman Catholic.
Political Career: Monterey Park City Council, 1974-80, mayor, 1974-75; Calif. Assembly, 1981-82.
Capitol Office: 109 Cannon Bldg. 20515; 225-5464.

California 30th: San Gabriel Valley — El Monte and Alhambra. The district vote for Ronald Reagan was 55% in 1984.

CQ Voting Studies

	Presidential Support	Party Unity	Voting Participation
1986	18%	82%	89%
1985	19%	88%	91%

Interest Groups

	ADA	ACU	AFL-CIO	CCUS
1986	85%	n/a	100%	7%
1985	80%	5%	100%	19%

Committees

Education and Labor
Government Operations
Select Children, Youth and Families

Elections

1986	General	64%	Primary	81%
1984	General	52%	Primary	75%

Robert T. Matsui (D-Calif.)

Of Sacramento — Elected 1978

Born: Sept. 17, 1941, Sacramento, Calif.
Education: U. of California, Berkeley, A.B. 1963; Hastings College of Law, J.D. 1966.
Occupation: Lawyer.
Family: Wife, Doris Okada; one child.
Religion: Methodist.
Political Career: Sacramento City Council, 1971-78.
Capitol Office: 2419 Rayburn Bldg. 20515; 225-7163.

California 3rd: Most of Sacramento and Eastern Suburbs. The district vote for Ronald Reagan was 55% in 1984.

CQ Voting Studies

	Presidential Support	Party Unity	Voting Participation
1986	20%	94%	97%
1985	20%	94%	96%

Interest Groups

	ADA	ACU	AFL-CIO	CCUS
1986	95%	n/a	79%	17%
1985	90%	5%	94%	18%

Committees

Ways and Means
Select Narcotics Abuse and Control

Elections

1986	General	76%	Primary	u/o
1984	General	100%	Primary	92%

Nicholas Mavroules (D-Mass.)

Of Peabody — Elected 1978

Born: Nov. 1, 1929, Peabody, Mass.
Education: Graduated from Peabody High School, 1947.
Occupation: Personnel supervisor.
Family: Wife, Mary Silva; three children.
Religion: Greek Orthodox.
Political Career: Peabody City Council, 1958-61 and 1964-65; mayor of Peabody, 1968-79; candidate for Peabody City Council, 1955; candidate for mayor of Peabody, 1961.
Capitol Office: 2432 Rayburn Bldg. 20515; 225-8020.

Massachusetts 6th: North Shore — Lynn and Peabody. The district vote for Ronald Reagan was 55% in 1984; 44% in 1980.

Committees

Armed Services
Small Business

CQ Voting Studies

	Presidential Support	Party Unity	Voting Participation
1986	19%	87%	92%
1985	20%	87%	94%

Interest Groups

	ADA	ACU	AFL-CIO	CCUS
1986	85%	n/a	93%	24%
1985	85%	10%	94%	27%

Elections

1986	General	u/o	Primary	u/o
1984	General	70%	Primary	u/o

Romano L. Mazzoli (D-Ky.)

Of Louisville — Elected 1970

Born: Nov. 2, 1932, Louisville, Ky.
Education: Notre Dame U., B.S. 1954; U. of Louisville, J.D. 1960.
Military Career: Army, 1954-56.
Occupation: Lawyer; law professor.
Family: Wife, Helen Dillon; two children.
Religion: Roman Catholic.
Political Career: Ky. Senate, 1968-70; sought Democratic nomination for mayor of Louisville, 1969.
Capitol Office: 2246 Rayburn Bldg. 20515; 225-5401.

Kentucky 3rd: Louisville and Suburbs. The district vote for Ronald Reagan was 52% in 1984; 43% in 1980.

Committees

District of Columbia
Judiciary
Small Business

CQ Voting Studies

	Presidential Support	Party Unity	Voting Participation
1986	40%	78%	98%
1985	48%	74%	97%

Interest Groups

	ADA	ACU	AFL-CIO	CCUS
1986	50%	n/a	64%	24%
1985	55%	33%	47%	50%

Elections

1986	General	74%	Primary	u/o
1984	General	68%	Primary	88%

Al McCandless (R-Calif.)

Of Bermuda Dunes — Elected 1982

Born: July 23, 1927, Brawley, Calif.
Education: U. of California at Los Angeles, B.A. 1951.
Military Career: Marines, 1945-46, 1950-52.
Occupation: Automobile dealer.
Family: Wife, Gail Wamsley Glass; five children.
Religion: Protestant.
Political Career: Riverside County Supervisor, 1970-1982; candidate for Calif. Assembly, 1975.
Capitol Office: 435 Cannon Bldg. 20515; 225-5330.

California 37th: Riverside County. The district vote for Ronald Reagan was 65% in 1984.

Committees

Banking, Finance and Urban Affairs
Government Operations

Elections

1986	General	64%	Primary	85%
1984	General	64%	Primary	82%

CQ Voting Studies

	Presidential Support	Party Unity	Voting Participation
1986	77%	84%	94%
1985	74%	89%	94%

Interest Groups

	ADA	ACU	AFL-CIO	CCUS
1986	5%	n/a	7%	94%
1985	5%	86%	0%	91%

Frank McCloskey (D-Ind.)

Of Bloomington — Elected 1982

Born: June 12, 1939, Philadelphia, Pa.
Education: Indiana U., A.B. 1968, J.D. 1971.
Military Career: Air Force, 1957-1961.
Occupation: Lawyer; journalist.
Family: Wife, Roberta Ann Barker; two children.
Religion: Roman Catholic.
Political career: Democratic nominee for Ind. House, 1970; mayor of Bloomington, 1972-1983.
Capitol Office: 127 Cannon Bldg. 20515; 225-4636.

Indiana 8th: Southwest — Evansville. The district vote for Ronald Reagan was 61% in 1984; 54% in 1980.

Committees

Armed Services
Post Office and Civil Service

Elections

1986	General	53%	Primary	89%
1984	General	50%	Primary	88%

CQ Voting Studies

	Presidential Support	Party Unity	Voting Participation
1986	24%	84%	97%
1985	29%	89%	99%

Interest Groups

	ADA	ACU	AFL-CIO	CCUS
1986	55%	n/a	86%	50%
1985	68%	28%	76%	30%

Bill McCollum (R-Fla.)

Of Altamonte Springs — Elected 1980

Born: July 12, 1944, Brooksville, Fla.
Education: U. of Florida, B.A. 1965, J.D. 1968.
Military Career: Navy, 1969-72; Naval Reserve, 1972 to present.
Occupation: Lawyer.
Family: Wife, Ingrid Seebohm; three children.
Religion: Episcopalian.
Political Career: Chairman, Seminole County Republican Executive Committee, 1976-80.
Capitol Office: 1507 Longworth Bldg. 20515; 225-2176.

Florida 5th: North Central — Orlando and Northern Suburbs. The district vote for Ronald Reagan was 71% in 1984; 62% in 1980.

Committees

Banking, Finance and Urban Affairs
Judiciary
Select Iran-contra

Elections

1986	General	u/o	Primary	u/o
1984	General	u/o	Primary	u/o

CQ Voting Studies

	Presidential Support	Party Unity	Voting Participation
1986	84%	81%	97%
1985	80%	82%	96%

Interest Groups

	ADA	ACU	AFL-CIO	CCUS
1986	0%	n/a	7%	82%
1985	5%	90%	6%	90%

Dave McCurdy (D-Okla.)

Of Norman — Elected 1980

Born: March 30, 1950, Canadian, Texas.
Education: U. of Oklahoma, B.A. 1972, J.D. 1975.
Military Career: Air Force Reserve, 1969-72.
Occupation: Lawyer.
Family: Wife, Pamela Plumb; three children.
Religion: Lutheran.
Political Career: Okla. asst. state attorney general, 1975-77.
Capitol Office: 409 Cannon Bldg. 20515; 225-6165.

Oklahoma 4th: Southwest — Part of Oklahoma City. The district vote for Ronald Reagan was 69% in 1984; 59% in 1980.

Committees

Armed Services
Science, Space and Technology
Select Intelligence

Elections

1986	General	76%	Primary	81%
1984	General	64%	Primary	u/o

CQ Voting Studies

	Presidential Support	Party Unity	Voting Participation
1986	31%	70%	92%
1985	44%	68%	95%

Interest Groups

	ADA	ACU	AFL-CIO	CCUS
1986	35%	n/a	42%	80%
1985	30%	52%	35%	64%

Joseph M. McDade (R-Pa.)

Of Scranton — Elected 1962

Born: Sept. 29, 1931, Scranton, Pa.
Education: U. of Notre Dame, B.A. 1953; U. of Pennsylvania, LL.B. 1956.
Occupation: Lawyer.
Family: Wife, Mary Teresa O'Brien; four children.
Religion: Roman Catholic.
Political Career: No previous office.
Capitol Office: 2370 Rayburn Bldg. 20515; 225-3731.

Pennsylvania 10th: Northeast — Scranton. The district vote for Ronald Reagan was 61% in 1984; 54% in 1980.

Committees

Appropriations
Small Business   (Ranking)

Elections

1986	General	75%	Primary	u/o
1984	General	77%	Primary	u/o

CQ Voting Studies

	Presidential Support	Party Unity	Voting Participation
1986	49%	31%	88%
1985	59%	44%	91%

Interest Groups

	ADA	ACU	AFL-CIO	CCUS
1986	45%	n/a	93%	35%
1985	20%	57%	75%	38%

Bob McEwen (R-Ohio)

Of Hillsboro — Elected 1980

Born: Jan. 12, 1950, Hillsboro, Ohio.
Education: U. of Miami (Fla.), B.B.A. 1972; graduate work, Ohio State U. College of Law, 1973-74.
Occupation: Real estate developer.
Family: Wife, Elizabeth Boebinger; four children.
Religion: Protestant.
Political Career: Ohio House, 1975-81.
Capitol Office: 329 Cannon Bldg. 20515; 225-5705.

Ohio 6th: South Central — Portsmouth and Chillicothe.

Committees

Public Works and Transportation
Veterans' Affairs
Select Intelligence

Elections

1986	General	72%	Primary	u/o
1984	General	74%	Primary	u/o

CQ Voting Studies

	Presidential Support	Party Unity	Voting Participation
1986	67%	63%	88%
1985	69%	79%	93%

Interest Groups

	ADA	ACU	AFL-CIO	CCUS
1986	5%	n/a	31%	79%
1985	15%	85%	6%	79%

Raymond J. McGrath (R-N.Y.)

Of Valley Stream — Elected 1980

Born: March 27, 1942, Valley Stream, N.Y.
Education: State U. of New York, Brockport, B.S. 1963; New York U., M.A. 1968.
Occupation: Physical education teacher; public official.
Family: Separated; one child.
Religion: Roman Catholic.
Political Career: New York Assembly, 1977-81.
Capitol Office: 205 Cannon Bldg. 20515; 225-5516.

New York 5th: Long Island — Southwestern Nassau County. The district vote for Ronald Reagan was 60% in 1984; 55% in 1980.

Committee

Ways and Means

CQ Voting Studies

	Presidential Support	Party Unity	Voting Participation
1986	60%	61%	91%
1985	64%	62%	89%

Interest Groups

	ADA	ACU	AFL-CIO	CCUS
1986	20%	n/a	43%	69%
1985	20%	71%	41%	52%

Elections

1986	General	65%	Primary	u/o
1984	General	62%	Primary	u/o

Matthew F. McHugh (D-N.Y.)

Of Ithaca — Elected 1974

Born: Dec. 6, 1938, Philadelphia, Pa.
Education: Mount St. Mary's College, B.S. 1960; Villanova U., J.D. 1963.
Occupation: Lawyer.
Family: Wife, Eileen Alanna Higgins; three children.
Religion: Roman Catholic.
Political Career: Tompkins County District Attorney, 1969-72.
Capitol Office: 2335 Rayburn Bldg. 20515; 225-6335.

New York 28th: Southern Tier — Binghamton and Ithaca. The district vote for Ronald Reagan was 61% in 1984; 49% in 1980.

Committees

Appropriations
Select Children, Youth and Families
Select Intelligence

CQ Voting Studies

	Presidential Support	Party Unity	Voting Participation
1986	23%	91%	98%
1985	25%	92%	96%

Interest Groups

	ADA	ACU	AFL-CIO	CCUS
1986	80%	n/a	71%	17%
1985	85%	10%	94%	18%

Elections

1986	General	67%	Primary	u/o
1984	General	57%	Primary	u/o

Stewart B. McKinney   (R-Conn.)

Of Westport — Elected 1970

Born: Jan. 30, 1931, Pittsburgh, Pa.
Education: Attended Princeton U., 1949-51;
  Yale U., B.A. 1958.
Military Career: Air Force, 1951-55.
Occupation: Tire retailer.
Family: Wife, Lucie Cunningham; five children.
Religion: Episcopalian.
Political Career: Conn. House, 1967-71.
Capitol Office: 237 Cannon Bldg. 20515; 225-5541.

Connecticut 4th: Southwest — Stamford and Bridgeport.
The district vote for Ronald Reagan was 63% in 1984; 54% in
1980.

Committees

Banking, Finance and Urban Affairs
District of Columbia   (Ranking)
Small Business
Select Narcotics Abuse and Control

Elections

| 1986 | General | 53% | Primary | u/o |
| 1984 | General | 70% | Primary | u/o |

CQ Voting Studies

	Presidential Support	Party Unity	Voting Participation
1986	31%	19%	92%
1985	28%	29%	77%

Interest Groups

	ADA	ACU	AFL-CIO	CCUS
1986	85%	n/a	92%	47%
1985	55%	13%	80%	57%

J. Alex McMillan   (R-N.C.)

Of Charlotte — Elected 1984

Born: May 9, 1932, Charlotte, N.C.
Education: U. of North Carolina, B.A. 1954; U. of Virginia,
  M.B.A. 1958.
Military Career: Army, 1954-56.
Occupation: Food store executive.
Family: Wife, Caroline Houston; two children.
Religion: Presbyterian.
Political Career: Mecklenburg County Commission, 1972-
74.
Capitol Office: 401 Cannon Bldg. 20515; 225-1976.

North Carolina 9th: West Central — Charlotte. The district
vote for Ronald Reagan was 65% in 1984; 49% in 1980.

Committees

Banking, Finance and Urban Affairs
Small Business
Joint Economic

Elections

| 1986 | General | 51% | Primary | u/o |
| 1984 | General | 50% | Primary | 58% |

CQ Voting Studies

	Presidential Support	Party Unity	Voting Participation
1986	66%	69%	97%
1985	79%	81%	98%

Interest Groups

	ADA	ACU	AFL-CIO	CCUS
1986	10%	n/a	36%	100%
1985	5%	81%	6%	91%

Tom McMillen   (D-Md.)

Of Crofton — Elected 1986

Born: May 26, 1952, Elmira, N.Y.
Education: U. of Maryland, B.S. 1974; Oxford U., M.A. 1978.
Occupation: Professional basketball player; electronic equipment distributor.
Family: Single.
Religion: Roman Catholic.
Political Career: No previous office.
Capitol Office: 1508 Longworth Bldg. 20515; 225-8090.

Maryland 4th: Anne Arundel and Southern Prince George's Counties. The district vote for Ronald Reagan was 59% in 1984; 50% in 1980.

Committees

Banking, Finance and Urban Affairs
Science, Space and Technology

Elections

1986	General	50%	Primary	66%

Jan Meyers   (R-Kan.)

Of Overland Park — Elected 1984

Born: July 20, 1928, Lincoln, Neb.
Education: William Woods College, A.F.A. 1948; U. of Nebraska, B.A. 1951.
Occupation: Homemaker.
Family: Husband, Louis "Dutch" Meyers; two children.
Religion: Methodist.
Political Career: Overland Park City Council, 1967-72; Kansas Senate, 1973-85; sought Republican U.S. Senate nomination, 1978.
Capitol Office: 315 Cannon Bldg. 20515; 225-2865.

Kansas 3rd: East — Kansas City. The district vote for Ronald Reagan was 63% in 1984; 55% in 1980.

Committees

Foreign Affairs
Small Business
Select Aging

CQ Voting Studies

	Presidential Support	Party Unity	Voting Participation
1986	59%	73%	99%
1985	68%	68%	96%

Interest Groups

	ADA	ACU	AFL-CIO	CCUS
1986	25%	n/a	14%	78%
1985	15%	71%	19%	86%

Elections

1986	General	u/o	Primary	u/o
1984	General	55%	Primary	35%

Kweisi Mfume (D-Md.)

Of Baltimore — Elected 1986

Born: Oct. 24, 1948, Baltimore, Md.
Education: Morgan State College, B.S. 1976; Johns Hopkins U., M.A. 1984.
Occupation: Radio station program director and talk show host.
Family: Divorced; five children.
Religion: Baptist.
Political Career: Baltimore City Council, 1979-87.
Capitol Office: 1107 Longworth Bldg., 20515; 225-4741.

Maryland 7th: Baltimore — West and Central. The district vote for Ronald Reagan was 18% in 1984; 17% in 1980.

Committees

Banking, Finance and Urban Affairs
Small Business
Select Hunger

Elections

1986	General	87%	Primary	44%

CQ Voting Studies

	Presidential Support	Party Unity	Voting Participation
1986	26%	82%	94%
1985	41%	78%	95%

Interest Groups

	ADA	ACU	AFL-CIO	CCUS
1986	55%	n/a	64%	47%
1985	45%	48%	59%	48%

Daniel A. Mica (D-Fla.)

Of West Palm Beach — Elected 1978

Born: Feb. 4, 1944, Binghamton, N.Y.
Education: Attended U. of Florida, 1961; Miami Dade Jr. College, A.A. 1965; Florida Atlantic U., B.A. 1966.
Occupation: Congressional aide.
Family: Wife, Martha Fry; four children.
Religion: Roman Catholic.
Political Career: No previous office.
Capitol Office: 2455 Rayburn Bldg. 20515; 225-3001.

Florida 14th: Southeast — Parts of Palm Beach and West Palm Beach. The district vote for Ronald Reagan was 61% in 1984; 57% in 1980.

Committees

Foreign Affairs
Veterans' Affairs
Select Aging

Elections

1986	General	74%	Primary	u/o
1984	General	55%	Primary	u/o

Robert H. Michel (R-Ill.)

Of Peoria — Elected 1956

Born: March 2, 1923, Peoria, Ill.
Education: Bradley U., B.S. 1948.
Military Career: Army, 1942-46.
Occupation: Congressional aide.
Family: Wife, Corinne Woodruff; four children.
Religion: Apostolic Christian.
Political Career: No previous office.
Capitol Office: 2112 Rayburn Bldg. 20515; 225-6201.

Illinois 18th: Central — Peoria. The district vote for Ronald Reagan was 60% in 1984; 61% in 1980.

CQ Voting Studies

	Presidential Support	Party Unity	Voting Participation
1986	74%	73%	92%
1985	85%	78%	94%

Interest Groups

	ADA	ACU	AFL-CIO	CCUS
1986	5%	n/a	8%	88%
1985	5%	86%	6%	81%

Committee

Minority Leader

Elections

1986	General	62%	Primary	u/o
1984	General	61%	Primary	u/o

Clarence E. Miller (R-Ohio)

Of Lancaster — Elected 1966

Born: Nov. 1, 1917, Lancaster, Ohio.
Education: Graduated from Lancaster H.S., 1935.
Occupation: Electrical engineer.
Family: Widower; two children.
Religion: Methodist.
Political Career: Lancaster City Council, 1957-63; mayor of Lancaster, 1963-65.
Capitol Office: 2208 Rayburn Bldg. 20515; 225-5131.

Ohio 10th: Southeast — Lancaster and Zanesville.

CQ Voting Studies

	Presidential Support	Party Unity	Voting Participation
1986	77%	83%	97%
1985	70%	79%	91%

Interest Groups

	ADA	ACU	AFL-CIO	CCUS
1986	5%	n/a	14%	78%
1985	0%	89%	0%	85%

Committee

Appropriations

Elections

1986	General	70%	Primary	u/o
1984	General	73%	Primary	u/o

George Miller (D-Calif.)

Of Martinez — Elected 1974

Born: May 17, 1945, Richmond, Calif.
Education: San Francisco State College, B.A. 1968; U. of California Law School, J.D. 1972.
Occupation: Lawyer.
Family: Wife, Cynthia Caccavo; two children.
Religion: Roman Catholic.
Political Career: Democratic nominee for California Senate, 1969.
Capitol Office: 2228 Rayburn Bldg. 20515; 225-2095.

California 7th: Most of Contra Costa County and Richmond. The district vote for Ronald Reagan was 52% in 1984.

Committees

Budget
Interior and Insular Affairs
Select Children, Youth and Families   (Chairman)

Elections

1986	General	67%	Primary	u/o
1984	General	67%	Primary	u/o

CQ Voting Studies

	Presidential Support	Party Unity	Voting Participation
1986	14%	84%	87%
1985	16%	84%	89%

Interest Groups

	ADA	ACU	AFL-CIO	CCUS
1986	90%	n/a	91%	15%
1985	95%	10%	80%	19%

John R. Miller (R-Wash.)

Of Seattle — Elected 1984

Born: May 23, 1938, New York, N.Y.
Education: Bucknell U., B.A. 1959; Yale U., M.A., LL.B. 1964.
Military Career: Army, 1960-61; Army Reserve, 1961-69.
Occupation: Lawyer.
Family: Wife, June Marion Makar.
Religion: Jewish.
Political Career: Seattle City Council, 1972-80, president, 1978-80; candidate for Seattle mayor, 1977; independent candidate for state attorney general, 1980.
Capitol Office: 1224 Longworth Bldg. 20515; 225-6311.

Washington 1st: Northern Seattle and Suburbs. The district vote for Ronald Reagan was 57% in 1984.

Committees

Foreign Affairs
Merchant Marine and Fisheries

Elections

1986	General	51%	Primary	53%
1984	General	56%	Primary	30%

CQ Voting Studies

	Presidential Support	Party Unity	Voting Participation
1986	56%	60%	98%
1985	64%	65%	97%

Interest Groups

	ADA	ACU	AFL-CIO	CCUS
1986	40%	n/a	36%	67%
1985	25%	67%	24%	86%

Norman Y. Mineta (D-Calif.)

Of San Jose — Elected 1974

Born: Nov. 12, 1931, San Jose, Calif.
Education: U. of California, Berkeley, B.S. 1953.
Military Career: Army, 1953-56.
Occupation: Insurance executive.
Family: Wife, May Hinoki; two children.
Religion: Methodist.
Political Career: San Jose City Council, 1967-71; Mayor of San Jose, 1971-75.
Capitol Office: 2350 Rayburn Bldg. 20515; 225-2631.

California 13th: Santa Clara County — San Jose and Santa Clara. The district vote for Ronald Reagan was 58% in 1984.

Committees

Public Works and Transportation
Science, Space and Technology

Elections

1986	General	70%	Primary	u/o
1984	General	65%	Primary	u/o

CQ Voting Studies

	Presidential Support	Party Unity	Voting Participation
1986	22%	95%	97%
1985	21%	95%	97%

Interest Groups

	ADA	ACU	AFL-CIO	CCUS
1986	95%	n/a	79%	18%
1985	80%	5%	94%	18%

Joe Moakley (D-Mass.)

Of Boston — Elected 1972

Born: April 27, 1927, Boston, Mass.
Education: Attended U. of Miami; Suffolk U., J.D. 1956.
Military Career: Navy, 1943-46.
Occupation: Lawyer.
Family: Wife, Evelyn Duffy.
Religion: Roman Catholic.
Political Career: Mass. House, 1953-65; Mass. Senate, 1965-69; Boston City Council, 1971-73; sought Democratic nomination for U.S. House, 1970.
Capitol Office: 221 Cannon Bldg. 20515; 225-8273.

Massachusetts 9th: Boston and Southern Suburbs. The district vote for Ronald Reagan was 48% in 1984; 42% in 1980.

Committee

Rules

Elections

1986	General	u/o	Primary	74%
1984	General	u/o	Primary	88%

CQ Voting Studies

	Presidential Support	Party Unity	Voting Participation
1986	16%	87%	91%
1985	23%	80%	86%

Interest Groups

	ADA	ACU	AFL-CIO	CCUS
1986	85%	n/a	100%	18%
1985	90%	5%	100%	23%

Guy V. Molinari (R-N.Y.)

Of Staten Island — Elected 1980

Born: Nov. 23, 1928, New York, N.Y.
Education: Wagner College, B.A. 1949; New York Law School, LL.B. 1951.
Military Career: Marine Corps, 1951-53.
Occupation: Lawyer.
Family: Wife, Marguerite Wing; one child.
Religion: Roman Catholic.
Political Career: N.Y. Assembly, 1975-81.
Capitol Office: 208 Cannon Bldg. 20515; 225-3371.

New York 14th: Staten Island and Southwest Brooklyn. The district vote for Ronald Reagan was 66% in 1984; 56% in 1980.

Committee

Public Works and Transportation

Elections

1986	General	68%	Primary	u/o
1984	General	70%	Primary	u/o

CQ Voting Studies

	Presidential Support	Party Unity	Voting Participation
1986	69%	75%	99%
1985	64%	74%	99%

Interest Groups

	ADA	ACU	AFL-CIO	CCUS
1986	15%	n/a	36%	72%
1985	30%	67%	35%	64%

Alan B. Mollohan (D-W. Va.)

Of Fairmont — Elected 1982

Born: May 14, 1943, Fairmont, W.Va.
Education: College of William and Mary, A.B. 1966; West Virginia U. School of Law, J.D. 1970.
Military Service: Army Reserve, 1970-present.
Occupation: Lawyer.
Family: Wife, Barbara Whiting; four children.
Religion: Baptist.
Political Career: No previous office.
Capitol Office: 516 Cannon Bldg. 20515; 225-4172.

West Virginia 1st: Northern Panhandle — Wheeling. The district vote for Ronald Reagan was 57% in 1984; 47% in 1980.

Committees

Appropriations
Standards of Official Conduct

Elections

1986	General	u/o	Primary	u/o
1984	General	54%	Primary	u/o

CQ Voting Studies

	Presidential Support	Party Unity	Voting Participation
1986	36%	79%	94%
1985	40%	82%	99%

Interest Groups

	ADA	ACU	AFL-CIO	CCUS
1986	50%	n/a	100%	24%
1985	55%	38%	82%	23%

G. V. "Sonny" Montgomery (D-Miss.)

Of Meridian — Elected 1966

Born: Aug. 5, 1920, Meridian, Miss.
Education: Mississippi State U., B.S. 1943.
Military Career: Army, 1943-46; National Guard, 1946-80, active duty 1951-52.
Occupation: Insurance executive.
Family: Single.
Religion: Episcopalian.
Political Career: Miss. Senate, 1956-66.
Capitol Office: 2184 Rayburn Bldg. 20515; 225-5031.

Mississippi 3rd: South Central — Meridian. The district vote for Ronald Reagan was 66% in 1984.

CQ Voting Studies

	Presidential Support	Party Unity	Voting Participation
1986	58%	53%	98%
1985	66%	53%	98%

Interest Groups

	ADA	ACU	AFL-CIO	CCUS
1986	5%	n/a	29%	76%
1985	15%	76%	18%	82%

Committees

Armed Services
Veterans' Affairs (Chairman)

Elections

1986	General	u/o	Primary	u/o
1984	General	u/o	Primary	u/o

Jim Moody (D-Wis.)

Of Milwaukee — Elected 1982

Born: Sept. 2, 1935, Richlands, Va.
Education: Haverford College, B.A. 1957; Harvard U., M.P.A. 1967; U. of California, Berkeley, Ph.D. 1973.
Occupation: Economist.
Family: Divorced.
Religion: Protestant.
Political Career: Wis. House, 1977-79; Wis. Senate, 1979-83.
Capitol Office: 1721 Longworth Bldg. 20515; 225-3571.

Wisconsin 5th: Northern Milwaukee and Suburbs — Wauwatosa. The district vote for Ronald Reagan was 39% in 1984; 37% in 1980.

CQ Voting Studies

	Presidential Support	Party Unity	Voting Participation
1986	18%	87%	94%
1985	20%	89%	94%

Interest Groups

	ADA	ACU	AFL-CIO	CCUS
1986	90%	n/a	86%	18%
1985	80%	0%	100%	18%

Committee

Ways and Means

Elections

1986	General	u/o	Primary	u/o
1984	General	98%	Primary	u/o

Carlos J. Moorhead (R-Calif.)

Of Glendale — Elected 1972

Born: May 6, 1922, Long Beach, Calif.
Education: U.C.L.A., B.A. 1943; U. of Southern California, J.D. 1949.
Military Career: Army, 1942-45; Army Reserve, 1945-82.
Occupation: Lawyer.
Family: Wife, Valery Joan Tyler; five children.
Religion: Presbyterian.
Political Career: Calif. Assembly, 1967-73.
Capitol Office: 2346 Rayburn Bldg. 20515; 225-4176.

California 22nd: Glendale, Part of Burbank and Part of Pasadena. The district vote for Ronald Reagan was 72% in 1984.

Committees

Energy and Commerce
Judiciary

Elections

1986	General	76%	Primary	u/o
1984	General	85%	Primary	u/o

CQ Voting Studies

	Presidential Support	Party Unity	Voting Participation
1986	82%	92%	99%
1985	80%	96%	99%

Interest Groups

	ADA	ACU	AFL-CIO	CCUS
1986	0%	n/a	7%	100%
1985	5%	90%	0%	95%

Constance A. Morella (R-Md.)

Of Bethesda — Elected 1986

Born: Feb. 12, 1931, Somerville, Mass.
Education: Boston U., B.A. 1954; American U., M.A. 1967.
Occupation: College professor.
Family: Husband, Anthony C. Morella; nine children.
Religion: Roman Catholic.
Political Career: Md. House, 1979-87; sought GOP nomination for U.S. House, 1980.
Capitol Office: 1024 Longworth Bldg. 20515; 225-5341.

Maryland 8th: Montgomery County. The district vote for Ronald Reagan was 49% in 1984; 47% in 1980.

Committees

Post Office and Civil Service
Science, Space and Technology
Select Aging

Elections

1986	General	53%	Primary	68%

Bruce A. Morrison (D-Conn.)

Of Hamden — Elected 1982

Born: Oct. 8, 1944, New York, N.Y.
Education: Massachusetts Institute of Technology, B.S. 1965; U. of Illinois, M.S. 1970; Yale U., J.D. 1973.
Occupation: Lawyer.
Family: Wife, Jane Phillips.
Religion: Lutheran.
Political Career: No previous office.
Capitol Office: 437 Cannon Bldg. 20515; 225-3661.

Connecticut 3rd: South — New Haven. The district vote for Ronald Reagan was 59% in 1984; 50% in 1980.

Committees

Banking, Finance and Urban Affairs
Judiciary
Select Children, Youth and Families

CQ Voting Studies

	Presidential Support	Party Unity	Voting Participation
1986	16%	81%	86%
1985	28%	89%	92%

Interest Groups

	ADA	ACU	AFL-CIO	CCUS
1986	80%	n/a	93%	27%
1985	90%	5%	100%	24%

Elections

| 1986 | General | 70% | Primary | u/o |
| 1984 | General | 53% | Primary | u/o |

Sid Morrison (R-Wash.)

Of Zillah — Elected 1980

Born: May 13, 1933, Yakima, Wash.
Education: Attended Yakima Valley College, 1951; Washington State U., B.S. 1954.
Military Career: Army, 1954-56.
Occupation: Fruit grower; nurseryman.
Family: Wife, Marcella Britton; four children.
Religion: Methodist.
Political Career: Wash. House, 1967-75; Wash. Senate, 1975-81.
Capitol Office: 1434 Longworth Bldg. 20515; 225-5816.

Washington 4th: Central — Yakima and Tri-Cities. The district vote for Ronald Reagan was 63% in 1984.

Committees

Agriculture
Science, Space and Technology
Select Hunger

CQ Voting Studies

	Presidential Support	Party Unity	Voting Participation
1986	59%	56%	98%
1985	59%	72%	98%

Interest Groups

	ADA	ACU	AFL-CIO	CCUS
1986	25%	n/a	38%	67%
1985	25%	71%	29%	82%

Elections

| 1986 | General | 72% | Primary | 72% |
| 1984 | General | 76% | Primary | u/o |

Robert J. Mrazek   (D-N.Y.)

Of Centerport — Elected 1982

Born: Nov. 6, 1945, Newport, R.I.
Education: Cornell U., B.A. 1967.
Military Career: Navy, 1967-69.
Occupation: Congressional aide.
Family: Wife, Catherine Susan Gurick; two children.
Religion: Methodist.
Political Career: Suffolk County Legislature, 1976-83; sought Democratic nomination for U.S. House, 1972; Democratic nominee for N.Y. Senate, 1978.
Capitol Office: 306 Cannon Bldg. 20515; 225-5956.

New York 3rd: Long Island — Parts of Nassau and Suffolk Counties. The district vote for Ronald Reagan was 64% in 1984; 55% in 1980.

Committee

Appropriations

CQ Voting Studies

	Presidential Support	Party Unity	Voting Participation
1986	17%	86%	94%
1985	24%	87%	94%

Interest Groups

	ADA	ACU	AFL-CIO	CCUS
1986	80%	n/a	85%	31%
1985	90%	19%	81%	43%

Elections

1986	General	56%	Primary	u/o
1984	General	51%	Primary	u/o

Austin J. Murphy   (D-Pa.)

Of Monongahela — Elected 1976

Born: June 17, 1927, North Charleroi, Pa.
Education: Duquesne U., B.A. 1949; U. of Pittsburgh, LL.B. 1952.
Military Career: Marine Corps, 1944-46; Marine Corps Reserve, 1948-50.
Occupation: Lawyer.
Family: Wife, Ramona McNamara; six children.
Religion: Roman Catholic.
Political Career: Pa. House, 1959-71; Pa. Senate, 1971-77.
Capitol Office: 2210 Rayburn Bldg. 20515; 225-4665.

Pennsylvania 22nd: Southwest — Washington. The district vote for Ronald Reagan was 38% in 1984; 42% in 1980.

Committees

Education and Labor
Interior and Insular Affairs

CQ Voting Studies

	Presidential Support	Party Unity	Voting Participation
1986	21%	75%	95%
1985	36%	78%	97%

Interest Groups

	ADA	ACU	AFL-CIO	CCUS
1986	70%	n/a	93%	33%
1985	60%	19%	76%	36%

Elections

1986	General	u/o	Primary	88%
1984	General	79%	Primary	86%

John P. Murtha   (D-Pa.)

Of Johnstown — Elected 1974

Born: June 17, 1932, New Martinsville, W.Va.
Education: U. of Pittsburgh, B.A. 1962; graduate work, Indiana U., Pa.
Military Career: Marine Corps, 1952-55, 1966-67.
Occupation: Car wash operator.
Family: Wife, Joyce Bell; three children.
Religion: Roman Catholic.
Political Career: Pa. House, 1969-74.
Capitol Office: 2423 Rayburn Bldg. 20515; 225-2065.

Pennsylvania 12th: Southwest — Johnstown. The district vote for Ronald Reagan was 51% in 1984; 49% in 1980.

CQ Voting Studies

	Presidential Support	Party Unity	Voting Participation
1986	42%	76%	91%
1985	52%	77%	95%

Interest Groups

	ADA	ACU	AFL-CIO	CCUS
1986	40%	n/a	93%	25%
1985	45%	50%	82%	14%

Committee

Appropriations

Elections

1986	General	67%	Primary	81%
1984	General	69%	Primary	u/o

John T. Myers   (R-Ind.)

Of Covington — Elected 1966

Born: Feb. 8, 1927, Covington, Ind.
Education: Indiana State U., B.S. 1951.
Military Career: Army, 1945-46.
Occupation: Banker; farmer.
Family: Wife, Carol Carruthers; two children.
Religion: Episcopalian.
Political Career: No previous office.
Capitol Office: 2372 Rayburn Bldg. 20515; 225-5805.

Indiana 7th: West Central — Terre Haute and Lafayette. The district vote for Ronald Reagan was 66% in 1984; 59% in 1980.

CQ Voting Studies

	Presidential Support	Party Unity	Voting Participation
1986	67%	54%	98%
1985	69%	58%	96%

Interest Groups

	ADA	ACU	AFL-CIO	CCUS
1986	20%	n/a	36%	50%
1985	20%	71%	18%	73%

Committees

Appropriations
Post Office and Civil Service
Standards of Official Conduct

Elections

1986	General	68%	Primary	88%
1984	General	67%	Primary	u/o

David R. Nagle (D-Iowa)

Of Cedar Falls — Elected 1986

Born: April 15, 1943, Grinnell, Iowa.
Education: U. of Northern Iowa, B.A. 1965; U. of Iowa Law School, LL.B. 1968.
Occupation: Lawyer.
Family: Wife, Diane Lewis; one child.
Religion: Roman Catholic.
Political Career: Black Hawk County Democratic chairman, 1978-82; Iowa Democratic chairman, 1982-85.
Capitol Office: 214 Cannon Bldg. 20515; 225-3301.

Iowa 3rd: North Central — Waterloo and Iowa City. The district vote for Ronald Reagan was 52% in 1984; 49% in 1980.

Committees

Agriculture
Science, Space and Technology

Elections

1986	General	55%	Primary	51%

William H. Natcher (D-Ky.)

Of Bowling Green — Elected 1953

Born: Sept. 11, 1909, Bowling Green, Ky.
Education: Western Kentucky State College, A.B. 1930; Ohio State U., LL.B. 1933.
Military Career: Navy, 1942-45.
Occupation: Lawyer.
Family: Wife, Virginia Reardon; two children.
Religion: Baptist.
Political Career: Warren County attorney, 1937-49; commonwealth attorney of Allen and Warren counties, 1951-53.
Capitol Office: 2333 Rayburn Bldg. 20515; 225-3501.

Kentucky 2nd: West Central — Owensboro. The district vote for Ronald Reagan was 63% in 1984; 50% in 1980.

Committee

Appropriations

Elections

1986	General	u/o	Primary	79%
1984	General	62%	Primary	71%

CQ Voting Studies

	Presidential Support	Party Unity	Voting Participation
1986	29%	89%	100%
1985	30%	87%	100%

Interest Groups

	ADA	ACU	AFL-CIO	CCUS
1986	65%	n/a	93%	28%
1985	60%	24%	76%	23%

Stephen L. Neal   (D-N.C.)

Of Winston-Salem — Elected 1974

Born: Nov. 7, 1934, Winston-Salem, N.C.
Education: Attended U. of California, Santa Barbara, 1954-56; U. of Hawaii, A.B. 1959.
Occupation: Mortgage banker; publisher.
Family: Wife, Rachel Landis Miller; two children.
Religion: Presbyterian.
Political Career: No previous office.
Capitol Office: 2463 Rayburn Bldg. 20515; 225-2071.

North Carolina 5th: Northwest — Winston-Salem. The district vote for Ronald Reagan was 64% in 1984; 52% in 1980.

Committees

Banking, Finance and Urban Affairs
Government Operations

Elections

1986	General	54%	Primary	u/o	
1984	General	51%	Primary	90%	

CQ Voting Studies

	Presidential Support	Party Unity	Voting Participation
1986	28%	75%	94%
1985	36%	72%	90%

Interest Groups

	ADA	ACU	AFL-CIO	CCUS
1986	65%	n/a	71%	50%
1985	50%	33%	53%	48%

Bill Nelson   (D-Fla.)

Of Melbourne — Elected 1978

Born: Sept. 29, 1942, Miami, Fla.
Education: Yale U., B.A. 1965; U. of Virginia, J.D. 1968.
Military Career: Army Reserve, 1965-71.
Occupation: Lawyer.
Family: Wife, Grace Cavert; two children.
Religion: Episcopalian.
Political Career: Fla. House, 1973-79.
Capitol Office: 2404 Rayburn Bldg. 20515; 225-3671.

Florida 11th: East — Melbourne and Part of Orange County. The district vote for Ronald Reagan was 74% in 1984; 61% in 1980.

Committees

Banking, Finance and Urban Affairs
Science, Space and Technology

Elections

1986	General	73%	Primary	u/o	
1984	General	61%	Primary	86%	

CQ Voting Studies

	Presidential Support	Party Unity	Voting Participation
1986	43%	69%	99%
1985	55%	47%	73%

Interest Groups

	ADA	ACU	AFL-CIO	CCUS
1986	15%	n/a	43%	61%
1985	30%	71%	47%	54%

Bill Nichols (D-Ala.)

Of Sylacauga — Elected 1966

Born: Oct. 16, 1918, Becker, Miss.
Education: Auburn U., B.S. 1939, M.A. 1941.
Military Career: Army, 1942-47.
Occupation: Fertilizer and cotton gin executive.
Family: Wife, Carolyn Funderburk; three children.
Religion: Methodist.
Political Career: Ala. House, 1959-63; Ala. Senate, 1963-67,
Capitol Office: 2405 Rayburn Bldg. 20515; 225-3261.

Alabama 3rd: East — Anniston and Auburn. The district vote for Ronald Reagan was 61% in 1984; 46% in 1980.

Committee

Armed Services

Elections

1986	General	81%	Primary	u/o
1984	General	96%	Primary	u/o

CQ Voting Studies

	Presidential Support	Party Unity	Voting Participation
1986	49%	36%	74%
1985	61%	55%	91%

Interest Groups

	ADA	ACU	AFL-CIO	CCUS
1986	10%	n/a	46%	73%
1985	10%	67%	24%	71%

Howard C. Nielson (R-Utah)

Of Provo — Elected 1982

Born: Sept. 12, 1924, Richfield, Utah.
Education: U. of Utah, B.S. 1947; U. of Oregon, M.S. 1949; Stanford U., M.B.A. 1956; Ph.D. 1958.
Military Career: Air Force, 1943-46.
Occupation: Professor of statistics.
Family: Wife, Julia Adams; seven children.
Religion: Mormon.
Political Career: Utah House, 1967-75, Speaker, 1973-75.
Capitol Office: 1229 Longworth Bldg. 20515; 225-7751.

Utah 3rd: Provo and Rural Utah. The district vote for Ronald Reagan was 77% in 1984; 77% in 1980.

Committees

Energy and Commerce
Government Operations

Elections

1986	General	67%	Primary	u/o
1984	General	75%	Primary	u/o

CQ Voting Studies

	Presidential Support	Party Unity	Voting Participation
1986	74%	84%	99%
1985	84%	89%	99%

Interest Groups

	ADA	ACU	AFL-CIO	CCUS
1986	5%	n/a	14%	89%
1985	5%	90%	0%	100%

Henry J. Nowak (D-N.Y.)
Of Buffalo — Elected 1974

Born: Feb. 21, 1935, Buffalo, N.Y.
Education: Canisius College, B.B.A. 1957; U. Of Buffalo, J.D. 1961.
Military Career: Army, 1957-62.
Occupation: Lawyer.
Family: Wife, Rose Santa Lucia; two children.
Religion: Roman Catholic.
Political Career: Erie County comptroller, 1966-75.
Capitol Office: 2240 Rayburn Bldg. 20515; 225-3306.

New York 33rd: West — Buffalo. The district vote for Ronald Reagan was 37% in 1984; 30% in 1980.

CQ Voting Studies

	Presidential Support	Party Unity	Voting Participation
1986	18%	92%	98%
1985	23%	89%	96%

Interest Groups

	ADA	ACU	AFL-CIO	CCUS
1986	95%	n/a	100%	28%
1985	80%	10%	100%	27%

Committees

Public Works and Transportation
Science, Space and Technology

Elections

1986	General	85%	Primary	89%
1984	General	78%	Primary	u/o

Mary Rose Oakar (D-Ohio)
Of Cleveland — Elected 1976

Born: March 5, 1940, Cleveland, Ohio.
Education: Ursuline College, B.A. 1962; John Carroll U., M.A. 1966.
Occupation: High school English and drama teacher.
Family: Single.
Religion: Roman Catholic.
Political Career: Cleveland City Council, 1973-77.
Capitol Office: 2231 Rayburn Bldg. 20515; 225-5871.

Ohio 20th: Cleveland — Central and West Suburbs.

CQ Voting Studies

	Presidential Support	Party Unity	Voting Participation
1986	16%	92%	93%
1985	18%	94%	97%

Interest Groups

	ADA	ACU	AFL-CIO	CCUS
1986	95%	n/a	93%	12%
1985	80%	5%	94%	23%

Committees

Banking, Finance and Urban Affairs
House Administration
Post Office and Civil Service
Select Aging

Elections

1986	General	85%	Primary	94%
1984	General	u/o	Primary	u/o

James L. Oberstar (D-Minn.)

Of Chisholm — Elected 1974

Born: Sept. 10, 1934, Chisholm, Minn.
Education: College of St. Thomas, B.A. 1956; College of Europe, M.A. 1957.
Occupation: Language teacher; congressional aide.
Family: Wife, Marilynn Jo Garlick; four children.
Religion: Roman Catholic.
Political Career: No previous office.
Capitol Office: 2351 Rayburn Bldg. 20515; 225-6211.

Minnesota 8th: Northeast — Duluth. The district vote for Ronald Reagan was 40% in 1984; 37% in 1980.

Committees

Budget
Public Works and Transportation

Elections

1986	General	72%	Primary	u/o
1984	General	67%	Primary	65%

CQ Voting Studies

	Presidential Support	Party Unity	Voting Participation
1986	18%	92%	96%
1985	16%	91%	96%

Interest Groups

	ADA	ACU	AFL-CIO	CCUS
1986	85%	n/a	93%	6%
1985	95%	5%	100%	18%

David R. Obey (D-Wis.)

Of Wausau — Elected 1969

Born: Oct. 3, 1938, Okmulgee, Okla.
Education: U. of Wisconsin, B.S. 1960, M.A. 1962.
Occupation: Real estate broker.
Family: Wife, Joan Lepinski; two children.
Religion: Roman Catholic.
Political Career: Wis. Assembly, 1963-69.
Capitol Office: 2217 Rayburn Bldg. 20515; 225-3365.

Wisconsin 7th: Northwest — Wausau and Superior. The district vote for Ronald Reagan was 53% in 1984; 45% in 1980.

Committees

Appropriations
Joint Economic

Elections

1986	General	63%	Primary	u/o
1984	General	61%	Primary	u/o

CQ Voting Studies

	Presidential Support	Party Unity	Voting Participation
1986	19%	92%	97%
1985	15%	93%	97%

Interest Groups

	ADA	ACU	AFL-CIO	CCUS
1986	85%	n/a	93%	12%
1985	90%	5%	94%	18%

James R. Olin (D-Va.)

Of Roanoke — Elected 1982

Born: Feb. 28, 1920, Chicago, Ill.
Education: Attended Deep Springs College (Calif.), 1941; Cornell U., B.E.E. 1943.
Military Career: Army, 1943-46.
Occupation: Retired electronics executive.
Family: Wife, Phyllis Avery; five children.
Religion: Unitarian.
Political Career: Rotterdam (N.Y.) town supervisor, Schenectady County supervisor, 1953-55.
Capitol Office: 1238 Longworth Bldg. 20515; 225-5431.

Virginia 6th: West — Roanoke and Lynchburg. The district vote for Ronald Reagan was 66% in 1984; 51% in 1980.

Committees

Agriculture
Small Business

Elections

1986	General	70%	Primary	u/o
1984	General	54%	Primary	u/o

CQ Voting Studies

	Presidential Support	Party Unity	Voting Participation
1986	36%	71%	97%
1985	41%	72%	96%

Interest Groups

	ADA	ACU	AFL-CIO	CCUS
1986	55%	n/a	57%	56%
1985	50%	38%	41%	67%

Solomon P. Ortiz (D-Texas)

Of Corpus Christi — Elected 1982

Born: June 3, 1937, Robstown, Texas.
Education: Attended Del Mar College, 1966-67.
Military Career: Army, 1960-62.
Occupation: Law enforcement official.
Family: Divorced; two children.
Religion: Methodist.
Political Career: Nueces County Constable, 1965-68; Nueces County Commissioner, 1969-76; Nueces County Sheriff, 1977-82.
Capitol Office: 1524 Longworth Bldg. 20515; 225-7742.

Texas 27th: Gulf Coast — Corpus Christi and Brownsville. The district vote for Ronald Reagan was 52% in 1984; 47% in 1980.

Committees

Armed Services
Merchant Marine and Fisheries
Select Narcotics Abuse and Control

Elections

1986	General	u/o	Primary	85%
1984	General	64%	Primary	u/o

CQ Voting Studies

	Presidential Support	Party Unity	Voting Participation
1986	36%	78%	92%
1985	36%	76%	90%

Interest Groups

	ADA	ACU	AFL-CIO	CCUS
1986	45%	n/a	85%	29%
1985	60%	33%	88%	16%

Major R. Owens (D-N.Y.)

Of Brooklyn — Elected 1982

Born: June 28, 1936, Collierville, Tenn.
Education: Morehouse College, B.A. 1956; Atlanta U., M.S. 1957.
Occupation: Librarian.
Family: Divorced; three children.
Religion: Baptist.
Political Career: N.Y. Senate, 1975-83.
Capitol Office: 114 Cannon Bldg. 20515; 225-6231.

New York 12th: Central Brooklyn — Crown Heights. The district vote for Ronald Reagan was 14% in 1984; 35% in 1980.

Committees

Education and Labor
Government Operations

CQ Voting Studies

	Presidential Support	Party Unity	Voting Participation
1986	11%	89%	91%
1985	16%	86%	87%

Interest Groups

	ADA	ACU	AFL-CIO	CCUS
1986	95%	n/a	93%	20%
1985	95%	0%	100%	14%

Elections

1986	General	91%	Primary	78%
1984	General	91%	Primary	67%

Wayne Owens (D-Utah)

Of Salt Lake City — Elected 1986

Born: May 2, 1937, Panguitch, Utah.
Education: Attended U. of Utah, 1958-61; U. of Utah Law School, J.D. 1964.
Occupation: Lawyer.
Family: Wife, Marlene Wessel; five children.
Religion: Mormon.
Political Career: U.S. House, 1973-75; Democratic nominee for U.S. Senate, 1974; Democratic nominee for governor, 1984.
Capitol Office: 1728 Longworth Bldg. 20515; 225-3011.

Utah 2nd: Salt Lake City. The district vote for Ronald Reagan was 68% in 1984; 66% in 1980.

Committees

Foreign Affairs
Interior and Insular Affairs

Elections

1986	General	56%	Primary	u/o

Michael G. Oxley   (R-Ohio)

Of Findlay — Elected 1981

Born: Feb. 11, 1944, Findlay, Ohio.
Education: Miami U. (Ohio), B.A. 1966; Ohio State U., J.D. 1969.
Occupation: FBI agent; lawyer.
Family: Wife, Patricia Pluguez; one child.
Religion: Lutheran.
Political Career: Ohio House, 1973-81.
Capitol Office: 1108 Longworth Bldg. 20515; 225-2676.

Ohio 4th: West Central — Lima and Findlay.

Committees

Energy and Commerce
Select Narcotics Abuse and Control

CQ Voting Studies

	Presidential Support	Party Unity	Voting Participation
1986	80%	85%	93%
1985	75%	88%	95%

Interest Groups

	ADA	ACU	AFL-CIO	CCUS
1986	0%	n/a	7%	100%
1985	10%	86%	0%	91%

Elections

1986	General	81%	Primary	u/o
1984	General	78%	Primary	u/o

Ron Packard   (R-Calif.)

Of Oceanside — Elected 1982

Born: Jan. 19, 1931, Meridian, Idaho.
Education: Attended Brigham Young U., 1948-50; attended Portland State U., 1952-53; U. of Oregon, D.M.D. 1957.
Military Career: Navy, 1957-59.
Occupation: Dentist.
Family: Wife, Roma Jean Sorenson; seven children.
Religion: Mormon.
Political Career: Carlsbad School Board, 1960-72; Carlsbad City Council, 1976-78; mayor of Carlsbad, 1978-82.
Capitol Office: 316 Cannon Bldg. 20515; 225-3906.

California 43rd: Northern San Diego County and Southern Orange County. The district vote for Ronald Reagan was 74% in 1984.

Committees

Public Works and Transportation
Science, Space and Technology
Select Children, Youth and Families

CQ Voting Studies

	Presidential Support	Party Unity	Voting Participation
1986	83%	79%	96%
1985	75%	85%	96%

Interest Groups

	ADA	ACU	AFL-CIO	CCUS
1986	5%	n/a	7%	94%
1985	10%	86%	6%	95%

Elections

1986	General	75%	Primary	u/o
1984	General	74%	Primary	77%

Leon E. Panetta (D-Calif.)

Of Carmel Valley — Elected 1976

Born: June 28, 1938, Monterey, Calif.
Education: U. of Santa Clara, B.A. 1960, J.D. 1963.
Military Career: Army, 1963-65.
Occupation: Lawyer.
Family: Wife, Sylvia Marie Varni; three children.
Religion: Roman Catholic.
Political Career: No previous office.
Capitol Office: 339 Cannon Bldg. 20515; 225-2861.

California 16th: Central Coast — Salinas and Monterey. The district vote for Ronald Reagan was 53% in 1984.

Committees

Agriculture
House Administration
Select Hunger

Elections

1986	General	80%	Primary	94%
1984	General	71%	Primary	u/o

CQ Voting Studies

	Presidential Support	Party Unity	Voting Participation
1986	20%	87%	95%
1985	20%	88%	96%

Interest Groups

	ADA	ACU	AFL-CIO	CCUS
1986	85%	n/a	85%	31%
1985	75%	14%	71%	32%

Stan Parris (R-Va.)

Of Springfield — Elected 1980

Born: Sept. 9, 1929, Champaign, Ill.
Education: U. of Illinois, B.S. 1950; George Washington U., J.D. 1958.
Military Career: Air Force, 1950-54.
Occupation: Lawyer; automobile dealer; commercial pilot; banker.
Family: Wife, Martha Merriam; three children.
Religion: Episcopalian.
Political Career: Fairfax County Board of Supervisors, 1964-67; Va. House, 1969-73; U.S. House, 1973-75; defeated for re-election to U.S. House, 1974.
Capitol Office: 1526 Longworth Bldg. 20515; 225-4376.

Virginia 8th: D.C. Suburbs and Alexandria. The district vote for Ronald Reagan was 61% in 1984; 55% in 1980.

Committees

Banking, Finance and Urban Affairs
District of Columbia
Select Narcotics Abuse and Control

Elections

1986	General	62%	Primary	u/o
1984	General	56%	Primary	u/o

CQ Voting Studies

	Presidential Support	Party Unity	Voting Participation
1986	70%	71%	93%
1985	64%	69%	95%

Interest Groups

	ADA	ACU	AFL-CIO	CCUS
1986	5%	n/a	25%	71%
1985	15%	67%	35%	76%

Charles Pashayan Jr. (R-Calif.)

Of Fresno — Elected 1978

Born: March 27, 1941, Fresno, Calif.
Education: Pomona College, B.A. 1963; U. of California Hastings Law School, J.D. 1968; Oxford U., England, B.Litt. 1977.
Military Career: Army, 1968-70.
Occupation: Lawyer; auto supply dealer.
Family: Wife, Sallie Christian.
Religion: Episcopalian.
Political Career: No previous office.
Capitol Office: 129 Cannon Bldg. 20515; 225-3341.

California 17th: Southern San Joaquin Valley. The district vote for Ronald Reagan was 63% in 1984.

Committees

Interior and Insular Affairs
Post Office and Civil Service
Standards of Official Conduct

Elections

1986	General	60%	Primary	u/o
1984	General	72%	Primary	u/o

CQ Voting Studies

	Presidential Support	Party Unity	Voting Participation
1986	58%	62%	95%
1985	59%	75%	94%

Interest Groups

	ADA	ACU	AFL-CIO	CCUS
1986	25%	n/a	77%	56%
1985	5%	80%	19%	85%

Liz Patterson (D-S.C.)

Of Spartanburg — Elected 1986

Born: Nov. 18, 1939, Columbia, S.C.
Education: Columbia College, B.A. 1961; attended U. of South Carolina, 1961-62.
Occupation: Legislative aide; Peace Corps recruiting officer.
Family: Husband, Dwight Fleming Patterson Jr.; three children.
Religion: United Methodist.
Political Career: Spartanburg County Council, 1975-76; S.C. Senate, 1979-87.
Capitol Office: 1022 Longworth Bldg. 20515; 225-6030.

South Carolina 4th: Northwest — Greenville and Spartanburg. The district vote for Ronald Reagan was 70% in 1984; 54% in 1980.

Committees

Banking, Finance and Urban Affairs
Veterans' Affairs
Select Hunger

Elections

1986	General	52%	Primary	u/o

Don J. Pease (D-Ohio)

Of Oberlin — Elected 1976

Born: Sept. 26, 1931, Toledo, Ohio.
Education: Ohio U., B.S. 1953, M.A. 1955; attended U. of Durham, England, 1954-55.
Military Career: Army, 1955-57.
Occupation: Newspaper editor.
Family: Wife, Jeanne Wendt; one child.
Religion: Methodist.
Political Career: Oberlin City Council, 1962-64; Ohio Senate, 1965-67 and 1975-77; Ohio House, 1969-75; sought re-election to Ohio Senate, 1966.
Capitol Office: 1127 Longworth Bldg. 20515; 225-3401.

Ohio 13th: North — Lorain.

Committee

Ways and Means

Elections

1986	General	63%	Primary	77%
1984	General	66%	Primary	78%

CQ Voting Studies

	Presidential Support	Party Unity	Voting Participation
1986	26%	92%	99%
1985	28%	93%	99%

Interest Groups

	ADA	ACU	AFL-CIO	CCUS
1986	75%	n/a	79%	17%
1985	70%	14%	82%	38%

Timothy J. Penny (D-Minn.)

Of New Richland — Elected 1982

Born: Nov. 19, 1951, Albert Lea, Minn.
Education: Winona State U., B.A. 1974; graduate work at U. of Minnesota, 1975.
Military Career: Naval Reserve, 1986-present.
Occupation: Sales representative.
Family: Wife, Barbara Christianson; four children.
Religion: Lutheran.
Political Career: Minn. Senate, 1977-83.
Capitol Office: 436 Cannon Bldg. 20515; 225-2472.

Minnesota 1st: Southeast — Rochester and Mankato. The district vote for Ronald Reagan was 55% in 1984; 53% in 1980.

Committees

Agriculture
Education and Labor
Veterans' Affairs
Select Hunger

Elections

1986	General	72%	Primary	93%
1984	General	57%	Primary	u/o

CQ Voting Studies

	Presidential Support	Party Unity	Voting Participation
1986	34%	61%	100%
1985	25%	53%	100%

Interest Groups

	ADA	ACU	AFL-CIO	CCUS
1986	75%	n/a	64%	50%
1985	60%	24%	47%	50%

Claude Pepper (D-Fla.)

Of Miami — Elected 1962

Born: Sept. 8, 1900, Chambers County, Ala.
Education: U. of Alabama, A.B. 1921; Harvard U., LL.B. 1924.
Occupation: Lawyer.
Family: Widowed.
Religion: Baptist.
Political Career: Fla. House, 1929-31; U.S. Senate, 1936-51; sought Democratic nomination to U.S. Senate, 1934, 1958; sought renomination to U.S. Senate, 1950.
Capitol Office: 2239 Rayburn Bldg. 20515; 225-3931.

Florida 18th: Southeast — Miami and Miami Beach. The district vote for Ronald Reagan was 60% in 1984; 52% in 1980.

Committees

Rules (Chairman)
Select Aging

CQ Voting Studies

	Presidential Support	Party Unity	Voting Participation
1986	30%	80%	89%
1985	26%	81%	86%

Interest Groups

	ADA	ACU	AFL-CIO	CCUS
1986	70%	n/a	100%	25%
1985	60%	32%	100%	15%

Elections

1986	General	74%	Primary	u/o
1984	General	61%	Primary	u/o

Carl C. Perkins (D-Ky.)

Of Hindman — Elected 1984

Born: Aug. 6, 1954, Washington, D.C.
Education: Davidson College, B.A. 1976; U. of Louisville, J.D. 1979.
Occupation: Lawyer.
Family: Wife, Cathy Whittaker.
Religion: Baptist.
Political Career: Kentucky House, 1982-84.
Capitol Office: 1004 Longworth Bldg. 20515; 225-4935.

Kentucky 7th: East — Ashland. The district vote for Ronald Reagan was 49% in 1984; 43% in 1980.

Committees

Education and Labor
Public Works and Transportation
Science, Space and Technology

CQ Voting Studies

	Presidential Support	Party Unity	Voting Participation
1986	22%	89%	99%
1985	20%	94%	100%

Interest Groups

	ADA	ACU	AFL-CIO	CCUS
1986	80%	n/a	93%	17%
1985	85%	10%	88%	23%

Elections

1986	General	79%	Primary	u/o
1984	General	74%	Primary	*

** Rep. Perkins did not run in the primary.*

Thomas E. Petri (R-Wis.)

Of Fond du Lac — Elected 1979

Born: May 28, 1940, Marinette, Wis.
Education: Harvard U., B.A. 1962, J.D. 1965.
Occupation: Lawyer.
Family: Wife, Anne Neal.
Religion: Lutheran.
Political Career: Wis. Senate, 1973-79; Republican nominee for U.S. Senate, 1974.
Capitol Office: 2443 Rayburn Bldg. 20515; 225-2476.

Wisconsin 6th: Central — Oshkosh, Fond du Lac and Manitowoc. The district vote for Ronald Reagan was 62% in 1984; 54% in 1980.

Committees

Education and Labor
Public Works and Transportation
Standards of Official Conduct

Elections

1986	General	u/o	Primary	u/o
1984	General	76%	Primary	u/o

CQ Voting Studies

	Presidential Support	Party Unity	Voting Participation
1986	73%	74%	99%
1985	61%	60%	97%

Interest Groups

	ADA	ACU	AFL-CIO	CCUS
1986	5%	n/a	0%	94%
1985	30%	62%	35%	59%

Owen B. Pickett (D-Va.)

Of Virginia Beach — Elected 1986

Born: Aug. 31, 1930, Richmond, Va.
Education: Virginia Polytechnic Institute and State U., B.S. 1952; U. of Richmond Law School, LL.B. 1955.
Occupation: Lawyer.
Family: Wife, Sybil Catherine Kelly; three children.
Religion: Baptist.
Political Career: Va. House, 1973-87; withdrew from seeking Democratic nomination for U.S. Senate, 1982.
Capitol Office: 1429 Longworth Bldg. 20515; 225-4215.

Virginia 2nd: Norfolk and Virginia Beach. The district vote for Ronald Reagan was 63% in 1984; 52% in 1980.

Committees

Armed Services
Merchant Marine and Fisheries

Elections

1986	General	54%	Primary	u/o

J. J. Pickle   (D-Texas)

Of Austin — Elected 1963

Born: Oct. 11, 1913, Roscoe, Texas.
Education: U. of Texas, B.A. 1938.
Military Career: Navy, 1942-45.
Occupation: Public relations and advertising executive.
Family: Wife, Beryl Bolton McCarroll; three children.
Religion: Methodist.
Political Career: No previous office.
Capitol Office: 242 Cannon Bldg. 20515; 225-4865.

Texas 10th: Central — Austin. The district vote for Ronald Reagan was 58% in 1984; 46% in 1980.

Committees

Ways and Means
Joint Taxation

CQ Voting Studies

	Presidential Support	Party Unity	Voting Participation
1986	39%	63%	89%
1985	40%	82%	97%

Interest Groups

	ADA	ACU	AFL-CIO	CCUS
1986	40%	n/a	43%	44%
1985	50%	38%	65%	43%

Elections

1986	General	72%	Primary	81%
1984	General	u/o	Primary	u/o

John Edward Porter   (R-Ill.)

Of Winnetka — Elected 1980

Born: June 1, 1935, Evanston, Ill.
Education: Attended Massachusetts Institute of Technology, 1953-54; Northwestern U., B.S., B.A. 1957; U. of Michigan, J.D. 1961.
Military Career: Army Reserve, 1958-64.
Occupation: Lawyer.
Family: Wife, Kathryn Cameron; five children.
Religion: Presbyterian.
Political Career: Ill. House, 1973-79; Republican nominee for U.S. House, 1978; Republican nominee for Cook County circuit court judge, 1970.
Capitol Office: 1131 Longworth Bldg. 20515; 225-4835.

Illinois 10th: North and Northwest Suburbs — Waukegan. The district vote for Ronald Reagan was 68% in 1984; 59% in 1980.

Committee

Appropriations

CQ Voting Studies

	Presidential Support	Party Unity	Voting Participation
1986	59%	68%	96%
1985	68%	71%	96%

Interest Groups

	ADA	ACU	AFL-CIO	CCUS
1986	15%	n/a	7%	94%
1985	20%	71%	24%	82%

Elections

1986	General	75%	Primary	u/o
1984	General	73%	Primary	u/o

David E. Price (D-N.C.)

Of Chapel Hill — Elected 1986

Born: Aug. 17, 1940, Johnson City, Tenn.
Education: U. of North Carolina, B.A. 1961; Yale U., B.D. 1964, Ph.D. 1969.
Occupation: Educator.
Family: Wife, Lisa Kanwit; two children.
Religion: Baptist.
Political Career: N.C. Democratic Party chairman, 1983-84.
Capitol Office: 1223 Longworth Bldg. 20515; 225-1784.

North Carolina 4th: Central — Raleigh and Chapel Hill. The district vote for Ronald Reagan was 60% in 1984; 47% in 1980.

Committees

Banking, Finance and Urban Affairs
Science, Space and Technology

Elections

1986	General	56%	Primary	48%

Melvin Price (D-Ill.)

Of Belleville — Elected 1944

Born: Jan. 1, 1905, East St. Louis, Ill.
Education: Attended St. Louis U., 1923-25.
Military Career: Army, 1943-44.
Occupation: Journalist.
Family: Wife, Geraldine Freelin; one child.
Religion: Roman Catholic.
Political Career: St. Clair County Board of Supervisors, 1929-31.
Capitol Office: 2110 Rayburn Bldg. 20515; 225-5661.

Illinois 21st: Southwest — East St. Louis and Alton. The district vote for Ronald Reagan was 53% in 1984; 50% in 1980.

Committee

Armed Services

Elections

1986	General	50%	Primary	53%
1984	General	60%	Primary	u/o

CQ Voting Studies

	Presidential Support	Party Unity	Voting Participation
1986	27%	91%	97%
1985	33%	73%	81%

Interest Groups

	ADA	ACU	AFL-CIO	CCUS
1986	65%	n/a	100%	29%
1985	40%	29%	100%	29%

Carl D. Pursell   (R-Mich.)

Of Plymouth — Elected 1976

Born: Dec. 19, 1932, Imlay City, Mich.
Education: Eastern Michigan U., B.A. 1956, M.A. 1961.
Military Career: Army 1957-59, Army Reserve 1959-65.
Occupation: High school teacher; real estate salesman; owner of office supply business.
Family: Wife, Peggy Jean Brown; three children.
Religion: Baptist.
Political Career: Wayne County Commission, 1969-70; Mich. Senate, 1971-77; sought Republican nomination for Mich. Senate, 1966.
Capitol Office: 1414 Longworth Bldg. 20515; 225-4401.

Michigan 2nd: Southeast — Ann Arbor and Jackson. The district vote for Ronald Reagan was 64% in 1984; 52% in 1980.

Committee

Appropriations

CQ Voting Studies

	Presidential Support	Party Unity	Voting Participation
1986	51%	50%	96%
1985	56%	57%	91%

Interest Groups

	ADA	ACU	AFL-CIO	CCUS
1986	45%	n/a	43%	76%
1985	15%	71%	21%	75%

Elections

1986	General	59%	Primary	u/o
1984	General	69%	Primary	u/o

James H. Quillen   (R-Tenn.)

Of Kingsport — Elected 1962

Born: Jan. 11, 1916, near Gate City, Va.
Education: Graduated from Dobyns-Bennett High School, 1934.
Military Career: Navy, 1942-46.
Occupation: Newspaper publisher; real estate and insurance salesman; banker.
Family: Wife, Cecile Cox.
Religion: Methodist.
Political Career: Tenn. House, 1955-63.
Capitol Office: 102 Cannon Bldg. 20515; 225-6356.

Tennessee 1st: Northeast — Tri-cities. The district vote for Ronald Reagan was 71% in 1984; 61% in 1980.

Committee

Rules   (Ranking)

CQ Voting Studies

	Presidential Support	Party Unity	Voting Participation
1986	62%	49%	90%
1985	68%	56%	89%

Interest Groups

	ADA	ACU	AFL-CIO	CCUS
1986	20%	n/a	38%	60%
1985	15%	81%	18%	67%

Elections

1986	General	70%	Primary	88%
1984	General	u/o	Primary	u/o

Nick J. Rahall II (D-W. Va.)

Of Beckley — Elected 1976

Born: May 20, 1949, Beckley, W. Va.
Education: Duke U., A.B. 1971; graduate work, George Washington U., 1972.
Occupation: Broadcasting executive; travel agent.
Family: Divorced; three children.
Religion: Presbyterian.
Political Career: No previous office.
Capitol Office: 343 Cannon Bldg. 20515; 225-3452.

West Virginia 4th: South and West — Huntington and Beckley. The district vote for Ronald Reagan was 49% in 1984; 40% in 1980.

Committees

Interior and Insular Affairs
Public Works and Transportation

Elections

1986	General	71%	Primary	u/o
1984	General	67%	Primary	u/o

CQ Voting Studies

	Presidential Support	Party Unity	Voting Participation
1986	21%	90%	96%
1985	20%	88%	94%

Interest Groups

	ADA	ACU	AFL-CIO	CCUS
1986	90%	n/a	93%	17%
1985	80%	5%	88%	18%

Charles B. Rangel (D-N.Y.)

Of Manhattan — Elected 1970

Born: June 11, 1930, New York, N.Y.
Education: New York U. School of Commerce, B.S. 1957; St. John's School of Law, LL.B. 1960.
Military Career: Army, 1948-52.
Occupation: Lawyer.
Family: Wife, Alma Carter; two children.
Religion: Roman Catholic.
Political Career: N.Y. Assembly, 1967-71; sought Democratic nomination for N.Y. City Council president, 1969.
Capitol Office: 2330 Rayburn Bldg. 20515; 225-4365.

New York 16th: Manhattan — Harlem. The district vote for Ronald Reagan was 16% in 1984; 17% in 1980.

Committees

Ways and Means
Select Narcotics Abuse and Control (Chairman)

Elections

1986	General	98%	Primary	u/o
1984	General	97%	Primary	u/o

CQ Voting Studies

	Presidential Support	Party Unity	Voting Participation
1986	17%	89%	91%
1985	16%	89%	90%

Interest Groups

	ADA	ACU	AFL-CIO	CCUS
1986	100%	n/a	93%	11%
1985	90%	0%	100%	10%

Arthur Ravenel Jr. (R-S.C.)

Of Mount Pleasant — Elected 1986

Born: March 29, 1927, St. Andrews Parish, S.C.
Education: College of Charleston, B.A. 1950.
Military Career: Marine Corps, 1945-46.
Occupation: Businessman.
Family: Wife, Jean Rickenbaker; six children.
Religion: French Huguenot.
Political Career: S.C. House, 1953-59; S.C. Senate, 1981-87.
Capitol Office: 1730 Longworth Bldg. 20515; 225-3176.

South Carolina 1st: South — Charleston. The district vote for Ronald Reagan was 64% in 1984; 53% in 1980.

Committee

Armed Services

Elections

1986	General	52%	Primary	57%

Richard Ray (D-Ga.)

Of Perry — Elected 1982

Born: Feb. 2, 1927, Fort Valley, Ga.
Education: Attended U. of Georgia, 1956.
Military Career: Navy, 1944-45.
Occupation: Exterminator; Senate aide.
Family: Wife, Barbara Elizabeth Giles; three children.
Religion: Methodist.
Political Career: Perry City Council, 1962-64; mayor of Perry, 1964-70.
Capitol Office: 425 Cannon Bldg. 20515; 225-5901.

Georgia 3rd: West Central — Columbus. The district vote for Ronald Reagan was 55% in 1984; 37% in 1980.

Committees

Armed Services
Small Business

Elections

1986	General	u/o	Primary	u/o
1984	General	81%	Primary	68%

CQ Voting Studies

	Presidential Support	Party Unity	Voting Participation
1986	56%	50%	98%
1985	56%	54%	98%

Interest Groups

	ADA	ACU	AFL-CIO	CCUS
1986	10%	n/a	21%	88%
1985	15%	71%	25%	82%

Ralph Regula   (R-Ohio)

Of Navarre — Elected 1972

Born: Dec. 3, 1924, Beach City, Ohio.
Education: Mount Union College, B.A. 1948; William McKinley School of Law, LL.B. 1952.
Military Career: Navy, 1944-46.
Occupation: Lawyer.
Family: Wife, Mary Rogusky; three children.
Religion: Episcopalian.
Political Career: Ohio House, 1965-67; Ohio Senate, 1967-73.
Capitol Office: 2209 Rayburn Bldg. 20515; 225-3876.

Ohio 16th: Northeast — Canton.

Committees

Appropriations
Select Aging

Elections

1986	General	76%	Primary	u/o
1984	General	72%	Primary	u/o

CQ Voting Studies

	Presidential Support	Party Unity	Voting Participation
1986	56%	56%	98%
1985	60%	57%	98%

Interest Groups

	ADA	ACU	AFL-CIO	CCUS
1986	15%	n/a	71%	61%
1985	25%	52%	35%	59%

John J. Rhodes III   (R-Ariz.)

Of Mesa — Elected 1986

Born: Sept. 8, 1943, Mesa, Ariz.
Education: Yale U., B.A. 1965; U. of Arizona, J.D. 1968.
Military Career: Army, 1968-70.
Occupation: Lawyer.
Family: Wife, Ann Chase; four children.
Religion: Protestant.
Political Career: Vice president, board of directors, Central Arizona Water Conservation District, 1983-87; Mesa School Board, 1972-76; GOP District Chairman, 1973-75.
Capitol Office: 510 Cannon Bldg. 20515; 225-2635.

Arizona 1st: Eastern Phoenix, Tempe and Mesa. The district vote for Ronald Reagan was 72% in 1984; 63% in 1980.

Committees

Interior and Insular Affairs
Small Business

Elections

1986	General	71%	Primary	45%

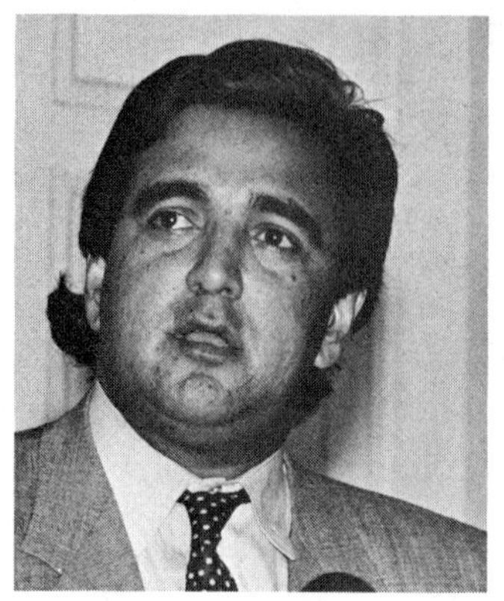

Bill Richardson (D-N.M.)

Of Santa Fe — Elected 1982

Born: Nov. 15, 1947, Pasadena, Calif.
Education: Tufts U., B.A. 1970, M.A. 1971.
Occupation: Business consultant.
Family: Wife, Barbara Flavin.
Religion: Roman Catholic.
Political Career: Executive director, New Mexico Democratic Party, 1978-80; Democratic nominee for U.S. House, 1980.
Capitol Office: 332 Cannon Bldg. 20515; 225-6190.

New Mexico 3rd: North and West — Farmington and Santa Fe. The district vote for Ronald Reagan was 53% in 1984; 52% in 1980.

Committees

Education and Labor
Energy and Commerce
Interior and Insular Affairs
Select Aging

CQ Voting Studies

	Presidential Support	Party Unity	Voting Participation
1986	24%	90%	97%
1985	25%	89%	95%

Interest Groups

	ADA	ACU	AFL-CIO	CCUS
1986	75%	n/a	100%	41%
1985	70%	14%	76%	32%

Elections

1986	General	71%	Primary	u/o
1984	General	61%	Primary	77%

Tom Ridge (R-Pa.)

Of Erie — Elected 1982

Born: Aug. 26, 1945, Munhall, Pa.
Education: Harvard College, B.A. 1967; Dickinson School of Law, J.D. 1972.
Military Career: Army, 1968-70.
Occupation: Lawyer.
Family: Wife, Michele Moore; one child.
Religion: Roman Catholic.
Political Career: No previous office.
Capitol Office: 1714 Longworth Bldg. 20515; 225-5406.

Pennsylvania 21st: Northwest — Erie. The district vote for Ronald Reagan was 53% in 1984; 49% in 1980.

Committees

Banking, Finance and Urban Affairs
Veterans' Affairs
Select Aging

CQ Voting Studies

	Presidential Support	Party Unity	Voting Participation
1986	47%	59%	97%
1985	44%	60%	96%

Interest Groups

	ADA	ACU	AFL-CIO	CCUS
1986	35%	n/a	64%	61%
1985	30%	48%	47%	73%

Elections

1986	General	81%	Primary	u/o
1984	General	65%	Primary	u/o

Matthew J. Rinaldo (R-N.J.)

Of Union — Elected 1972

Born: Sept. 1, 1931, Elizabeth, N.J.
Education: Rutgers U., B.S. 1953; Seton Hall U., M.B.A. 1959; New York U., Ph.D. 1979.
Occupation: Industrial relations consultant.
Family: Single.
Religion: Roman Catholic.
Political Career: Union County Board of Freeholders, 1963-64; N.J. Senate, 1968-72.
Capitol Office: 2469 Rayburn Bldg. 20515; 225-5361.

New Jersey 7th: North and Central — Elizabeth. The district vote for Ronald Reagan was 63% in 1984.

Committees

Energy and Commerce
Select Aging   (Ranking)

Elections

1986	General	80%	Primary	u/o
1984	General	74%	Primary	u/o

CQ Voting Studies

	Presidential Support	Party Unity	Voting Participation
1986	40%	34%	96%
1985	50%	43%	94%

Interest Groups

	ADA	ACU	AFL-CIO	CCUS
1986	45%	n/a	100%	28%
1985	55%	52%	81%	41%

Don Ritter (R-Pa.)

Of Coopersburg — Elected 1978

Born: Oct. 21, 1940, New York, N.Y.
Education: Lehigh U., B.S. 1961; Massachusetts Institute of Technology, M.S. 1963, Sc.D. 1966.
Occupation: Engineering consultant; professor.
Family: Wife, Edith Duerksen; two children.
Religion: Unitarian.
Political Career: No previous office.
Capitol Office: 2447 Rayburn Bldg. 20515; 225-6411.

Pennsylvania 15th: East — Allentown and Bethlehem. The district vote for Ronald Reagan was 57% in 1984; 50% in 1980.

Committees

Energy and Commerce
Science, Space and Technology

Elections

1986	General	57%	Primary	u/o
1984	General	58%	Primary	u/o

CQ Voting Studies

	Presidential Support	Party Unity	Voting Participation
1986	70%	65%	94%
1985	75%	71%	93%

Interest Groups

	ADA	ACU	AFL-CIO	CCUS
1986	10%	n/a	57%	94%
1985	10%	86%	38%	82%

Pat Roberts (R-Kan.)

Of Dodge City — Elected 1980

Born: April 20, 1936, Topeka, Kan.
Education: Kansas State U., B.A. 1958.
Military Career: Marine Corps, 1958-62.
Occupation: Journalist; congressional aide.
Family: Wife, Franki Fann; three children.
Religion: Methodist.
Political Career: No previous office.
Capitol Office: 1314 Longworth Bldg. 20515; 225-2715.

Kansas 1st: West — Salina and Dodge City. The district vote for Ronald Reagan was 74% in 1984; 66% in 1980.

CQ Voting Studies

	Presidential Support	Party Unity	Voting Participation
1986	69%	87%	98%
1985	63%	83%	95%

Interest Groups

	ADA	ACU	AFL-CIO	CCUS
1986	0%	n/a	7%	94%
1985	15%	71%	12%	95%

Committees

Agriculture
House Administration

Elections

1986	General	76%	Primary	u/o
1984	General	76%	Primary	u/o

Tommy F. Robinson (D-Ark.)

Of Jacksonville — Elected 1984

Born: March 7, 1942, Little Rock, Ark.
Education: U. of Arkansas, Little Rock, B.A. 1976.
Military Career: Navy, 1959-63.
Occupation: Law enforcement officer.
Family: Wife, Carolyn Barber; six children.
Religion: Methodist.
Political Career: Pulaski County (Little Rock) sheriff, 1980-84.
Capitol Office: 1541 Longworth Bldg. 20515; 225-2506.

Arkansas 2nd: Central — Little Rock. The district vote for Ronald Reagan was 60% in 1984; 48% in 1980.

CQ Voting Studies

	Presidential Support	Party Unity	Voting Participation
1986	46%	54%	96%
1985	45%	66%	95%

Interest Groups

	ADA	ACU	AFL-CIO	CCUS
1986	25%	n/a	86%	44%
1985	40%	57%	63%	45%

Committees

Armed Services
Education and Labor
Veterans' Affairs
Select Aging

Elections

1986	General	75%	Primary	78%
1984	General	47%	Primary	53% *

Primary runoff.

Peter W. Rodino Jr.   (D-N.J.)

Of Newark — Elected 1948

Born: June 7, 1909, Newark, N.J.
Education: U. of Newark (Rutgers), LL.B. 1937.
Military Career: Army, 1941-46.
Occupation: Lawyer.
Family: Widowed; two children.
Religion: Roman Catholic.
Political Career: Democratic nominee for N.J. Assembly, 1940; Democratic nominee for U.S. House, 1946.
Capitol Office: 2462 Rayburn Bldg. 20515; 225-3436.

New Jersey 10th: Newark. The district vote for Ronald Reagan was 25% in 1984.

Committees

Judiciary   (Chairman)
Select Iran-contra
Select Narcotics Abuse and Control

CQ Voting Studies

	Presidential Support	Party Unity	Voting Participation
1986	16%	84%	87%
1985	16%	80%	86%

Interest Groups

	ADA	ACU	AFL-CIO	CCUS
1986	100%	n/a	100%	19%
1985	100%	5%	100%	19%

Elections

1986	General	u/o	Primary	60%
1984	General	84%	Primary	76%

Robert A. Roe   (D-N.J.)

Of Pompton Lakes — Elected 1969

Born: Feb. 28, 1924, Wayne, N.J.
Education: Attended Oregon State U. and Washington State U.
Military Career: Army, World War II.
Occupation: Construction company owner; engineer.
Family: Single.
Religion: Roman Catholic.
Political Career: Wayne Township committeeman, 1955-56; mayor of Wayne Township, 1956-61; Passaic County freeholder, 1959-63; sought Democratic nomination for governor, 1977 and 1981.
Capitol Office: 2243 Rayburn Bldg. 20515; 225-5751.

New Jersey 8th: North — Paterson. The district vote for Ronald Reagan was 58% in 1984.

Committees

Public Works and Transportation
Science, Space and Technology   (Chairman)
Select Intelligence

CQ Voting Studies

	Presidential Support	Party Unity	Voting Participation
1986	22%	89%	95%
1985	18%	89%	94%

Interest Groups

	ADA	ACU	AFL-CIO	CCUS
1986	75%	n/a	100%	18%
1985	75%	11%	94%	29%

Elections

1986	General	63%	Primary	96%
1984	General	63%	Primary	89%

Buddy Roemer (D-La.)

Of Bossier City — Elected 1980

Born: October 4, 1943, Shreveport, La.
Education: Harvard U., B.A. 1964, M.B.A. 1967.
Occupation: Banker; data processing executive.
Family: Wife, Patti Crocker; three children.
Religion: Methodist.
Political Career: Democratic nominee for U.S. House, 1978.
Capitol Office: 103 Cannon Bldg. 20515; 225-2777.

Louisiana 4th: Northwest — Shreveport. The district vote for Ronald Reagan was 65% in 1984; 54% in 1980.

Committees

Banking, Finance and Urban Affairs
Small Business

CQ Voting Studies

	Presidential Support	Party Unity	Voting Participation
1986	50%	40%	95%
1985	66%	27%	99%

Interest Groups

	ADA	ACU	AFL-CIO	CCUS
1986	35%	n/a	43%	61%
1985	25%	81%	31%	77%

Elections

1986	General	†	Primary	†
1984	General	†	Primary	†

† *In Louisiana a candidate unopposed in the primary and general elections is declared elected.*

Harold Rogers (R-Ky.)

Of Somerset — Elected 1980

Born: Dec. 31, 1937, Barrier, Ky.
Education: Attended Western Kentucky U., 1956-57; U. of Kentucky, B.A. 1962, LL.B. 1964.
Military Career: Army National Guard, 1956-64.
Occupation: Lawyer.
Family: Wife, Shirley McDowell; three children.
Religion: Baptist.
Political Career: Commonwealth attorney, Pulaski and Rockcastle counties, 1969-79; Republican nominee for lt. gov., 1979.
Capitol Office: 206 Cannon Bldg. 20515; 225-4601.

Kentucky 5th: Southeast — Middlesboro. The district vote for Ronald Reagan was 69% in 1984; 61% in 1980.

Committees

Appropriations
Budget

CQ Voting Studies

	Presidential Support	Party Unity	Voting Participation
1986	70%	76%	99%
1985	64%	75%	96%

Interest Groups

	ADA	ACU	AFL-CIO	CCUS
1986	10%	n/a	43%	67%
1985	10%	76%	18%	76%

Elections

1986	General	u/o	Primary	u/o
1984	General	76%	Primary	u/o

Charlie Rose (D-N.C.)

Of Fayetteville — Elected 1972

Born: Aug. 10, 1939, Fayetteville, N.C.
Education: Davidson College, B.A. 1961; U. of North Carolina Law School, LL.B. 1964.
Occupation: Lawyer.
Family: Wife, Joan Teague; two children.
Religion: Presbyterian.
Political Career: Chief district court prosecutor, 12th Judicial District, 1967-71; sought Democratic nomination for U.S. House, 1970.
Capitol Office: 2230 Rayburn Bldg. 20515; 225-2731.

North Carolina 7th: Southeast — Fayetteville and Wilmington. The district vote for Ronald Reagan was 57% in 1984; 44% in 1980.

Committees

Agriculture
House Administration

Elections

1986	General	66%	Primary	u/o
1984	General	59%	Primary	84%

CQ Voting Studies

	Presidential Support	Party Unity	Voting Participation
1986	29%	78%	88%
1985	28%	84%	95%

Interest Groups

	ADA	ACU	AFL-CIO	CCUS
1986	55%	n/a	67%	44%
1985	60%	17%	56%	25%

Dan Rostenkowski (D-Ill.)

Of Chicago — Elected 1958

Born: Jan. 2, 1928, Chicago, Ill.
Education: Attended Loyola U., 1948-51.
Military Career: Army, 1946-48.
Occupation: Insurance executive.
Family: Wife, LaVerne Pirkins; four children.
Religion: Roman Catholic.
Political Career: Ill. House, 1953-55; Ill. Senate, 1955-59.
Capitol Office: 2111 Rayburn Bldg. 20515; 225-4061.

Illinois 8th: Chicago — North and Northwest Sides. The district vote for Ronald Reagan was 51% in 1984; 34% in 1980.

Committees

Ways and Means (Chairman)
Joint Taxation (Chairman)

Elections

1986	General	79%	Primary	87%
1984	General	71%	Primary	88%

CQ Voting Studies

	Presidential Support	Party Unity	Voting Participation
1986	19%	84%	85%
1985	28%	82%	88%

Interest Groups

	ADA	ACU	AFL-CIO	CCUS
1986	65%	n/a	86%	35%
1985	75%	20%	81%	36%

Toby Roth (R-Wis.)

Of Appleton — Elected 1978

Born: Oct. 10, 1938, Strasburg, N.D.
Education: Marquette U., B.A. 1961.
Military Career: Army Reserve, 1962-69.
Occupation: Real estate broker.
Family: Wife, Barbara Fischer; three children.
Religion: Roman Catholic.
Political Career: Wis. Assembly, 1973-79.
Capitol Office: 2352 Rayburn Bldg. 20515; 225-5665.

Wisconsin 8th: Northeast — Green Bay and Appleton. The district vote for Ronald Reagan was 63% in 1984; 55% in 1980.

Committees

Banking, Finance and Urban Affairs
Foreign Affairs

Elections

1986	General	67%	Primary	u/o
1984	General	68%	Primary	u/o

CQ Voting Studies

	Presidential Support	Party Unity	Voting Participation
1986	68%	79%	94%
1985	55%	76%	89%

Interest Groups

	ADA	ACU	AFL-CIO	CCUS
1986	0%	n/a	8%	81%
1985	10%	80%	13%	95%

Marge Roukema (R-N.J.)

Of Ridgewood — Elected 1980

Born: Sept. 19, 1929, Newark, N.J.
Education: Montclair State College, B.A. 1951, graduate work, 1951-53; Rutgers U., 1975.
Occupation: High school government and history teacher.
Family: Husband, Richard Roukema; two children.
Religion: Protestant.
Political Career: Ridgewood Board of Education, 1970-73; Republican nominee for U.S. House, 1978.
Capitol Office: 303 Cannon Bldg. 20515; 225-4465.

New Jersey 5th: North and West — Ridgewood. The district vote for Ronald Reagan was 71% in 1984.

Committees

Banking, Finance and Urban Affairs
Education and Labor
Select Hunger   (Ranking)

Elections

1986	General	75%	Primary	75%
1984	General	71%	Primary	u/o

CQ Voting Studies

	Presidential Support	Party Unity	Voting Participation
1986	56%	62%	96%
1985	49%	56%	98%

Interest Groups

	ADA	ACU	AFL-CIO	CCUS
1986	30%	n/a	43%	78%
1985	45%	40%	29%	68%

J. Roy Rowland (D-Ga.)

Of Dublin — Elected 1982

Born: Feb. 3, 1926, Wrightsville, Ga.
Education: Attended Emory University, 1943, South Georgia College, 1946-47, U. of Georgia, 1947-48; Medical College of Georgia, M.D. 1952.
Military Career: Army, 1944-46.
Occupation: Physician.
Family: Wife, Luella Price; three children.
Religion: Methodist.
Political Career: Ga. House, 1977-83.
Capitol Office: 423 Cannon Bldg. 20515; 225-6531.

Georgia 8th: South Central — Macon and Waycross. The district vote for Ronald Reagan was 52% in 1984; 34% in 1980.

Committees

Public Works and Transportation
Veterans' Affairs
Select Children, Youth and Families

Elections

1986	General	85%	Primary	u/o
1984	General	u/o	Primary	u/o

CQ Voting Studies

	Presidential Support	Party Unity	Voting Participation
1986	44%	73%	100%
1985	50%	75%	99%

Interest Groups

	ADA	ACU	AFL-CIO	CCUS
1986	40%	n/a	50%	56%
1985	30%	67%	41%	45%

John G. Rowland (R-Conn.)

Of Waterbury — Elected 1984

Born: May 24, 1957, Waterbury, Conn.
Education: Villanova U., B.S. 1979.
Occupation: Insurance agent.
Family: Wife, Deborah J. Nabhan; one child.
Religion: Roman Catholic.
Political Career: Conn. House, 1981-85.
Capitol Office: 512 Cannon Bldg. 20515; 225-3822.

Connecticut 5th: West — Waterbury and Danbury. The district vote for Ronald Reagan was 67% in 1984; 53% in 1980.

Committees

Armed Services
Veterans' Affairs

Elections

1986	General	61%	Primary	u/o
1984	General	54%	Primary	u/o

CQ Voting Studies

	Presidential Support	Party Unity	Voting Participation
1986	61%	59%	99%
1985	71%	76%	97%

Interest Groups

	ADA	ACU	AFL-CIO	CCUS
1986	35%	n/a	79%	72%
1985	10%	76%	24%	86%

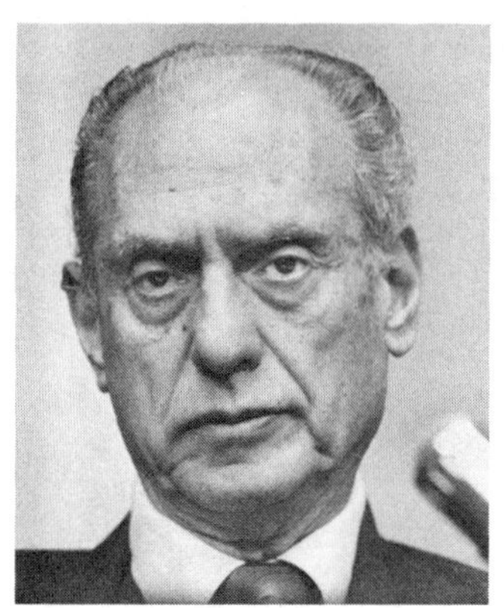

Edward R. Roybal   (D-Calif.)

Of Pasadena — Elected 1962

Born: Feb. 10, 1916, Albuquerque, N.M.
Education: Attended U. of California, Los Angeles, 1935; Southwestern U. School of Law, 1952.
Military Career: Army, 1944-45.
Occupation: Social worker; public health educator.
Family: Wife, Lucille Beserra; three children.
Religion: Roman Catholic.
Political Career: Los Angeles City Council, 1949-62; Democratic candidate for Calif. lieutenant governor, 1954.
Capitol Office: 2211 Rayburn Bldg. 20515; 225-6235.

California 25th: Central and East Los Angeles. The district vote for Ronald Reagan was 39% in 1984.

Committees

Appropriations
Select Aging   (Chairman)

CQ Voting Studies

	Presidential Support	Party Unity	Voting Participation
1986	16%	88%	94%
1985	16%	89%	91%

Interest Groups

	ADA	ACU	AFL-CIO	CCUS
1986	95%	n/a	85%	19%
1985	95%	5%	94%	15%

Elections

1986	General	78%	Primary	89%
1984	General	72%	Primary	86%

Marty Russo   (D-Ill.)

Of South Holland — Elected 1974

Born: Jan. 23, 1944, Chicago, Ill.
Education: DePaul U., B.A. 1965, J.D. 1967.
Occupation: Lawyer.
Family: Wife, Karen Jorgenson; two children.
Religion: Roman Catholic.
Political Career: Assistant Cook County state's attorney, 1971-73.
Capitol Office: 2233 Rayburn Bldg. 20515; 225-5736.

Illinois 3rd: Southwest Chicago and Suburbs. The district vote for Ronald Reagan was 65% in 1984; 49% in 1980.

Committees

Budget
Ways and Means

CQ Voting Studies

	Presidential Support	Party Unity	Voting Participation
1986	18%	81%	93%
1985	23%	82%	94%

Interest Groups

	ADA	ACU	AFL-CIO	CCUS
1986	65%	n/a	86%	38%
1985	70%	14%	82%	36%

Elections

1986	General	66%	Primary	91%
1984	General	64%	Primary	u/o

Martin Olav Sabo   (D-Minn.)

Of Minneapolis — Elected 1978

Born: Feb. 28, 1938, Crosby, N.D.
Education: Augsburg College, B.A. 1959; graduate work, U. of Minnesota, 1960.
Occupation: Public official.
Family: Wife, Sylvia Ann Lee; two children.
Religion: Lutheran.
Political Career: Minn. House, 1961-79, Speaker, 1973-79.
Capitol Office: 2201 Rayburn Bldg. 20515; 225-4755.

Minnesota 5th: Minneapolis and Suburbs. The district vote for Ronald Reagan was 37% in 1984; 28% in 1980.

Committee

Appropriations

Elections

1986	General	74%	Primary	91%
1984	General	70%	Primary	u/o

CQ Voting Studies

	Presidential Support	Party Unity	Voting Participation
1986	20%	95%	98%
1985	16%	98%	99%

Interest Groups

	ADA	ACU	AFL-CIO	CCUS
1986	95%	n/a	93%	11%
1985	95%	5%	94%	18%

Patricia Saiki   (R-Hawaii)

Of Honolulu — Elected 1986

Born: May 28, 1930, Hilo, Hawaii.
Education: U. of Hawaii, Manoa, B.S. 1952.
Occupation: Legislative aide; teacher.
Family: Husband, Stanley Saiki; five children.
Religion: Episcopalian.
Political Career: Hawaii House, 1969-75; Hawaii Senate, 1975-83; Republican nominee for lt. governor, 1982; Hawaii Republican Party chairman, 1983-85.
Capitol Office: 1407 Longworth Bldg. 20515; 225-2726.

Hawaii 1st: Honolulu. The district vote for Ronald Reagan was 55% in 1984.

Committees

Banking, Finance and Urban Affairs
Merchant Marine and Fisheries
Select Aging

Elections

1986	General	61%	Primary	u/o

Fernand J. St Germain (D-R.I.)

Of Woonsocket — Elected 1960

Born: Jan. 9, 1928, Blackstone, Mass.
Education: Providence College, Ph.B. 1948; Boston U., LL.B. 1955.
Military Career: Army, 1949-52.
Occupation: Lawyer.
Family: Wife, Rachel O'Neill; two children.
Religion: Roman Catholic.
Political Career: Rhode Island House, 1953-61.
Capitol Office: 2108 Rayburn Bldg. 20515; 225-4911.

Rhode Island 1st: East — Part of Providence and Pawtucket. The district vote for Ronald Reagan was 50% in 1984; 37% in 1980.

Committee

Banking, Finance and Urban Affairs   (Chairman)

CQ Voting Studies

	Presidential Support	Party Unity	Voting Participation
1986	21%	87%	92%
1985	20%	82%	88%

Interest Groups

	ADA	ACU	AFL-CIO	CCUS
1986	80%	n/a	100%	35%
1985	70%	10%	100%	20%

Elections

1986	General	58%	Primary	u/o
1984	General	69%	Primary	u/o

Gus Savage (D-Ill.)

Of Chicago — Elected 1980

Born: Oct. 30, 1925, Detroit, Mich.
Education: Roosevelt U., B.A. 1951; graduate work in political science, 1952; attended Chicago-Kent College of Law, 1952-53.
Military Career: Army, 1943-46.
Occupation: Newspaper publisher.
Family: Widowed; two children.
Religion: Baptist.
Political Career: Sought Democratic nomination for U.S. House, 1968 and 1970.
Capitol Office: 1121 Longworth Bldg. 20515; 225-0773.

Illinois 2nd: South Side Chicago and Harvey. The district vote for Ronald Reagan was 16% in 1984; 23% in 1980.

Committees

Public Works and Transportation
Small Business

CQ Voting Studies

	Presidential Support	Party Unity	Voting Participation
1986	14%	79%	84%
1985	13%	85%	88%

Interest Groups

	ADA	ACU	AFL-CIO	CCUS
1986	95%	n/a	100%	7%
1985	100%	5%	100%	18%

Elections

1986	General	83%	Primary	52%
1984	General	83%	Primary	45%

Thomas C. Sawyer   (D-Ohio)

Of Akron — Elected 1986

Born: Aug. 15, 1945, Akron, Ohio.
Education: U. of Akron, B.A. 1968, M.A. 1970.
Occupation: Teacher.
Family: Wife, Joyce Handler; one child.
Religion: Presbyterian.
Political Career: Ohio House, 1977-83; Akron mayor, 1983-87.
Capitol Office: 1338 Longworth Bldg. 20515; 225-5231.

Ohio 14th: Northeast — Akron.

Committees

Education and Labor
Government Operations
Select Children, Youth and Families

Elections

1986	General	54%	Primary	49%

H. James Saxton   (R-N.J.)

Of Vincentown — Elected 1984

Born: Jan. 22, 1943, Scranton, Pa.
Education: East Stroudsburg (Pa.) State College, B.A. 1965; Temple U., graduate studies, 1967-68.
Occupation: Owner of realty company.
Family: Wife, Helen Gadomski; two children.
Religion: Methodist.
Political Career: N.J. Assembly, 1976-82; N.J. Senate, 1982-84.
Capitol Office: 324 Cannon Bldg. 20515; 225-4765.

New Jersey 13th: South and Central. The district vote for Ronald Reagan was 65% in 1984.

Committees

Banking, Finance and Urban Affairs
Merchant Marine and Fisheries
Select Aging

Elections

1986	General	65%	Primary	u/o
1984	General	61%	Primary	45%

CQ Voting Studies

	Presidential Support	Party Unity	Voting Participation
1986	64%	67%	99%
1985	61%	81%	99%

Interest Groups

	ADA	ACU	AFL-CIO	CCUS
1986	30%	n/a	57%	56%
1985	15%	81%	12%	82%

Dan L. Schaefer (R-Colo.)

Of Lakewood — Elected 1983

Born: Jan. 25, 1936, Gutenberg, Iowa.
Education: Niagara U., B.A. 1961; graduate work at Potsdam State U. (N.Y.), 1961-64.
Military Career: Marine Corps, 1955-57.
Occupation: Public relations consultant.
Family: Wife, Mary Lenney; four children.
Religion: Roman Catholic.
Political Career: Colorado House, 1977-79; Colorado Senate, 1979-83, president pro tempore, 1981-83.
Capitol Office: 1317 Longworth Bldg. 20515; 225-7882.

Colorado 6th: Denver Suburbs — Aurora and Lakewood. The district vote for Ronald Reagan was 68% in 1984; 60% in 1980.

Committee

Energy and Commerce

CQ Voting Studies

	Presidential Support	Party Unity	Voting Participation
1986	76%	84%	95%
1985	76%	84%	96%

Interest Groups

	ADA	ACU	AFL-CIO	CCUS
1986	0%	n/a	15%	88%
1985	10%	80%	13%	91%

Elections

1986	General	66%	Primary	u/o
1984	General	89%	Primary	u/o

James H. Scheuer (D-N.Y.)

Of Queens — Elected 1964

Born: Feb. 6, 1920, New York, N.Y.
Education: Swarthmore College, A.B. 1942; Harvard Business School, M.A. 1943; Columbia U. Law School, LL.B. 1948.
Military Career: Army, 1943-45.
Occupation: Lawyer.
Family: Wife, Emily Malino; four children.
Religion: Jewish.
Political Career: Sought Democratic nomination for mayor of New York, 1969; defeated for renomination to U.S. House, 1972; returned to House, 1974.
Capitol Office: 2466 Rayburn Bldg. 20515; 225-5471.

New York 8th: Northern Queens, Eastern Bronx and Western Nassau County. The district vote for Ronald Reagan was 48% in 1984; 47% in 1980.

Committees

Energy and Commerce
Science, Space and Technology
Joint Economic
Select Narcotics Abuse and Control

CQ Voting Studies

	Presidential Support	Party Unity	Voting Participation
1986	18%	88%	94%
1985	19%	90%	93%

Interest Groups

	ADA	ACU	AFL-CIO	CCUS
1986	95%	n/a	100%	18%
1985	90%	0%	100%	23%

Elections

1986	General	90%	Primary	u/o
1984	General	63%	Primary	u/o

Claudine Schneider   (R-R.I.)

Of Narragansett — Elected 1980

Born: March 25, 1947, Pittsburgh, Pa.
Education: Windham College, B.A. 1969; graduate work, U. of Rhode Island, 1975.
Occupation: Television producer and moderator.
Family: Divorced.
Religion: Roman Catholic.
Political Career: Republican nominee for U.S. House, 1978.
Capitol Office: 1512 Longworth Bldg. 20515; 225-2735.

Rhode Island 2nd: West — Western Providence and Warwick. The district vote for Ronald Reagan was 53% in 1984; 38% in 1980.

Committees

Merchant Marine and Fisheries
Science, Space and Technology
Select Aging

Elections

1986	General	72%	Primary	u/o
1984	General	68%	Primary	u/o

CQ Voting Studies

	Presidential Support	Party Unity	Voting Participation
1986	31%	29%	90%
1985	34%	31%	91%

Interest Groups

	ADA	ACU	AFL-CIO	CCUS
1986	80%	n/a	100%	47%
1985	55%	26%	63%	44%

Patricia Schroeder   (D-Colo.)

Of Denver — Elected 1972

Born: July 30, 1940, Portland, Ore.
Education: U. of Minnesota, B.A. 1961; Harvard U., J.D. 1964.
Occupation: Lawyer; law instructor.
Family: Husband, James Schroeder; two children.
Religion: United Church of Christ.
Political Career: No previous office.
Capitol Office: 2410 Rayburn Bldg. 20515; 225-4431.

Colorado 1st: Denver. The district vote for Ronald Reagan was 47% in 1984; 41% in 1980.

Committees

Armed Services
Judiciary
Post Office and Civil Service
Select Children, Youth and Families

Elections

1986	General	68%	Primary	u/o
1984	General	62%	Primary	u/o

CQ Voting Studies

	Presidential Support	Party Unity	Voting Participation
1986	19%	66%	95%
1985	30%	58%	97%

Interest Groups

	ADA	ACU	AFL-CIO	CCUS
1986	95%	n/a	86%	29%
1985	80%	19%	71%	55%

Bill Schuette (R-Mich.)

Of Sanford — Elected 1984

Born: Oct. 13, 1953, Midland, Mich.
Education: Georgetown U., B.A. 1976; U. of San Francisco School of Law, J.D. 1979.
Occupation: Lawyer.
Family: Single.
Religion: Episcopalian.
Political Career: No previous office.
Capitol Office: 415 Cannon Bldg. 20515; 225-3561.

Michigan 10th: North Central — Midland. The district vote for Ronald Reagan was 67% in 1984; 55% in 1980.

Committees

Agriculture
Select Aging

Elections

1986	General	51%	Primary	u/o
1984	General	50%	Primary	u/o

CQ Voting Studies

	Presidential Support	Party Unity	Voting Participation
1986	60%	76%	95%
1985	68%	85%	98%

Interest Groups

	ADA	ACU	AFL-CIO	CCUS
1986	10%	n/a	23%	73%
1985	5%	81%	6%	68%

Richard T. Schulze (R-Pa.)

Of Berwyn — Elected 1974

Born: Aug. 7, 1929, Philadelphia, Pa.
Education: Attended U. of Houston, 1949-50; Villanova U., 1952; Temple U., 1968.
Military Career: Army, 1951-53.
Occupation: Household appliance dealer.
Family: Wife, Nancy Lockwood; four children.
Religion: Presbyterian.
Political Career: Pa. House, 1969-75.
Capitol Office: 2369 Rayburn Bldg. 20515; 225-5761.

Pennsylvania 5th: Western Philadelphia Suburbs — Chester. The district vote for Ronald Reagan was 67% in 1984; 58% in 1980.

Committee

Ways and Means

Elections

1986	General	66%	Primary	u/o
1984	General	73%	Primary	89%

CQ Voting Studies

	Presidential Support	Party Unity	Voting Participation
1986	58%	60%	88%
1985	64%	68%	91%

Interest Groups

	ADA	ACU	AFL-CIO	CCUS
1986	15%	n/a	46%	81%
1985	10%	71%	29%	82%

Charles E. Schumer (D-N.Y.)

Of Brooklyn — Elected 1980

Born: Nov. 23, 1950, Brooklyn, N.Y.
Education: Harvard U., B.A. 1971, J.D. 1974.
Occupation: Lawyer.
Family: Wife, Iris Weinshall; one child.
Religion: Jewish.
Political Career: N.Y. Assembly, 1975-81.
Capitol Office: 126 Cannon Bldg. 20515; 225-6616.

New York 10th: Central and Southern Brooklyn — Flatbush. The district vote for Ronald Reagan was 48% in 1984; 44% in 1980.

Committees

Banking, Finance and Urban Affairs
Budget
Judiciary

Elections

1986	General	93%	Primary	u/o
1984	General	72%	Primary	u/o

CQ Voting Studies

	Presidential Support	Party Unity	Voting Participation
1986	17%	88%	94%
1985	28%	84%	93%

Interest Groups

	ADA	ACU	AFL-CIO	CCUS
1986	85%	n/a	86%	29%
1985	90%	14%	93%	32%

F. James Sensenbrenner Jr. (R-Wis.)

Of Menomonee Falls — Elected 1978

Born: June 14, 1943, Chicago, Ill.
Education: Stanford U., A.B. 1965; U. of Wisconsin Law School, J.D. 1968.
Occupation: Lawyer.
Family: Wife, Cheryl Warren; two children.
Religion: Episcopalian.
Political Career: Wis. Assembly, 1969-75; Wis. Senate, 1975-79.
Capitol Office: 2444 Rayburn Bldg. 20515; 225-5101.

Wisconsin 9th: Milwaukee Suburbs and Sheboygan. The district vote for Ronald Reagan was 64% in 1984; 58% in 1980.

Committees

Judiciary
Science, Space and Technology
Select Narcotics Abuse and Control

Elections

1986	General	78%	Primary	u/o
1984	General	73%	Primary	u/o

CQ Voting Studies

	Presidential Support	Party Unity	Voting Participation
1986	73%	89%	99%
1985	68%	87%	98%

Interest Groups

	ADA	ACU	AFL-CIO	CCUS
1986	0%	n/a	7%	89%
1985	20%	71%	6%	86%

Philip R. Sharp (D-Ind.)

Of Muncie — Elected 1974

Born: July 15, 1942, Baltimore, Md.
Education: Georgetown U., B.S. 1964; graduate work, Oxford U., 1966; Georgetown U., Ph.D. 1974.
Occupation: Political science professor.
Family: Wife, Marilyn Augburn; two children.
Religion: Methodist.
Political Career: Democratic nominee for U.S. House, 1970 and 1972.
Capitol Office: 2452 Rayburn Bldg. 20515; 225-3021.

Indiana 2nd: East Central — Muncie and Richmond. The district vote for Ronald Reagan was 67% in 1984; 61% in 1980.

Committees

Energy and Commerce
Interior and Insular Affairs

CQ Voting Studies

	Presidential Support	Party Unity	Voting Participation
1986	24%	81%	96%
1985	43%	76%	97%

Interest Groups

	ADA	ACU	AFL-CIO	CCUS
1986	65%	n/a	86%	41%
1985	65%	38%	71%	50%

Elections

1986	General	62%	Primary	94%
1984	General	53%	Primary	92%

E. Clay Shaw Jr. (R-Fla.)

Of Fort Lauderdale — Elected 1980

Born: April 19, 1939, Miami, Fla.
Education: Stetson Univ., B.A. 1961, J.D. 1966; U. of Alabama, M.A. 1963.
Occupation: Nurseryman; lawyer.
Family: Wife, Emilie Costar; four children.
Religion: Roman Catholic.
Political Career: Fort Lauderdale assistant city attorney, 1968; chief city prosecutor, 1968-69; associate municipal judge, 1969-71; city commissioner, 1971-73; vice mayor, 1973-75; mayor, 1975-81.
Capitol Office: 440 Cannon Bldg. 20515; 225-3026.

Florida 15th: Southeast — Fort Lauderdale. The district vote for Ronald Reagan was 59% in 1984; 57% in 1980.

Committees

Judiciary
Public Works and Transportation
Select Narcotics Abuse and Control

CQ Voting Studies

	Presidential Support	Party Unity	Voting Participation
1986	79%	86%	96%
1985	70%	88%	97%

Interest Groups

	ADA	ACU	AFL-CIO	CCUS
1986	5%	n/a	7%	87%
1985	5%	81%	18%	81%

Elections

1986	General	u/o	Primary	u/o
1984	General	66%	Primary	u/o

Norman D. Shumway   (R-Calif.)

Of Stockton — Elected 1978

Born: July 28, 1934, Phoenix, Ariz.
Education: Stockton Junior College, A.A. 1954; U. of Utah, B.S. 1960; U. of California Hastings College of Law, J.D. 1963.
Occupation: Lawyer.
Family: Wife, Luana June Schow; six children.
Religion: Mormon.
Political Career: San Joaquin County Supervisor, 1975-79.
Capitol Office: 1203 Longworth Bldg. 20515; 225-2511.

California 14th: Northeastern California — Part of San Joaquin County. The district vote for Ronald Reagan was 64% in 1984.

Committees

Banking, Finance and Urban Affairs
Merchant Marine and Fisheries
Select Aging

Elections

1986	General	73%	Primary	u/o
1984	General	73%	Primary	u/o

CQ Voting Studies

	Presidential Support	Party Unity	Voting Participation
1986	86%	82%	97%
1985	79%	88%	97%

Interest Groups

	ADA	ACU	AFL-CIO	CCUS
1986	0%	n/a	7%	94%
1985	15%	95%	12%	91%

Bud Shuster   (R-Pa.)

Of Everett — Elected 1972

Born: Jan. 23, 1932, Glassport, Pa.
Education: U. of Pittsburgh, B.S. 1954; Duquesne U., M.B.A. 1960; American U., Ph.D. 1967.
Military Career: Army, 1954-56.
Occupation: Corporate executive.
Family: Wife, Patricia Rommel; five children.
Religion: United Church of Christ.
Political Career: No previous office.
Capitol Office: 2268 Rayburn Bldg. 20515; 225-2431.

Pennsylvania 9th: South Central — Altoona. The district vote for Ronald Reagan was 67% in 1984; 60% in 1980.

Committees

Public Works and Transportation
Select Intelligence

Elections

1986	General	u/o	Primary	u/o
1984	General	67%	Primary	u/o

CQ Voting Studies

	Presidential Support	Party Unity	Voting Participation
1986	77%	85%	96%
1985	66%	86%	97%

Interest Groups

	ADA	ACU	AFL-CIO	CCUS
1986	5%	n/a	29%	94%
1985	10%	81%	24%	86%

Gerry Sikorski (D-Minn.)

Of Stillwater — Elected 1982

Born: April 26, 1948, Breckenridge, Minn.
Education: U. of Minnesota, B.A. 1970, J.D. 1973.
Military Career: Naval Reserve, 1984-present.
Occupation: Lawyer.
Family: Wife, Susan Erkel; one child.
Religion: Roman Catholic.
Political Career: Minn. Senate, 1977-83; Democratic nominee for U.S. House, 1978.
Capitol Office: 414 Cannon Bldg. 20515; 225-2271.

Minnesota 6th: Northern and Eastern Twin Cities Suburbs. The district vote for Ronald Reagan was 52% in 1984; 43% in 1980.

Committees

Energy and Commerce
Post Office and Civil Service
Select Children, Youth and Families

CQ Voting Studies

	Presidential Support	Party Unity	Voting Participation
1986	17%	79%	97%
1985	23%	70%	98%

Interest Groups

	ADA	ACU	AFL-CIO	CCUS
1986	85%	n/a	100%	33%
1985	75%	14%	88%	27%

Elections

1986	General	64%	Primary	u/o
1984	General	60%	Primary	88%

Norman Sisisky (D-Va.)

Of Petersburg — Elected 1982

Born: June 9, 1927, Baltimore, Md.
Education: Virginia Commonwealth U., B.S. 1949.
Military Career: Navy, 1945-46.
Occupation: Beer and soft drink distributor.
Family: Wife, Rhoda Brown; four children.
Religion: Jewish.
Political Career: Va. House, 1974-82.
Capitol Office: 426 Cannon Bldg. 20515; 225-6365.

Virginia 4th: Southeast — Chesapeake and Portsmouth. The district vote for Ronald Reagan was 56% in 1984; 46% in 1980.

Committees

Armed Services
Small Business
Select Aging

CQ Voting Studies

	Presidential Support	Party Unity	Voting Participation
1986	39%	75%	97%
1985	39%	76%	97%

Interest Groups

	ADA	ACU	AFL-CIO	CCUS
1986	45%	n/a	57%	56%
1985	40%	38%	47%	36%

Elections

1986	General	u/o	Primary	u/o
1984	General	u/o	Primary	u/o

David E. Skaggs (D-Colo.)

Of Boulder — Elected 1986

Born: Feb. 22, 1943, Cincinnati, Ohio.
Education: Wesleyan U., B.A. 1964; Yale U. Law School, LL.B. 1967.
Military Career: Marine Corps, 1968-71; Marine Corps Reserve, 1971-75.
Occupation: Lawyer.
Family: Wife, Laura Driscoll; one child; two stepchildren.
Religion: Congregationalist.
Political Career: Colo. House, 1981-87; minority leader, 1983-85.
Capitol Office: 1723 Longworth Bldg. 20515; 225-2161.

Colorado 2nd: Northern Denver Suburbs and Boulder. The district vote for Ronald Reagan was 60% in 1984; 50% in 1980.

Committees

Government Operations
Public Works and Transportation
Select Children, Youth and Families

Elections

1986	General	51%	Primary	58%

Joe Skeen (R-N.M.)

Of Picacho — Elected 1980

Born: June 30, 1927, Roswell, N.M.
Education: Texas A&M U., B.S. 1950.
Military Career: Navy, 1945-46; Air Force Reserve, 1949-52.
Occupation: Rancher.
Family: Wife, Mary Jones; two children.
Religion: Roman Catholic.
Political Career: Republican state chairman, 1962-65; N.M. Senate, 1961-71, minority leader, 1965-71; Republican nominee for lt. governor of N.M., 1970; Republican nominee for governor, 1974, 1978.
Capitol Office: 1007 Longworth Bldg. 20515; 225-2365.

New Mexico 2nd: South and East — Las Cruces and Roswell. The district vote for Ronald Reagan was 66% in 1984; 60% in 1980.

Committee

Appropriations

CQ Voting Studies

	Presidential Support	Party Unity	Voting Participation
1986	68%	79%	99%
1985	68%	81%	98%

Interest Groups

	ADA	ACU	AFL-CIO	CCUS
1986	10%	n/a	7%	67%
1985	0%	76%	6%	86%

Elections

1986	General	63%	Primary	u/o
1984	General	74%	Primary	u/o

Ike Skelton (D-Mo.)

Of Lexington — Elected 1976

Born: Dec. 20, 1931, Lexington, Mo.
Education: Attended Wentworth Military Academy, 1949-51; U. of Edinburgh, 1951-53; U. of Missouri, B.A. 1953, LL.B. 1956.
Occupation: Lawyer.
Family: Wife, Susan Anding; three children.
Religion: Christian Church.
Political Career: Chairman, Lafayette County Democratic Committee, 1962-66; Mo. Senate, 1971-77.
Capitol Office: 2453 Rayburn Bldg. 20515; 225-2876.

Missouri 4th: West — Kansas City Suburbs and Jefferson City. The district vote for Ronald Reagan was 67% in 1984; 56% in 1980.

Committees

Armed Services
Small Business
Select Aging

CQ Voting Studies

	Presidential Support	Party Unity	Voting Participation
1986	48%	66%	93%
1985	44%	66%	93%

Interest Groups

	ADA	ACU	AFL-CIO	CCUS
1986	35%	n/a	86%	47%
1985	40%	50%	63%	33%

Elections

1986	General	u/o	Primary	u/o
1984	General	67%	Primary	u/o

Jim Slattery (D-Kan.)

Of Topeka — Elected 1982

Born: Aug. 4, 1948, Good Intent, Kan.
Education: Attended Netherlands School of International Economics and Business, 1969-70; Washburn U., B.S. 1970, J.D. 1974.
Military Career: Army National Guard, 1970-75.
Occupation: Realtor.
Family: Wife, Linda Smith; two children.
Religion: Roman Catholic.
Political Career: Kansas House, 1973-79.
Capitol Office: 1440 Longworth Bldg. 20515; 225-6601.

Kansas 2nd: Topeka and Lawrence. The district vote for Ronald Reagan was 63% in 1984; 56% in 1980.

Committees

Budget
Energy and Commerce

CQ Voting Studies

	Presidential Support	Party Unity	Voting Participation
1986	34%	68%	98%
1985	43%	71%	99%

Interest Groups

	ADA	ACU	AFL-CIO	CCUS
1986	45%	n/a	57%	56%
1985	55%	33%	53%	36%

Elections

1986	General	71%	Primary	u/o
1984	General	60%	Primary	u/o

D. French Slaughter Jr.   (R-Va.)

Of Culpeper — Elected 1984

Born: May 20, 1925, Culpeper County, Va.
Education: Attended Virginia Military Institute, 1942-1943;
 U. of Virginia, B.A., LL.B. 1953.
Military Career: U.S. Army, 1943-47.
Occupation: Lawyer.
Family: Widowed; two children.
Religion: Episcopalian.
Political Career: Va. House, 1958-78.
Capitol Office: 319 Cannon Bldg. 20515; 225-6561.

Virginia 7th: North — Charlottesville and Winchester. The
district vote for Ronald Reagan was 69% in 1984; 61% in
1980.

Committees

Judiciary
Science, Space and Technology
Small Business

Elections

1986	General	u/o	Primary	u/o
1984	General	57%	Primary	u/o

CQ Voting Studies

	Presidential Support	Party Unity	Voting Participation
1986	80%	86%	97%
1985	74%	90%	99%

Interest Groups

	ADA	ACU	AFL-CIO	CCUS
1986	0%	n/a	21%	94%
1985	0%	86%	12%	95%

Louise M. Slaughter   (D-N.Y.)

Of Fairport — Elected 1986

Born: Aug. 14, 1929, Harlan County, Ky.
Education: U. of Kentucky, B.S. 1951, M.S. 1953.
Occupation: Market researcher.
Family: Husband, Robert Slaughter; three children.
Religion: Episcopalian.
Political Career: Monroe County legislator, 1975-79; N.Y.
 Assembly, 1983-87.
Capitol Office: 1313 Longworth Bldg. 20515; 225-3615.

New York 30th: West — Part of Rochester and Batavia.
The district vote for Ronald Reagan was 44% in 1984; 44% in
1980.

Committees

Government Operations
Public Works and Transportation
Select Aging

Elections

1986	General	51%	Primary	81%

Christopher H. Smith (R-N.J.)

Of Hamilton Square — Elected 1980

Born: March 4, 1953, Rahway, N.J.
Education: Trenton State College, B.A. 1975.
Occupation: Sporting goods wholesaler.
Family: Wife, Marie Hahn; three children.
Religion: Roman Catholic.
Political Career: Republican nominee for U.S. House, 1978.
Capitol Office: 422 Cannon Bldg. 20515; 225-3765.

New Jersey 4th: Central — Trenton. The district vote for Ronald Reagan was 59% in 1984.

Committees

Foreign Affairs
Veterans' Affairs
Select Aging

Elections

1986	General	62%	Primary	u/o
1984	General	61%	Primary	u/o

CQ Voting Studies

	Presidential Support	Party Unity	Voting Participation
1986	46%	32%	99%
1985	45%	43%	97%

Interest Groups

	ADA	ACU	AFL-CIO	CCUS
1986	45%	n/a	93%	33%
1985	65%	52%	88%	41%

Denny Smith (R-Ore.)

Of Salem — Elected 1980

Born: Jan. 19, 1938, Ontario, Ore.
Education: Willamette U., B.A. 1961.
Military Career: Air Force, 1958-60, 1962-67.
Occupation: Newspaper publisher; airline pilot.
Family: Wife, Kathleen Barrett; six children.
Religion: Protestant.
Political Career: No previous office.
Capitol Office: 1213 Longworth Bldg. 20515; 225-5711.

Oregon 5th: Willamette Valley — Salem and Corvallis. The district vote for Ronald Reagan was 59% in 1984; 49% in 1980.

Committees

Budget
Interior and Insular Affairs

CQ Voting Studies

	Presidential Support	Party Unity	Voting Participation
1986	74%	86%	94%
1985	76%	87%	94%

Elections

1986	General	60%	Primary	89%
1984	General	54%	Primary	77%

Interest Groups

	ADA	ACU	AFL-CIO	CCUS
1986	0%	n/a	15%	88%
1985	10%	95%	18%	95%

Lamar Smith (R-Texas)

Of San Antonio — Elected 1986

Born: Nov. 19, 1947, San Antonio.
Education: Yale U., B.A. 1969; Southern Methodist U. School of Law, J.D. 1975.
Occupation: Lawyer; rancher.
Family: Wife, Jane Shoults; two children.
Religion: Christian Scientist.
Political Career: Texas House, 1981-83; Bexar County commissioner, 1983-85.
Capitol Office: 509 Cannon Bldg. 20515; 225-4236.

Texas 21st: San Antonio Suburbs, San Angelo and Midland. The district vote for Ronald Reagan was 78% in 1984.

Committees

Judiciary
Science, Space and Technology

Elections

1986	General	61%	Primary	31%

Larry Smith (D-Fla.)

Of Hollywood — Elected 1982

Born: April 25, 1941, Brooklyn, N.Y.
Education: New York U., B.A. 1963; Brooklyn Law School, LL.B. 1964, J.D., 1967.
Occupation: Lawyer.
Family: Wife, Sheila Cohen; two children.
Religion: Jewish.
Political Career: Fla. House, 1979-83.
Capitol Office: 113 Cannon Bldg. 20515; 225-7931.

Florida 16th: Southeast — Hollywood and Part of Dade County. The district vote for Ronald Reagan was 61% in 1984; 57% in 1980.

Committees

Foreign Affairs
Judiciary
Select Narcotics Abuse and Control

Elections

1986	General	70%	Primary	u/o
1984	General	56%	Primary	u/o

CQ Voting Studies

	Presidential Support	Party Unity	Voting Participation
1986	27%	88%	96%
1985	30%	88%	94%

Interest Groups

	ADA	ACU	AFL-CIO	CCUS
1986	65%	n/a	100%	27%
1985	55%	35%	94%	33%

Neal Smith (D-Iowa)

Of Altoona — Elected 1958

Born: March 23, 1920, Hedrick, Iowa.
Education: Attended U. of Missouri, 1945-46; Syracuse U., 1946-47; Drake U., LL.B. 1950.
Military Career: Army Air Corps, 1942-45.
Occupation: Farmer; lawyer.
Family: Wife, Beatrix Havens; two children.
Religion: Methodist.
Political Career: Sought Democratic nomination for U.S. House, 1956.
Capitol Office: 2373 Rayburn Bldg. 20515, 225-4426.

Iowa 4th: Central — Des Moines and Ames. The district vote for Ronald Reagan was 49% in 1984; 45% in 1980.

CQ Voting Studies

	Presidential Support	Party Unity	Voting Participation
1986	22%	80%	94%
1985	30%	85%	96%

Interest Groups

	ADA	ACU	AFL-CIO	CCUS
1986	70%	n/a	83%	22%
1985	75%	10%	75%	24%

Committees

Appropriations
Small Business

Elections

1986	General	68%	Primary	89%
1984	General	61%	Primary	u/o

Robert C. Smith (R-N.H.)

Of Tuftonboro — Elected 1984

Born: March 30, 1941, Trenton, N.J.
Education: Lafayette College, B.A. 1965.
Military Career: Navy, 1965-67.
Occupation: Real estate broker.
Family: Wife, Mary Jo Hutchinson; three children.
Religion: Congregationalist.
Political Career: Gov. Wentworth Regional School Board (Wolfeboro, N.H.), 1978-84; sought Republican nomination for U.S. House, 1980; Republican nominee for U.S. House, 1982.
Capitol Office: 115 Cannon Bldg. 20515; 225-5456.

New Hampshire 1st: East — Manchester. The district vote for Ronald Reagan was 70% in 1984; 60% in 1980.

CQ Voting Studies

	Presidential Support	Party Unity	Voting Participation
1986	82%	96%	100%
1985	84%	91%	99%

Interest Groups

	ADA	ACU	AFL-CIO	CCUS
1986	0%	n/a	14%	100%
1985	5%	90%	18%	95%

Committees

Science, Space and Technology
Veterans' Affairs

Elections

1986	General	56%	Primary	50%
1984	General	59%	Primary	42%

Robert F. Smith (R-Ore.)

Of Burns — Elected 1982

Born: June 16, 1931, Portland, Ore.
Education: Willamette U., B.A. 1953.
Occupation: Cattle rancher.
Family: Wife, Kaye Tomlinson; three children.
Religion: Presbyterian.
Political Career: Ore. House 1961-73, Speaker, 1969-73; Ore. Senate 1973-82, minority leader, 1977-82.
Capitol Office: 118 Cannon Bldg. 20515; 225-6730.

Oregon 2nd: East and Southwest — Bend and Medford. The district vote for Ronald Reagan was 63% in 1984; 58% in 1980.

Committees

Agriculture
Select Hunger

Elections

1986	General	60%	Primary	u/o
1984	General	57%	Primary	u/o

CQ Voting Studies

	Presidential Support	Party Unity	Voting Participation
1986	66%	82%	95%
1985	63%	82%	96%

Interest Groups

	ADA	ACU	AFL-CIO	CCUS
1986	5%	n/a	14%	100%
1985	20%	75%	12%	90%

Virginia Smith (R-Neb.)

Of Chappell — Elected 1974

Born: June 30, 1911, Randolph, Iowa.
Education: U. of Nebraska, B.A. 1936.
Occupation: Farmer.
Family: Husband, Haven Smith.
Religion: Methodist.
Political Career: No previous office.
Capitol Office: 2202 Rayburn Bldg. 20515; 225-6435.

Nebraska 3rd: Central and West — Grand Island. The district vote for Ronald Reagan was 78% in 1984; 72% in 1980.

Committee

Appropriations

Elections

1986	General	70%	Primary	u/o
1984	General	83%	Primary	u/o

CQ Voting Studies

	Presidential Support	Party Unity	Voting Participation
1986	64%	62%	94%
1985	58%	65%	97%

Interest Groups

	ADA	ACU	AFL-CIO	CCUS
1986	10%	n/a	8%	81%
1985	10%	62%	12%	73%

Olympia J. Snowe   (R-Maine)
Of Auburn — Elected 1978

Born: Feb. 21, 1947, Augusta, Maine.
Education: U. of Maine, B.A. 1969.
Occupation: Concrete company executive; public official.
Family: Widowed.
Religion: Greek Orthodox.
Political Career: Maine House, 1973-77; Maine Senate, 1977-79.
Capitol Office: 2464 Rayburn Bldg. 20515; 225-6306.

Maine 2nd: North — Lewiston and Bangor. The district vote for Ronald Reagan was 62% in 1984; 46% in 1980.

CQ Voting Studies

	Presidential Support	Party Unity	Voting Participation
1986	44%	53%	99%
1985	48%	56%	99%

Interest Groups

	ADA	ACU	AFL-CIO	CCUS
1986	50%	n/a	64%	61%
1985	35%	48%	53%	59%

Committees

Foreign Affairs
Joint Economic
Select Aging

Elections

1986	General	77%	Primary	u/o
1984	General	76%	Primary	u/o

Stephen J. Solarz   (D-N.Y.)
Of Brooklyn — Elected 1974

Born: Sept. 12, 1940, New York, N.Y.
Education: Brandeis U., A.B. 1962; Columbia U., M.A. 1967.
Occupation: Public official.
Family: Wife, Nina Koldin; two children.
Religion: Jewish.
Political Career: N.Y. Assembly, 1969-75; sought Democratic nomination for Brooklyn borough president, 1973.
Capitol Office: 1536 Longworth Bldg. 20515; 225-2361.

New York 13th: Western and Southern Brooklyn — Bensonhurst and Brooklyn Heights. The district vote for Ronald Reagan was 48% in 1984; 43% in 1980.

CQ Voting Studies

	Presidential Support	Party Unity	Voting Participation
1986	18%	89%	93%
1985	24%	89%	93%

Interest Groups

	ADA	ACU	AFL-CIO	CCUS
1986	90%	n/a	86%	20%
1985	90%	14%	94%	20%

Committees

Education and Labor
Foreign Affairs
Post Office and Civil Service
Joint Economic

Elections

1986	General	82%	Primary	u/o
1984	General	66%	Primary	u/o

Gerald B. H. Solomon   (R-N.Y.)

Of Glens Falls — Elected 1978

Born: Aug. 14, 1930, Okeechobee, Fla.
Education: Attended Siena College, 1949-50; St. Lawrence U. 1952-53.
Military Career: Marine Corps, 1951-52.
Occupation: Insurance salesman.
Family: Wife, Freda Parker; five children.
Religion: Presbyterian.
Political Career: Warren County Legislature, 1968-72; N.Y. Assembly, 1973-79.
Capitol Office: 2342 Rayburn Bldg. 20515; 225-5614.

New York 24th: Upper Hudson Valley — Saratoga Springs. The district vote for Ronald Reagan was 69% in 1984; 54% in 1980.

CQ Voting Studies

	Presidential Support	Party Unity	Voting Participation
1986	79%	84%	93%
1985	70%	86%	91%

Interest Groups

	ADA	ACU	AFL-CIO	CCUS
1986	0%	n/a	21%	83%
1985	15%	84%	25%	86%

Committees

Foreign Affairs
Veterans' Affairs   (Ranking)

Elections

1986	General	71%	Primary	u/o
1984	General	73%	Primary	u/o

Floyd Spence   (R-S.C.)

Of Lexington — Elected 1970

Born: April 9, 1928, Columbia, S.C.
Education: U. of South Carolina, A.B. 1952, J.D. 1956.
Military Career: Navy, 1952-54.
Occupation: Lawyer.
Family: Widowed; four children.
Religion: Lutheran.
Political Career: S.C. House, 1957-63; S.C. Senate, 1967-71, minority leader 1967-71; Republican nominee for U.S. House, 1962.
Capitol Office: 2113 Rayburn Bldg. 20515; 225-2452.

South Carolina 2nd: Central — Columbia. The district vote for Ronald Reagan was 62% in 1984; 54% in 1980.

CQ Voting Studies

	Presidential Support	Party Unity	Voting Participation
1986	69%	75%	98%
1985	61%	84%	98%

Interest Groups

	ADA	ACU	AFL-CIO	CCUS
1986	10%	n/a	43%	76%
1985	0%	81%	12%	95%

Committees

Armed Services
Standards of Official Conduct   (Ranking)
Select Aging

Elections

1986	General	54%	Primary	u/o
1984	General	62%	Primary	u/o

John M. Spratt Jr. (D-S.C.)

Of York — Elected 1982

Born: Nov. 1, 1942, Charlotte, N.C.
Education: Davidson College, A.B. 1964; Oxford U., M.A. 1966; Yale U., LL.B. 1969.
Military Career: Army, 1969-71.
Occupation: Lawyer; insurance executive.
Family: Wife, Jane Stacy; three children.
Religion: Presbyterian.
Political Career: No previous office.
Capitol Office: 1118 Longworth Bldg. 20515; 225-5501.

South Carolina 5th: North Central — Rock Hill. The district vote for Ronald Reagan was 62% in 1984; 45% in 1980.

Committees

Armed Services
Government Operations

CQ Voting Studies

	Presidential Support	Party Unity	Voting Participation
1986	28%	84%	97%
1985	41%	79%	97%

Interest Groups

	ADA	ACU	AFL-CIO	CCUS
1986	60%	n/a	64%	59%
1985	35%	38%	38%	57%

Elections

1986	General	u/o	Primary	u/o
1984	General	92%	Primary	u/o

Harley O. Staggers Jr. (D-W. Va.)

Of Keyser — Elected 1982

Born: Feb. 22, 1951, Washington, D.C.
Education: Harvard U., B.A. 1974; West Virginia U. School of Law, J.D. 1977.
Occupation: Lawyer.
Family: Leslie Sergy.
Religion: Roman Catholic.
Political Career: Sought Democratic nomination to U.S. House, 1980; W.Va. Senate, 1981-83.
Capitol Office: 1504 Longworth Bldg. 20515; 225-4331.

West Virginia 2nd: East — Morgantown and Eastern Panhandle. The district vote for Ronald Reagan was 58% in 1984; 47% in 1980.

Committees

Agriculture
Judiciary
Veterans' Affairs

CQ Voting Studies

	Presidential Support	Party Unity	Voting Participation
1986	18%	89%	97%
1985	29%	88%	98%

Interest Groups

	ADA	ACU	AFL-CIO	CCUS
1986	80%	n/a	100%	28%
1985	70%	19%	82%	38%

Elections

1986	General	70%	Primary	86%
1984	General	56%	Primary	81%

Richard H. Stallings (D-Idaho)

Of Rexburg — Elected 1984

Born: Oct. 7, 1940, Ogden, Utah.
Education: Weber State College, B.S. 1965; Utah State U., M.A. 1968.
Occupation: History professor.
Family: Wife, Ranae Garner; three children.
Religion: Mormon.
Political Career: Democratic nominee for Idaho House, 1974 and 1978; Democratic nominee for U.S. House, 1982.
Capitol Office: 1221 Longworth Bldg. 20515; 225-5531.

Idaho 2nd: East — Pocatello and Idaho Falls. The district vote for Ronald Reagan was 77% in 1984; 71% in 1980.

Committees

Agriculture
Science, Space and Technology
Select Aging

Elections

1986	General	54%	Primary	u/o
1984	General	50%	Primary	u/o

CQ Voting Studies

	Presidential Support	Party Unity	Voting Participation
1986	42%	62%	96%
1985	41%	69%	94%

Interest Groups

	ADA	ACU	AFL-CIO	CCUS
1986	45%	n/a	57%	71%
1985	35%	40%	44%	55%

Arlan Stangeland (R-Minn.)

Of Barnesville — Elected 1977

Born: Feb. 8, 1930, Fargo, N.D.
Education: High school graduate.
Occupation: Farmer.
Family: Wife, Virginia Trowbridge; seven children.
Religion: Lutheran.
Political Career: Minn. House, 1967-75; Barnesville school board, 1976-77.
Capitol Office: 2245 Rayburn Bldg. 20515; 225-2165.

Minnesota 7th: Northwest — St. Cloud and Moorhead. The district vote for Ronald Reagan was 57% in 1984; 50% in 1980.

Committees

Agriculture
Public Works and Transportation

Elections

1986	General	50%	Primary	u/o
1984	General	57%	Primary	u/o

CQ Voting Studies

	Presidential Support	Party Unity	Voting Participation
1986	68%	71%	92%
1985	65%	82%	96%

Interest Groups

	ADA	ACU	AFL-CIO	CCUS
1986	10%	n/a	21%	59%
1985	15%	81%	0%	67%

Fortney H. "Pete" Stark   (D-Calif.)

Of Oakland — Elected 1972

Born: Nov. 11, 1931, Milwaukee, Wis.
Education: Massachusetts Institute of Technology, B.S., 1953; U. of California, M.B.A., 1960.
Military Career: Air Force, 1955-57.
Occupation: Banker.
Family: Divorced; four children.
Religion: Unitarian.
Political Career: Sought Democratic nomination for Calif. Senate, 1969.
Capitol Office: 1125 Longworth Bldg. 20515; 225-5065.

California 9th: Suburban Alameda County — Hayward. The district vote for Ronald Reagan was 50% in 1984.

Committees

District of Columbia
Ways and Means
Joint Economic
Select Narcotics Abuse and Control

Elections

1986	General	70%	Primary	89%
1984	General	70%	Primary	u/o

CQ Voting Studies

	Presidential Support	Party Unity	Voting Participation
1986	18%	86%	88%
1985	18%	89%	91%

Interest Groups

	ADA	ACU	AFL-CIO	CCUS
1986	95%	n/a	77%	12%
1985	90%	11%	94%	14%

Charles W. Stenholm   (D-Texas)

Of Stamford — Elected 1978

Born: Oct. 26, 1938, Stamford, Texas.
Education: Attended Tarleton State Jr. College, 1957-59; Texas Tech U., B.S. 1961, M.S. 1962.
Occupation: Cotton grower.
Family: Wife, Cynthia Ann Watson; three children.
Religion: Lutheran.
Political Career: No previous office.
Capitol Office: 1226 Longworth Bldg. 20515; 225-6605.

Texas 17th: West Central — Abilene. The district vote for Ronald Reagan was 68% in 1984; 51% in 1980.

Committees

Agriculture
Veterans' Affairs

Elections

1986	General	u/o	Primary	u/o
1984	General	u/o	Primary	88%

CQ Voting Studies

	Presidential Support	Party Unity	Voting Participation
1986	66%	32%	99%
1985	66%	35%	99%

Interest Groups

	ADA	ACU	AFL-CIO	CCUS
1986	5%	n/a	21%	78%
1985	20%	90%	24%	86%

Louis Stokes (D-Ohio)

Of Warrensville Heights— Elected 1968

Born: Feb. 23, 1925, Cleveland, Ohio.
Education: Attended Western Reserve U., 1946-48; Cleveland Marshall Law School, J.D. 1953.
Military Career: Army, 1943-46.
Occupation: Lawyer.
Family: Wife, Jeanette Francis; four children.
Religion: African Methodist Episcopalian.
Political Career: No previous office.
Capitol Office: 2365 Rayburn Bldg. 20515; 225-7032.

Ohio 21st: Cleveland — East and Cleveland Heights.

Committees

Appropriations
Select Intelligence (Chairman)
Select Iran-contra

Elections

1986	General	82%	Primary	u/o
1984	General	82%	Primary	u/o

CQ Voting Studies

	Presidential Support	Party Unity	Voting Participation
1986	11%	87%	90%
1985	15%	93%	93%

Interest Groups

	ADA	ACU	AFL-CIO	CCUS
1986	100%	n/a	93%	12%
1985	95%	0%	100%	24%

Samuel S. Stratton (D-N.Y.)

Of Schenectady — Elected 1958

Born: Sept. 27, 1916, Yonkers, N.Y.
Education: U. of Rochester, A.B. 1937; Haverford College, M.A. 1938; Harvard U., M.A. 1940.
Military Career: Navy, 1942-46 and 1951-53.
Occupation: Broadcast journalist; college instructor.
Family: Wife, Joan Wolfe; five children.
Religion: Presbyterian.
Political Career: Schenectady City Council, 1950-56; mayor of Schenectady, 1956-59; Democratic nominee for N.Y. Assembly, 1950.
Capitol Office: 2205 Rayburn Bldg. 20515; 225-5076.

New York 23rd: Hudson and Mohawk Valleys — Albany and Schenectady. The district vote for Ronald Reagan was 53% in 1984; 40% in 1980.

Committee

Armed Services

Elections

1986	General	u/o	Primary	u/o
1984	General	78%	Primary	u/o

CQ Voting Studies

	Presidential Support	Party Unity	Voting Participation
1986	50%	60%	90%
1985	59%	74%	98%

Interest Groups

	ADA	ACU	AFL-CIO	CCUS
1986	45%	n/a	86%	29%
1985	40%	55%	76%	30%

Gerry E. Studds   (D-Mass.)

Of Cohasset — Elected 1972

Born: May 12, 1937, Mineola, N.Y.
Education: Yale U., B.A. 1959, M.A.T. 1961.
Occupation: High school teacher.
Family: Single.
Religion: Episcopalian.
Political Career: Democratic nominee for U.S. House, 1970.
Capitol Office: 1501 Longworth Bldg. 20515; 225-3111.

Massachusetts 10th: South Shore, Southeast and Cape Cod. The district vote for Ronald Reagan was 55% in 1984; 48% in 1980.

Committees

Foreign Affairs
Merchant Marine and Fisheries

CQ Voting Studies

	Presidential Support	Party Unity	Voting Participation
1986	16%	93%	96%
1985	21%	93%	96%

Interest Groups

	ADA	ACU	AFL-CIO	CCUS
1986	95%	n/a	86%	19%
1985	100%	10%	100%	27%

Elections

1986	General	65%	Primary	76%
1984	General	56%	Primary	61%

Bob Stump   (R-Ariz.)

Of Tolleson — Elected 1976

Born: April 4, 1927, Phoenix, Ariz.
Education: Arizona State U., B.S. 1951.
Military Career: Navy, 1943-46.
Occupation: Farmer.
Family: Divorced; three children.
Religion: Seventh-day Adventist.
Political Career: Ariz. House, 1959-67; Ariz. Senate, 1967-77, Senate president, 1975-77.
Capitol Office: 211 Cannon Bldg. 20515; 225-4576.

Arizona 3rd: North and West — Glendale, Flagstaff and Part of Phoenix. The district vote for Ronald Reagan was 71% in 1984; 67% in 1980.

Committees

Armed Services
Veterans' Affairs

CQ Voting Studies

	Presidential Support	Party Unity	Voting Participation
1986	88%	92%	98%
1985	84%	93%	99%

Interest Groups

	ADA	ACU	AFL-CIO	CCUS
1986	0%	n/a	8%	100%
1985	0%	100%	0%	95%

Elections

1986	General	u/o	Primary	u/o
1984	General	72%	Primary	u/o

Don Sundquist (R-Tenn.)

Of Memphis — Elected 1982

Born: March 15, 1936, Moline, Ill.
Education: Augustana College (Ill.), B.A. 1957.
Military Career: Naval Reserve, 1957-59.
Occupation: Owner of printing, advertising and marketing firm.
Family: Wife, Martha Swanson; three children.
Religion: Lutheran.
Political Career: No previous office.
Capitol Office: 230 Cannon Bldg. 20515; 225-2811.

Tennessee 7th: West Central — Clarksville and Part of Shelby County. The district vote for Ronald Reagan was 66% in 1984; 56% in 1980.

Committees

Budget
Public Works and Transportation

Elections

1986	General	72%	Primary	u/o
1984	General	u/o	Primary	u/o

CQ Voting Studies

	Presidential Support	Party Unity	Voting Participation
1986	74%	86%	98%
1985	75%	87%	97%

Interest Groups

	ADA	ACU	AFL-CIO	CCUS
1986	5%	n/a	14%	72%
1985	15%	81%	18%	91%

Mac Sweeney (R-Texas)

Of Wharton — Elected 1984

Born: Sept. 15, 1955, Wharton, Texas.
Education: U. of Texas, B.A. 1978.
Occupation: Congressional aide; White House personnel administrator.
Family: Wife, Cathy Hellmann; one child.
Religion: Methodist.
Political Career: No previous office.
Capitol Office: 1713 Longworth Bldg. 20515; 225-2831.

Texas 14th: Southeast and Gulf Coast. The district vote for Ronald Reagan was 67% in 1984; 57% in 1980.

Committees

Armed Services
Merchant Marine and Fisheries

Elections

1986	General	52%	Primary	u/o
1984	General	51%	Primary	60% *

** Primary runoff.*

CQ Voting Studies

	Presidential Support	Party Unity	Voting Participation
1986	67%	70%	88%
1985	78%	79%	94%

Interest Groups

	ADA	ACU	AFL-CIO	CCUS
1986	5%	n/a	23%	94%
1985	10%	90%	0%	95%

Al Swift (D-Wash.)

Of Bellingham — Elected 1978

Born: Sept. 12, 1935, Tacoma, Wash.

Education: Attended Whitman College, 1953-55; Central Washington College, B.A. 1957.

Occupation: Broadcaster; television news and public affairs director.

Family: Wife, Paula Jean Jackson; two children.

Religion: Unitarian.

Political Career: No previous office.

Capitol Office: 1502 Longworth Bldg. 20515; 225-2605.

Washington 2nd: Northwest — Everett and Part of Olympic Peninsula. The district vote for Ronald Reagan was 55% in 1984.

CQ Voting Studies

	Presidential Support	Party Unity	Voting Participation
1986	19%	93%	97%
1985	26%	93%	98%

Interest Groups

	ADA	ACU	AFL-CIO	CCUS
1986	90%	n/a	79%	18%
1985	75%	14%	76%	27%

Committees

Energy and Commerce
House Administration

Elections

1986	General	73%	Primary	72%
1984	General	59%	Primary	85%

Pat Swindall (R-Ga.)

Of Dunwoody — Elected 1984

Born: Oct. 18, 1950, Gadsden, Ala.

Education: U. of Georgia, B.A. 1972; U. of Georgia Law School, J.D. 1975.

Occupation: Lawyer; furniture store owner.

Family: Wife, Kimberly Schiesser; two children.

Religion: Presbyterian.

Political Career: No previous office.

Capitol Office: 331 Cannon Bldg. 20515; 225-4272.

Georgia 4th: Atlanta Suburbs — De Kalb County. The district vote for Ronald Reagan was 66% in 1984; 43% in 1980.

CQ Voting Studies

	Presidential Support	Party Unity	Voting Participation
1986	82%	94%	98%
1985	79%	93%	97%

Interest Groups

	ADA	ACU	AFL-CIO	CCUS
1986	0%	n/a	14%	94%
1985	5%	86%	6%	95%

Committees

Banking, Finance and Urban Affairs
Judiciary
Select Aging

Elections

1986	General	53%	Primary	u/o
1984	General	53%	Primary	91%

Mike Synar (D-Okla.)

Of Muskogee — Elected 1978

Born: Oct. 17, 1950, Vinita, Okla.
Education: U. of Oklahoma, B.B.A. 1972; Northwestern U., M.S. 1973; U. of Oklahoma Law School, LL.B. 1977.
Occupation: Rancher; real estate broker; lawyer.
Family: Single.
Religion: Episcopalian.
Political Career: No previous office.
Capitol Office: 2441 Rayburn Bldg. 20515; 225-2701.

Oklahoma 2nd: Northeast — Tulsa and Muskogee. The district vote for Ronald Reagan was 64% in 1984; 55% in 1980.

CQ Voting Studies

	Presidential Support	Party Unity	Voting Participation
1986	24%	83%	94%
1985	25%	88%	98%

Interest Groups

	ADA	ACU	AFL-CIO	CCUS
1986	70%	n/a	57%	22%
1985	75%	14%	53%	36%

Committees

Energy and Commerce
Government Operations
Judiciary
Select Aging

Elections

1986	General	73%	Primary	84%
1984	General	74%	Primary	88%

Robin Tallon (D-S.C.)

Of Florence — Elected 1982

Born: Aug. 8, 1946, Hemingway, S.C.
Education: Attended U. of South Carolina, 1964-65.
Occupation: Clothing store owner.
Family: Wife, Amelia Louise Johns; three children.
Religion: Methodist.
Political Career: S.C. House, 1981-83.
Capitol Office: 432 Cannon Bldg. 20515; 225-3315.

South Carolina 6th: East — Florence. The district vote for Ronald Reagan was 57% in 1984; 46% in 1980.

CQ Voting Studies

	Presidential Support	Party Unity	Voting Participation
1986	40%	59%	93%
1985	41%	69%	96%

Interest Groups

	ADA	ACU	AFL-CIO	CCUS
1986	40%	n/a	71%	44%
1985	45%	48%	53%	50%

Committees

Agriculture
Merchant Marine and Fisheries

Elections

1986	General	75%	Primary	90%
1984	General	60%	Primary	74%

Tom Tauke (R-Iowa)

Of Dubuque — Elected 1978

Born: Oct. 11, 1950, Dubuque, Iowa.
Education: Loras College, B.A. 1972; U. of Iowa, J.D. 1974.
Occupation: Lawyer.
Family: Beverly Hubble; one child.
Religion: Roman Catholic.
Political Career: Iowa House, 1975-79.
Capitol Office: 2244 Rayburn Bldg. 20515; 225-2911.

Iowa 2nd: Northeast — Cedar Rapids. The district vote for Ronald Reagan was 53% in 1984; 49% in 1980.

CQ Voting Studies

	Presidential Support	Party Unity	Voting Participation
1986	53%	71%	96%
1985	52%	77%	99%

Interest Groups

	ADA	ACU	AFL-CIO	CCUS
1986	30%	n/a	21%	88%
1985	35%	57%	24%	82%

Committees

Education and Labor
Energy and Commerce
Select Aging

Elections

1986	General	61%	Primary	u/o
1984	General	64%	Primary	u/o

W. J. "Billy" Tauzin (D-La.)

Of Thibodaux — Elected 1980

Born: June 14, 1943, Chackbay, La.
Education: Nicholls State U., B.A. 1964; Louisiana State U., J.D. 1967.
Occupation: Lawyer.
Family: Wife, Gayle Clement; five children.
Religion: Roman Catholic.
Political Career: La. House, 1971-80.
Capitol Office: 222 Cannon Bldg. 20515; 225-4031.

Louisana 3rd: South Central — Houma and New Iberia. The district vote for Ronald Reagan was 66% in 1984.

CQ Voting Studies

	Presidential Support	Party Unity	Voting Participation
1986	49%	56%	100%
1985	54%	55%	94%

Interest Groups

	ADA	ACU	AFL-CIO	CCUS
1986	20%	n/a	50%	72%
1985	25%	65%	53%	65%

Committees

Energy and Commerce
Merchant Marine and Fisheries

Elections

1986	General	†	Primary	†
1984	General	†	Primary	†

† *In Louisiana a candidate unopposed in the primary and general elections is declared elected.*

Gene Taylor (R-Mo.)

Of Sarcoxie — Elected 1972

Born: Feb. 10, 1928, Sarcoxie, Mo.
Education: Southwest Missouri State College, 1945-47.
Military Career: National Guard, 1948-49.
Occupation: Automobile dealer.
Family: Wife, Dorothy Wooldridge; two children.
Religion: Methodist.
Political Career: Sarcoxie Board of Education, 1954-64; mayor of Sarcoxie, 1954-60.
Capitol Office: 2134 Rayburn Bldg. 20515; 225-6536.

Missouri 7th: Southwest — Springfield and Joplin. The district vote for Ronald Reagan was 69% in 1984; 60% in 1980.

Committees

Post Office and Civil Service   (Ranking)
Rules

Elections

1986	General	67%	Primary	u/o
1984	General	70%	Primary	u/o

CQ Voting Studies

	Presidential Support	Party Unity	Voting Participation
1986	68%	65%	95%
1985	66%	76%	94%

Interest Groups

	ADA	ACU	AFL-CIO	CCUS
1986	5%	n/a	21%	71%
1985	10%	81%	18%	76%

Robert Lindsay Thomas (D-Ga.)

Of Statesboro — Elected 1982

Born: Nov. 20, 1943, Patterson, Ga.
Education: U. of Georgia, B.A. 1965.
Military Career: Ga. Air National Guard, 1966-72.
Occupation: Farmer; investment banker.
Family: Wife, Melinda Ann Fry; three children.
Religion: Methodist.
Political Career: No previous office.
Capitol Office: 431 Cannon Bldg. 20515; 225-5831.

Georgia 1st: Southeast — Savannah and Brunswick. The district vote for Ronald Reagan was 59% in 1984; 42% in 1980.

Committees

Agriculture
Merchant Marine and Fisheries

Elections

1986	General	u/o	Primary	u/o
1984	General	82%	Primary	u/o

CQ Voting Studies

	Presidential Support	Party Unity	Voting Participation
1986	47%	72%	99%
1985	50%	75%	99%

Interest Groups

	ADA	ACU	AFL-CIO	CCUS
1986	25%	n/a	43%	61%
1985	25%	67%	41%	45%

William M. Thomas   (R-Calif.)

Of Bakersfield — Elected 1978

Born: Dec. 6, 1941, Wallace, Idaho.
Education: San Francisco State U., B.A. 1963, M.A. 1965.
Occupation: Political science professor.
Family: Wife, Sharon Lynn Hamilton; two children.
Religion: Baptist.
Political Career: Calif. Assembly, 1975-79.
Capitol Office: 2402 Rayburn Bldg. 20515; 225-2915.

California 20th: Bakersfield and San Luis Obispo. The district vote for Ronald Reagan was 69% in 1984.

Committees

Budget
House Administration
Ways and Means

Elections

1986	General	72%	Primary	u/o
1984	General	71%	Primary	u/o

CQ Voting Studies

	Presidential Support	Party Unity	Voting Participation
1986	76%	82%	91%
1985	61%	79%	92%

Interest Groups

	ADA	ACU	AFL-CIO	CCUS
1986	10%	n/a	21%	93%
1985	10%	86%	13%	95%

Esteban Edward Torres   (D-Calif.)

Of La Puente — Elected 1982

Born: Jan. 27, 1930, Miami, Ariz.
Education: East Los Angeles Community College, A.A. 1961; California State U. at Los Angeles, B.A. 1963; graduate work, U. of Maryland, 1965, American U., 1966.
Military Career: Army, 1949-53.
Occupation: Auto worker; labor official; international trade executive.
Family: Wife, Arcy Sanchez; five children.
Religion: Roman Catholic.
Political Career: Sought Democratic nomination for U.S. House, 1974.
Capitol Office: 1740 Longworth Bldg. 20515; 225-5256.

California 34th: Los Angeles Suburbs — Norwalk. The district vote for Ronald Reagan was 59% in 1984.

Committees

Banking, Finance and Urban Affairs
Small Business

Elections

1986	General	60%	Primary	u/o
1984	General	60%	Primary	81%

CQ Voting Studies

	Presidential Support	Party Unity	Voting Participation
1986	18%	91%	94%
1985	18%	90%	92%

Interest Groups

	ADA	ACU	AFL-CIO	CCUS
1986	90%	n/a	93%	18%
1985	75%	10%	94%	24%

Robert G. Torricelli (D-N.J.)

Of Englewood — Elected 1982

Born: Aug. 26, 1951, Paterson, N.J.
Education: Rutgers U., A.B. 1974, J.D. 1977; Harvard U.,
  M.P.A. 1980.
Occupation: Lawyer.
Family: Wife, Susan Holloway.
Religion: Methodist.
Political Career: No previous office.
Capitol Office: 317 Cannon Bldg. 20515; 225-5061.

New Jersey 9th: North — Fort Lee and Hackensack. The
district vote for Ronald Reagan was 59% in 1984.

Committees

Foreign Affairs
Science, Space and Technology

Elections

1986	General	69%	Primary	97%
1984	General	63%	Primary	94%

CQ Voting Studies

	Presidential Support	Party Unity	Voting Participation
1986	19%	85%	92%
1985	24%	87%	92%

Interest Groups

	ADA	ACU	AFL-CIO	CCUS
1986	70%	n/a	100%	13%
1985	80%	5%	100%	19%

Edolphus Towns (D-N.Y.)

Of Brooklyn — Elected 1982

Born: July 21, 1934, Chadbourn, N.C.
Education: North Carolina A&T U., B.S. 1956; Adelphi U.,
  M.S.W. 1973.
Military Career: Army, 1956-58.
Occupation: Social worker; teacher.
Family: Wife, Gwen Forbes; two children.
Religion: Protestant.
Political Career: Deputy Brooklyn borough president, 1977-
  82 (appointed).
Capitol Office: 1726 Longworth Bldg. 20515; 225-5936.

New York 11th: Northern Brooklyn — Bedford-Stuyvesant.
The district vote for Ronald Reagan was 21% in 1984; 25% in
1980.

Committees

Government Operations
Public Works and Transportation
Select Narcotics Abuse and Control

Elections

1986	General	88%	Primary	u/o
1984	General	85%	Primary	65%

CQ Voting Studies

	Presidential Support	Party Unity	Voting Participation
1986	14%	81%	89%
1985	11%	81%	84%

Interest Groups

	ADA	ACU	AFL-CIO	CCUS
1986	95%	n/a	100%	15%
1985	95%	5%	93%	15%

James A. Traficant Jr. (D-Ohio)

Of Poland — Elected 1984

Born: May 8, 1941, Youngstown, Ohio.
Education: U. of Pittsburgh, B.S. 1963; Youngstown State U., M.S. (administration) 1973, M.S. (counseling) 1976.
Occupation: Law enforcement official.
Family: Wife, Patricia Choppa; two children.
Religion: Roman Catholic.
Political Career: Mahoning County sheriff, 1981-85.
Capitol Office: 128 Cannon Bldg. 20515; 225-5261.

Ohio 17th: Northeast — Youngstown and Warren.

Committees

Public Works and Transportation
Science, Space and Technology

CQ Voting Studies

	Presidential Support	Party Unity	Voting Participation
1986	10%	87%	99%
1985	13%	87%	94%

Interest Groups

	ADA	ACU	AFL-CIO	CCUS
1986	95%	n/a	100%	28%
1985	95%	0%	100%	27%

Elections

1986	General	72%	Primary	76%
1984	General	53%	Primary	56%

Bob Traxler (D-Mich.)

Of Bay City — Elected 1974

Born: July 21, 1931, Kawkawlin, Mich.
Education: Michigan State U., B.A. 1952; Detroit College of Law, LL.B. 1959.
Military Career: Army, 1953-55.
Occupation: Lawyer.
Family: Divorced; three children.
Religion: Episcopalian.
Political Career: Mich. House, 1963-74.
Capitol Office: 2366 Rayburn Bldg. 20515; 225-2806.

Michigan 8th: East — Bay City and Saginaw. The district vote for Ronald Reagan was 60% in 1984; 52% in 1980.

Committees

Appropriations
Select Hunger

CQ Voting Studies

	Presidential Support	Party Unity	Voting Participation
1986	19%	79%	89%
1985	26%	83%	89%

Interest Groups

	ADA	ACU	AFL-CIO	CCUS
1986	80%	n/a	100%	29%
1985	80%	5%	88%	27%

Elections

1986	General	73%	Primary	93%
1984	General	64%	Primary	u/o

Morris K. Udall (D-Ariz.)

Of Tucson — Elected 1961

Born: June 15, 1922, St. Johns, Ariz.
Education: U. of Arizona, J.D. 1949.
Military Career: Army Air Corps, 1942-46.
Occupation: Lawyer.
Family: Wife, Ella Royston; six children.
Religion: Mormon.
Political Career: Pima County attorney, 1952-54; sought Democratic nomination for president, 1976.
Capitol Office: 235 Cannon Bldg. 20515; 225-4065.

Arizona 2nd: Southwest — Western Tucson, Southern Phoenix and Yuma. The district vote for Ronald Reagan was 51% in 1984; 44% in 1980.

Committees

Foreign Affairs
Interior and Insular Affairs (Chairman)
Post Office and Civil Service

Elections

1986	General	76%	Primary	73%
1984	General	88%	Primary	86%

CQ Voting Studies

	Presidential Support	Party Unity	Voting Participation
1986	19%	89%	93%
1985	16%	84%	89%

Interest Groups

	ADA	ACU	AFL-CIO	CCUS
1986	85%	n/a	86%	13%
1985	80%	0%	88%	20%

Fred Upton (R-Mich.)

Of St. Joseph — Elected 1986

Born: April 23, 1953, St. Joseph, Mich.
Education: U. of Mich., B.A. 1975.
Occupation: Legislative affairs specialist.
Family: Wife, Amey Rulon-Miller.
Religion: Protestant.
Political Career: No previous office.
Capitol Office: 1607 Longworth Bldg. 20515; 225-3761.

Michigan 4th: Southwest — Holland, Benton Harbor and St. Joseph. The district vote for Ronald Reagan was 68% in 1984; 60% in 1980.

Committees

Public Works and Transportation
Small Business
Select Hunger

Elections

1986	General	63%	Primary	55%

Tim Valentine (D-N.C.)

Of Nashville — Elected 1982

Born: March 15, 1926, Nashville, N.C.
Education: The Citadel, A.B. 1948; U. of North Carolina, LLB. 1952.
Military Career: Army Air Corps, 1944-46.
Occupation: Lawyer.
Family: Widowed; four children.
Religion: Baptist.
Political Career: N.C. House, 1955-61; state Democratic chairman, 1966-68.
Capitol Office: 1510 Longworth Bldg. 20515; 225-4531.

North Carolina 2nd: North Central — Durham and Rocky Mount. The district vote for Ronald Reagan was 53% in 1984; 43% in 1980.

Committees

Public Works and Transportation
Science, Space and Technology

CQ Voting Studies

	Presidential Support	Party Unity	Voting Participation
1986	41%	67%	98%
1985	46%	71%	97%

Interest Groups

	ADA	ACU	AFL-CIO	CCUS
1986	30%	n/a	43%	65%
1985	35%	48%	35%	59%

Elections

1986	General	74%	Primary	u/o
1984	General	68%	Primary	52%

Guy Vander Jagt (R-Mich.)

Of Luther — Elected 1966

Born: Aug. 26, 1931, Cadillac, Mich.
Education: Hope College, A.B. 1953; Yale U., B.D. 1955; Bonn U., Rotary Fellowship, 1956; U. of Michigan, LL.B. 1960.
Occupation: Lawyer.
Family: Wife, Carol Doorn; one child.
Religion: Presbyterian.
Political Career: Mich. Senate, 1965-66.
Capitol Office: 2409 Rayburn Bldg. 20515; 225-3511.

Michigan 9th: West — Muskegon and Traverse City. The district vote for Ronald Reagan was 69% in 1984; 59% in 1980.

Committee

Ways and Means

CQ Voting Studies

	Presidential Support	Party Unity	Voting Participation
1986	62%	76%	88%
1985	65%	74%	91%

Interest Groups

	ADA	ACU	AFL-CIO	CCUS
1986	0%	n/a	14%	89%
1985	5%	79%	6%	89%

Elections

1986	General	64%	Primary	u/o
1984	General	71%	Primary	u/o

Bruce F. Vento (D-Minn.)

Of St. Paul — Elected 1976

Born: Oct. 7, 1940, St. Paul, Minn.
Education: U. of Minnesota, A.A. 1961; Wisconsin State U.,
   B.S. 1965; graduate work, U. of Minnesota, 1965-70.
Occupation: Science teacher.
Family: Wife, Mary Jean Moore; three children.
Religion: Roman Catholic.
Political Career: Minn. House, 1971-77.
Capitol Office: 2304 Rayburn Bldg. 20515; 225-6631.

Minnesota 4th: St. Paul and Suburbs. The district vote for
Ronald Reagan was 41% in 1984; 34% in 1980.

Committees

Banking, Finance and Urban Affairs
Interior and Insular Affairs
Select Aging

CQ Voting Studies

	Presidential Support	Party Unity	Voting Participation
1986	19%	94%	99%
1985	21%	95%	97%

Interest Groups

	ADA	ACU	AFL-CIO	CCUS
1986	90%	n/a	93%	28%
1985	95%	5%	100%	18%

Elections

1986	General	73%	Primary	89%
1984	General	74%	Primary	91%

Peter J. Visclosky (D-Ind.)

Of Merrillville — Elected 1984

Born: Aug. 13, 1949, Gary, Indiana.
Education: Indiana U., B.S. 1970; Notre Dame U., J.D. 1973;
   Georgetown U., LL.M. 1982.
Occupation: Lawyer.
Family: Wife, Ann Marie O'Keefe.
Religion: Roman Catholic.
Political Career: No previous office.
Capitol Office: 420 Cannon Bldg. 20515; 225-2461.

Indiana 1st: Industrial Belt — Gary and Hammond. The
district vote for Ronald Reagan was 43% in 1984; 45% in
1980.

Committees

Education and Labor
Interior and Insular Affairs
Public Works and Transportation

CQ Voting Studies

	Presidential Support	Party Unity	Voting Participation
1986	19%	93%	100%
1985	30%	90%	99%

Interest Groups

	ADA	ACU	AFL-CIO	CCUS
1986	90%	n/a	93%	33%
1985	80%	5%	71%	36%

Elections

1986	General	74%	Primary	57%
1984	General	71%	Primary	35%

Harold L. Volkmer   (D-Mo.)

Of Hannibal — Elected 1976

Born: April 4, 1931, Jefferson City, Mo.
Education: U. of Missouri, LL.B. 1955.
Military Career: Army, 1955-57.
Occupation: Lawyer.
Family: Wife, Shirley Ruth Braskett; three children.
Religion: Roman Catholic.
Political Career: Marion County prosecuting attorney, 1960-66; Mo. House, 1967-77.
Capitol Office: 2411 Rayburn Bldg. 20515; 225-2956.

Missouri 9th: Northeast — Columbia. The district vote for Ronald Reagan was 64% in 1984; 54% in 1980.

Committees

Agriculture
Science, Space and Technology
Select Aging

CQ Voting Studies

	Presidential Support	Party Unity	Voting Participation
1986	33%	79%	98%
1985	30%	77%	98%

Interest Groups

	ADA	ACU	AFL-CIO	CCUS
1986	45%	n/a	79%	33%
1985	40%	33%	59%	36%

Elections

1986	General	57%	Primary	u/o
1984	General	53%	Primary	u/o

Barbara F. Vucanovich   (R-Nev.)

Of Reno — Elected 1982

Born: June 22, 1921, Camp Dix, N.J.
Education: Attended Manhattanville College, 1938-39.
Occupation: Travel agent; congressional aide.
Family: Husband, George F. Vucanovich; five children.
Religion: Roman Catholic.
Political Career: No previous office.
Capitol Office: 312 Cannon Bldg. 20515; 225-6155.

Nevada 2nd: North — Reno and the Cow Counties. The district vote for Ronald Reagan was 70% in 1984; 65% in 1980.

Committees

House Administration
Interior and Insular Affairs
Select Children, Youth and Families

CQ Voting Studies

	Presidential Support	Party Unity	Voting Participation
1986	69%	84%	96%
1985	70%	87%	96%

Interest Groups

	ADA	ACU	AFL-CIO	CCUS
1986	0%	n/a	7%	89%
1985	10%	86%	13%	95%

Elections

1986	General	58%	Primary	u/o
1984	General	71%	Primary	u/o

Doug Walgren   (D-Pa.)

Of Mount Lebanon — Elected 1976

Born: Dec. 28, 1940, Rochester, N.Y.
Education: Dartmouth College, B.A. 1963; Stanford U. Law School, LL.B. 1966.
Occupation: Lawyer.
Family: Wife, Carmala Vincent; three children.
Religion: Roman Catholic.
Political Career: Democratic nominee for U.S. House, 1970, 1972 special election, 1972 general election.
Capitol Office: 2241 Rayburn Bldg. 20515; 225-2135.

Pennsylvania 18th: Pittsburgh Suburbs. The district vote for Ronald Reagan was 58% in 1984; 56% in 1980.

Committees

Energy and Commerce
Science, Space and Technology

Elections

1986	General	63%	Primary	u/o
1984	General	63%	Primary	u/o

CQ Voting Studies

	Presidential Support	Party Unity	Voting Participation
1986	13%	83%	94%
1985	25%	89%	95%

Interest Groups

	ADA	ACU	AFL-CIO	CCUS
1986	85%	n/a	86%	41%
1985	70%	10%	88%	29%

Robert S. Walker   (R-Pa.)

Of East Petersburg — Elected 1976

Born: Dec. 23, 1942, Bradford, Pa.
Education: Millersville State College, B.S. 1964; U. of Delaware, M.A. 1968.
Military Career: Pa. National Guard, 1967-73.
Occupation: High school teacher; congressional aide.
Family: Wife, Sue Albertson.
Religion: Presbyterian.
Political Career: No previous office.
Capitol Office: 2445 Rayburn Bldg. 20515; 225-2411.

Pennsylvania 16th: Southeast — Lancaster. The district vote for Ronald Reagan was 74% in 1984; 66% in 1980.

Committees

Government Operations
Science, Space and Technology

Elections

1986	General	75%	Primary	u/o
1984	General	78%	Primary	84%

CQ Voting Studies

	Presidential Support	Party Unity	Voting Participation
1986	82%	96%	99%
1985	80%	93%	99%

Interest Groups

	ADA	ACU	AFL-CIO	CCUS
1986	0%	n/a	14%	94%
1985	15%	86%	12%	91%

Wes Watkins (D-Okla.)

Of Ada — Elected 1976

Born: Dec. 15, 1938, DeQueen, Ark.
Education: Oklahoma State U., B.S. 1960, M.S. 1961.
Military Career: Okla. Air National Guard, 1961-67.
Occupation: Real estate salesman; home builder.
Family: Wife, Elizabeth Lou Rogers; three children.
Religion: Presbyterian.
Political Career: Okla. Senate, 1975-77.
Capitol Office: 2348 Rayburn Bldg. 20515; 225-4565.

Oklahoma 3rd: Southeast — "Little Dixie". The district vote for Ronald Reagan was 62% in 1984; 51% in 1980.

Committee

Appropriations

Elections

1986	General	78%	Primary	85%
1984	General	78%	Primary	u/o

CQ Voting Studies

	Presidential Support	Party Unity	Voting Participation
1986	32%	75%	96%
1985	43%	73%	96%

Interest Groups

	ADA	ACU	AFL-CIO	CCUS
1986	40%	n/a	64%	29%
1985	50%	48%	47%	45%

Henry A. Waxman (D-Calif.)

Of Los Angeles — Elected 1974

Born: Sept. 12, 1939, Los Angeles, Calif.
Education: U.C.L.A., B.A. 1961, J.D. 1964.
Occupation: Lawyer.
Family: Wife, Janet Kessler; two children.
Religion: Jewish.
Political Career: Calif. Assembly, 1969-75.
Capitol Office: 2418 Rayburn Bldg. 20515; 225-3976.

California 24th: Hollywood and Part of San Fernando Valley. The district vote for Ronald Reagan was 44% in 1984.

Committees

Energy and Commerce
Government Operations
Select Aging

Elections

1986	General	u/o	Primary	u/o
1984	General	63%	Primary	87%

CQ Voting Studies

	Presidential Support	Party Unity	Voting Participation
1986	12%	87%	92%
1985	28%	86%	89%

Interest Groups

	ADA	ACU	AFL-CIO	CCUS
1986	95%	n/a	92%	20%
1985	95%	16%	94%	27%

Vin Weber (R-Minn.)

Of North Mankato — Elected 1980

Born: July 24, 1952, Slayton, Minn.
Education: Attended U. of Minnesota, 1970-74.
Occupation: Publisher.
Family: Divorced.
Religion: Roman Catholic.
Political Career: Republican nominee for Minn. Senate, 1976.
Capitol Office: 106 Cannon Bldg. 20515; 225-2331.

Minnesota 2nd: Southwest — Willmar. The district vote for Ronald Reagan was 57% in 1984; 52% in 1980.

Committee

Appropriations

Elections

1986	General	52%	Primary	u/o
1984	General	63%	Primary	u/o

CQ Voting Studies

	Presidential Support	Party Unity	Voting Participation
1986	69%	80%	97%
1985	64%	79%	92%

Interest Groups

	ADA	ACU	AFL-CIO	CCUS
1986	15%	n/a	21%	72%
1985	15%	85%	20%	76%

Ted Weiss (D-N.Y.)

Of Manhattan — Elected 1976

Born: Sept. 17, 1927, in Hungary.
Education: Syracuse U., B.A. 1951, LL.B. 1952.
Military Career: Army, 1946-47.
Occupation: Lawyer.
Family: Wife, Sonya Hoover; two children.
Religion: Jewish.
Political Career: N.Y. City Council, 1962-77; sought Democratic nomination for U.S. House, 1966, 1968.
Capitol Office: 2442 Rayburn Bldg. 20515; 225-5635.

New York 17th: West Side Manhattan — Part of the Bronx. The district vote for Ronald Reagan was 25% in 1984; 28% in 1980.

Committees

Foreign Affairs
Government Operations
Select Children, Youth and Families

Elections

1986	General	86%	Primary	83%
1984	General	82%	Primary	85%

CQ Voting Studies

	Presidential Support	Party Unity	Voting Participation
1986	12%	81%	85%
1985	23%	93%	97%

Interest Groups

	ADA	ACU	AFL-CIO	CCUS
1986	95%	n/a	79%	25%
1985	100%	5%	100%	18%

Curt Weldon   (R-Pa.)

Of Aston — Elected 1986

Born: July 22, 1947, Marcus Hook, Pa.
Education: West Chester State College, B.A. 1969; attended Cheney U. of Pennsylvania, Temple U., Cabrini College, St. Joseph's U., 1969-73; Delaware Valley College of Science and Agriculture, A.A.S. 1972.
Occupation: Teacher.
Family: Wife, Mary Gallagher; five children.
Religion: Protestant.
Political Career: Mayor, Marcus Hook, 1977-82; Delaware County Council, 1981-86; GOP nominee for U.S. House, 1984.
Capitol Office: 1233 Longworth Bldg. 20515; 225-2011

Pennsylvania 7th: Southwest Philadelphia Suburbs. The district vote for Ronald Reagan was 62% in 1984; 56% in 1980.

Committees

Armed Services
Merchant Marine and Fisheries

Elections

1986	General	61%	Primary	u/o

Alan Wheat   (D-Mo.)

Of Kansas City — Elected 1982

Born: Oct. 16, 1951, San Antonio, Texas.
Education: Grinnell College, B.A. 1972.
Occupation: Public official.
Family: Single.
Religion: Church of Christ.
Political Career: Mo. House, 1977-83.
Capitol Office: 1204 Longworth Bldg. 20515; 225-4535.

Missouri 5th: Kansas City and Eastern Suburbs. The district vote for Ronald Reagan was 46% in 1984; 40% in 1980.

Committees

District of Columbia
Rules
Select Children, Youth and Families

CQ Voting Studies

	Presidential Support	Party Unity	Voting Participation
1986	14%	96%	99%
1985	15%	97%	99%

Interest Groups

	ADA	ACU	AFL-CIO	CCUS
1986	95%	n/a	86%	22%
1985	100%	0%	100%	14%

Elections

1986	General	72%	Primary	u/o
1984	General	66%	Primary	u/o

Bob Whittaker   (R-Kan.)

Of Augusta — Elected 1978

Born: Sept. 18, 1939, Eureka, Kan.
Education: Attended U. of Kansas, 1957-59;
Emporia State College, 1959; Illinois College of Optometry,
B.S., D.O. 1962.
Occupation: Optometrist.
Family: Wife, Marlene Faye Arnold; three children.
Religion: Christian Church.
Political Career: Kansas House, 1975-77.
Capitol Office: 2436 Rayburn Bldg. 20515; 225-3911.

Kansas 5th: Southeast — Emporia and Pittsburg. The district vote for Ronald Reagan was 67% in 1984; 59% in 1980.

Committee

Energy and Commerce

Elections

1986	General	71%	Primary	u/o
1984	General	74%	Primary	u/o

CQ Voting Studies

	Presidential Support	Party Unity	Voting Participation
1986	67%	83%	97%
1985	58%	79%	94%

Interest Groups

	ADA	ACU	AFL-CIO	CCUS
1986	10%	n/a	15%	94%
1985	10%	81%	12%	86%

Jamie L. Whitten   (D-Miss.)

Of Charleston — Elected 1941

Born: April 18, 1910, Cascilla, Miss.
Education: Attended U. of Mississippi, 1927-32.
Occupation: Grammar school teacher and principal; lawyer; author.
Family: Wife, Rebecca Thompson; two children.
Religion: Presbyterian.
Political Career: Miss. House, 1931-33; district attorney, 17th district, 1933-41.
Capitol Office: 2314 Rayburn Bldg., 20515; 225-4306.

Mississippi 1st: North — Clarksdale. The district vote for Ronald Reagan was 62% in 1984.

Committee

Appropriations (Chairman)

Elections

1986	General	66%	Primary	77%
1984	General	88%	Primary	88%

CQ Voting Studies

	Presidential Support	Party Unity	Voting Participation
1986	30%	76%	92%
1985	33%	79%	92%

Interest Groups

	ADA	ACU	AFL-CIO	CCUS
1986	55%	n/a	69%	31%
1985	55%	26%	75%	20%

Pat Williams (D-Mont.)

Of Helena — Elected 1978

Born: Oct. 30, 1937, Helena, Mont.
Education: Attended U. of Montana, 1956-57; William Jewell College, 1958; U. of Denver, B.A. 1961; graduate work, Western Mont. College, 1962.
Military Career: Army, 1960-61; National Guard, 1962-69.
Occupation: Elementary and secondary school teacher.
Family: Wife, Carol Griffith; three children.
Religion: Roman Catholic.
Political Career: Mont. House, 1967-71; sought Democratic nomination for U.S. House, 1974.
Capitol Office: 2457 Rayburn Bldg. 20515; 225-3211.

Montana 1st: Western Mountains — Helena and Missoula. The district vote for Ronald Reagan was 58% in 1984; 55% in 1980.

Committees

Budget
Education and Labor

CQ Voting Studies

	Presidential Support	Party Unity	Voting Participation
1986	12%	76%	88%
1985	18%	76%	85%

Interest Groups

	ADA	ACU	AFL-CIO	CCUS
1986	85%	n/a	92%	20%
1985	95%	10%	94%	23%

Elections

1986	General	62%	Primary	u/o
1984	General	66%	Primary	u/o

Charles Wilson (D-Texas)

Of Lufkin — Elected 1972

Born: June 1, 1933, Trinity, Texas.
Education: Attended Sam Houston State U., 1950-51; U.S. Naval Academy, B.S. 1956.
Military Career: Navy, 1956-60.
Occupation: Lumberyard manager.
Family: Divorced.
Religion: Methodist.
Political Career: Texas House, 1961-67; Texas Senate, 1967-73.
Capitol Office: 2265 Rayburn Bldg. 20515; 225-2401.

Texas 2nd: East — Lufkin and Orange. The district vote for Ronald Reagan was 58% in 1984; 48% in 1980.

Committees

Appropriations
Select Intelligence

CQ Voting Studies

	Presidential Support	Party Unity	Voting Participation
1986	38%	61%	81%
1985	40%	63%	74%

Interest Groups

	ADA	ACU	AFL-CIO	CCUS
1986	35%	n/a	92%	27%
1985	40%	55%	75%	44%

Elections

1986	General	67%	Primary	u/o
1984	General	59%	Primary	55%

Bob Wise (D-W. Va.)

Of Clendenin — Elected 1982

Born: Jan. 6, 1948, Washington, D.C.
Education: Duke U., A.B. 1970; Tulane U. School of Law, J.D. 1975.
Occupation: Lawyer.
Family: Wife, Sandra Casber.
Religion: Episcopalian.
Political Career: W.Va. Senate, 1981-83.
Capitol Office: 1421 Longworth Bldg. 20515; 225-2711.

West Virginia 3rd: Central — Charleston. The district vote for Ronald Reagan was 56% in 1984; 46% in 1980.

Committees

Education and Labor
Government Operations
Public Works and Transportation
Select Aging

CQ Voting Studies

	Presidential Support	Party Unity	Voting Participation
1986	23%	88%	96%
1985	26%	84%	95%

Interest Groups

	ADA	ACU	AFL-CIO	CCUS
1986	75%	n/a	93%	22%
1985	70%	10%	82%	32%

Elections

1986	General	65%	Primary	u/o
1984	General	68%	Primary	91%

Frank R. Wolf (R-Va.)

Of Vienna — Elected 1980

Born: Jan. 30, 1939, Philadelphia, Pa.
Education: Pennsylvania State U., B.A. 1961; Georgetown U., LL.B. 1965.
Military Career: Army, 1962-63, Reserve, 1963-67.
Occupation: Lawyer.
Family: Wife, Carolyn Stover; five children.
Religion: Presbyterian.
Political Career: Sought Republican nomination for U.S. House, 1976; Republican nominee for U.S. House, 1978.
Capitol Office: 130 Cannon Bldg. 20515; 225-5136.

Virginia 10th: D.C. Suburbs — Arlington County. The district vote for Ronald Reagan was 59% in 1984; 53% in 1980.

Committees

Appropriations
Select Children, Youth and Families

CQ Voting Studies

	Presidential Support	Party Unity	Voting Participation
1986	67%	74%	99%
1985	70%	72%	98%

Interest Groups

	ADA	ACU	AFL-CIO	CCUS
1986	5%	n/a	21%	67%
1985	15%	71%	24%	73%

Elections

1986	General	60%	Primary	u/o
1984	General	63%	Primary	u/o

Howard Wolpe (D-Mich.)

Of Lansing — Elected 1978

Born: Nov. 2, 1939, Los Angeles, Calif.
Education: Reed College, B.A. 1960; Massachusetts Institute of Technology, Ph.D. 1967.
Occupation: Political science professor.
Family: Divorced; one child.
Religion: Jewish.
Political Career: Kalamazoo City Commission, 1969-72; Mich. House, 1973-77; Democratic nominee for U.S. House, 1976.
Capitol Office: 1535 Longworth Bldg. 20515; 225-5011.

Michigan 3rd: South Central — Lansing and Kalamazoo. The district vote for Ronald Reagan was 63% in 1984; 52% in 1980.

Committees

Budget
Foreign Affairs

CQ Voting Studies

	Presidential Support	Party Unity	Voting Participation
1986	16%	91%	97%
1985	21%	91%	97%

Interest Groups

	ADA	ACU	AFL-CIO	CCUS
1986	90%	n/a	93%	33%
1985	85%	10%	94%	20%

Elections

1986	General	60%	Primary	u/o
1984	General	53%	Primary	u/o

George C. Wortley (R-N.Y.)

Of Fayetteville — Elected 1980

Born: Dec. 8, 1926, Syracuse, N.Y.
Education: Attended Kings Point Academy, 1945-46; Syracuse U., B.S. 1948.
Military Career: Navy, 1945-46.
Occupation: Newspaper publisher.
Family: Wife, Barbara Hennessy; three children.
Religion: Roman Catholic.
Political Career: Republican nominee for U.S. House, 1976.
Capitol Office: 229 Cannon Bldg. 20515; 225-3701.

New York 27th: Central — Syracuse. The district vote for Ronald Reagan was 60% in 1984; 51% in 1980.

Committees

Banking, Finance and Urban Affairs
Select Aging
Select Children, Youth and Families

CQ Voting Studies

	Presidential Support	Party Unity	Voting Participation
1986	63%	53%	96%
1985	65%	62%	93%

Interest Groups

	ADA	ACU	AFL-CIO	CCUS
1986	20%	n/a	57%	65%
1985	15%	80%	35%	82%

Elections

1986	General	50%	Primary	u/o
1984	General	57%	Primary	u/o

Jim Wright (D-Texas)

Of Fort Worth — Elected 1954

Born: Dec. 22, 1922, Fort Worth, Texas.
Education: Attended Weatherford College, 1939-40; U. of Texas 1940-41.
Military Career: Army Air Corps, 1941-45.
Occupation: Advertising executive.
Family: Wife, Betty Hay; four children.
Religion: Presbyterian.
Political Career: Texas House, 1947-49; Mayor of Weatherford, 1950-54; candidate for U.S. Senate, special election, 1961.
Capitol Office: 1236 Longworth Bldg. 20515; 225-5071.

Texas 12th: Fort Worth and Northwest Tarrant County. The district vote for Ronald Reagan was 59% in 1984; 49% in 1980.

Committee

Speaker of the House

Elections

1986	General	69%	Primary	91%
1984	General	u/o	Primary	u/o

CQ Voting Studies

	Presidential Support	Party Unity	Voting Participation
1986	19%	83%	89%
1985	23%	81%	87%

Interest Groups

	ADA	ACU	AFL-CIO	CCUS
1986	80%	n/a	100%	31%
1985	50%	13%	80%	37%

Ron Wyden (D-Ore.)

Of Portland — Elected 1980

Born: May 3, 1949, Wichita, Kan.
Education: Stanford U., A.B. 1971; U. of Oregon, J.D. 1974.
Occupation: Lawyer.
Family: Wife, Laurie Oseran; one child.
Religion: Jewish.
Political Career: No previous office.
Capitol Office: 1406 Longworth Bldg. 20515; 225-4811.

Oregon 3rd: Eastern Portland and Suburbs. The district vote for Ronald Reagan was 46% in 1984; 40% in 1980.

Committees

Energy and Commerce
Small Business
Select Aging

Elections

1986	General	86%	Primary	95%
1984	General	72%	Primary	u/o

CQ Voting Studies

	Presidential Support	Party Unity	Voting Participation
1986	23%	89%	99%
1985	26%	84%	99%

Interest Groups

	ADA	ACU	AFL-CIO	CCUS
1986	80%	n/a	79%	28%
1985	60%	29%	71%	59%

Chalmers P. Wylie   (R-Ohio)

Of Worthington — Elected 1966

Born: Nov. 23, 1920, Norwich, Ohio.
Education: Attended Otterbein College, 1939-40; Ohio State U., 1940-43; Harvard U., J.D. 1948.
Military Career: Army, 1943-45; Army Reserve, 1945-53; National Guard, 1958-78.
Occupation: Lawyer.
Family: Wife, Marjorie Siebold; two children.
Religion: Methodist.
Political Career: Columbus city attorney, 1954-57; Ohio House, 1961-67.
Capitol Office: 2310 Rayburn Bldg. 20515; 225-2015.

Ohio 15th: Central — Western Columbus and Suburbs.

Committees

Banking, Finance and Urban Affairs   (Ranking)
Veterans' Affairs
Joint Economic   (Ranking)

Elections

1986	General	64%	Primary	u/o
1984	General	72%	Primary	u/o

CQ Voting Studies

	Presidential Support	Party Unity	Voting Participation
1986	63%	58%	95%
1985	68%	61%	92%

Interest Groups

	ADA	ACU	AFL-CIO	CCUS
1986	15%	n/a	31%	71%
1985	10%	76%	29%	73%

Sidney R. Yates   (D-Ill.)

Of Chicago — Elected 1948

Born: Aug. 27, 1909, Chicago, Ill.
Education: U. of Chicago, Ph.B. 1931, J.D. 1933.
Military Career: Navy, 1944-46.
Occupation: Lawyer.
Family: Wife, Adeline Holleb; one child.
Religion: Jewish.
Political Career: Democratic nominee for U.S. Senate, 1962.
Capitol Office: 2234 Rayburn Bldg. 20515; 225-2111.

Illinois 9th: Chicago — North Side Lakefront and Northern Suburbs. The district vote for Ronald Reagan was 45% in 1984; 37% in 1980.

Committee

Appropriations

Elections

1986	General	72%	Primary	84%
1984	General	68%	Primary	80%

CQ Voting Studies

	Presidential Support	Party Unity	Voting Participation
1986	18%	88%	92%
1985	31%	93%	95%

Interest Groups

	ADA	ACU	AFL-CIO	CCUS
1986	90%	n/a	85%	12%
1985	100%	10%	88%	20%

Gus Yatron (D-Pa.)

Of Reading — Elected 1968

Born: Oct. 16, 1927, Reading, Pa.
Education: Attended Kutztown State Teachers College, 1950.
Occupation: Professional boxer; ice cream manufacturer.
Family: Wife, Millie Menzies; two children.
Religion: Greek Orthodox.
Political Career: Reading School Board, 1955-61; Pa. House, 1957-61; Pa. Senate, 1961-69.
Capitol Office: 2267 Rayburn Bldg. 20515; 225-5546.

Pennsylvania 6th: Southeast — Reading. The district vote for Ronald Reagan was 64% in 1984; 56% in 1980.

Committees

Foreign Affairs
Post Office and Civil Service

Elections

1986	General	69%	Primary	u/o	
1984	General	u/o	Primary	88%	

CQ Voting Studies

	Presidential Support	Party Unity	Voting Participation
1986	22%	80%	97%
1985	44%	80%	97%

Interest Groups

	ADA	ACU	AFL-CIO	CCUS
1986	65%	n/a	100%	38%
1985	50%	33%	69%	36%

C. W. Bill Young (R-Fla.)

Of St. Petersburg — Elected 1970

Born: Dec. 16, 1930, Harmarville, Pa.
Education: Attended Pennsylvania public schools.
Military Career: National Guard, 1948-57.
Occupation: Insurance executive.
Family: Wife, Beverly F. Angelo; three children, two stepchildren.
Religion: Methodist.
Political Career: Fla. Senate, 1961-71, minority leader, 1967-71.
Capitol Office: 2407 Rayburn Bldg. 20515; 225-5961.

Florida 8th: West — St. Petersburg. The district vote for Ronald Reagan was 63% in 1984; 53% in 1980.

Committee

Appropriations

Elections

1986	General	u/o	Primary	u/o	
1984	General	80%	Primary	u/o	

CQ Voting Studies

	Presidential Support	Party Unity	Voting Participation
1986	72%	75%	94%
1985	74%	80%	93%

Interest Groups

	ADA	ACU	AFL-CIO	CCUS
1986	5%	n/a	8%	67%
1985	5%	71%	24%	76%

Don Young (R-Alaska)

Of Fort Yukon — Elected 1973

Born: June 9, 1933, Meridian, Calif.

Education: Yuba Junior College, A.A. 1952; Chico State College, Calif., B.A. 1958.

Military Career: Army, 1955-57.

Occupation: Elementary school teacher; riverboat captain.

Family: Wife, Lula Fredson; two children.

Religion: Episcopalian.

Political Career: Fort Yukon City Council, 1960-64; mayor of Fort Yukon, 1964-68; Alaska House, 1967-71; Alaska Senate, 1971-73; Republican nominee for U.S. House, 1972.

Capitol Office: 2331 Rayburn Bldg. 20515; 225-5765.

Alaska: At-large. The district vote for Ronald Reagan was 67% in 1984; 54% in 1980.

CQ Voting Studies

	Presidential Support	Party Unity	Voting Participation
1986	61%	63%	93%
1985	51%	62%	94%

Interest Groups

	ADA	ACU	AFL-CIO	CCUS
1986	20%	n/a	62%	56%
1985	30%	62%	53%	45%

Committees

Interior and Insular Affairs   (Ranking)
Merchant Marine and Fisheries
Post Office and Civil Service

Elections

1986	General	58%	Primary	92%
1984	General	55%	Primary	u/o

Non-Voting Members of The House of Representatives

Non-voting delegates are not exactly members of the House, but they are part of the legislative process. They make speeches, serve on committees, and hold chairmanships.

The only thing delegates are not allowed to do is to vote on the House floor.

Following are profiles of the delegates, who serve in the House on a non-voting basis.

Ben Blaz (R)

Of Guam — Elected 1984

Born: Feb. 14, 1928, Agana, Guam.

Education: U. of Notre Dame, B.S. 1951; George Washington U., M.A. 1963; Naval War College, 1971.

Military Career: Marines, 1951-80.

Occupation: Retired brigadier general.

Family: Wife, Ann Evers; two children.

Religion: Roman Catholic.

Political Career: No previous office.

Capitol office: 1130 Longworth Bldg. 20515; 225-1188.

Committees: Armed Services; Foreign Affairs; Interior and Insular Affairs; Select Aging.

Ron de Lugo (D)

Of the Virgin Islands — Elected 1972

Born: August 2, 1930, Englewood, N.J.

Education: Attended Colegio San Jose.

Military Career: Army, 1948-50.

Occupation: Radio journalist.

Family: Wife, Sheila Paieworsky; four children.

Religion: Roman Catholic.

Political Career: V.I. Senate, 1956-66; delegate to Democratic National Convention, 1956, 1960, 1964, 1968; Democratic national committeeman, 1959; administrator for St. Croix, 1961; Washington representative for V.I., 1968; candidate for Virgin Islands governor, 1978.

Capitol Office: 2238 Rayburn Bldg. 20515; 225-1790.

Committees: Interior and Insular Affairs; Post Office and Civil Service; Public Works and Transportation.

Walter E. Fauntroy (D)

Of Washington, D.C. — Elected 1971

Born: Feb. 6, 1933, Washington, D.C.

Education: Virginia Union U., B.A. 1955; Yale U. Divinity School, B.D. 1958.

Occupation: Pastor.

Family: Wife, Dorothy Simms; one child.

Religion: Baptist.

Political Career: No previous office.

Capitol office: 2135 Rayburn Bldg. 20515; 225-8050.

Committees: Banking, Finance and Urban Affairs; District of Columbia; Select Narcotics, Abuse and Control.

Fofō I. F. Sunia (D)

Of American Samoa — Elected 1980

Born: March 13, 1937, Fagasa, American Samoa.

Education: U. of Hawaii, B.A. 1960.

Occupation: Tourism director.

Religion: Samoan Christian Congregational Church.

Family: Wife, Aioletuna Ta'amu; eight children.

Political Career: Samoan affairs liaison officer for governor; election commissioner, 1961-1966; American Samoa Senate, 1970-78.

Capitol Office: 1206 Longworth Bldg. 20515; 225-8577.

Committees: Interior and Insular Affairs; Foreign Affairs; Public Works and Transportation.

Jaime B. Fuster (Pop. Dem.)

Of Puerto Rico — Elected 1984
Resident Commissioner

Born: Jan. 12, 1941, Guayama, P.R.

Education: U. of Notre Dame, B.A. 1962; U. of Puerto Rico Law School, J.D. 1965; Columbia U. Law School, LL.M. 1966; Harvard Law School, S.J.D. candidacy 1974.

Occupation: Law professor; university administrator.

Family: Wife, Mary Jo Zalduondo; two children.

Religion: Roman Catholic.

Political Career: No previous office.

Capitol Office: 427 Cannon Bldg. 20515; 225-2615.

Committees: Interior and Insular Affairs; Foreign Affairs.

State Delegations and Members' Chief Aides

ALABAMA

Senate

Richard C. Shelby (D, 92) .... Rick Roberts
Howell Heflin (D, 90) ... Carlton Betenbaugh

Representatives

1. Sonny Callahan (R) .... Randy Hinaman
2. William L. Dickinson (R) . H. Clay Swanzy
3. Bill Nichols (D) .... Winston T. Lett
4. Tom Bevill (D) .... Donald R. Smith
5. Ronnie G. Flippo (D) ... William E. Rasco
6. Ben Erdreich (D) .... Judy Weinstein
7. Claude Harris (D) .... Walter Braswell

ALASKA

Senate

Frank H. Murkowski (R, 92) Dennis Fradley
Ted Stevens (R, 90) .... Greg Chapados

Representative

AL Don Young (R) .... C. J. Zane

ARIZONA

Senate

Dennis DeConcini (D, 88) .... Gene Karp
John McCain (R, 92) .... Chris Koch

Representatives

1. John J. Rhodes III (R) .... Jack Seum
2. Morris K. Udall (D) . Robert A. Neuman
3. Bob Stump (R) .... Lisa A. Jackson
4. Jon Kyl (R) Kelly Johnston
5. Jim Kolbe (R) ... Richard (Rowdy) Yeates

ARKANSAS

Senate

Dale Bumpers (D, 92) .... Mary E. Davis
David Pryor (D, 90) .... Don W. Harrell

Representatives

1. Bill Alexander (D) .... Dorothy Thomas
2. Tommy F. Robinson (D) . Louise D. Hilsen
3. John Paul Hammerschmidt (R)
   .... Raymond Reid
4. Beryl Anthony Jr. (D) .... Carol Garison

CALIFORNIA

Senate

Alan Cranston (D, 92) ..... Roy F. Greenaway
Pete Wilson (R, 88) .... Bob White

Representatives

1. Douglas H. Bosco (D) .. Mitch B. Stogner
2. Wally Herger (R) .... John Magill
3. Robert T. Matsui (D) . Edgar A. Hatcher IV
4. Vic Fazio (D) ...... Christopher M. Humes
5. Sala Burton (D) .... Nancy M. Leong
6. Barbara Boxer (D) .... Sam Chapman
7. George Miller (D) .... John A. Lawrence
8. Ronald V. Dellums (D) Carlottia A. Scott
9. Fortney H. "Pete" Stark (D)
   .... William Vaughan
10. Don Edwards (D) .... Roberta Haeberle
11. Tom Lantos (D) .... Robert R. King
12. Ernie Konnyu (R) .... Dick Leggitt
13. Norman Y. Mineta (D) . Susanne Elfving
14. Norman D. Shumway (R)
    .... Christopher Seeger
15. Tony Coelho (D) .. Frederick W. Hatfield
16. Leon E. Panetta (D) .... J. Diana Marino
17. Charles Pashayan Jr. (R) Norman Turnette
18. Richard H. Lehman (D) ..... Steven J. Jost
19. Robert J. Lagomarsino (R) Susan Gerrick
20. William M. Thomas (R)
    ...... Catherine Abernathy
21. Elton Gallegly (R) .... Mike Sedell
22. Carlos J. Moorhead (R)   Alice K. Andersen
23. Anthony C. Beilenson (D) . Janet Faulstich
24. Henry A. Waxman (D) .... Philip Schiliro
25. Edward R. Roybal (D) .. Jorge J. Lambrinos
26. Howard L. Berman (D) .... Gene Smith
27. Mel Levine (D)   William G. Andresen Jr.
28. Julian C. Dixon (D) ... Andrea T. Holmes
29. Augustus F. Hawkins (D) . Mark J. Molli
30. Matthew G. Martinez (D) . Maxine Grant
31. Mervyn M. Dymally (D) . David Johnson
32. Glenn M. Anderson (D)
    .... Jerimiah Bresnahan
33. David Dreier (R) .... Brad Smith
34. Esteban Edward Torres (D) ... Bob Alcock
35. Jerry Lewis (R) .... Arlene Willis
36. George E. Brown Jr. (D) .... Skip Stiles
37. Al McCandless (R) .. Signy Ellerton-Jones
38. Bob Dornan (R) .... Brian O. Bennett

39. William E. Dannemeyer (R)
.... Bengt Naslund
40. Robert E. Badham (R) .... Kathy W. Hill
41. Bill Lowery (R) ...... Benjamin A. Haddad
42. Dan Lungren (R) .... Victor E. Arnold-Bik
43. Ron Packard (R) .... Nancy H. Mason
44. Jim Bates (D) .... Sally N. McConnell
45. Duncan L. Hunter (R) ... John P. Palafoutas

COLORADO

Senate

William L. Armstrong (R, 90) . Howard Propst
Timothy E. Wirth (D, 92) .... Paige Reffe

Representatives

1. Patricia Schroeder (D) ...... Daniel J. Buck
2. David Skaggs (D) .... Tom Gillooly
3. Ben Nighthorse Campbell (D)
.... Sherrie Wolff
4. Hank Brown (R) .... Joel D. Kassiday
5. Joel Hefley (R) ....
6. Dan L. Schaefer (R) .... Larry W. Dye

CONNECTICUT

Senate

Christopher J. Dodd (D, 92) ... Ed Silverman
Lowell P. Weicker Jr. (R, 88) ... Meredith Fauls

Representatives

1. Barbara B. Kennelly (D) ..Michael Prucker
2. Sam Gejdenson (D) .... Sarah A. Farrell
3. Bruce A. Morrison (D) .... Paul J. Drolet
4. Stewart B. McKinney (R) ... Barbara Rapp
5. John G. Rowland (R) John A. Mastropietro
6. Nancy L. Johnson (R)
...... Kathleen Harrington

DELAWARE

Senate

Joseph R. Biden Jr. (D, 90) .... Tim Ridley
William V. Roth Jr. (R, 88) John M. Duncan

Representative

AL Thomas R. Carper (D) ... Edward J. Freel

FLORIDA

Senate

Lawton Chiles (D, 88) . Richard T. Farrell Jr.
Bob Graham (D, 92) .... Buddy Shorstein

Representatives

1. Earl Hutto (D) ...... Randolph L. Knepper
2. Bill Grant (D) .... Herb Wadsworth

3. Charles E. Bennett (D) ...... Ramon L. Day
4. Bill Chappell Jr. (D) ... Shephard W. Hill
5. Bill McCollum (R) ...... Vaughn S. Forrest
6. Buddy MacKay (D) .... Greg Farmer
7. Sam Gibbons (D) .... Janice F. Stoorza
8. C. W. Bill Young (R) .. George N. Cretekos
9. Michael Bilirakis (R) Sandra D. Hanbury
10. Andy Ireland (R) ...... Katharine Calhoun
11. Bill Nelson (D) ...... James F. Southerland
12. Tom Lewis (R) .... Karen Hogan
13. Connie Mack (R) .... Michael P. Forbes
14. Daniel A. Mica (D) ...... Suzanne M. Stoll
15. E. Clay Shaw Jr. (R) .... Wendy Strong
16. Larry Smith (D) .... Gary Edwards
17. William Lehman (D) Marsha Runningen
18. Claude Pepper (D) . Frances H. Campbell
19. Dante B. Fascell (D) Charles R. O'Regan

GEORGIA

Senate

Wyche Fowler Jr. (D, 92) . Marc Wetherhorn
Sam Nunn (D, 90) .... Zada Johnson

Representatives

1. Robert Lindsay Thomas (D) Robert Hurt
2. Charles Hatcher (D) .. Robert L. Redding
3. Richard Ray (D) Douglas W. Hopkins
4. Pat Swindall (R) .... Ken Willis
5. John Lewis (D) .... Clarence Bishop
6. Newt Gingrich (R) .... Mary N. Brown
7. George "Buddy" Darden (D)
.... R. Brent Gilroy
8. J. Roy Rowland (D) .... Selby McCash
9. Ed Jenkins (D) .... Carl Barrett
10. Doug Barnard Jr. (D) ..... Billye Hansford

HAWAII

Senate

Daniel K. Inouye (D, 92) ...... Patrick DeLeon
Spark M. Matsunaga (D, 88) Cherry Matano

Representatives

1. Patricia F. Saiki (R) ...... Arthur J. Arnold
2. Daniel K. Akaka (D) .... James K. Sakai

IDAHO

Senate

James A. McClure (R, 90)
.... Tod Neuenschwander
Steve Symms (R, 92) .... Samuel J. Routson

Representatives

1. Larry E. Craig (R) .... Joe Karpinski
2. Richard H. Stailings (D) . Gary R. Catron

ILLINOIS

Senate

Alan J. Dixon (D, 92) .... Eugene Callahan
Paul Simon (D, 90) .... Floyd J. Fithian

Representatives

1. Charles A. Hayes (D) .. Harriet C. Pritchett
2. Gus Savage (D) .... Louanner Peters
3. Marty Russo (D) .... Ed Greelegs
4. Jack Davis (R) .... Ted Cormaney
5. William O. Lipinski (D) Bonnie A. Reiss
6. Henry J. Hyde (R) .... Judy Wolverton
7. Cardiss Collins (D) . Rufus H. (Bud) Myers
8. Dan Rostenkowski (D) . Virginia Fletcher
9. Sidney R. Yates (D) .. Mary Anderson Bain
10. John Edward Porter (R)
                         .... Gordon MacDougall
11. Frank Annunzio (D) ..... Anna Azhderian
12. Philip M. Crane (R) . Robert C. Coleman
13. Harris W. Fawell (R) .... Alan B. Mertz
14. Dennis Hastert (R) .... Scott Palmer
15. Edward R. Madigan (R) . Diane R. Liesman
16. Lynn Martin (R) ... Frances C. McNaught
17. Lane Evans (D) .... Dennis J. King
18. Robert H. Michel (R) .. Carol A. Dearden
19. Terry L. Bruce (D) .... Dave Gerrie
20. Richard J. Durbin (D) .... Milan Yager
21. Melvin Price (D) .... Mike Mansfield
22. Kenneth J. Gray (D) James M. O'Dell III

INDIANA

Senate

Richard G. Lugar (R, 88) .. Charles N. Andreae
Dan Quayle (R, 92) ... Thomas J. Duesterberg

Representatives

1. Peter J. Visclosky (D) .... Ronald Gyure
2. Philip R. Sharp (D) .... Michael B. Kraft
3. John Hiler (R) .... John H. Gautier
4. Dan Coats (R) .... G. Thomas Long
5. Jim Jontz (D) .... Deb Smuljan
6. Dan Burton (R) .... Linda Decker
7. John T. Myers (R) .... Ronald L. Hardman
8. Frank McCloskey (D) ... Nancy L. Allison
9. Lee H. Hamilton (D) .... Casey Miller
10. Andrew Jacobs Jr. (D) ... David S. Wildes

IOWA

Senate

Charles E. Grassley (R, 92) . Robert Ludwiczak
Tom Harkin (D, 90) .... Robert J. Waters

Representatives

1. Jim Leach (R) .... Bill Tate
2. Tom Tauke (R) .... Gem E. Meyer
3. David R. Nagle (D) .... Tim Raftis
4. Neal Smith (D) .... Tom H. Dawson
5. Jim Lightfoot (R) .... Mark R. Anderson
6. Fred Grandy (R) .... Craig Tufty

KANSAS

Senate

Robert Dole (R, 92) .... Mike Pettit
Nancy Landon Kassebaum (R, 90) Dave Bartel

Representatives

1. Pat Roberts (R) .... D. Leroy Towns
2. Jim Slattery (D) .... Brent J. Budowsky
3. Jan Meyers (R) ..... Kathleen Sloan Musil
4. Dan Glickman (D) .... Scott S. Fleming
5. Bob Whittaker (R) .... Chuck Pike

KENTUCKY

Senate

Wendell H. Ford (D, 92) .. James T. Fleming
Mitch McConnell (R, 90) .... Janet Mullins

Representatives

1. Carroll Hubbard Jr. (D)   Lorraine Grant
2. William H. Natcher (D) ....
3. Romano L. Mazzoli (D) .... Sarah L. Luna
4. Jim Bunning (R) .... Dave York
5. Harold Rogers (R) .... Marty T. Driesler
6. Larry J. Hopkins (R) ..... Larry VanHoose
7. Carl C. Perkins (D) ..... David M. Whalin

LOUISIANA

Senate

J. Bennett Johnston (D, 90) .... Jim Oakes
John B. Breaux (D, 92) .... G. Wayne Smith

Representatives

1. Bob Livingston (R) .... J. Allen Martin
2. Lindy (Mrs. Hale) Boggs (D)
                         .... Peg Kavaljian
3. W. J. "Billy" Tauzin (D) ....
4. Buddy Roemer (D) .... Len Sanderson
5. Jerry Huckaby (D) ... Lou Gehrig Burnett
6. Richard H. Baker (R) .... Kim Carpenter
7. Jimmy Hayes (D) .... Willy Meaux
8. Clyde C. Holloway (R) .... Ed Buckman

MAINE

Senate

William S. Cohen (R, 90) .. Thomas A. Daffron
George J. Mitchell (D, 88) Richard Arenberg

Representatives

1. Joseph E. Brennan (D) .. David Redmond

2. Olympia J. Snowe (R) ...... Kirk E. Walder

MARYLAND

Senate

Barbara A. Mikulski (D, 92)   Diane Thompson
Paul S. Sarbanes (D, 88) ...... Marvin F. Moss

Representatives

 1. Roy Dyson (D) .... Tom M. Pappas
 2. Helen Delich Bentley (R) .... Pat Wait
 3. Benjamin L. Cardin (D)   David Koshgarian
 4. Tom McMillen (D) .... Jerry Grant
 5. Steny H. Hoyer (D) ...... Eleanor G. Lewis
 6. Beverly B. Byron (D) ..... Brenton E. Ayer
 7. Kweisi Mfume (D) .... Ruth Simms
 8. Constance A. Morella (R) . David Nathan

MASSACHUSETTS

Senate

Edward M. Kennedy (D, 88) .. Ranny Cooper
John Kerry (D, 90) .... L.D. Tim Barnicle

Representatives

 1. Silvio O. Conte (R) .... Patrick J. Larkin
 2. Edward P. Boland (D)   Patrick J. Donoghue
 3. Joseph D. Early (D)   Francis W. Shannon
 4. Barney Frank (D) .... Douglas Cahn
 5. Chester G. Atkins (D) ..... Linda J. Hartke
 6. Nicholas Mavroules (D) .... M. C. Keegan
 7. Edward J. Markey (D) ....
 8. Joseph P. Kennedy II (D)
 .... Chuck McDermott
 9. Joe Moakley (D) .... John J. Weinfurter
10. Gerry E. Studds (D) . Steven C. Schwadron
11. Brian J. Donnelly (D) .... Frank Tirrell

MICHIGAN

Senate

Carl Levin (D, 90) .... Gordon C. Kerr
Donald W. Riegle Jr. (D, 88)   James N. Arbury

Representatives

 1. John Conyers Jr. (D) .... Heidi Napper
 2. Carl D. Pursell (R) ... William R. McBride
 3. Howard Wolpe (D) ..... Keith E. Laughlin
 4. Fred Upton (R) .... Lynn Sachs
 5. Paul B. Henry (R) .... Mary Lobisco
 6. Bob Carr (D) .... Mark H. Miller
 7. Dale E. Kildee (D) .... John H. Morrill
 8. Bob Traxler (D) .... Roger R. Szemraj
 9. Guy Vander Jagt (R) . James M. Sparling Jr.
10. Bill Schuette (R) .... David L. Camp
11. Robert W. Davis (R) .... Bill Mengebier
12. David E. Bonior (D) ..... Sarah Dufendach
13. George W. Crockett Jr. (D)
 .... Joan Willoughby

14. Dennis M. Hertel (D) . Raymond O'Malley
15. William D. Ford (D) .... David W. Geiss
16. John D. Dingell (D) .... John Orlando
17. Sander M. Levin (D)   Kathryn O'L Higgins
18. William S. Broomfield (R)   John R. Sinclair

MINNESOTA

Senate

Rudy Boschwitz (R, 90) .... Gary G. Russell
Dave Durenberger (R, 88) .... Douglas Kelley

Representatives

 1. Timothy J. Penny (D) ...... Steve Kingsley
 2. Vin Weber (R) .... Dan Meyer
 3. Bill Frenzel (R) .... Patricia C. Eveland
 4. Bruce F. Vento (D) . Lawrence J. Romans
 5. Martin Olav Sabo (D) . David A. Bieging
 6. Gerry Sikorski (D) . Dennis M. McGrann
 7. Arlan Stangeland (R) . Maurice Hausheer
 8. James L. Oberstar (D) ..... Tom R. Reagan

MISSISSIPPI

Senate

Thad Cochran (R, 90) .... William N. LaForge
John C. Stennis (D, 88) .. William E. Cresswell

Representatives

 1. Jamie L. Whitten (D) .. Marion F. Bishop
 2. Mike Espy (D) .... Robert Bush
 3. G. V. "Sonny" Montgomery (D)
 .... Andre Clemandot
 4. Wayne Dowdy (D) ... William H. Wright
 5. Trent Lott (R) .... Tom H. Anderson Jr.

MISSOURI

Senate

John C. Danforth (R, 88) . Alex Netchvolodoff
Christopher S. "Kit" Bond (R, 92)
 .... Warren Erdman

Representatives

 1. William L. Clay (D)   Jerome W. Williams
 2. Jack Buechner (R) .... Tom Hockaday
 3. Richard A. Gephardt (D) .. Steve Murphy
 4. Ike Skelton (D) .... John J. Pollard III
 5. Alan Wheat (D) .. Margaret E. Broadaway
 6. E. Thomas Coleman (R) . Dennis Lambert
 7. Gene Taylor (R) .... Gerald L. Henson
 8. Bill Emerson (R) .... Bill Coffield
 9. Harold L. Volkmer (D) ... James Spurling

MONTANA

Senate

Max Baucus (D, 90) .... Roger Schlickeisen
John Melcher (D, 88) ..... Ronald P. Richards

Representatives
1. Pat Williams (D) .... Jon Weintraub
2. Ron Marlenee (R) .... Glenn Marx

NEBRASKA

Senate
J. James Exon (D, 90) .... Loren B. Belker
Edward Zorinsky (D, 88) . Aletha A. Collinson

Representatives
1. Doug Bereuter (R) .... Helen M. Sramek
2. Hal Daub (R) .... David E. Heineman
3. Virginia Smith (R) . Jeralyn Parker Finke

NEVADA

Senate
Chic Hecht (R, 88) .... Glen N. Mauldin
Harry Reid (D, 92) .... Reynaldo Martinez

Representatives
1. James Bilbray (D) .... James Mulhall
2. Barbara F. Vucanovich (R) ... L. W. Likins

NEW HAMPSHIRE

Senate
Gordon J. Humphrey (R, 90) Frank T.J. Bray
Warren B. Rudman (R, 92) . G. Allan Walker

Representatives
1. Robert C. Smith (R) .... Patrick J. Pettey
2. Judd Gregg (R) .... Robert H. Barker

NEW JERSEY

Senate
Bill Bradley (D, 90) .... Marcia S. Aronoff
Frank R. Lautenberg (D, 88) ...... Eve Lubalin

Representatives
1. James J. Florio (D) .... Peter E. Newbould
2. William J. Hughes (D) ... Jonathan B. Spear
3. James J. Howard (D) .... William T. Deitz
4. Christopher H. Smith (R)
...... Martin Dannenfelser
5. Marge Roukema (R) .... Cindy Vosper
6. Bernard J. Dwyer (D) .... Lyle B. Dennis
7. Matthew J. Rinaldo (R) ...... Dave Bunton
8. Robert A. Roe (D) .... Alan Friedman
9. Robert G. Torricelli (D) . Victoria Durbin
10. Peter W. Rodino Jr. (D) .. Charles Scalera
11. Dean A. Gallo (R) .... Tamzin McMinn
12. Jim Courter (R) .... Mac Carey
13. H. James Saxton (R) ...... Ralph M. Shrom
14. Frank J. Guarini (D) .... Todd Eachus

NEW MEXICO

Senate
Jeff Bingaman (D, 88) ... Vincent C. Murphy
Pete V. Domenici (R, 90) .... J. Paul Gilman

Representatives
1. Manuel Lujan Jr. (R) .... Lucy Salazar
2. Joe Skeen (R) .... Suzanne Eisold
3. Bill Richardson (D) Melanie Kenderdine

NEW YORK

Senate
Alfonse M. D'Amato (R, 92) . Michael Kinsella
Daniel Patrick Moynihan (D, 88)
.... Paul Browne

Representatives
1. George J. Hochbrueckner (D)
.... Andrew Kennedy
2. Thomas J. Downey (D) John Peter Olinger
3. Robert J. Mrazek (D) .... Thomas V. Barry
4. Norman F. Lent (R)   Michael S. Scrivner
5. Raymond J. McGrath (R) Arthur DeCelle
6. Floyd H. Flake (D) .... Edwin Reed
7. Gary L. Ackerman (D) .. Jedd I. Moskowitz
8. James H. Scheuer (D) . Thomas W. Geng
9. Thomas J. Manton (D) .. David E. Springer
10. Charles E. Schumer (D) J. Wayne Dillehay
11. Edolphus Towns (D) .... Carolyn J. Smith
12. Major R. Owens (D) .... Maria Cuprill
13. Stephen J. Solarz (D) ...... Michael Lewan
14. Guy V. Molinari (R) ..... Robert Dizard Jr.
15. Bill Green (R) .... Sheila J. Greenwald
16. Charles B. Rangel (D) . George A. Dalley
17. Ted Weiss (D) .... Michael D. Timmeny
18. Robert Garcia (D) .... Mildred Perez
19. Mario Biaggi (D) .... Robert B. Blancato
20. Joseph J. DioGuardi (R) .. Kieran Mahoney
21. Hamilton Fish Jr. (R) ...... Nicholas Hayes
22. Benjamin A. Gilman (R) . Richard J. Garon
23. Samuel S. Stratton (D) ..... Mary B. Leslie
24. Gerald B. H. Solomon (R) Arthur A. Jutton
25. Sherwood Boehlert (R) Steven B. Kelmar
26. David O'B. Martin (R) .... Cary R. Brick
27. George C. Wortley (R) Rosemarie Woods
28. Matthew F. McHugh (D)
.... Thomas Parkhurst
29. Frank Horton (R) .... Ruby G. Moy
30. Louise M. Slaughter (D) ... Clayton Lewis
31. Jack F. Kemp (R) .... Dave Hoppe
32. John J. LaFalce (D)
Dan Crane, Gary Luczak
33. Henry J. Nowak (D) .. Ronald J. Maselka
34. Amory Houghton (R) .... Gary Madson

NORTH CAROLINA

Senate

Terry Sanford (D, 92) .... Paul Bick
Jesse Helms (R, 90) .... Clint Fuller

Representatives

1. Walter B. Jones (D) .... Floyd J. Lupton
2. Tim Valentine (D) .... Ed Nagy
3. H. Martin Lancaster (D) Howard R. Barker
4. David E. Price (D) .. Michelle Smith Nofer
5. Stephen L. Neal (D) .... Jackie Brincefield
6. Howard Coble (R) .... Marshall R. Hurley
7. Charlie Rose (D) ..... Andrea Turner-Scott
8. W. G. "Bill" Hefner (D) . William McEwen
9. J. Alex McMillan (R) .... Frank H. Hill
10. Cass Ballenger (R) .... Max Veale
11. James McClure Clarke (D) . Dennis Clark

NORTH DAKOTA

Senate

Kent Conrad (D, 92) .... Jim Margolis
Quentin N. Burdick (D, 88) .. David M. Strauss

Representative

AL Byron L. Dorgan (D) .... Andrew Kentz

OHIO

Senate

John Glenn (D, 92) .... Phil Upschulte
Howard M. Metzenbaum (D, 88)   Peter Harris

Representatives

1. Thomas A. Luken (D) . Hannah Margetich
2. Bill Gradison (R) .... Margaret P. Totten
3. Tony P. Hall (D) .... George M. Lowrey
4. Michael G. Oxley (R) James K. Conzelman
5. Delbert L. Latta (R) ..... Joan M. Southard
6. Bob McEwen (R) .... Charles Greener
7. Michael DeWine (R) .. Laurel A. Pressler
8. Donald E. "Buzz" Lukens (R) John Hishta
9. Marcy Kaptur (D) Theodore Mastroianni
10. Clarence E. Miller (R) ...... Bob Reintsema
11. Dennis E. Eckart (D) Gordan Jack Dover
12. John R. Kasich (R) .... Don Thibaut
13. Don J. Pease (D) .... J. William Goold
14. Thomas C. Sawyer (D) ... James M. Dolan
15. Chalmers P. Wylie (R) ... Benson H. Hart
16. Ralph Regula (R) .... Carol D. Hall
17. James A. Traficant Jr. (D) . Barbara Allen
18. Douglas Applegate (D) ...... James R. Hart
19. Edward F. Feighan (D)
                        George Stephanopoulos
20. Mary Rose Oakar (D)   Nancy A. Lea Mond
21. Louis Stokes (D) .... Hal D. Payne

OKLAHOMA

Senate

David L. Boren (D, 90) .... Charles L. Ward
Don Nickles (R, 92) .... Doyce Boesch

Representatives

1. James M. Inhofe (R) .. Richard Soudriette
2. Mike Synar (D) .... Clifton Peter Rose
3. Wes Watkins (D) .... Emily K. Ray
4. Dave McCurdy (D) Stephen K. Patterson
5. Mickey Edwards (R) Vicki L. F. Martyak
6. Glenn English (D) .... Scott B. Ingham

OREGON

Senate

Mark O. Hatfield (R, 90) ... Gerald W. Frank
Bob Packwood (R, 92) .... Etta Fielek

Representatives

1. Les AuCoin (D) .... Bob Crane
2. Robert F. Smith (R) . Stephen G. Sprague
3. Ron Wyden (D) .... Lois L. Davis
4. Peter A. DeFazio (D) .... Doug Marker
5. Denny Smith (R) .... John D. Heubusch

PENNSYLVANIA

Senate

John Heinz (R, 88) .... Cliff Shannon
Arlen Specter (R, 92) .... Neil Manne

Representatives

1. Thomas M. Foglietta (D) Phillip Rotondi
2. William H. Gray III (D) .... Michael Reed
3. Robert A. Borski (D) ...... Alan Slomowitz
4. Joe Kolter (D) .... Gerald W. Weaver
5. Richard T. Schulze (R) ... Sharon Borg Wall
6. Gus Yatron (D) .... Joseph P. Gemmell
7. Curt Weldon (R) .... Russ Schriefer
8. Peter H. Kostmayer (D) . F. H. Brewer III
9. Bud Shuster (R) .... Ann M. Eppard
10. Joseph M. McDade (R)
                        .... Deborah Weatherly
11. Paul E. Kanjorski (D) ...... W. Robert Hall
12. John P. Murtha (D) ...... Philip Giomariso
13. Lawrence Coughlin (R) Joseph Mahoney
14. William J. Coyne (D) .. Coleman J. Conroy
15. Don Ritter (R) ..... James H. Cromwell Jr.
16. Robert S. Walker (R) .... John W. Howard
17. George W. Gekas (R) .... Ed Uravic
18. Doug Walgren (D) .. Jonathan W. Delano
19. Bill Goodling (R) ...... James M. Eagen III
20. Joseph M. Gaydos (D) Bernard Mandella
21. Tom Ridge (R) .... Mark Holman
22. Austin J. Murphy (D)
                        .. Frederick McLuckie Jr.

23. William F. Clinger Jr. (R) . Marc G. Stanley

RHODE ISLAND

Senate
John H. Chafee (R, 88) .... Robert Hurley
Claiborne Pell (D, 90) .. Thomas G. Hughes Jr.

Representatives
1. Fernand J. St Germain (D)
.... Richard Maurano
2. Claudine Schneider (R)
.... Elizabeth Raisbeck

SOUTH CAROLINA

Senate
Ernest F. Hollings (D, 92) .. Ashley O. Thrift
Strom Thurmond (R, 90) . Thaddeaus E. Strom

Representatives
1. Arthur Ravenel Jr. (R) .. Ben Underwood
2. Floyd Spence (R) .... Kenneth L. Black
3. Butler Derrick (D) .... Leo Coco
4. Liz Patterson (D) .... Rita Hayes
5. John M. Spratt Jr. (D) .. Ellen W. Buchanan
6. Robin Tallon (D) .... Marva A. Smalls

SOUTH DAKOTA

Senate
Thomas A. Daschle (D, 92) .... Peter Rouse
Larry Pressler (R, 90) .... Eleanor Rhodes

Representative
AL Tim Johnson (D) .... Drey Samuelson

TENNESSEE

Senate
Albert Gore Jr. (D, 90) .... Peter S. Knight
Jim Sasser (D, 88) .... John Callahan

Representatives
1. James H. Quillen (R) Frances Light Currie
2. John J. Duncan (R) Patricia D. Robinson
3. Marilyn Lloyd (D) .... Sue Carlton
4. Jim Cooper (D) .... David A. Withrow
5. Bill Boner (D) .... Douglas S. Johnston Jr.
6. Bart Gordon (D) .... Timothy C. Kernan
7. Don Sundquist (R) Thomas J. McNamara
8. Ed Jones (D) .... Kelly M. Sharbel Jr.
9. Harold E. Ford (D) .... A. Jay Cooper Jr.

TEXAS

Senate
Lloyd Bentsen (D, 88) .... Michael Levy
Phil Gramm (R, 90) .... Ruth Cymber

Representatives
1. Jim Chapman (D) .... William K. Moore
2. Charles Wilson (D) .... Charlie Schnabel
3. Steve Bartlett (R) ...... Mary Jane Maddox
4. Ralph M. Hall (D) .... James D. Cole
5. John Bryant (D) .... Randy White
6. Joe L. Barton (R) .... Beth McPherson
7. Bill Archer (R) .... Phillip D. Moseley
8. Jack Fields (R) ..... Robert E. H. Ferguson
9. Jack Brooks (D) .... Sharon Matts
10. J. J. Pickle (D) .... John S. Bender
11. Marvin Leath (D) .... John D. Canatsey
12. Jim Wright (D) .... Marshall L. Lynam
13. Beau Boulter (R) .... Kim McKernan
14. Mac Sweeney (R) ...... Suzanne K. Scholte
15. E. "Kika" de la Garza (D)
.... Celia Hare Martin
16. Ronald D. Coleman (D) ... Paul F. Rogers
17. Charles W. Stenholm (D) .... Lois Auer
18. Mickey Leland (D) . William J. Taylor III
19. Larry Combest (R) William M. Thornberry
20. Henry B. Gonzalez (D) ...... Gail J. Beagle
21. Lamar Smith (R) .... John Rampmann
22. Thomas D. DeLay (R) .... Ken Carroll
23. Albert G. Bustamante (D)
.... Ella Wong-Rusinko
24. Martin Frost (D) .... Dolly A. McClary
25. Michael A. Andrews (D) .... Bill Miller
26. Dick Armey (R) .... Kerry Knott
27. Solomon P. Ortiz (D) . Florencio Rendon

UTAH

Senate
Jake Garn (R, 92) .... Jeff M. Bingham
Orrin G. Hatch (R, 88) .... Dee Benson

Representatives
1. James V. Hansen (R) ...... James C. Barker
2. Wayne Owens (D) .... Tod H. Cohen
3. Howard C. Nielson (R) ...... L. Reid Ivins

VERMONT

Senate
Patrick J. Leahy (D, 92) .... Ellen Lovell
Robert T. Stafford (R, 88) ... Neal J. Houston

Representative
AL James M. Jeffords (R) . Susan M. Boardman

VIRGINIA

Senate
Paul S. Trible Jr. (R, 88) ..... Mark Greenberg
John W. Warner (R, 90) .... Susan Magill

Representatives

1. Herbert H. Bateman (R) ... John I. Brooks
2. Owen B. Pickett (D) ...... William K. Hart
3. Thomas J. Bliley Jr. (R) M. Boyd Marcus Jr.
4. Norman Sisisky (D) . Dennis W. Johnson
5. Dan Daniel (D) .... W. Fred Fletcher
6. James R. Olin (D) .... Bill Black
7. D. French Slaughter Jr. (R) . George White
8. Stan Parris (R) .... Dick Leggitt
9. Frederick C. Boucher (D) . Andrew Wright
10. Frank R. Wolf (R) .... William C. Mims

WASHINGTON

Senate

Daniel J. Evans (R, 88) .... Bill Jacobs
Brock Adams (D, 92) .... Ellen Globokar

Representatives

1. John R. Miller (R) .... Herbert S. Stone
2. Al Swift (D) .... Drew D. Pettus
3. Don Bonker (D) .... Mark D. Murray
4. Sid Morrison (R) .... Gretchen White
5. Thomas S. Foley (D) .... Heather S. Foley
6. Norman D. Dicks (D) .... Diane Anello
7. Mike Lowry (D) .... Don Wolgamott
8. Rod Chandler (R) .... John Giese

WEST VIRGINIA

Senate

Robert C. Byrd (D, 88) .... Joan Drummond
John D. Rockefeller IV (D, 90) ... Ira S. Shapiro

Representatives

1. Alan B. Mollohan (D) . C. Louise Ingram
2. Harley O. Staggers Jr. (D) James Rhodes
3. Bob Wise (D) .... Dan McGinn
4. Nick J. Rahall II (D) ...... John A. Kunkel

WISCONSIN

Senate

Bob Kasten (R, 92) .... Dawn G. Martinez

William Proxmire (D, 88) . Ronald L. Tammen

Representatives

1. Les Aspin (D) .... Penny E. Gentilly
2. Robert W. Kastenmeier (D) .. Kaz Oshiki
3. Steve Gunderson (R) .... John L. Frank
4. Gerald D. Kleczka (D) ...... James M. Hill
5. Jim Moody (D) .... Marcus Kunian
6. Thomas E. Petri (R) .... Gene E. Kussart
7. David R. Obey (D) ...... Elliott M. Fiedler
8. Toby Roth (R) .... George Ann Way
9. F. James Sensenbrenner Jr. (R)
... John Schrote

WYOMING

Senate

Alan K. Simpson (R, 90) .... Donald Hardy
Malcolm Wallop (R, 88) .... William U. Hill

Representative

AL Dick Cheney (R) .... Patricia Howe

DELEGATES

American Samoa

Fofō I. F. Sunia (D) .... Matthew K. Iuli

District of Columbia

Walter E. Fauntroy (D) .... Johnny Barnes

Guam

Ben Blaz (R) .... Robin Grove

Virgin Islands

Ron de Lugo (D) .... Sheila M. Ross

RESIDENT COMMISSIONER

Puerto Rico

Jaime B. Fuster (Pop. Dem.)
...Carmen Delgado Votaw

TV Guide to Senate Floor Action

Cable television viewers accustomed to watching the normally fastpaced, well orchestrated action of the House of Representatives have found that the Senate operates quite differently.

In contrast to the 435 member House, where the leadership sets the agenda for the week and usually makes it stick, the Senate often operates at the mercy of its 100 members.

Many of the Senate rules are designed to assure that members who hold minority views have a chance to make their point.

One determined senator can take advantage of the rules to delay action for days or weeks on legislation he opposes.

The Senate often meanders through hours of cursory debate and quorum calls, during which a clerk slowly calls the role. No one answers, not even members who are present.

(Last October, Arkansas Democrat Sen. David Pryor calculated that the Senate had spent about one-quarter of its time in quorum calls and the equivalent of another full work week waiting for stragglers to vote after the voting period had expired.) Senate leaders hope that the presence of television cameras, which have been allowed only since June 2, will lead to a more efficient Senate.

Proceedings are broadcast by the Cable-Satellite Public Affairs Network (C-SPAN).

Typical Day

A typical day in the Senate might go like this:

- The Senate is **called to order** by the presiding officer. The constitutional presiding officer, the vice president, seldom is in attendance. Usually the president pro tempore presides over the opening minutes of the Senate session.

During the course of the day, other members of the majority party take turns presiding over the Senate for an hour at a time. Whoever is in the chair is addressed as Mr. (or Madame) President.

- The Senate chaplain delivers the **opening prayer.**

- The majority leader and the minority leader are recognized for opening remarks. The majority leader usually announces his plan for the day's business, which is developed in consultation with the minority leadership.

- Several senators, usually fewer than half a dozen, who have requested time in advance are recognized for **special orders,** during which they may speak about any topic for five minutes. (Before TV came to the Senate, special orders were 15 minutes.) Some senators ask for special order time every day.

- After special orders, the Senate usually conducts **morning business.** During morning business — which need not be in the morning — members conduct routine administrative chores. They introduce bills and receive reports from committees and messages from the president.

- After morning business, the Senate begins work on **legislative or executive** matters. If the majority leader wants the Senate to begin work on a piece of legislation, he normally asks for unanimous consent to call up the measure.

If any member objects, the leader may make a debatable **motion** that the Senate begin work on the bill.

The debatable motion gives opponents the opportunity to launch a **filibuster**, or extended debate, even before the Senate officially begins work on the bill.

Sponsors of the bill may file a **cloture petition** seeking to shut off debate.

Under normal circumstances, the Senate votes on the petition two days after it is filed. To terminate debate, 60 votes are needed, regardless of how many members are voting.

Even after cloture is invoked, debate on the motion can continue for 30 hours. In addition, opponents can keep a filibuster going by demanding votes on all amendments filed before cloture.

A few measures, such as the budget resolution and conference reports, are privileged and a motion to consider them is not debatable.

After the Senate begins work on a bill, floor debate is generally handled by **managers,** usually the chairman and the ranking minority member of the committee with jurisdiction over the measure.

Some measures are considered under a **time agreement** in which the Senate unanimously agrees to limit debate and to divide the time in some prearranged fashion. Usually, however, legislation is considered with no limit on debate.

In the absence of a time agreement, any

senator may seek recognition from the chair, and once recognized, may speak for as long as he or she wishes.

Unless the Senate has unanimously agreed to limit **amendments**, senators may offer as many as they wish. Generally, amendments need not be **germane**, or directly related, to the bill.

Most bills are passed by a voice vote with only a handful of senators present.

Any member can request a **roll call**, or recorded vote, on an amendment or on final passage of a measure. Although Senate rules require a **"sufficient second"** by at least 11 members, the presiding officer often orders a roll call vote when fewer members second the request.

The Senate leadership tries to schedule roll call votes at a time convenient to members; thus few votes are held on Mondays or Fridays, when members are often in their home states.

Senate roll calls are casual affairs. Few members answer the clerk as their names are called. Instead, senators stroll in from the cloakrooms or their offices and congregate in the well (the area between the front row of desks and the desk occupied by the presiding officer and the other officials of the Senate). When they are ready to vote, senators catch the eye of the clerk and vote, often by indicating thumbs-up or thumbs-down.

Roll call votes are supposed to last 15 minutes, but a study by Pryor last year revealed that the average vote lasts about 23 minutes. Some have dragged on for more than an hour, as members waited for stragglers to arrive from other appointments around town.

● Often, near the end of the day the majority leader and the minority leader quickly move through a **"wrap-up"** period, during which minor bills that previously have been cleared by all members are passed by unanimous consent.

It is not uncommon for the Senate to pass as many as a dozen bills on the Senate **calendar** in just a few minutes during the wrap-up.

● Just before the Senate finishes its work for the day, the majority leader will seek unanimous consent for his agenda for the next session — when the Senate will convene, which senators will be given special orders and, sometimes, specific time agreements for consideration of legislation.

TV Guide to House Floor Proceedings

The House of Representatives has supplanted soap operas as preferred daytime viewing for millions of Americans.

Since the House opened its chambers to television in 1979, C-SPAN has brought the often rambunctious antics of the 435 congressmen and the representatives of the District of Columbia, Puerto Rico, Guam, American Samoa and the Virgin Islands to life with far more impact than history books.

Because its membership is so large, the House has developed rigid rules to expedite its business. As a result, the House is actually more manageable and efficient than the Senate, with just 100 members.

There is little "dead" air — no quorum calls or desultory speeches as in the Senate. Members, who usually have less than five minutes to make their points, must get right to the heart of the issue.

In just one or two days, the House can pass major legislation that would take weeks in the Senate.

Typical Day

A typical day in the House might go like this:

- The chaplain delivers the **opening prayer.**
- The speaker approves the *Journal,* the record of the previous day's proceedings. Often a member will demand a roll call vote on the approval of the *Journal.* The vote gives party leaders an opportunity to find out which members are absent. On days when hotly contested legislation is to be considered, the absence of just a few members might alter the outcome of a vote.
- After some procedural activities — receiving messages from the Senate or the president, granting committees permission to file reports or to meet during the session, etc. — members are recognized for **one minute speeches.**

On a typical day, 10 or 20 members come to the well to deliver their brief statements, which can be on any topic — current events, a bill due on the floor that day, a tribute to a prominent constituent or a Republican harangue against some action of the Democratic leadership.

- The House then turns to its legislative business.

Virtually every major bill is considered under a **rule** that sets forth guidelines for floor action. The rule, which is a resolution reported by the Rules Committee, sets a time limit for general debate on the bill and specifies which, if any, amendments are permitted.

The Rules panel works closely with the Democratic leadership: Democrats hold nine of the 13 seats on the committee and all Democratic members are appointed by the Speaker (with the approval of the Democratic Caucus).

The rule is generally approved with little opposition. However, rules are occasionally defeated by members opposed to the bill, or by members who want a more favorable rule that will allow them to offer their amendments.

Sometimes members approve an **open rule,** which permits unlimited amendments, or a **closed rule,** which permits no amendments. However, most major bills are considered under a **modified open/closed rule,** which permits only specific amendments identified in the rule.

Privileged matters such as conference reports, the budget resolution and appropriations bills can come to the floor without a rule.

After the rule is adopted, the House resolves into the Committee of the Whole House on the State of the Union (known simply as the **Committee of the Whole)** to consider the bill. The Speaker relinquishes the gavel to a chairman, who presides over the Committee.

The debate time is controlled by the **managers** of the bill, usually the chairman and ranking minority member of the standing committee with jurisdiction over the measure. After time for general debate has expired, amendments that are permitted under the rule can be offered.

Debate on the amendments is conducted under a **five-minute rule:** Supporters are limited to five minutes and opponents get five minutes. However, members may obtain additional time for debate by offering pro-forma amendments to "strike the last word."

Voting is by voice (the usual procedure); division (members stand to be counted); teller (a seldom-used procedure in which members walk past designated tellers); or by electronic device. When members vote electronically, they insert a plastic card into one of many voting stations on the House floor and press a button to record a "yea," a "nay" or a "present". Their vote is immediately recorded on a big screen on the wall above the Speaker's desk and tabulated, giving a running vote total.

Most electronic votes last 15 minutes.

Votes cannot technically be taken without a **quorum** (although they often are because no one objects). A point of order that a quorum is not present mandates an electronic vote. A quorum in the Committeee of the Whole is 100; a House quorum is 218.

After the amending process is complete, the Committee "rises," and the chairman reports to the Speaker on the actions taken.

Acting once again as the House, the members vote on final passage of the bill, sometimes after voting on a motion to recommit the bill to its committee of origin.

• On many non-controversial bills, the House leadership wants to speed up action, bypassing the Rules Committee and the Committee of the Whole.

It can do that by waiving, or "suspending" the rules. Bills under **suspension**, sometimes as many as a dozen at a time, are usually brought up early in the week.

Suspensions cannot be amended. Debate is limited to 40 minutes. Then members are asked to vote on whether they want to suspend the rules and pass the bill. A single vote accomplishes both steps. A two-thirds vote is needed to suspend the House rules, making it a gamble sometimes to bring up legislation under suspension.

If a bill is defeated under the two-thirds requirement, it often is brought back to the floor later under regular procedures, where only a simple majority is sufficient.

To accommodate many members who not returned from their districts on Mondays, recorded votes on suspensions are ordinarily delayed until Tuesday. Roughly half the measures under suspension are passed by voice vote.

• Measures that are even less controversial are placed on the **consent calendar** or are passed by **unanimous consent.** These measures, such as resolutions expressing congratulations to a winning sports team, expressing support for a Soviet dissident, or approving a minor transfer of government land, are cleared through the leadership of both parties. a single objecton on the floor can block passage.

• After the House completes its legislative business, members are allowed to speak for up to 60 minutes under **special orders.** They must reserve the time in advance but can speak on any topic. The television cameras record the speeches, which often are made to an almost deserted chamber.

Glossary of Legislative Terms

This is an abridged glossary based on glossaries appearing in Congressional Quarterly's Guide to Congress *and the annual* Congressional Quarterly Almanacs.

Amendment — A proposal to alter the language or provisions in a bill or in another amendment.

Amendment in the Nature of a Substitute — An amendment that seeks to replace either the entire text of a bill or a large portion of it.

Appropriations Bill — A bill that gives legal authority to spend or obligate money from the Treasury. An appropriations bill generally cannot provide more money than has been authorized for a particular program under separate legislation.

Authorization Bill — Basic, substantive legislation that establishes or continues the legal operation of a federal program or agency, either indefinitely or for a specific period of time. An authorization normally is a prerequisite for an appropriation, and sets a ceiling for it.

Bills — Most legislative proposals before Congress are in the form of bills designated by HR in the House of Representatives and S in the Senate, according to the chamber in which they originate, and by a number assigned in the order in which they are introduced during the two-year period of a Congress. "Public bills" deal with general questions and become public laws if approved by Congress and signed by the president. "Private bills" deal with such matters as an individual's claim against the government or special immigration request, and become private laws if approved and signed.

Bills Introduced — Any number of members may join in introducing a bill or resolution. The first member listed is the sponsor of the bill; the others are cosponsors.

Bills Referred — When introduced, a bill is referred to the committee or committees that have jurisdiction over the subject of the bill.

Budget — The document sent to Congress by the president early each year estimating government revenue and expenditures for the ensuing fiscal year.

Budget Reconciliation — The 1974 budget act provides for a "reconciliation" procedure for bringing tax and appropriations bills into conformity with congressional budget resolutions. Congress instructs its legislative committees to approve measures adjusting revenues and expenditures by a certain amount by a given deadline. The recommendations of these committees are consolidated without change by the Budget committees into an omnibus reconciliation bill, which then must be approved by both houses of Congress.

By Request — A phrase used when a member introduces a bill at the request of an executive agency or private organization but does not necessarily endorse it.

Calendar — An agenda of business awaiting action by the chamber. The House uses five calendars — the Consent, Discharge, House, Private and Union calendars, according to the type of bill involved. The Senate uses only a legislative and an executive calendar.

Cloture — The process in the Senate for ending a filibuster by other than unanimous consent. A petition to limit debate must be signed by 16 senators, and the motion to invoke cloture then must be agreed to by three-fifths of the Senate's membership.

Committee of the Whole — The working title of what is formally "The Committee of the Whole House on the State of the Union." To expedite business, the House resolves itself into the Committee of the

Whole to consider amendments to most major bills. The Speaker is supplanted with a "chairman" who presides over debate and voting on amendments. When work on a measure is complete, the Committee "rises," the Speaker returns to the chair and the full House then votes on passage of the legislation.

Concurrent Resolution — A statement expressing the sense of Congress on some issue. Designated H Con Res or S Con Res, depending on the chamber of origin, it must be adopted by both houses, but it does not go to the president or have the force of law.

Conference — A meeting between selected members of the House and Senate to reconcile differences between the two chambers' versions of the same legislation.

Congressional Record — The daily printed account of all proceedings in the House and Senate, with a substantially verbatim account of debate. Members are allowed to revise their spoken remarks.

Continuing Resolution — A joint resolution to continue appropriations for a department or agency when a fiscal year is beginning and Congress has not enacted the department's regular appropriations bill.

Division Vote — A vote in which all members present who favor a bill are asked to stand, followed by all those opposed. No record is kept of how members voted (also called "standing vote").

Entitlement Program — A federal program such as Social Security or unemployment compensation that guarantees a certain level of benefits to all persons who meet eligibility requirements set by law.

Executive Calendar — This is the non-legislative calendar of the Senate, on which presidential documents such as treaties and nominations are listed.

Filibuster — A time-delaying strategy of debate, quorum calls, amendments and other procedures used by a minority to defeat or achieve compromise on a proposition favored by the majority.

Fiscal Year — Financial operations of the government are carried out over a 12-month period beginning Oct. 1 each year. Fiscal 1987 began Oct. 1, 1986, and will end Sept. 30, 1987.

Five-Minute Rule — A debate-limiting rule of the House which, while the Committee of the Whole sits, allows a member offering an amendment to speak for five minutes in its favor, followed by an opponent who also speaks for five minutes.

Floor Manager — A member who has the task of steering legislation through floor debate and the amending process to a final vote in the chamber.

Germane — Pertaining to the subject matter of the measure at hand.

Hopper — Box on the House clerk's desk where members deposit bills and resolutions to be introduced.

Joint Resolution — A resolution requiring approval by both the House and Senate. It becomes law if signed by the president or passed over his veto. Differing in no substantive way from a bill, a joint resolution is often used to address a limited matter. A joint resolution also is used for a constitutional amendment, which requires passage by two-thirds of each chamber but does not go to the president.

Marking Up a Bill — Working on legislation in committee or subcommittee, approving, amending or rejecting each provision and the bill as a whole.

Morning Hour — Time set aside for the conduct of routine business. The House rarely has a morning hour.

One-Minute Speeches — Delivered at the beginning of a legislative day in the House, these may cover any topic but are limited to one minute in duration.

Pair — A "gentleman's agreement" between two lawmakers who are on opposite sides of an issue, made in advance of a vote to cancel out the effects of absences. Notices of pairs are printed in the *Congressional Record*.

Parliamentarian — Each chamber employs several parliamentarians to assist the presiding officer in making rulings and conducting the business of the chamber.

Point of Order — An objection raised by a member that the chamber is departing from rules governing its conduct of business. The chair then must rule on whether objection is justified.

President of the Senate — The vice president of the United States presides over the Senate. In his absence, a president pro tempore presides.

President Pro Tempore — The presiding officer of the Senate in the absence of the vice president of the United States.

Previous Question — A motion that, if approved, has the effect of cutting off all debate, preventing further amendments and forcing a vote on the pending matter.

Quorum — The number of members whose presence is necessary for transaction of business. In the Senate, a majority of the membership comprises a quorum. In the House, a quorum also is a majority of the members, except in Committee of the Whole, where it is 100 members.

Readings of Bills — Traditionally, a bill had to be read aloud three times before passage. In modern practice, a bill is considered to have been read first upon introduction, second upon floor consideration and third after all floor debate. Seldom are bills actually read aloud in their entirety.

Recommit to Committee — A motion made after a bill has been debated to return it to the committee that reported it. Recommittal usually is a death blow to a bill, unless done with instructions to adopt a particular amendment and report the bill back to the chamber.

Reconsider a Vote — A motion to reconsider the vote by which an action was taken has the effect, until disposed of, of putting the action in abeyance. Such a motion can be made only by a member who voted on the prevailing side.

Recorded Vote — A vote on which a public record is kept of each member's stand. In the Senate, this is accomplished through a roll-call of the senators. The House uses an electronic voting system, and a recorded vote can be obtained on demand of one-fifth of a quorum (44 members) of the full House, or one-fourth (25) during Committee of the Whole.

Report — Both a verb and a noun as a congressional term. After completing a markup of a bill, a committee reports its recommendations to the chamber along with the measure. It usually publishes a written report containing an explanation of the bill as approved and the committee's reasons for its action.

Rider — An amendment, usually not germane, which a sponsor offers to a bill to enhance the amendment's chances of enactment.

Rules — The term has two congressional meanings. Both houses of Congress have standing rules governing procedure. In the House, the term also refers to resolutions reported by the Rules Committee, which upon approval by the full House, governs the length and terms of debate for most bills considered on the floor.

Secretary of the Senate — The chief administrative officer of the Senate.

Strike Out the Last Word — In the House's Committee of the Whole, when debate is limited by the five-minute rule, a member may gain recognition from the chair by moving to "strike out the last word" of the amendment or section of a bill under consideration. The motion is pro forma, requires no vote and does not alter the measure being debated. Members also use "strike out the requisite number of words."

Supplemental Appropriations Bill — Legislation appropriating added funds for a department during the current fiscal year after its regular appropriations bill has been enacted.

Suspend the Rules — A time-saving procedure used for considering bills in the House under which no amendments may be offered and debate is limited to 20 minutes per side. A two-thirds vote is required for passage under suspension of the rules, a procedure reserved mostly for non-controversial bills.

Table a Bill — A motion to "lay on the table" effectively kills a bill if approved.

Unanimous Consent — The Senate and House can do almost anything it wishes, regardless of its rules, upon unanimous consent of the chamber. But objection from a single member can block action.

Unanimous Consent Agreement — Also called a time limitation agreement, it is an agreement negotiated by the Senate leadership to govern one or more aspects of action on a measure. In effect, it is similar to a rule in the House.

Voice Vote — Members answer "aye" or "no" in chorus and the presiding officer decides the result. No record is made of how individual members voted.

Yeas and Nays — A recorded vote (see above).

Yield — When a member has been recognized to speak, no other member may speak unless he obtains permission from the member recognized. Requests are made in the form, "Will the gentleman yield?"

Map of Capitol Hill

(Dotted line indicates the city's quadrants, which are noted in the corner of the map)

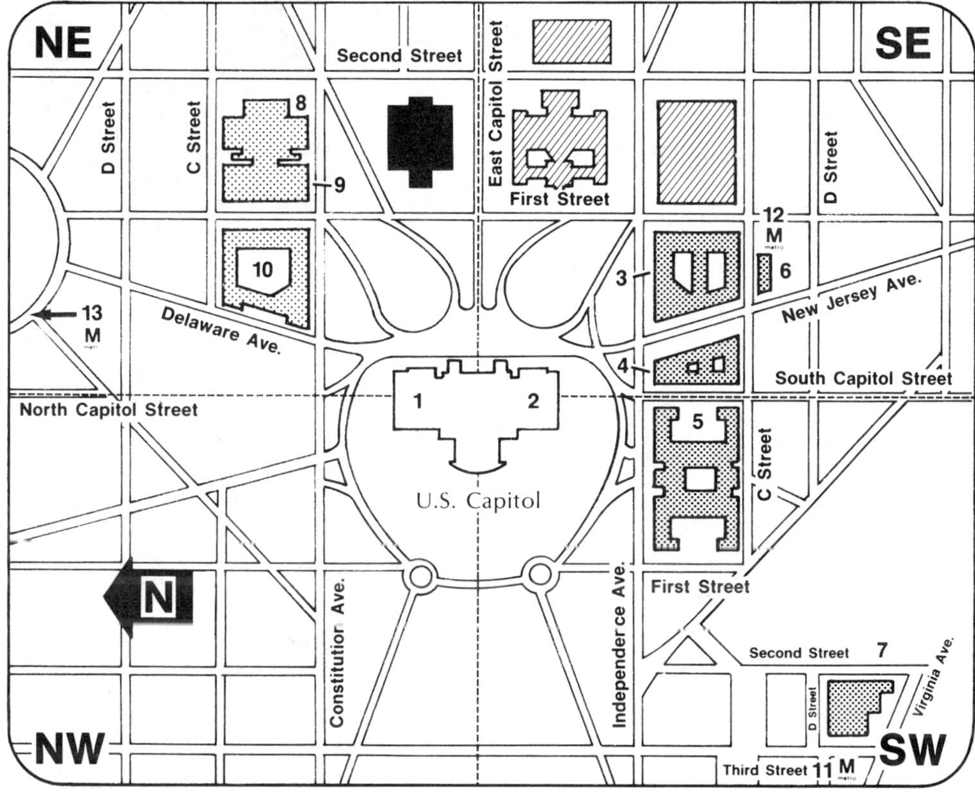

☐ U.S. Capitol,
Washington, D.C. 20510 20515*
- 1 Senate Wing
- 2 House Wing

☒ House Office Buildings,
Washington, D.C. 20515
- 3 Cannon
- 4 Longworth
- 5 Rayburn
- 6 House Annex No. 1
- 7 House Annex No. 2

* Mail sent to the U.S. Capitol should bear
the ZIP code of the chamber to which it
is addressed.

☒ Senate Office Buildings,
Washington, D.C. 20510
- 8 Hart
- 9 Dirksen
- 10 Russell

■ Supreme Court
Washington, D.C. 20543

☐ Library of Congress,
Washington, D.C. 20540

Ⓜ Subway System
- 11 Federal Center SW Station
- 12 Capitol South Station
- 13 Union Station Station